The Politics of Rescue

Henry L. Feingold

The Politics of Rescue

The Roosevelt Administration and the Holocaust, 1938–1945

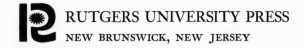 RUTGERS UNIVERSITY PRESS
NEW BRUNSWICK, NEW JERSEY

Copyright © 1970 by Rutgers University, the State University of New Jersey
Library of Congress Catalog Card Number: 75-127049
SBN: 8135-0664-6
Manufactured in the United States of America by Quinn & Boden Company, Inc.,
  Rahway, New Jersey

Dedicated to the memory of a true lover of Zion,
Marcus M. Feingold, my father

Contents

Preface

Artists, writers and dramatists have long since recognized that the world of Auschwitz and the reaction of those who witnessed it contain a key to understanding our time in history. Historians, who are often the last to discover such seminal happenings, hesitate even after three decades to probe for the meaning of the Holocaust.* It is mentioned cursorily in modern textbooks, where it is usually linked to the larger insanity of World War II, and except for some works which attempt to find a pattern in the massive collection of data now available, no synthesis has yet appeared. The reaction of those who witnessed the Holocaust has been left to moralists like Rolf Hochhuth and Arthur Morse † whose works resemble prosecutors' briefs before the court of public opinion. This book, which examines the reaction of the Roosevelt Administration to the Holocaust, attempts to move beyond the moral aspect to examine the political context in which America's response was conceived.

To go beyond the moral aspect is not to ignore it. One soon discovers that the role of witness is burdened with a moral freight that cannot be ignored. The reaction of victims to their fate, which at one time preoccupied writers on the Holocaust, remains morally fairly simple since choice was circumscribed. Whether they resisted

* A term used to refer to the destruction of European Jewry during the war years.
† Rolf Hochhuth, *The Deputy*, New York: Grove Press, 1964; Arthur D. Morse, *While Six Million Died: A Chronicle of American Apathy*, New York: Random House, 1967.

heroically in the Warsaw ghetto or hid hopefully in the attics of Amsterdam or dug their graves passively at Babi Yar, victims were, with few exceptions, ultimately compelled to assume the role assigned by the central casting agent in Berlin. But in the case of witnesses such as the Roosevelt Administration, alternative courses of action—helping the victims, indifference and even complicity in their destruction—were, in theory at least, open. The existence of choice is accompanied by questions of morality.

In the case of the Roosevelt Administration, the moral imperatives inherent in its role as witness were more pronounced than usual. A morally charged democratic rhetoric traditionally accompanied and sometimes cloaked baser motives of national policy. Such rhetoric, which included concern for the "forgotten man" and reminders that "hunger was not debatable" received a new lease on life. America, especially the America of Roosevelt, was expected to muster more concern for the unfortunates than nations without humanitarian pretensions. For those who assumed that the New Deal was what its rhetoric said it was, the accumulation of evidence of indifference and even complicity in the Final Solution is difficult to accept. The temptation to scream out in righteous anger that the promise of America has been betrayed is irresistible. I have tried, not always successfully, I fear, to avoid such fulminations, not only because I am aware that they are partly based on a misreading of American, especially New Deal, history but because they make us no wiser about why the Roosevelt Administration's rescue effort was so meager. A "deputy" for the Roosevelt Administration is easily written. The rescue story is replete with examples of indifference, sabotage of rescue initiatives, and seeming compliance with the goals of the Final Solution. But appalling as it may sound, that is a self-evident truth for which there are six million pieces of evidence. After one is done with documenting that fact, there remain gnawing questions that require answers if some understanding is to be found for the choices which the Roosevelt Administration made during the Holocaust. The accusation that the Roosevelt Administration did not do enough has no meaning until we determine how much might have been done. Yet it was precisely the question of what was possible which was at the heart of the argument between rescue advocates and State Department officials. Even today, with all our perspective, it is still difficult to determine possibilities.

One still wants to know what forces prevented a more human response. What was their motivation and what tactics did they use to thwart a more active rescue effort? Why was it relatively easy to intern the Nisei, an event which bears some parallels to the Germans' early concentration of the Jews, whereas it proved extremely difficult for the Administration to move on the rescue front, even when its intentions were good? In a broader context, it would be interesting to find out how it happened that the forces for life were so consistently outmatched by darker impulses. The energy, resources, and will committed to rescue never remotely matched the Nazi commitment to liquidation of the Jews. In short, we need to go beyond simply another sermon on man's inhumanity to man.

This work takes the story of the Roosevelt Administration's rescue program from 1938, when the third and most serious wave of anti-Jewish violence began in Germany, to the early months of 1945 when the problem of rescue gave way to organizing a relief program for those who had survived. Within this period there are four subdivisions. From the *Anschluss* in March 1938 to the invasion of Poland in September 1939 when, spurred by Roosevelt's initiative, an attempt was made to bring order into the refugee chaos. During the following period which ended with the attack on Pearl Harbor in December 1941, the United States as a leading neutral avidly searched for resettlement havens even while restrictionist elements in Congress and the Department of State succeeded in establishing prohibitive regulations for rescue actions. The period between December 1941 and November 1943 was marked by a growing gulf between the rescue advocates and the State Department which led to a series of sharp confrontations within the Administration. The final period takes us to the early months of 1945. It was the scene of massive public agitation to remove the rescue operation from the State Department to a newly created agency, the War Refugee Board, devoted exclusively to the rescue of Jews.

This work covers the war period which is in its own right one of extreme complexity. The examination of the rescue theme with only casual reference to the wartime context of which it was part creates some sticky problems. Those in government responsible for policy decisions thought in terms of winning the war. Often they cited the exigencies of the war as the rationale for not taking certain steps. This was true to some extent in the question of shipping for refugees and bombing of the camps and railroad lines. By isolating the rescue theme we are giving it a priority which few decision makers were willing to give it during the war. That, in fact, is precisely what this book is all about. Why was the rescue of the Jews given such a low priority? To what extent were those opposed to rescue able to use the argument of wartime exigencies as an excuse for doing nothing?

On the domestic scene, too, the rescue issue was complicated, perhaps needlessly, by Roosevelt's own apprehensions and assumptions, especially about ethnic politics. The result was a certain element of deviousness in Roosevelt's position. One can in fact trace Roosevelt's path from those who insisted that the refugee presented a threat to national security to those who insisted that the humanitarian roots of the New Deal had to be watered by something more than rhetoric. The President appeared at home in either camp. Neither side knew for certain where Roosevelt would stand at a given moment. This absence of a specific mandate, which some observers see as the most typical aspect of Roosevelt's style of administration, was very apparent on the rescue question. Decision making was rarely clear cut. Roosevelt remained above the battle and when he did intervene directly his advice had a visionary quality made possible by being nowhere anchored to the basic facts of the case. The effect was that the agencies and departments responsible for administering the various elements which made up the rescue program found themselves in the unceasing conflict of overlapping authorities following divergent policies. Under Harold Ickes the Department of Interior simply did not share the State Department's phobia regarding refugee spies. The same was true of other conflicts, some of which might have been resolved had Roosevelt acted more the lion and less the fox.

Naturally, in an issue where life and death hung in the balance, every step taken by the Administration was bound to be emotionally charged. The stakes for all involved in making or attempting to influence rescue policy and administration were high, and accusations of duplicity and worse were not long in coming. Almost three decades have passed since these events yet the passion they arouse shows few signs of waning. I am as much subjected to them as anyone else. My own impatience with the listless manner in which the State Department approached the rescue problem has, I fear, crept into the narrative. I feel that more might have been done but I am also aware that there were many factors in the rescue situation which were simply beyond the Roosevelt Administration's control. Not the least of these was Berlin's determination to liquidate the Jews and the great difficulty of assigning to a modern nation-state a humanitarian mission to rescue a foreign minority for which it had no legal responsibility. It is a moral and humanitarian response we seek from the Roosevelt Administration. Such responses are rare in history and practically nonexistent during wartime. The villain of the piece, in the last analysis, may not be the State Department or even certain officials but the nature of the nation-state itself.

A word of appreciation is in order to Dr. E. T. Parks of the State Department's Historical Office, who granted me permission to examine the Department's archives and returned my notes in record-breaking time. I believe I was the first researcher to have been granted such access. I hope he does not feel that I have abused the privilege. Miss Elizabeth B. Drewry, formerly of the Franklin D. Roosevelt Library, and her staff of archivists were helpful in familiarizing me with the Library's mass of material on the rescue theme. There were many others who were helpful and I am grateful to all of them. A special debt is due to Professor Henry B. Parkes of the History Department of New York University who served as midwife for the birth of the doctoral dissertation on which this work is based. He patiently and cheerfully bore the rantings of a feverish student delving into the morbidities of the Holocaust.

The errors which have remained undetected, and there are bound to be some, are of course the author's responsibility.

Henry L. Feingold

New York
November 1969

The Politics of Rescue

1

The Refugee-Rescue Crisis

The massive refugee problem of the 1930's and the problem of rescue during the war years originated in the Nazi quest for a solution to its "Jewish problem." After the advent of Nazism in 1933 the world witnessed a display of national paranoia as Germany imagined itself in mortal combat with a powerful and corrupting Jewry, proceeded to make the solution of its Jewish problem the *idée fixe* in an otherwise sham ideology, and culminated its struggle for survival by liquidating a small, unarmed, relatively gifted minority of its own loyal citizens.

Solution by annihilation was inherent in Hitler's thinking, although plans for the systematic slaughter of Jews were not made until the Wannsee Conference in January 1942.[1] The first phase of oppression after he became Fuehrer and Chancellor of the Third Reich, though marked by atrocities, was devoted primarily to ridding Germany of Jews by forced emigration. Willing or unwilling recipients of a heavy influx of penniless refugees, the nations bordering the Reich were hardly able to ignore Berlin's racial machinations, but across the Atlantic no such problem developed. The accident of geography coupled with a highly restrictive immigration law effectively curtailed the refugee flow. Between 1932 and 1938 the United States actually sustained a net loss of immigrants.[2] Yet it was this country, rather than those bordering Germany, which in March 1938 took the initiative in calling a special international conference on the worsening refugee situation. Franklin D. Roosevelt's motivations and the subsequent actions of his Administration are best viewed within the context of

3

the refugee crisis brought on by Nazi Germany's anti-Jewish policy. It was this policy that forced the American Jewish community to come to the aid of its beleaguered European brethren and it was from the President directly that Jews expected succor.

THE SITUATION IN THE REICH

The attack on German Jewry began in earnest in September 1935, when the Nazi regime systematically began to force that well-assimilated group out of the national entity through the enactment of the Nuremberg Laws. The implementation of these increasingly severe anti-Jewish measures was at first far from orderly. Periods of severe repression were followed by periods of respite as the Nazi administrative machine struggled to coordinate and focus its activities. The erratic course of the exodus of German Jewry can be traced to these alternating periods. For German Jewry, a group particularly disinclined to uproot itself, the periods of respite afforded momentary security and even hope that all might be well again, that the Nazi menace was but a temporary aberration. When such hopes turned out to be illusory the despair of Germany's Jews knew no equal.[3]

The lack of *gleichschaltung* or coordination, so uncharacteristic of German bureaucracy, was caused partly by the problem of implementing such unprecedented legislation against a well-integrated Jewish community. Distinguishing between Aryan Germans and Jews proved a formidable task. Moreover, the Nazi hierarchy did not yet share precise plans or even common assumptions regarding the solution of the "Jewish problem." Practical-minded leaders such as Hjalmar Schacht, president of the Reichsbank, Wilhelm Frick, Minister of the Interior, Walter Funk, Minister of the Economy, and Ludwig Beck, Chief of the General Staff, were primarily concerned with restoring the Reich's economy so that the rearmament program could go forward. Thinking exclusively in economic terms, they tended to link a solution to the "Jewish problem" with Germany's severe exchange crisis. Ultimately such an association became the basis of the ransom proposal of 1939. These operationalists were aware that expropriating the assets of less than 2 percent of the Reich's population could nevertheless lead to serious economic dislocation especially when the expropriatees were so well-placed in the economy. As early as August 25, 1935, Schacht warned against the *Einzelaktionen* (random Nazi-sponsored actions of violence against Jews), which he asserted were interfering with the rearmament program.[4] For Nazi visionaries such as Josef Goebbels, Minister of Propaganda, Reinhard Heydrich, Minister of Security, Joachim von Ribbentrop, Minister of Foreign Affairs, and Heinrich Himmler, Minister of the Interior, such economic disadvantages originating in the anti-Jewish depredations hardly mattered. The real problem of the Reich, the holy work to which it was dedicated, was the elimination of the international Communist conspiracy which they viewed as anchored somehow in a body called international Jewry. Hardly disturbed by the nonproletarian character of German Jewry, they sought to rid Germany of her Jews at any price, using the tactics of the "Green Border," and ultimately the death camp. ("Green Border" was a slang expression used by the Gestapo for the act of picking up foreign-born Jews living in Germany, holding them incommunicado, and then dumping them penniless over the border. The most notorious of such incidents occurred on October 28, 1938, when the Gestapo simply dumped a group of Jews into the no man's land near the Polish border town of Sbonszyn.) Between 1933 and 1939 neither faction was able to prevail within the party and impose its anti-Jewish program on the country. Above both groups stood Hitler, after the Roehm murder and the purge of the SA virtually unopposed, who clearly tended toward the extremist position on matters concerning Jews but at the same time displaying a remarkable indifference toward the administration of anti-Jewish measures.[5] In short, the chaotic refugee situation was itself in some ways a clear reflection of the muddled priorities within the Nazi party which only the stringencies of war would untangle. Moreover, while Nazi wrath was directed against "international Jewry," the ability to act was limited for the moment to Germany with its rather small Jewish community of 350,000 souls.[6]

Although virulent anti-Semitic rhetoric had been part of German life since 1880, German Jewry's reaction was one of bewilderment. Anti-Semitism had not prevented the rapid Germanization of Jews, who played an active role in the social and cultural life of the nation. Lulled into a false sense of security, some awaited the return of the Germany they loved, the Germany of Goethe and Heine, while still others no doubt hoped to accommodate themselves to the new situation. A small group thought that the depredations were intended against the thousands of Polish Jews residing in the Reich for whom they shared Hitler's distaste. It was this last tendency that spurred the wrath of Rabbi Stephen Wise, leader of the reinvigorated American Jewish Congress, whose pro-Zionist membership was composed largely of Jews of East European descent. Apprehensive that the Nazi depredations were committed against Eastern Jews, Wise feared that some German Jewish leaders were attempting to steer them in that direction.[7] It is difficult to envisage a powerless Jewish community having such influence with the Nazis. Wise was probably more annoyed at the increasing pressure from German Jews to halt the noisy mass protests and boycotts, sponsored by the American Jewish Congress, which they felt were endangering their already tenuous position. The growing number of Jews who chose to leave the homeland were attacked by the Organization of Jewish War Veterans who proclaimed proudly, "Nobody can rob us of our German fatherland."[8] But it was to little avail, for the highest degree of loyalty could not halt the onslaught nor could patriotic German Jews realize that their desire for accommodation had the effect of deepening the divisions within American Jewry, on which they would soon come to depend. Such exhortations, moreover, did not prevent those seeking to leave, especially the younger people, from finding a way into exile. Between 1933 and 1940 the birth rate in the Jewish community declined sharply so that by 1938 it was in an "age senilization" with 73.7 percent over forty.[9] Had the Nazis waited another generation the movement of German Jews abroad and natural attrition would have solved the "Jewish problem" for them. They of course did not and these factors instead developed into a road block to the rescue of German Jewry. That community proved to be a poor risk for mass resettlement not only psychologically and financially but demographically as well. It was precisely in the area of resettlement that the hope for immediate rescue lay.

THE CRISIS AND AMERICAN JEWRY

Faced with the crisis in Germany, American Jewry found itself reluctantly accepting the role of special pleader before the Roosevelt Administration. American influence and power might again offer some hope for deliverance, as in the past. Here was a society which allowed, indeed encouraged, the art of projecting pressure by organ-

ized groups, an art which American Jewry hastily now set out to
learn. No hyphenate group could have been better equipped for the
task.[10] Few Jews questioned the widely held belief that the New Deal
was peculiarly sensitive to human misery. The rich organizational life
of the 4,770,000 Jews of the United States, concentrated in the important urban centers of the Northeast, was further stimulated by the
Nazi threat.[11] The American Jew was likely to be better informed,
especially on foreign policy matters, better educated, and politically
more active than his fellow American.[12] Jews outpaced all other
groups in mobility and were recovering from the effects of the Depression at a faster rate.[13] The economic position of American Jewry
was similar to that of German Jewry in whose behalf it acted. A dis-
proportionate number had settled in commerce and hardly any in
agriculture. Underrepresented in basic industry such as the manufacture of steel, Jews were prominent in that section of the economy
where manufacturing and trade converge, such as wholesaling. Contrary to widely held belief, no section of the American economy, with
the exception of the garment industry, was dominated by Jews.[14]
Nevertheless, domestic anti-Semites echoing a Nazi theme found a
ready audience in America, and throughout the crisis Jewish defense
organizations continued to be plagued by images of conspiratorial
Jewish economic domination of the nation.

In matters of foreign policy the effect of the Nazi "cold pogrom"
was to intensify Jewish international-mindedness. But although Jews
tended to give verbal support to American involvement in world
affairs during the 1930's, they were in fact cautious in advocating
direct intervention when the opportunity arose, as during the Spanish
Civil War.[15] They shared with other Americans the fear of war, and
many were as anxious as the most devoted pacifist to give the appeasement policy a fair trial. Nor were Jews immune from the notion of
conspiracy in history, then popular among certain historians. The *Reconstructionist*, a publication aimed at the growing Jewish professional stratum, echoed the "merchant of death" theory popularized
by the Nye Committee hearings when it asserted in 1935 that "our
real danger is that the interests that would profit by our participation
in the [Ethiopian] war . . . will be able to beguile us with plausible,
idealistic reasons for joining it." [16]

Jewish voters had begun to switch their allegiance from the Republican Party during the presidential campaign of 1928. The move was so precipitous that it tended to outpace the more entrenched leadership of the community. From 1932 they were consistently loyal to the New Deal and unlike other ethnic groups, their ardor increased rather than diminished after the election of 1936.[17] So strong was Roosevelt's hold on the Jewish voter that even the traditionally radical elements in the community succumbed. The American Labor Party was formed to furnish a vehicle for these voters who wanted to cast their ballots for this high-born Episcopalian without compromising their credentials as radicals by voting for a capitalist party.[18] The spontaneous outpouring of Jewish support for Roosevelt reflected a strong identification with the welfare state concept to which most Jews subscribed. Its significance for our story can hardly be overestimated. The Jewish "love affair" with Roosevelt corresponded in time to the refugee-rescue crisis and had a profound bearing on it. It meant that political leverage based on the threat of the withdrawal of Jewish votes was not available to Jewish leadership, who were forced to depend on the less certain rewards for political loyalty.[19] Moreover Jewish reluctance to openly question the credibility of New Deal humanitarianism on the rescue issue contributed notably to the ominous silence which surrounded the destruction of Europe's Jews.

Insecurity generated by the spread of virulent anti-Semitism abroad and at home was a prime ingredient of American Jewish life in the 1930's. "The apprehensiveness of American Jews," wrote the authors of an authoritative *Fortune* study in 1936, "has become one of the important influences in the social life of our time." [20] Jews became aware that by example and by offering funds and leadership, the Nazi Party had succeeded in sparking a wave of domestic anti-Semitism, which, when combined with the social tensions generated by the Depression, might undo their hard-won gains.[21] It was not only that Father Charles E. Coughlin had a radio audience of 3.5 million but that the Catholic hierarchy did not often challenge the Canadian-born priest's views and that public opinion polls indicated that Coughlin and a growing group of rabid anti-Semites enunciated what a sizable portion of their countrymen felt. A public opinion survey taken in April 1939 showed that 42.3 percent of the general population believed that hostility towards Jews stemmed from unfavorable Jewish characteristics. Seven months later another poll indicated that

Jews ranked second only to Italians as the group considered to be the worst citizens.[22] The more assimilated Jews were especially distressed by this development. The American Jewish Committee, an elitist organization comprising principally the older German Jewish element, preferred to play down the idea of a Jewish vote or even a Jewish point of view, lest the nativists' charge that the New Deal was little more than a "Jew Deal" gain credence.

The close association between the Jewish community and the Roosevelt Administration was more easily denied than concealed. The special loyalty of the Jewish voter, the common interest in economic and social reform, served as a constant reminder of the close ties between the two. Moreover, Roosevelt had appointed more Jews to high places than any prior chief executive. Some Jews recited the list of Jewish names in the Administration like a litany, but for others the names of Bernard Baruch, Ben Cohen, Felix Frankfurter, Sidney Hillman, Herbert Lehman, David Lilienthal, Isador Lubin, Henry Morgenthau, Jr., David Niles, Anna Rosenberg, and Samuel Rosenman were a source of embarrassment. Roosevelt had also raised the number of Jewish appointments to the federal judiciary and while there were an even greater number of Catholic appointments, the proportionate share of such positions now held by Jews rose conspicuously.[23] Jews also began to appear in greater numbers in Congress. The Seventy-fifth Congress returned ten Jews in the first session and six in the second of whom three occupied important leadership positions. Sol Bloom was chairman of the House Foreign Affairs Committee, Samuel Dickstein was chairman of the House Committee on Immigration and Naturalization, and Emanuel Celler was chairman of the House Judiciary Committee. With such an embarrassment of political riches it was easy to believe that Jews formed a strong unified political force on the American scene, but such unity was more apparent than real.

Nazi-inspired criticism of "international Jewry" tended to conceal the fact that diversity rather than unity was characteristic of Jewish communities everywhere. Jews had never achieved a definition of their status on which all elements could agree. In the American Jewish community the divisions between "uptown" and "downtown" had barely been bridged when the refugee crisis was upon it. The designations "uptown" and "downtown" can conveniently classify the primary division within the community. The former refers to the well-to-do, assimilated descendants of German-Jewish immigrants of the nineteenth century. Its religious preference was reform Judaism and its organizational expression was the American Jewish Committee. The term "downtown" is associated with the post-1881 immigration which brought millions of Jews from Eastern Europe to American shores. Less well assimilated and generally less affluent, "downtown" Jewry was anxious to retain the various expressions of Jewish culture. Within this division such disparate groups as the political Zionists, Yiddishists, Socialist-Labor Bundists, and a strong element of traditional Orthodox Jews lived in uncomfortable proximity. The strong Zionist thrust of the 1930's, represented partly by the American Jewish Congress, was anchored here.

By 1939 all Jewish groups were aware of the gloomy prospect for German Jewry, but there were few leaders like Stephen Wise who sensed that the Nazi onslaught threatened all European Jewry. Little agreement existed on the degree of danger and what should be done about it. The crisis in Germany deepened the divisions within the American Jewish community rather than serving as a catalyst. No unified plan of action emerged; instead, half-forgotten conflicts were given a new lease on life.

Three primary issues can be isolated from the welter of arguments that wracked American Jewry in the thirties. One conflict revolved around the nature of the Jewish response to the Nazi onslaught. The second concerned the manner in which unity within the community might be achieved, and the third hinged on the role of Zionism in the American Jewish community. Not so neatly separated, these conflicts were the contemporary expression of the traditional socioeconomic division within American Jewry.

The militant sections of American Jewry, spurred on by the Zionist-oriented American Jewish Congress, met the Nazi challenge with innumerable protest rallies which soon developed into a formalized ritual. Protest demonstrations were held in local Jewish communities, drawing in non-Jewish organizations and personalities wherever possible. A mass rally at New York's Madison Square Garden, during which a resolution to the President was adopted, culminated such rallies. If such activities had little discernible influence on policy, they did serve to release pent-up emotions.

The boycott of German goods, organized after the Nazi regime imposed a boycott on Jewish businesses on April 1, 1933, was another weapon in the arsenal of the militants. Led by Samuel Untermeyer, the boycott movement spread to other Jewish and non-Jewish groups. By 1934 a world-wide boycott organization was established in Geneva. The difficulty of implementing the boycott did not deter its supporters, who sensed an opportunity to wring more civilized behavior from Berlin by posing a threat to Germany's critical exchange balance while simultaneously mobilizing the Jewish community. Boycott proponents, mustering statistics to demonstrate that the drop of the Reich's exports to the 1919 level while the trade picture for other nations showed general improvement in 1938, were not quite convincing since it proved difficult to trace the decline to the boycott.[24] Not until the early months of 1939 was their faith in the boycott redeemed, when the Reich itself linked the treatment of Jews to the improvement of its exchange position.

The American Jewish Committee and the B'nai B'rith repelled by useless emotional displays, shunned the boycott. Their leaders questioned its effectiveness, using as evidence requests from German Jewish leaders that the boycott be suspended because it did more harm than good. It was pointed out that the boycott itself was a subtle confirmation of the Nazi thesis of an international Jewish conspiracy.[25] For the Zionist supporters of the boycott the most compromising piece of evidence was the Haavara agreement which the Anglo-Palestine Bank, representing the economic interests of the *Yishuv* (Palestine Jewry) had with Germany. By means of this agreement the Jewish Agency, the legal political and administrative agent of Palestine Jewry under the British mandate, was able to derive some benefit from blocked accounts of potential German-Jewish immigrants to Palestine. The blocked reichsmarks were paid to a German exporter of agricultural and industrial machinery for Palestine. Upon his arrival in Palestine the immigrant or his representative was reimbursed by the Jewish Agency in pounds sterling. The arrangement proved economically useful to both parties, but it created a paradox for the world Zionist movement. While the business-as-usual attitude of the *Yishuv* created a captive market for German goods, organizations which supported the Zionist position in America spared no effort to boycott them.

Behind the fracas over the response to the Nazi threat were basic conflicts about the nature of the Jewish community. In social position and life style the American Jewish Committee membership resembled the leadership class of German Jewry, its ancestral prototype. Both groups held to the assumptions that the Nazi regime could be dealt with in the traditional manner, quiet behind-the-scene activity based on the intercession of influential Jews and friendly powers. Assuming a role much like that of the *shtadlan*, or court Jew during the Middle Ages, the committee spared no effort to direct the Administration's attention to the depredations committed against Jews in Germany and to the difficulties caused by the complexity of the visa procedure. A well-organized campaign to educate the public on the nature of the Nazi movement was undertaken. Cyrus Adler, president of the Committee in 1933 and a well-known scholar of Semitic languages, attempted to convince Secretary of State Cordell Hull that some intercession was called for.[26] Well-documented briefs tracing the precedent for government intercession on behalf of mistreated minorities were prepared for the State Department.[27] But Hull, who expressed sympathy with the goals of the petitioners, maintained a legalistic posture throughout the early phase of the crisis. Inquiries and representations were made with increasing frequency to the Wilhelmstrasse but the argument of the German Foreign Office that the fate of German Jewry was an internal question proved difficult to challenge.

By the midthirties the American Jewish Committee's leadership was challenged by the rapidly growing American Jewish Congress. The issue was the Committee's generally elitist point of view and its preference for restrained tactics against Nazi depredations. The Committee, as an organization of influential Jews rather than organization purporting to represent the Jewish masses, shunned the proposal of a nation-wide election within the American Jewish community. The election idea smacked too much of "a state within a state" and would arouse questions of dual loyalty, about which they were extremely sensitive. It suggested instead some loose federation of organizations, acting together for limited ends, while allowing each group to maintain its organizational integrity. The leaders of the American Jewish Congress proved far more sensitive to the meaning of what was happening in Germany and far less concerned about questions of loyalty. Unity of all Jews was imperative, exhorted Rabbi

Stephen Wise repeatedly, because "world Jewry, not German Jewry [was] under attack." [28] The Committee's legalistic response was a species of "self anesthesia" for it could not but perceive that the Nazi regime was impervious to legalistic reasoning based on a concern for human life. The character of the depredations was the surest proof of that.

The 300 national organizations and the thousands of local ones were thus never able to act in unison, but by 1938 it was apparent that the Jewish public leaned toward the more militant Congress position. By avoiding emotional displays the Committee lost considerable good will among the Jewish masses. The Zionist movement, with no such aversion, was able to increase its membership from 15,000 in 1930 to 400,000 in 1940.[29] The logic of the Congress position was compelling for people who watched German Jewry being slowly devastated by Nazi racialism and feared that the same thing was developing here. Emotional displays were excusable when one felt helpless in the face of catastrophe. "What else can we do but scream," observed one Jewish commentator, "Jewish power lies in screaming . . . we are powerless." [30]

Roosevelt, who thrived politically on such inside information, was alerted to the altered power situation in the Jewish community by numerous Zionist-inclined members of his inner circle.[31] Felix Frankfurter, whom Roosevelt had appointed to the Supreme Court at some political risk, and Justice Louis Brandeis, whom Roosevelt affectionately called "old Isaiah," were prominent in this role.[32] Outside the Administration the acknowledged spokesman for the Zionist cause was Rabbi Stephen Wise, who, almost single handed, had kept the American Jewish Congress alive during the 1920's. Wise was an early co-worker of Roosevelt's who chose to support Al Smith's nomination by the 1932 Democratic Convention. That misjudgment earned him the enmity of Louis McHenry Howe, Roosevelt's devoted secretary and political advisor. Not until Howe's influence waned in the mid-thirties was Wise able to reestablish his contact with the President. Thereafter Wise was in constant touch with the White House. The Roosevelt papers at Hyde Park contain numerous cables testifying to Wise's assiduous courting of the President. Few occasions passed without some laudatory telegram from Wise to Roosevelt.

In general, with the distinct exception of the left-wing Jewish

Labor Council, Jewish organizations were reluctant to advocate bringing refugees to American shores.[33] The lack of enthusiasm for such a solution is understandable if one considers that American Jews were subject to all the arguments in favor of restriction. Supplementing such logical reasons for restriction as the lack of jobs and even the need to maintain America's ethnic balance was a series of reasons peculiar to the Jewish community. The racist thrust of the national origins formula on which the quota system was based became for many additional evidence that it could happen here. Jewish anxiety about its position in the United States had reached extraordinary proportions in the thirties. Moreover, a Jewish-sponsored move to liberalize the law, such as the steps suggested by Congressman Samuel Dickstein during the Seventy-fifth and Seventy-sixth Congresses, had a tendency to elicit more restrictive measures whose antirefugee character was only thinly disguised. In addition, Jewish philanthropy was not equipped to handle hordes of penniless refugees, funds being depleted because of the Depression.[34] Central to all these reasons was the fear that the advocacy of a mass influx of Jewish refugees might establish a precedent, and other nations, such as Poland and Rumania, could declare their Jews surplus population and be assured that they would be resettled in the United States. Such a move might place a premium on the persecution of unpopular minorities. Cyrus Adler preferred that the Administration use its influence to secure the rights of minorities where they lived, by following the procedure outlined in the Treaty of Versailles. Failing that, non-Zionists were able to overcome their strong distaste for political Zionism long enough to support Palestine as a logical destination for refugees. "The old-fashioned anti-Zionist has become merely a non-Zionist," wrote a B'nai B'rith spokesman in 1935, "he looks with no hostility at the Palestine enterprise . . . if it will make good homes for the homeless he gives it money even." [35] Virtually any solution was preferable to bringing the refugees here. The community's lack of enthusiasm disheartened James G. McDonald, League of Nations High Commissioner for Refugees from Germany, who early warned the Jews of the impending catastrophe: "I cannot believe, no matter what the necessity at home, that American Jewry will fail to recognize that their coreligionists must be helped now," observed McDonald in the fall of 1935.[36] Like the Jews of

Germany, American Jews were slow to perceive the extent of the disaster about to overtake them.

Yet American Jewry was given ample warning of the price of disunity in the fund-raising sphere. By the 1930's fund raising had become the pivotal activity of American Jewish organizational life and an unending source of strife. The establishment of the United Jewish Appeal in 1939 to conduct one annual campaign on behalf of all overseas agencies outside Palestine marked a momentary unity which would not last. It did serve to permit nonpartisan agencies such as the American Joint Distribution Committee (AJDC) and Hebrew Immigrant Aid Society (HIAS) to carry out their important work throughout the crisis. Although the work of relief and rescue was not disrupted by internal strife, the diplomatic task of halting the refugee flow at its source was continually frustrated.

Probably no amount of pressure on the part of Jewish leaders could have succeeded in changing the immigration law or the Administration's Middle East policy; these were fixed. The disunity made a great deal of difference, however, in the area of visa administration and the compilation of special visa lists. Here snarls and blocks and miles of red tape were used by the second-echelon officials of the State Department to keep those refugees who had successfully run the gauntlet imposed by the consuls away from these shores. Leading this group was Breckinridge Long. Appointed Assistant Secretary of State for Special Problems in January 1940, he committed himself to halting completely the flow of refugees. It did not take him long to discover the disunity within American Jewry. Before he surrendered his strategic position in January 1944 he confided in his diary that "the Jewish organizations are all divided amid controversies . . . there is no cohesion nor any sympathetic collaboration—rather rivalry, jealousy and antagonism. . . ." [37] It was a startlingly accurate observation and although at other times Long was inclined to attribute immense power to American Jewry and bewail the absence of a countervailing Arab community in the United States, he was aware that disunity among the Jews was a blessing for his cause.

THE ROOSEVELT ADMINISTRATION AND THE REFUGEE CRISIS

Roosevelt was from the outset personally sympathetic to the plight of the refugees but his actions were tempered by the need to consider the wisdom of official government involvement in an "internal matter." To Ambassador William E. Dodd, his choice for the Berlin post, he confided that he preferred the use of "unofficial and personal influence" rather than government-to-government communication to moderate Berlin's racial policies.[38] His predilection for personal approach in diplomacy had no counterpart where domestic politics was concerned. Roosevelt knew that no exercise of personal charm could bring a change in the immigration law and no Administration attempt to do so was ever hinted at. Instead the Administration directed its attention to liberalizing the implementation of the law, especially the visa procedure. One of the steps taken by the Hoover Administration to assure that the labor force was not expanded during a period when employment opportunities were scarce was to discourage immigration by rigidly enforcing the "likely to become a public charge" (LPC) clause of the Immigration Act of 1917. The intending immigrant would now either have to possess enough money to support himself or produce affidavits guaranteeing his support by relatives or friends. Almost immediately after the new policy was instituted in September, 1930, the demand for visas dropped by 75 percent. Thereafter, although the number of visas issued rose steadily after 1934, the German quota remained underissued until 1939.[39] This remained true despite a ruling in December 1933 by the Attorney General that the Secretary of Labor may accept a bond in advance of issuing a visa rather than have the immigrant furnish a bond upon arrival. The hope was that such a step would remove an important stumbling block created by the LPC provision, since emigrants from Germany could not remove their property or capital. In December 1936, in view of the deepening refugee crisis, the State Department was ordered to revoke the Hoover Executive Order and to substitute a more liberal interpretation of the LPC clause. Roosevelt was kept informed of the refugee situation by political leaders with links in the Jewish community, among them Governor Herbert H. Lehman, who throughout the latter part of 1935 saw that the President was briefed on the incredible snarls in the visa procedure. It was probably due to Lehman's personal intercession that Roosevelt ordered the State Department to extend to the refugees crowding the understaffed consulates "the most humane treatment possible under the law." [40] Despite such exhortations the visa procedure caused much anguish within the Jewish community and much strife within the Administration.

The Anschluss of March 1938 not only brought on a drastic deterioration of the refugee situation by adding the 190,000 Jews of Austria but threatened further to complicate the visa situation by eliminating the Austrian quota. The Roosevelt Administration chose to combine the German and Austrian quotas despite the fact that such a step indirectly bestowed a legality on the German annexation. At the same time, despite growing opposition at home and a sudden jump in the unemployment figures, the Administration pressed forward with its new policy of giving special consideration to Jewish visa applicants in the Reich. Complaints regarding the visa procedure continued to flow into the White House and it soon became apparent that the Administration's good intentions remained largely rhetorical. They were being thwarted by the recalcitrance of the consular officials who legally held the final responsibility for determining whether visa applicants qualified.

By late 1938 and early 1939 the reaction pattern of the Administration seemed clear. It was carefully attempting to pick its way between two forces at minimal political risk. On the one hand there existed strong restrictionist sentiment generated by the Depression, and on the other a particularly loyal Jewish community allied with other liberal elements which was urging that the tradition of asylum for the persecuted of Europe be at least nominally maintained. Restrictionist sentiment was manifest in the flood of antialien proposals that poured into the House Committee on Immigration and Naturalization in the Seventy-sixth Congress and the refusal of a House Appropriation Subcommittee to vote funds to maintain the Canadian preexemption procedure. By preventing refugees here on visitors' visas from establishing residence in Canada to qualify for a regular visa, the Subcommittee hoped to eliminate an important path around the road blocks for regular visas on the consular level in Germany and Austria. At the same time a "spontaneous" pogrom on the night of November 9, during which thousands of Jewish businesses and synagogues were looted and burned, underlined the urgency of the refugee crisis. Roosevelt, taking great care to publicly guarantee that the quota itself remained inviolate, announced the extension of the visitors' visas of approximately 15,000 refugees on November 18. He "did not know that we have a right to put them on a ship and send them back to Germany under the present conditions." [41] It was, at the same time, a gesture of support for the rescue advocates and an acknowledgement of the political strength of the restrictionists.

On the diplomatic front, where involvement did not come at a political price, the precedent of concern for refugees had been established in October 1933, when the United States joined other nations in urging the League of Nations to establish a commission for refugees. James G. McDonald, then president of the Foreign Policy Association, became the first High Commissioner for Refugees from Germany but resigned dramatically in December 1935 after issuing a damning report on the League Commission's ineffectiveness and general world indifference to the refugees' plight. When, for example, the League called for an international conference to discuss the critical refugee situation in April 1936, Hull counseled FDR against American attendance lest the conference succeed in its goal of redefining the legal status of refugees so that their situation would be almost identical to that of ordinary immigrants.[42] The Immigration Act of 1924 did not distinguish between refugees and immigrants, and this lack of distinction became the State Department's primary instrument to restrict the refugee inflow.

Generally Roosevelt was content to let the State Department handle the refugee matter. He preferred to remain above the battle although he might occasionally make an inquiry or a suggestion. Such a procedure, Roosevelt had discovered in other areas, offered certain advantages, especially if the issue proved nettlesome. It allowed the agency involved to absorb much of the pressure and ire that might otherwise be directed at the White House. In the case of American Jewry it proved extremely effective. Roosevelt's benevolent image emerged from the war relatively unscathed.

Handling the day-to-day details originating in Berlin's racial policies sometimes proved a troublesome task for the Department. It involved seemingly endless wrangling with the Wilhelmstrasse. The provocative anti-Nazi speeches of prominent Americans, the economic boycott, the application of the Aryanization laws to the property of American Jews in Germany, became the daily fare of the diplomatic exchanges between the two nations.[43] Roosevelt's hope that a personal unofficial touch would help mitigate Nazi racialism proved groundless.

Instead, Ambassador William E. Dodd found himself virtually isolated in Berlin, unable even to utilize the few available sources of intelligence.[44] By mid-1938 relations between the two nations had reached a low ebb.

For Hull the Jewish-sponsored boycott of German goods posed special problems. His free-trade predilections naturally placed him in opposition to such tactics. They did not, however, stand in the way of his using the leverage the boycott gave him to remind the Wilhelmstrasse that a more humane treatment of Jews might result in better trade relations.[45] The German debt was used in a similar way. When in June 1934 the German Foreign Office requested a six-month moratorium, Hull told the German Ambassador that a more civilized racial policy might result in granting the moratorium.[46] Still, there were limits beyond which Hull would not go. When Hugh R. Wilson, Dodd's successor in Berlin, suggested to the President that a restraining influence on the Nazi regime might be exercised by blocking German funds in the hands of the Allied Property Custodian, Hull rejected the idea.[47]

Although Hull's relations with the Jewish community remained cordial, the Department itself aroused Jewish antipathy. Jewish sons had not been conspicuously successful in entering the foreign service and some were ready to share Ambassador Dodd's revelations that it was little more than a playground for the rich and well-born. As the crisis intensified, Hull, whose immunity from criticism was based partly on his choice of a Jewish mate, was found by some to lack initiative. The bureaucratic density of the Department had become a source of frustration. If there were a real will to help, a way would be found to cut through the endless regulations hampering the rescue effort. That was the gist of Congressman Emanuel Celler's criticism. Celler, who represented an almost all Jewish constituency in Brooklyn, echoed community sentiment when he accused the Department of having a "heartbeat muffled in protocol." [48]

Criticism in the liberal and Anglo-Jewish press did not disturb the Department as much as criticism and attempts to intervene in Department affairs from within the Administration. Much of the feud between Hull and Secretary of the Treasury Henry Morgenthau, Jr., had its roots in the refugee-rescue crisis. Morgenthau felt that "the State Department was simply not equipped, psychologically or administratively, for the refugee job." [49] The Treasury Department could do better, but not until January 1944 was Morgenthau able to persuade Roosevelt to let him try. In the meantime, he contented himself with doing what he could to bring pressure on Berlin. In 1937, against Hull's advice, he increased the countervailing duties on German goods, thereby thwarting Hull's reciprocal tariff policy. For Hull the action was evidence that Morgenthau was waging a "personal war" against the Nazi regime. [50] No such claim could be leveled against Harold Ickes, the Secretary of the Interior, who followed the Morgenthau example by refusing to release helium for sale in Germany. Such interdepartmental conflicts, often accompanied by personal recriminations, became a normal by-product of the conflict over rescue policy, but nowhere was it more pronounced than with the Treasury. Doubtless the Morgenthau plan, a particularly harsh policy for the treatment of postwar Germany, found some of its roots in prior conflicting approaches to what might have been done about the Final Solution.

THE UNITED STATES AND THE PALESTINE QUESTION

The increase in Zionist strength among American Jews in the 1930's reflected their widely held belief that unlimited immigration into Palestine offered the most practical solution to the refugee problem. The hope of gaining Roosevelt's support for such a policy was destined to be dashed. Roosevelt, though he frequently publicly admired the work done by Zionist pioneering in that area, would not seriously consider it as a possibility for the refugees. He felt keenly that the Middle East was a British sphere, and, as the war progressed, grew increasingly reluctant to risk a rift with the British over Palestine. Despite their growing strength and their close liaison with the Administration, the Zionists were unable to change the Middle East policy. While they turned to introducing an unceasing flow of pro-Zionist rescue resolutions in city and state legislatures, the State Department continued to follow a policy established by Secretary of State Charles Evans Hughes during the Harding Administration, of not considering the national homeland provision of the mandate as an American interest. Occasionally Zionist pressure was assuaged by the State Department directing an inquiry to London. For example, after the Peel Commission recommended partition in 1937, Anthony Eden, then British Foreign Secretary, was formally asked whether the United States would be consulted on any change in Palestine policy on the basis of being an interested party. Eden denied American responsibility and the State Department did not contest the matter. In March 1938 the President accepted without question a British-proposed limitation of the agenda of the forthcoming refugee conference which ruled out Palestine in the discussion of rescue alternatives.[51]

Again Roosevelt was able to use the State Department to deflect Zionist pressure. Delegations and letters were referred, as a matter of course, to the Department, which was asked to prepare noncommittal replies.[52] Meanwhile, the President felt no compunction about pledging his general support for the Zionist program and assuring Arab leaders at the same time that nothing would be done without their consent.[53] An astute pro-Zionist observer of the Administration's activities, Bartley Crum, went as far as claiming that every time support was pledged to the Zionists by the Administration the State Department automatically sent reassurances to the Arab nations.[54]

During the war the apprehension of the Joint Chiefs of Staff regarding the Allied strategic position, especially the military base at Dhahran and the security of the oil pipelines, served virtually to freeze Middle East policy. Behind much of American policy in the Middle East was the influence of American oil interests (Arabian-American Oil Company) whose loss would have been catastrophic to the war effort.[55]

Here then is the gloomy context in which the refugee crisis occurred. A modern nation in the grip of a passion to rid itself of its Jewish community at any price, a world as yet unaware of the murderous intent of the regime in Berlin; in the United States an Administration bound by the strictures of its immigration laws and inclined to the rhetoric rather than the substance of a humanitarian rescue policy; and a divided American Jewry, traumatized by domestic anti-Semitism, and reluctant to accept responsibility for its European brethren. Only the announcement by Roosevelt of plans to hold an intergovernmental refugee conference permitted some hope that the nations might yet do something for the hapless refugees.

The Evian Conference

On March 25, 1938, President Roosevelt informed newspapermen, gathered at his Warm Springs retreat for one of those informal press conferences in which he delighted, that he had decided to call an international conference on the refugee crisis.[1] The announcement must have confounded many people. The President had decided to move on the refugee issue when the employment rate had again reached a new low and the strength of the restrictionists in Congress was high. For the risk it entailed, tampering with the refugee issue, offered few advantages. Restrictionists, who considered the immigration law immutable, would certainly challenge the move. It seemed inconceivable that a sincere attempt to bring order out of the refugee chaos could be made without modifying the immigration law so that a distinction between refugees and immigrants could be drawn.

Nor was the hope for making an effective contribution more apparent on the foreign scene. The League of Nations already had three agencies, the High Commission for Refugees from Germany, the International Labor Organization, and the soon to be disbanded Nansen Office, struggling with different aspects of the refugee problem. Moreover, Germany's neighbors, burdened by a heavy refugee load, could not be expected to welcome an initiative by an extracontinental nation whose absorption capacity had hardly been put to the test. The British government, without whose support no effort to order the refugee chaos could hope to succeed, was under considerable pressure because of its Palestine policy. It could not be expected to welcome a conference which promised to intensify such pressure.

Roosevelt was keenly aware that he ran a political risk. "It is my hope," he informed Judge Irving Lehman, brother of the governor, "that the narrow isolationists will not use this move of ours for purely partisan objectives—but no one can tell." [2] Special care was taken to guarantee that the quota system would remain unchallenged. The twenty-nine nations invited were asked to help establish a special committee "for the purpose of facilitating the emigration from Germany and presumably Austria of political refugees," but "no country would be expected to receive greater number of emigrants than is permitted by its existing legislation." Nor would it cost anything since any new program would be financed by the private agencies. The functions of other League agencies were not to be preempted. The invitation promised not "to discourage or interfere with such work as is already being done on the refugee problem by existing agencies." [3] The Administration was making a gesture to the image of America as a refuge for the oppressed but it was also carefully reassuring those who no longer held to such a belief.

After the Anschluss Roosevelt may have felt that such a manifestation of concern was called for. Adolf Eichmann in Vienna, anxious to demonstrate to his superiors in Berlin how quickly the Jewish problem could be solved, was setting new records in the expulsion of Jews not only for speed but for cruelty.[4] Roosevelt was kept informed of the depredations by a steady flow of prominent refugees whose caliber impressed him and whose personal misfortunes aroused his sympathy.[5] There were other influences. Dorothy Thompson, who, almost singlehanded, aroused the American public to the plight of the refugees, was generally credited with having a considerable part in making the conference a reality.[6] Isador Lubin, presidential advisor, attributes the conference to Stephen Wise. "I am certain," writes Lubin, "that Franklin D. Roosevelt bringing up the problem in 1938 was the result of pressure upon him by Rabbi Wise, for whom he had a great deal of affection." [7] Frances Perkins, Secretary of Labor, finds that Roosevelt was favorably impressed by an economic theory that had been held by Jane Addams, which favored increased immigration because of its pump-priming effects on the economy.[8] Others saw in the invitation a subtle attempt by Roosevelt to alert public opinion to the growing menace of Nazism. The fear that public pressure would create proposals for more liberal immigration legislation and threaten the fragile political coalition of southern restrictionists and northern urban liberals played a role within the Administration. The State Department's Sumner Welles, it is thought, proposed the conference in order to forestall such a possibility.[9] Whatever the motivations for the invitation, the timing of it was Roosevelt's own, made against the backdrop of a deteriorating refugee situation.

When the announcement did come it caught the leaders of American Jewry completely by surprise.[10] Their jubilant reaction reached the President through dozens of wires and letters. Governor Herbert Lehman simply sent a note with the single word "splendid" on it, to which Roosevelt replied, "I only wish that we could do more." [11] Five major Jewish organizations, finding themselves temporarily united, informed the President of that phenomenon in their letter of congratulation: "These organizations frequently divided heretofore are united in requesting an interview with you." [12] They were referred to the State Department. The American Committee for the Protection of Minorities released an appeal through the press signed by 125 prominent Americans urging all nations to respond to the invitation and "unite with us in this great cooperative endeavor to ask the dictatorships to let the oppressed people go. . . ." [13] Overlooked was the Administration's careful hedging of the invitation which ruled out a refugee influx greater than permitted by existing law.

Such plaudits were somewhat tempered by the expected unfavorable reaction of restrictionists. Representative Thomas A. Jenkins, a leader of this group, castigated the President for having gone "on a visionary excursion into the warm fields of altruism. He forgets the cold winds of poverty and penury that are sweeping over the 'one third' of our people who are ill clothed, ill housed, ill fed." [14] Already Representative Samuel Dickstein had introduced legislation to modify the immigration law by mortgaging future quotas. He proposed to make the quotas for Germany for 1939, 1940, and 1941 available in 1938 and 1939, the increased admission to be balanced by some future curtailment of the quota. Here was a clear threat against which restrictionists would mobilize.

ORGANIZING THE PRESIDENT'S ADVISORY COMMITTEE

The Administration probably had no threat in mind. It supposed that private organizations would carry out the actual refugee work, the member governments to make available established diplomatic channels for purposes of communication. In order to mobilize these private organizations, their leaders were invited to meet the President at an informal White House conference on April 14. Included were Joseph Chamberlain, Law Professor and Chairman of the National Coordinating Committee; Samuel Cavert of the National Council of Churches of Christ in the U.S.A.; Archbishop Joseph Rummel of New Orleans, chairman of the Committee for Catholic Refugees from Germany; Louis Kennedy, president of the National Council for Catholic Men; Henry Morgenthau, Jr., Secretary of the Treasury; Bernard Baruch, presidential adviser; James G. McDonald, former League of Nations High Commissioner for Refugees from Germany; and later Rabbi Stephen Wise, president of the American Jewish Congress. The purpose, stated the invitation, is "to undertake a preliminary consideration of the most effective manner in which private individuals and organizations within the United States can cooperate with this government in the work to be undertaken by the international committee which will shortly be created to facilitate the emigration of political refugees from Austria and Germany." [15] The proposal that the federal government should help coordinate the private refugee organizations was not unprecedented. The National Coordinating Committee, predecessor to the National Refugee Service, which served as the steering agency for all private refugee work in the nation, had been organized in 1935 at the behest of the State Department.[16]

On April 14 the leaders of the several organizations met first with the President at the White House to be briefed on the objectives of the new committee and then moved to the State Department to discuss the agenda outlined by Undersecretary Welles. Unfortunately, the new committee's beginnings were not auspicious, its objectives were never clearly defined, and it depended for financial support on the very agencies it was supposed to coordinate. Some of its membership was poorly chosen. Baruch and Morgenthau, who were to represent the Jewish community, never became active and in fact never had participated in Jewish organizational life. On the other hand, Wise, who represented an increasingly important segment of American Jewry, had not been invited to the preliminary meeting. The error was soon rectified but the composition of the committee remained weighted in favor of non-Jewish refugee organizations even though Jews were entering the refugee stream in ever greater numbers. There was little eagerness on the part of potential leaders to head the new group. Not even the impressive title, President's Advisory Committee on Political Refugees (PACPR), could convince Hamilton Fish Armstrong, chairman of the prestigious Foreign Policy Association, to chair the new committee. He regretfully explained to the President that his interest was "after all [more] international relations than relief or philanthropy as such." [17] On May 16, 1938, when the PACPR met for a second time in the State Department, James G. McDonald was made chairman and Samuel Cavert secretary. Almost immediately work was begun on a survey of relief and resettlement opportunities. Thereafter Roosevelt seemed to have forgotten that such a committee existed and it worked almost exclusively through the State Department, where it became enmeshed in a bitter controversy over the promulgation of special visa lists.

FINAL PREPARATIONS FOR EVIAN

Meanwhile the responses to the invitation were pouring into the State Department. Cordial though they were, the major powers did not hide their apprehension. Britain asked for clarification of the President's intent and took care to protect her national interest by making her cooperation conditional: the Palestine question was not to be discussed at the conference. France, fearing that the American initiative would increase her heavy refugee burden, requested that the conference be held in executive session and that France, Britain, and the United States meet beforehand to assure a unity of views. [18] The replies of the Latin-American Republics, also cordial, usually contained some expression of their reluctance to accept more refugees. Cables came from Poland and Rumania requesting an invitation. Both were rejected because they were not potential receiving nations.

They sent observers to the conference as did the Union of South Africa. The failure to invite Portugal proved a serious oversight since the principal hope for mass resettlement at one point focused on Angola, a Portuguese possession. Luxembourg and Ireland expressed regret at not having been invited and Ireland did eventually attend. Alexander Troyanovsky, the Soviet Ambassador to the United States, true to type, saw in the conference a plot to encourage the sabotage activities of the Trotskyist *émigrés*. Only Italy turned the invitation down outright.[19] An unforeseen road block appeared when Switzerland, where Washington planned to hold the conference, requested that some other country be chosen. The Swiss felt a strong loyalty to the League agencies on refugees and were, moreover, extremely wary of antagonizing Berlin.

On Hull's advice Germany was not invited. It would be more effective, Hull reasoned, to make a unified proposal for a solution to the refugee problem rather than to negotiate with the felon about his misdeeds. The Wilhelmstrasse shared the general confusion regarding the purpose of the conference and gave no sign of willingness to cooperate. The German Foreign Office, however, was held in low esteem by the Nazi hierarchy, where such decisions were made. Hitler commented on the impending conference at an election speech in Königsberg. He spoke facetiously about his willingness to let Jews leave "even on luxury ships," but made no mention of relaxing laws on the transfer of capital and property, the principal hindrance to their exodus.[20]

Meanwhile, Sumner Welles had prepared a tentative agenda for the President's approval. It is conceivable that the ambivalence in American refugee policy can be traced to the Undersecretary. He was one of the few people in the State Department who seemed genuinely concerned for the welfare of the refugees and his energy and organizational talent figured prominently in the President's initiative. At the same time he was sensitive to restrictionist sentiment and went as far as to remind the President that the impression that the Administration was contemplating a change in the immigration laws ought to be avoided.[21] That caution was reflected in the preface of the agenda, which warned that the United States could not change its immigration laws and expected no one else to do so.[22] It also raised the following points:

(a) An examination of the possibilities for mass resettlement of refugees.

(b) Limitation of the scope of the conference to actual refugees from Germany and Austria.

(c) A pledge of cooperation with existing League of Nations refugee agencies.

(d) Plans for immediate aid to the most urgent cases.

(e) A confidential system to allow each nation at the conference to report on the number of refugees it was prepared to admit under its immigration regulations.

(f) Plans for a new system of furnishing stateless refugees with legal documents to replace the Nansen passport.

(g) The organization of an Intergovernmental Committee on Political Refugees (IGC) to deal with the crisis on a continuing basis.

Knowing that the importance of such conferences was judged by the rank of the delegation rather than the agenda, Welles suggested to Roosevelt that the Secretary of State, accompanied by Frances Perkins, George Messersmith, and himself make up the American delegation.[23] No doubt the President thought such a delegation too powerful, and nothing came of the suggestion. Instead the President selected Myron C. Taylor, a personal friend and former head of the United States Steel Company, to head the delegation. To stress the importance attached to the conference he was given the rank of Ambassador Extraordinary Plenipotentiary and assigned as technical advisors Robert Pell, of the State Department's Division of European Affairs, and George Brandt, formerly chief of the Department's Visa Division.

On July 6 the representatives of thirty-two nations met at the Hôtel Royal in Evian-les-Bains, France. In the nine days of the conference the atmosphere of confusion about the Administration's intent was intensified by the secrecy and private bargaining which characterized most of the proceedings. The confrontation of the three major powers resembled nothing so much as a poker game, observed one reporter.[24] A business-like atmosphere was maintained by the creation of two subcommittees, one to hear the recommendations of the private refugee organizations, which were well represented at the conference, and the other to make a confidential record of the offers of resettlement that were hopefully expected.

ORGANIZING AN INTERGOVERNMENTAL COMMITTEE

The motivation of the United States puzzled the delegates. Why did the United States not simply join in the work of existing League agencies? Henry Bérenger, the French delegate, after struggling heroically for an answer, finally divined that there really was no purpose: "we are simply a body which the President of the United States desired to create between America and the other continents." [25] More certain was Edouard Daladier, the French Premier, who informed Neville Chamberlain in November that he believed that Roosevelt was acting to soothe an aroused public opinion.[26]

Like France, Britain was skeptical of Roosevelt's motives but may have seen an opportunity to encourage a movement in Washington to assume more responsibility in the international arena. Nevertheless, Britain now faced the dilemma of participating in a conference whose objectives she did not support. Sir Neill Malcolm, the League of Nations High Commissioner for Refugees from Germany who had been specially invited to Evian, lost little time in putting a damper on the conference by expressing pessimism about solving the refugee problem without finding new homes for the refugees. Palestine was out of the question. The newspapers of July 9 told of renewed violence and a number of casualties in the area. London had been forced to send more troops. He could see little possibility of relief even with the creation of a new agency. The British position remained unchanged throughout the conference. At least the League Commission offered a graceful way to table the issue and avoid raising false hopes. London seemed determined to forestall creation of another refugee agency. She hoped to neutralize the American effort by insisting that the IGC be made a subsidiary of the British-dominated League Commission. The conflict over whether the IGC should be allowed to come to life was the chief preoccupation of the conference.

The State Department was prepared for British opposition to the creation of a new agency and had taken pains to assure London that no preemption of the work of other agencies was intended. Myron Taylor now repeated these assurances in his opening address.[27] In addition, the special invitation extended to Sir Neill Malcolm was

intended to demonstrate that the State Department took these assurances seriously. The British argument that no new agency was needed
was countered by pointing out that the League Commission had
become virtually impotent because it could not negotiate with Berlin,
where anything connected with the League was anathema. A new
agency like the IGC might at least attempt to solve the refugee
problem at its source. The point could hardly be disputed. In the
end the British, still sensitive to what they considered a clumsy
American intrusion which might create more problems than it solved,
gave in. The final resolution established the new agency and reiterated
a guarantee that it would cooperate with the existing League Commission.[28] It left for a future meeting delineation of areas of responsibility. The primary task of the new agency would be twofold. It
would undertake a search for resettlement havens and would seek
to negotiate with Berlin over the refugees. These were defined as all
persons from Germany and Austria "who must emigrate on account
of their political opinions or religious beliefs, or racial origins." [29]
The scope was broader than originally contemplated in the Welles
agenda because in order to negotiate with the German government
potential as well as actual refugees had to be included. The distinction
was a necessary fiction since there could be no legal responsibility
for potential refugees; they remained an "internal matter" until they
crossed the border. An optimistic closing address by Taylor notwithstanding, the creation of the IGC was the sole concrete achievement
of the conference.

THE RESETTLEMENT PROBLEM AT EVIAN

The success of the IGC in finding resettlement areas would determine
whether the refugee problem could be ordered. For the American
delegation the finding of such areas was far more difficult and entailed
a degree of embarrassment not foreseen in the relatively simple task
of establishing the IGC. The American bargaining position was not
enviable. Having no such areas available, she could offer only good intentions. In contrast, Britain and France, might, at least in theory, make
havens available in their overseas territories. Before the conference
began the American delegation searched for some way to strengthen
its position. Avra Warren suggested a way in which the number of

immigrants admitted might be made to appear larger than it really was. "For confidential bargaining purposes," he wrote to George Brandt, Breckinridge Long's executive assistant, "visitor's visas might be included in a fair comparison" with other countries.[30] Taylor's opening address made much of the generous American policy for the admission of refugees. "The American government," stated Taylor, "prides itself upon the liberality of its existing laws and practices. . . . I might point out that the American government has taken steps to consolidate the German and former Austrian quota so that a total of 27,370 immigrants may enter the United States on the German quota in one year."[31] Such sleight-of-hand deceived no one. The combination of the two quotas prevented the loss of one quota but did not add any new openings. Representatives of the private organizations may well have wondered why, even at the time of the conference, the German quota was still being underissued. Moreover, while it was true that in absolute terms the United States was accepting a greater number of refugees than any other receiving nation, the proportionate burden of the nations bordering the Reich was far greater if one calculated the rate on the ability to absorb immigrants or on the number of immigrants per hundred of native population. To these other receiving nations it might easily appear that the United States had called a refugee conference to persuade them to accept more refugees while itself maintaining a strict "keep out" policy.

Supplementing what was considered by the Administration to be a generous refugee policy was the hope that the Latin-American Republics would make resettlement havens available. This, in a sense, would be the American contribution, since she held a special position in the area somewhat analogous to Britain's position in the Commonwealth. Everything was done to encourage the republics. McDonald's suggestion of inviting only European countries was hastily abandoned and all the American republics were invited to Evian where they formed the largest regional bloc. In the next few months pressure was brought to bear on Chile, one of the more reluctant republics, to join the IGC, lest her example set a bad precedent. Helio Lobo, Brazil's delegate at Evian, was offered the office of vice-chairman of the IGC in the hope that it would encourage Brazil to open her vast interior to resettlement.[32] But at Evian it was apparent that the Latin-

American Republics could muster little enthusiasm for accepting penniless Jewish refugees.

On July 9 and 11 the Latin-American delegates rose, one by one, and with all the eloquence they could muster shattered any illusion on the possibility of resettlement in their areas. The delegate from Peru, Francisco Calderón, had not "forgotten the teachings of Nietzsche, that Jewish influence, like leaven or ferment, is of value to all nations." [33] Peru, however, had quite enough ferment, and her immigration law, like that of the United States, was designed to protect her racial composition. The delegate from Colombia, Luis Cano, while "not prepared to resign [himself] to the belief that two thousand years of Christian civilization must lead to this terrible catastrophe," promptly suggested that the remaining European colonies in Latin America would be ideal for resettlement. Colombia itself could offer nothing.[34] The Dominican delegate, Trujillo Molina, trusted "that our conference will be like a peaceful, limpid lake, whose health-giving waters assuage the thirst and add to the fertility of the lands that border it." [35] He compensated the conference by making the only substantial resettlement offer. Representatives of the Jewish organizations despaired as the solitary hope for immediate action drowned in a sea of Latin eloquence.

Behind the refusal to consider Latin-American territory for resettlement was the fear of German retaliation. Brazil, one of the likeliest areas, was already in conflict with Berlin over the rights of her large German minority; she had no need for German-speaking refugees. Nor would the American republics risk jeopardizing the lucrative barter agreements which made Germany one of Latin America's best customers. At Evian the Latin-American delegates would do nothing that could be construed as anti-German and threatened not to sign the final resolutions if a request to Berlin to allow refugees to remove more of their property were not softened.

Perhaps even more important in Latin-American reluctance was the occupational stratification of the refugees. Good farmers were needed in the area, not merchants or lawyers. There were, moreover, enough social tensions without importing large numbers of Jews. The delegate from Venezuela called it the desire for "demographic equilibrium," which translated freely meant no Jewish merchants, peddlers, or intellectuals.[36] The report of the technical subcommittee presented on July 14 showed that most of the Latin-American delegates had not even bothered to inform the committee of their immigration laws and of potential resettlement possibilities. Nor did anything come of a formula suggested by the Central-American Republics which would have assigned a quota of refugees to each nation based on economic and geographic resources. Bound by its immigration regulations, the American delegation could not entertain such a practical proposal.

THE ZIONIST REACTION TO THE EVIAN CONFERENCE

For Jews the Evian conference was a cruel disappointment. Consideration of a Zionist solution to the refugee problem had been ruled out and Latin America had failed to respond with an alternative. Evian, in the words of the delegate of New Zealand, became a "modern wailing wall." [37] The Anglo-Jewish press generally agreed with an estimate by Ira Hirschmann, a New York department store executive who left the conference for Vienna because he became convinced that Evian was "a facade behind which the civilized governments could hide their inability to act." [38] The conference confirmed what Zionists had claimed all along. Jews would have to depend on themselves in a world indifferent to their fate. Josef Beck, the Polish Foreign Minister, saw the development of an irresistible Zionist thrust among Jews which would make them increasingly disinclined to collaborate in other remedies.[39] The Zionist view of a beleaguered world Jewry surrounded by a murderous world community became a fixation which is still in evidence.

Zionist self-reliance did not of course mean that possibilities for influencing the course of events were overlooked. Despite British refusal to discuss Palestine at Evian they continued to shower the Administration with pro-Palestine appeals. Three days before the conference was scheduled to begin, Stephen Wise declared in a speech before the annual convention of the Zionist Organization of America that the conference would be a "dismal failure" unless Britain opened the doors of Palestine. Several days later the United Jewish Appeal, meeting at the Hotel Astor in New York, sent a similar plea directly to the delegates gathered at Evian. Such activities had little discernible effect. At the conference the Zionists faced an uphill fight, for not only was the British delegation implacable on the Palestine issue but the other Jewish organizations refused to unite under the Zionist banner. An attempt to draw up a joint memorandum recommending the Zionist solution to the refugee-rescue problem fell through and the Jewish organizations fell into bitter open dispute. Zionist clamor did, however, force Lord Winterton to address himself to the homeland issue and while he predictably ruled out Palestine, he opened up the enticing possibility for resettlement in Britain's African possessions for the non-Zionist representatives.[40]

Such long-range hopes increased the agony of one representative who came to Evian from Vienna with an immediate need to find asylum for 40,000 Viennese Jews. Dr. Heinrich Neumann was ostensibly dispatched to Evian by Adolf Eichmann with an incredible proposal to ransom Jews. Since Austria no longer existed, the conference technically could not discuss the offer, nor did they want to. News of the Neumann mission caused some consternation among the delegates and representatives of the private organizations. The authenticity of the offer and its source, about which a novel has recently been published, have never been firmly established.[41] In any case the Neumann plea differed only in urgency from the needs of other organizations representing Jews under Nazi hegemony and may actually have represented an Eichmann gambit to beat out his colleagues in making Vienna *Judenrein* (free of Jews). In general, private organizations that had direct contact with refugees were more inclined to stress the need for systematic emigration, whereas those farther away from the scene dwelt more on the need of finding a way to protect minorities where they were.[42]

A JEWISH QUESTION OR A REFUGEE PROBLEM?

The organization of a new refugee agency could not allay the fear that the conference may have damaged the rescue cause. During the conference attention was riveted on the worsening situation in Rumania and Poland. Evidence mounted that these Jewish communities would also be forced to join the refugee stream.[43] Observers from both nations were present at Evian and their governments had already made it clear that they expected equal opportunity with Germany to rid themselves of their Jews. Poland went so far as to hint to the State Department that suitable pogroms could occur to impress the powers with the urgency of its situation.[44] A Pandora's box would be opened if the receiving nations gave the impression that they were about to assume responsibility for any and all refugees. The nub of the problem was in the distinction between what Berlin called its Jewish problem and what the receiving nations preferred to call the problem of political refugees. While Berlin was solving its "Jewish problem" and Rumania and Poland were threatening to follow suit, one was hard pressed to find, either at Evian or in the State Department, any official recognition that the refugee crisis was in fact related directly to Berlin's racial machinations. Roosevelt was anxious to conceal the largely Jewish character of the refugee crisis. The invitation and the agenda referred to "political refugees" and the final resolutions drawn up at Evian spoke of "involuntary immigrants." The Administration took great care to give the PACPR an interdenominational membership and when the British inadvertently broke the rule by distinguishing between Jewish and non-Jewish refugees there was considerable distress in the State Department. No one spoke of Jews except Berlin.[45]

The Administration assumed that there would be more public support for the refugee effort if its Jewish character were played down. If a distinction between Jewish and non-Jewish refugees was made, it reasoned, only the latter would be resettled and Jews would be left stranded. Roosevelt had early in his Administration been made aware of the political liabilities which the label "Jew Deal" entailed.[46] Domestic anti-Semites would surely fix on the refugees as a likely target for their propaganda. Unforeseen by the Administration was the fact that euphemisms like "political refugee" would become an impediment to rescue and create something of a paradox. While Berlin was converting all "enemies," including Roosevelt, to the Jewish faith, the Roosevelt Administration was reconverting Jews, caught in the Nazi net, to a bland category called "political refugees." Washington's bureaucracy, like Berlin's, invented a terminology to camouflage what was happening and in doing so helped to muffle the rumbles of the Final Solution.

Maintaining the fiction, especially that the refugee problem was political in character, proved difficult. The effects of Nazi propaganda were widespread and spoke exclusively of Jews and rarely of political refugees. At Evian twenty of the thirty-nine private organizations represented Jewish interests. Most important, the composition of the refugees was the surest proof of the link between the Reich's Jewish problem and Roosevelt's "political refugee" problem. Of the estimated 660,000 refugees in July 1938, 300,000 were confessional Jews, 285,000 were non-Aryan Christians disqualified by part Jewish ancestry (first and second degree mixtures under the Nuremberg Laws), and 75,000 were Catholics.[47] As non-Jewish political undesirables made their way out of Germany or succumbed, the proportion of Jews would rise.

The delegates at Evian could not completely fathom the Jewish dimension to the refugee exodus. Only one delegate cautioned that disaster might overtake all European Jewry.[48] It was difficult to understand the Nazi obsession. How could one take seriously the Nazi charge that a small ageing Jewish community which had produced four Nobel Prize winners presented a danger to Germany's existence? There was an element of unreality and no doubt a hope that the Nazis would stop carrying on, and the vexing refugee problem would resolve itself.

AN EARLY GERMAN REACTION

Nazi authorities would probably have been gratified had the conference simply assumed responsibility for resettling the Jews of Germany and Austria. It was clear from the first days of the conference that no such desire existed on the part of the receiving nations. Officially Berlin denigrated the conference and in the Foreign Office a fear arose that it would become a focal point for anti-Nazi propaganda. Only two days after the conference opened Ernst Weizsäcker, who held the position of Secretary of State, the equivalent of an Under-Secretary in the U.S. State Department, presented a pessimistic estimate of the possibilities of success in solving the Jewish problem.[49] On July 12 the *Deutsche Diplomatische Korrespondenz*, the official organ of the Foreign Office, gloatingly observed that ". . . since in many foreign countries it was recently regarded as wholly incomprehensible why Germans did not wish to preserve in its population an element like the Jews . . . it appears astounding that countries seem in no way particularly anxious to make use of these elements themselves now that the opportunity offers." [50]

Such sarcasm could not fully conceal the Foreign Office's disappointment. The Nazi regime had permitted the *Reichsvetretung der Juden in Deutschland*, the Nazi-controlled Central Organization for German Jewry, to participate unofficially in the conference. Hugh Wilson's optimism about the Reich's eventual cooperation with the IGC was dimmed two weeks later by Berlin's first rejection of an offer to negotiate on the refugee issue.[51]

PROBLEMS IN ESTABLISHING NEGOTIATIONS WITH BERLIN

Berlin's adverse reaction did not deter the IGC from holding its first meeting on August 31 in London. A compromise with London resolved the problem of leadership. An American would be the director of the new agency and the chairman would be British. Appointed to the former position was George Rublee, a crony and fellow Groton alumnus of the President, to whom some attributed the remarkable success of Dwight W. Morrow in finding a formula to resolve the sticky Mexican Church-State dispute in 1928. At the time Rublee was legal advisor to the American Embassy in Mexico City. He had earned a reputation as an astute, persistent negotiator. Earl Winterton, a member of the House of Lords, was the shy and somewhat cautious choice of the Foreign Office. He had been leader of the British delegation at Evian, where he had established a reputation as a staunch anti-Zionist. A meeting between Rublee and Winterton at the latter's estate before the conference demonstrated to Rublee a continued lack of enthusiasm by the British regarding the American plan. Taylor had prepared him for that but the dismal performance of the London delegates was new to him. Only twenty-seven of the original thirty-two members of the IGC bothered to send a delegate and then it was usually a head of a trade mission who knew little about Evian and cared less. France was at first unwilling to send delegates, and Brazil never did. It became virtually impossible for the conference to complete the work of Evian and define with some precision what the mission of the IGC should be and how best to achieve it. The Roosevelt refugee-rescue initiative had reached a dead-end and the IGC seemed to have died aborning.

Urgent pleas to the State Department for some indication of what resettlement offers were already in hand resulted only in counsel for patience. A Rublee suggestion for tactics to generate more generosity by the American republics had no effect. Without some leverage, some assurance that the IGC had resettlement havens available, there could be no point in going to Berlin. Finally Rublee, at his wits' end, was forced to conceive of a hypothetical resettlement scheme which he could only hope would materialize later. The scheme called for the Latin-American Republics to absorb 250,000 additional refugees, the United States, Britain, and France would somehow find room for the remaining 250,000.[52] Roosevelt's good cheer and optimism that the nations were about to abandon their overcautious attitude towards the influx of refugees must have been small comfort to Rublee.[53] The Latin-American republics were in the midst of changing their immigration regulations towards greater restriction. In the United States a Roper poll indicated that restrictionist sentiment among the general public was rising sharply.[54]

British recalcitrance was an unending source of frustration. London had not abandoned plans to put the refugee mess back into the hands of the League of Nations High Commission, which was to be reorganized in September 1938. "To put the situation bluntly," Rublee wired Hull on October 12, 1938, "I have no indication that the Germans are reluctant to talk. It is apparent to me, however, that the British are reluctant to have me talk with the Germans." [55] Rublee expressed concern lest the British prevail and "the criticism of the Intergovernmental Committee and in particular of our government as a sponsor of the committee [mounts] in circles in close touch with the refugee situation." [56]

As exasperated as he may have been by the British and French attitude, Rublee had little difficulty in seeing their side. Both nations had judged the resettlement effort hopeless and, since the League Commission confined itself to helping actual refugees rather than potential ones, it at least held out the promise that they would not be burdened with additional refugees. More anxious to be helped than to be helpers, both nations only vaguely felt a moral responsibility towards the refugees. Why should Berlin's madness become the special responsibility of their governments? Moreover, if the contemplated negotiations with Berlin, for which the IGC was created, were successful, there would be more refugees to be absorbed. Rublee was forced to discount active British and French cooperation and proceed without it.

In Berlin, too, circumstances for negotiations were not encouraging.

Two months had passed since the London conference and State Department feelers had been met only by official coolness. Wilson, whose optimism that the Nazi hierarchy would ultimately agree to negotiate remained unimpaired, talked with Weizäcker on October 18 and thought he understood the reason for the delay. The division between Nazi moderates and fanatics had not yet been resolved and no decision on the extent of cooperation with the IGC could be made until it was.[57] Viewed in the context of the time Wilson's optimism was not far-fetched. September had after all seen negotiations with Hitler on the Sudeten problem. The appeasement policy had not yet lost its credibility. The belief was strong that there were men in the Nazi hierarchy anxious to maintain the sweet reasonableness of Munich. Surely if Berlin could negotiate on the Czech problem she would negotiate on refugees. Myron Taylor had even tried at Evian to link the solution of the refugee crisis to the appeasement policy by cautioning that failure to resolve it "may hinder seriously the process of appeasement in international relations."[58] The warning was directed as much to the delegates as it was to the Nazi moderates. On October 3, in a speech before the Foreign Policy Association, Taylor went as far as outlining a possible basis for a settlement. He estimated that German Jewish property in Germany was worth between two and six billion dollars. "Even the lower figure," he calculated, "would be more than enough to reestablish the half-million persons elsewhere, were it possible to use it."[59] The developments in late October and early November would force a downward estimate of the value of Jewish property in Germany.

Meanwhile, Roosevelt decided to take a hand in establishing contact with Berlin. He requested Neville Chamberlain to use his new understanding with Hitler to bring more flexibility on the refugee issue:

The Intergovernmental Committee has scrupulously avoided any emotional or critical approach to the problem and is on the contrary seeking a solution along strictly practical lines. While it may be too much to expect an early change in the basic racial policy of the German Government, nevertheless it would seem reasonable to anticipate that the German Government will assist the other governments upon which this problem has been forced by relaxing the pressure upon these people sufficiently to permit the arrangement of orderly emigration and by permitting them to take with them a reasonable percentage of their property.[60]

Chamberlain rebuffed the President. Such matters, he told Ambassador Joseph P. Kennedy, are best handled through formal diplomatic channels.[61]

Meanwhile, in Germany a new development led rescue advocates to believe that a favorable change towards the idea of negotiations was in the making. News that the 1937 German trade surplus had, by 1938, been converted into a 413,000,000-reichsmark deficit became known.[62] Almost simultaneously with the exchange report stories reached rescue advocates that the German Ministry of the Interior had annulled all passports held by Jews and substituted in their place emigration permits. From this it was deduced that the Nazi bureaucracy was setting the stage for some sort of offer and was holding German Jewry hostage in true underworld style. But there would be much more shifting of positions in Berlin before an agreement to negotiate would be given. Sponsors of the boycott, who were perhaps wont to attribute too much to Nazi concern about its exchange situation, had conveniently overlooked another ominous development. On October 2, Reinhard Heydrich, Chief of the Security Police and a staunch proponent of a radical solution to the Jewish problem, seized thousands of Polish Jews living in Germany and dumped them into the no man's land near the Polish border town of Sbonszyn.

November saw a further development of the radical trend apparent in the Sbonszyn incident. Among the deportees Heydrich had dumped over the German border was the father of a seventeen-year-old Jewish boy, Herschell Grynszpan. Young Grynszpan, half-crazed with anguish, shot Ernst vom Rath, Third Secretary of the German Embassy, in Paris. The shooting was made a *cause célèbre* by the wild men of the Nazi leadership. Goebbels, especially, saw in the death of vom Rath an opportunity to improve his own position. Capitalizing on the Jewish problem could be a mobility instrument within the hierarchy. He sparked a "spontaneous" orgy of arson and looting which has since become known as *Kristallnacht* or the "Night of the Broken Glass." Shortly before it was to take place, Heydrich sent a TWX message to all SS groups cautioning that only "such measures are to be taken which do not entail a danger to German life and property." [63] Unexpectedly the planned excesses got out of hand. "Beginning systematically in the early morning hours," the New York Times correspondent reported, "in almost every town and city in the country, the wrecking, looting and burning continued all day. Huge but mostly silent crowds looked on and the police confined themselves to regulating traffic and making wholesale arrests of Jews 'for their own protection.' " [64]

As the extent of the excesses became known, a bitter anti-Nazi reaction abroad caught the Nazi regime completely off guard. Hans Dieckhoff, the German Ambassador in Washington, frantically cabled Berlin that American public opinion "is without exception incensed against Germany . . . even the respectable patriotic circles which were thoroughly . . . anti-Semitic in their outlook also begin to turn away from us." [65] The boycott, too, received a new lease on life. From London Herbert von Dirksen was even more gloomy. The excesses had not only turned public opinion against Germany but had discredited Chamberlain and his appeasement policy.[66] The dispatches were not exaggerated. Public opinion polls reported a strong anti-German reaction in the United States.[67] The public outcry ran the gamut from protest rallieds to a bomb threat to the German Consulate in New York City, to which Mayor Fiorello H. La Guardia responded by assigning an all-Jewish police detail.[68]

Indeed, so intense was the public reaction that officials in the State Department feared that the Department would be forced into some kind of retaliation and incidentally some liberalization of the immigration law.

The German situation was uppermost in our minds [wrote J. Pierrepont Moffat, chief of the Division of European Affairs of the State Department on November 13] the wholesale confiscation, the atrocities, the increasing attacks . . . have aroused public opinion here to a point where if something is not done there will be a combustion. The difficulty was to find ways and means of making a gesture that would neither inherently hurt us nor provoke retaliation that would hurt us.[69]

George Messersmith, now an Assistant Secretary of State, shared Moffat's concern for finding the proper response, lest the Department fall behind the march of public opinion. To get "out in front" and attempt to guide it he suggested to Hull that Hugh Wilson be recalled for consultation "as a token of our disapproval of this wholesale inhumanity." [70] On November 18, Roosevelt followed through by announcing at his news conference that Wilson had been recalled.

Dieckhoff's recall followed as a matter of course, a small price to pay for assuaging public opinion. The effect of breaking a vital communications link on the possibility of negotiating the refugee issue went by the board in the excitement of the moment.

Informed by the State Department about a ground swell of public support for refugees, Roosevelt decided to use the moment to make another gesture. He told the gathered reporters on November 15 that he "could scarcely believe that such a thing [*Krystallnacht*] could occur in a twentieth century civilization." [71] To show his concern he was ordering the Labor Department to arrange a six-month extension of visitors' visas. (See footnote 41, Chapter 1.) But the Administration was not prepared to tamper with the quota system. An inquiry by Myron Taylor concerning the possibility of liberalizing the quota system brought a very explicit response from Samuel I. Rosenman, a member of Roosevelt's inner circle and a prominent member of the American Jewish Committee: "I do not believe it either *desirable* or *practicable* to recommend any change in the quota provision of our immigration law." [72] Taylor was prevailed upon to prick the bubble of hope that the radical change in the public mood had generated. He chose a radio address on November 25 to caution refugee advocates and to reassure the public that no attempt to change the immigration law was pending.

The Administration's sensitivity about the quota system was based on the recognition of the vigor of the congressional restrictionists. The winter of 1938 saw a bitter congressional debate on immigration in which the restrictionists clearly held the upper hand. The public reaction to *Krystallnacht* seemed to represent no more than a strong spectator sympathy for the underdog. The percentage opposed to changing the law had actually risen from 67.4 in 1938 to 83 in 1939. [73] Messersmith's concern about falling behind public opinion was matched by Roosevelt's caution about getting too far in front of it. The President's well-timed gesture of extending visitors' visas was a prudent middle course between the refugee enthusiasts and restrictionists.

In the Reich the Administration's cautious response appeared totally inadequate for the critical post-*Krystallnacht* situation. Many German Jews understood for the first time the hopelessness of their situation. Panicky crowds of Jews formed long lines every day before the

Embassy and the consulates. In May 1939 there were enough applications on file in the consulates of Germany, Austria and Czechoslovakia to fill the quota for the next half decade.[74]

Moderate Nazis were as appalled by *Kristallnacht* as civilized opinion in the receiving countries, but for different reasons. The pogrom had been counterproductive in every respect. The adverse reaction abroad would certainly lead to a strengthening of the boycott and if the exchange crisis worsened there would have to be a redefinition of the ambitious rearmament goals of Göring's four-year plan. Worse yet, the pogrom had resulted in considerable destruction of property, which not only placed the insurance companies in an embarrassing situation but affected the property inventory of the nation. A department store, whether Jewish-owned or not, was an important exchange facility whose destruction was costly to the nation. Such a pogrom was a luxury which the Reich could ill afford, especially when there was the alternative of simply nationalizing Jewish property. A way of making up the loss was needed and what better way than having the victims themselves compensate the nation while at the same time bringing the remaining Jewish property into the national coffers? At the suggestions of Goebbels, Göring leveled an "atonement fine" of a billion reichsmarks against the German Jewish community. The decree, promulgated on November 12, fixed each Jew's share at 20 percent of his registered property, which would be paid in four installments by all who possessed property worth more than 50,000 reichsmarks. Soon an additional 5 percent was added. On the same day all Jewish retail establishments were ordered closed. On December 3, Jews who owned real estate, industrial firms, and securities were notified of the government's intent to liquidate them. Thus during November and December 1938, substantially all remaining property in Jewish hands was in one way or other taken by the state. In addition, Jews wishing to emigrate were required to pay a security tax and a 25 percent "flight tax" on all property valued at more than 200,000 reichsmarks or yearly incomes over 20,000 reichsmarks. Considered with the earlier dismissal of Jews from the professions and proscriptions against employment of Jews in civil service, the decrees accelerated the pauperization of German Jewry. So grave had their economic plight become that the British chargé said he feared that "the civilized world is faced with the appalling sight of 500,000 people about to rot away in starvation." [75] That may have been an overstatement, but certainly Myron Taylor's hope of using Jewish capital to resettle German Jewry seemed no longer feasible.

The effect of *Krystallnacht* was twofold. It alerted the public to the drastic measures taken against Jews in Germany and left for them a residue of good will. At the same time, even the most Germanized Jew was now forced to think in terms of emigration. The increased need was not matched by increased opportunities. In Latin America the movement towards ever tighter admissions requirements continued, uninfluenced by the pogrom. In Britain too, nothing had changed. Neville Chamberlain's suggestion that some refugees might be settled in the former German colonies in Africa brought an outcry not only from Berlin, which somehow felt a claim to these areas, but also from Zionists who had strong negative reactions to anything that smacked of Germany or might again one day be German. When these factors are considered together with the pauperization of German Jewry, the effect of the pogrom was to cause a sharp deterioration in the refugee situation.

One unforeseen result would prove a boon to refugee advocates, however. The effects of the pogrom within the Reich had momentarily discredited the radical element of the Nazi party. Moderates again seemed to find a voice. In mid-December Hjalmar Schacht, head of the Reichsbank and spokesman for the moderates, paid an inconspicuous visit to London with a proposal for Rublee and Jewish leaders.

Negotiations with the Reich

For sheer absurdity the negotiations that took place in the early months of 1939 are difficult to match. Consider the situation—a modern nation enters into protracted negotiations with an international agency, which officially it does not recognize, over the disposition of a minority of its own citizens, who have, in fact, been remarkably productive in contributing to its culture.

NAZI POLITICS AND THE ISSUE OF NEGOTIATIONS WITH THE IGC

It was not recognition of the absurdity of the situation that compelled radicals like the new Foreign Minister, Joachim von Ribbentrop, to reject Ambassador Wilson's request of October 18 for negotiations with a curt comment, "visit out of the question." [1] Rather it was the belief that the offer represented a Jewish conspiracy to extract as much of the Jewish assets as possible while at the same time generating anti-Nazi propaganda. When Prentice Gilbert, the American chargé, approached Weizsäcker regarding the possibility of Rublee's visit to Berlin, he was nonplussed when Weizsäcker inquired about the percentage of "Jewish blood" in Rublee's veins. Such obtuseness was not uncommon in Nazi officialdom.

To be involved in Nazi politics meant to be preoccupied with the Jewish problem. As a high official in the Foreign Office, Weizsäcker could see how the Jewish question could be used as a power lever. When Konstantin von Neurath was Foreign Minister, two agencies, the Auslands Organization (an agency concerned with Germans living abroad) and the Büro Ribbentrop (Ribbentrop office) took shape within the Nazi party. Closer to the source of real power and more avid in their anti-Semitism, both agencies were able to usurp Foreign Office functions until in February 1938 the Nazification process was completed by the simple device of making Ribbentrop Foreign Minister.[2] Almost a year later, Ribbentrop, projecting his own experience, suspected that Schacht, in pushing for negotiations with the IGC over the strategic Jewish question, would usurp the Foreign Office function much as he had done. He knew that the moderates were secretly preparing to negotiate with Rublee and were armed with Hitler's personal order that "Jewish emigration was to be promoted by all means" as well as strong support from Reichsminister Göring.[3] The secret could not have been very well kept, for the French and the American Embassies soon got wind of it. There was little Ribbentrop could do against such impressive support; the moderates had captured the Jewish question. Ironically, his position bore a remarkable resemblance to that of Cordell Hull in the Roosevelt Administration. But Ribbentrop was patient; he would wait for the right moment to recapture the initiative. For the moment the events of November 9 had discredited the radicals.

The moderates, whose ranks had been joined by Hans Fishboeck, former Austrian Minister for Economic Affairs, hoped to use Otto Niemayer, the German agent for the Bank of England, to establish contact with the IGC. A plan to circumvent official diplomatic channels was dismissed when the moderates found Ribbentrop surprisingly cooperative. Instead Ernst Woermann, Weizsäcker's secretary, was allowed to arrange the contact directly through Dirksen in London. Hans Abshageen, a journalist and friend of Robert Pell, would serve as go-between. Ribbentrop had only one request: Absolute secrecy must be maintained and therefore George Rublee, whose mission to Europe was too well known, should not take part in the initial contact.[4] When Wilson next spoke to Ribbentrop on November 15, the change in atmosphere was apparent. Wilson must have been surprised when the Foreign Minister suggested that a preliminary meeting might be scheduled in Holland and spoke of the impending negotiations as if they were his own idea.[5]

An event, unforeseen by the moderates, gave Ribbentrop an opportunity to steal their thunder. He was scheduled to hold informal talks with Georges Bonnet, his French opposite number, in early December. The Quai d'Orsay had received a request from London to include the refugee issue in the talks. Dirksen was surprised that the British had "passed the baby on to Mr. Bonnet," and imagined that it was a response to pressure from Washington.[6] The result was that Ribbentrop was handed an opportunity to compromise the moderates' initiative, which he did not fail to use.

Meanwhile Hjalmar Schacht's visit to London was arranged through Montagu Norman, Governor of the Bank of England, and a third contact was planned by Fishboeck to take place in Brussels. From a refusal to recognize the IGC, Rublee was now overwhelmed with three negotiation opportunities. Schacht brought some order into the chaos by arranging a diplomatic illness for Fishboeck but there was nothing he could do about preventing the Bonnet-Ribbentrop discussion.

This took place on December 8 as scheduled. After exchanging views on the more important issues of the day, Bonnet led the discussion to the refugee issue. He told Ribbentrop that France was greatly concerned about Germany's solution of the Jewish question since it had resulted in an influx of Jewish refugees into France, which burdened the French economy. Could Germany do something about the situation? France, for example, was thinking of resettling 10,000 Jews in Madagascar. Ribbentrop was sympathetic to France's plight but Germany could do nothing because ridding herself of Jews was a question of national survival. Germany was anxious to bring order into the situation; "the difficulty lay in the fact that no country wished to receive them."[7] Bonnet then suggested that a way out of the dilemma would be to permit the Jews to depart with more of their capital. It was a mistake to allow Ribbentrop such an opening for he immediately went into a stock party diatribe to the effect that all Jewish property should be considered stolen since all Jews were criminals and they would have to leave Germany as they entered— penniless. The not very productive discussion created the false impression that such was the official position of Berlin, which may have been what Ribbentrop wanted to do. Roosevelt, for example, was so taken aback by Ribbentrop's diatribe that he asked Welles to confirm that Ribbentrop actually made such statements. "If there is any truth in it," he exclaimed, "the time will come when we can bring it out for the benefit of humanity." [8]

FACTORS AFFECTING THE RECEPTION OF THE SCHACHT PROPOSAL

Schacht's impending visit to London offered more cause for hope. The financial wizard had been instrumental in fashioning the barter agreements with Latin America and the Haavara agreement with the Anglo-Palestine Bank. The latter agreement, if extended, might serve as a basis for a solution since it offered the prime requisite for any agreement, a link between Germany's exchange situation and the orderly emigration of Jews. Schacht had in fact mentioned to leaders of British Jewry in 1935, a scheme to extricate German Jewry. It was very much like the Haavara agreement and foundered only when it became apparent that there would be no place to put the refugees and that it would cost too much money.[9] Those road blocks still existed in 1939.

The State Department did not have to speculate about the Schacht proposal. The American Minister to Rumania, Franklin Mott Gunther, had been informed by Otto Jeidel, formerly Schacht's assistant and now himself a refugee, of the likely outline of the Schacht proposal.[10] Jeidel cautioned that Berlin should be pressed to make a substantial contribution to the resettlement of the Jews. The French vice-chairman of the IGC, Henry Bérenger, expressed the same theme when he cautioned that Berlin intended not only to dump human beings "but also their goods in lieu of capital which the involuntary emigrants might wish to take with them abroad." [11] The British attaché George Forbes sounded the same fear of Berlin's intentions and suggested that "it might be advisable to hint at the right moment and in suitable quarters that proceeds of the fine [atonement fine leveled after *Krystallnacht*] should be applied to assisting emigration." [12] The mood in the receiving countries was one of hostility and suspicion which the Wilhelmstrasse's persistent reminders of the absence of resettlement havens did not mitigate.[13]

Rublee, concerned lest this failure to produce resettlement areas foredoom the impending discussions with Schacht, requested that the State Department redouble its efforts in Latin America. When in November it became apparent that resettlement schemes in Britain, France, and Holland would never progress beyond the discussion stage, he communicated his disillusionment to Hull: "The attack on the Jewish community on the one hand and the indifference of the participating governments on the other, has brought the affairs of the Intergovernmental Committee to a critical stage where in our opinion immediate action is required if the President's initiative is to lead to positive results." [14] He had already scaled down his optimistic earlier projections of the absorption of 500,000 people in Europe and Latin America. In October he hoped to come to Berlin with places for only 100,000 refugees in Europe and the United States. [15] By December even this scaled-down projection appeared unrealistic. Rublee gloomily pondered the possibility that the negotiations might be abortive. Once again the State Department urged the Latin-American republics to make space available. The dispatch carefully outlined the urgency of the situation, it spoke of the great talent among the refugees, of the asset such immigrants could be in developing their economies, and it appealed to their humanitarian instincts. But the republics would not relent. They could claim that they had actually doubled their admissions in 1938 when, by accepting 20,000 refugees, they admitted as many as they had in the previous five years. In the two principal receiving countries, Argentina and Brazil, the statistics told a different story. Argentina, which had accepted 5,178 Jewish refugees in 1937, reduced the inflow to 1,050 in 1938 and raised it again under pressure to 4,300 in 1939. Thereafter the number entering Argentina went down progressively to 384 in 1944. Brazil admitted 2,003 in 1937 and 530 in 1938. In the strategic year of 1939 she raised the number to 4,601 but thereafter the number of Jews admitted was lowered each year until in 1944 none entered. [16] The story is generally the same for the other republics. They responded in 1939 by admitting more refugees but nowhere near the 250,000 projected by Rublee and after 1939 the number of Jewish refugees admitted was cut each year. We shall see presently that the search for resettlement areas was no more successful. The resettlement failure was significant because it allowed the Nazi regime to claim that the world at large shared their revulsion to Jews as well as guilt in their death.

THE SCHACHT PROPOSAL

On December 14 Schacht appeared in London as a guest of Lord Norman. The purpose of his visit, the press was told, was to forestall

had warned when he first learned of the proposal's outlines, "the German Government to use our government's interest in the distress of German refugees as a lever to break up this policy and create additional spheres of bilateral influence." [18] Roosevelt liked the plan even less and echoed the criticism in the press when he wrote Taylor that Hitler was "asking the world to pay a ransom for the release of hostages in Germany and barter human misery for increased exports." [19] Nevertheless, Roosevelt too counseled against rejection of the plan out of hand.

American and British Jewish leadership opposed the continuing discussion on a scheme which they considered a moral outrage. Nahum Goldmann, leader of the World Jewish Congress, was particularly incensed at what appeared to be complicity of the democracies in the scheme. "I did not think that I was as much hurt by Hitler's measures as by the attitude of the Washington foreign office and those of other democracies." [20] If Hitler's attempt at extortion is successful, which minority would be next? Did anyone imagine that once Berlin tasted the fruits of such an arrangement she could resist the temptation of raising the price? That was the essence of Dorothy Parker's argument when she counseled the IGC to reject a heartless scheme which amounted to "nothing more or less than the extortion of ransom from the Jews of the whole world." [21] Lewis Strauss, a prominent Jew later called upon to help form the international corporation, was struck by the sheer malevolence of the proposal. Not only was Germany stealing the capital assets of German Jewry but it was trying to gain possession of the capital of Jews the world over and all for the "crime" of being Jewish.[22] Perhaps the most significant criticism originated with Joseph Tenenbaum, chairman of the Joint Boycott Council of the American Jewish Congress, when he was informed of details of the plan in August. Tenenbaum, who later became scholar of the Holocaust, urged Wise not to support the ransom proposal lest such "procedures . . . make the Jewish victims agents of the Nazi Government." [23] In sounding this note Tenenbaum unknowingly hit upon one of the principal themes of the postwar discussions on the Holocaust—Jewish cooperation in their own destruction. Wise passed on the warning to McDonald, alerting him to the implications of pressuring Jewish cooperation in the Schacht scheme.[24] The problem of whether Jews should have cooperated with a criminal government to save lives became a moral question only in retrospect. In the early months of 1939 no alternate means of rescue was available and few foresaw the possibility of mass murder.

At the time, Jewish leaders were more concerned with a practical problem: If there should be cooperation with Berlin would the ransom idea spread to Warsaw and Bucharest? These governments shared the assumption on which the Schacht plan was based, that there was an international Jewry with unlimited resources. In January 1939 Roosevelt was briefed on the possibility that these two nations would follow the Nazi pattern. Doubtlessly Roosevelt hoped to forestall a swelling of the refugee pool just at the moment when there was some hope that the existing refugee problem might be solved. "I do not believe," he wrote in a memorandum to the Secretary of State, "that the migration of 7,000,000 persons from their present homes and their resettlement in other parts of the world is either possible or essential to a solution of the problem." [25] If Warsaw and Bucharest could be denied the possibility of a reward the "exceedingly dark" situation of Jews might be improved.

Despite the reservations expressed by some officials and the hostility of Jewish leaders, the officers of the IGC decided to explore the Schacht proposal further. Lord Norman, under whose auspices the Schacht visit was made, was sent to Basel to determine whether further concessions might be won. He was to inform Schacht that the British government and the IGC were not impressed with the plan but were willing to negotiate further provided that a halt was called to the anti-Jewish actions within Germany. On January 9 Norman and Schacht met in Basel to clear the way for the Rublee visit to Berlin.

OPPOSITION TO SCHACHT PROPOSAL IN GERMANY
AND CONTINUED NEGOTIATIONS

The lack of enthusiasm for the Schacht plan in the democracies was matched by the opposition of extremists in the Reich. No sooner had Schacht returned to Berlin than Ribbentrop, still determined not to make concessions on German Jews, addressed a sharp reprimand to Schacht. There had been an intolerable breech of security. The *Boersen Zeitung*, an authoritative Swiss daily, had carried an accurate account of what transpired in London on December 19, 1938. More-

over, Schacht had stepped into a Foreign Office area of competence
with a contradictory policy. "For six months," complained Weizsäcker, "the subject had been under discussion between the foreign
diplomatic missions and the Foreign Ministry, and to date it [the possibility of negotiations] had been treated by us in an entirely negative
manner." [26] Now in one stroke Schacht's meddling in an area that was
rightfully the concern of the Foreign Office had upset the applecart.
Schacht was quite prepared for the tirade and responded by reminding
Weizsäcker that he was, after all, under direct orders of Reichsminister
Göring who had charged him directly with getting the economy
moving. The discussions on refugees were related directly to Anglo-
German trade relations. He could say no more until he reported to
the Fuehrer.[27] On January 2, Schacht was granted a long audience
with Hitler and must have been extremely convincing. He had, after
all, a plan to accomplish Hitler's two primary objectives, to shore up
the German economy, and to rid Germany of Jews, at one stroke.
Indeed, Hitler was so impressed with Schacht's achievement in London that he appointed him his special delegate for the promotion of
Jewish emigration. The Foreign Office was instructed to withdraw
opposition to the Rublee visit. The road was clear for the talks to
begin. On January 4, Schacht gleefully reported to Ribbentrop with
the Fuehrer's instructions. His victory over the former wine salesman
seemed complete.

At this juncture Rublee and Robert Pell appeared in Berlin. With
them they had brought a list of amendments which they hoped would
make the Schacht proposal more acceptable. The idea of a forced loan
through the issuance of bonds backed by the collateral of Jewish
property in the trust fund was not acceptable. Montagu Norman
pointed out that "seized Jewish property in Germany as security for
foreign investment is not worth a penny." [28] Such bonds were not
marketable, nor could receiving governments be expected to underwrite an act of confiscation. Schacht agreed to abandon the bond
scheme, reasoning that a massive act of expropriation would in any
case so depreciate the bonds and so dislocate the economy that the
advantage would be lost.[29] Instead, a plan which strongly resembled
the Haavara agreement was substituted. The emigrant, still furnished
with 10,000-reichsmarks credit, would hypothetically purchase capital
goods needed for resettlement, such as tractors or other machinery,

from German concerns. In theory these goods would then be purchased by the international corporation. This would result in an automatic increase in German export sales, with the banished Jews compelled to act as salesmen. The trust fund would also assume the cost of transportation provided German carriers were used. The use of such goods would be confined to resettlement projects, so that no inroads into conventional markets would be made. It was hoped that this provision would appease Hull, who feared Germany's use of the Jewish refugee to gain economic leverage.

Rublee was less successful in his request that Jews be allowed to take at least 20 percent of their capital with them as well as their personal property, with the exception of jewelry and art works. In return Rublee was prepared to press for an abandonment of the boycott. Schacht could agree that some categories of personal property might be removed but remained adamant in his refusal to allow 20 percent of Jewish-owned property to leave the Reich. He was prepared to make some other concessions, however. He could guarantee that no property owned by American Jews in Germany would be seized, thus eliminating a source of friction between the two nations. Also, the flight tax would be eliminated. But the atonement fine levied after *Krystallnacht* was something else; here Schacht would make no concessions. Nor could he extend the terms to cover non-Jewish refugees. The agreement was, after all, designed to solve the Reich's Jewish problem. He would try to get Jews released from concentration camps, but, of course, that was a different ministry and he could offer no guarantees. For the Jews remaining in Germany, Schacht could offer retraining facilities so that they could be transformed into useful subjects of the state.

Key to the changes was the new scheme for the forced sale of German goods, the crux of which was the establishment of a private international corporation under the auspices of the IGC, to be funded by wealthy Jews of the United States, Britain, and France. The corporation would be capitalized at $50 million for the first year, to finance resettlement ventures on a commercial basis, in the hope that these ventures could be made to show a profit after an initial period of experiment. When that occurred, investment in the international corporation could be carried under normal marketing procedures—the profit motive rather than philanthropy. Acceptance of the plan

by the IGC is an indication of how anxious refugee advocates had
become to solve the problem. The idea of a profit from resettlement
ventures was sheer illusion. Such profit had rarely even under the
most favorable circumstances materialized in the twentieth century.

After the basic agreement, there remained several details to be
ironed out. Since the servicing of the debt depended on an increase in
German exports, how would Berlin calculate such an increase? What
would be the relation between servicing the new debt and the still outstanding older debts? What provisions were there to make the trust
fund secure from seizure? Rublee was satisfied with the progress
being made and grew to respect Schacht's ability as a negotiator.
"Schacht defended the German position vigorously," he observed in
a dispatch to the State Department, "and made it quite plain to me
that he was presenting . . . a statement of program which the German Government intended to put into effect unilaterally." [30] After
three protracted meetings, the parties were ready to draw up a
memorandum, which Rublee would carry to the executive committee
of the IGC, who were waiting in Paris to give careful scrutiny to
the result of the negotiations.

At this juncture the negotiations, so painstakingly wrought, appeared
to collapse. On January 20 Schacht informed Rublee that he would
not be able to sign the memorandum which Rublee had prepared; he
had been forced to resign and his role as intermediary was at an end.
The resignation was not related to the negotiations but to Schacht's
stubborn refusal to inflate the German currency. Rublee witnessed
an extraordinary transition as the radicals regained control of the
Jewish question.

Almost immediately Ribbentrop took a hand in the negotiations.
Opposed to the agreement's conciliatory attitude toward Jews, Ernst
Eisenlohr, Schacht's assistant during the negotiations, was ordered not
to initial the memorandum and to make "no promises . . . to Mr.
Rublee concerning future treatment of Jews in Germany." [31] Ribbentrop was already negating some of the most important concessions
won by Rublee but the core of the plan, the trust fund and the private
international corporation, did not appear to be as nettlesome to him
as Schacht's timetable. For men like Ribbentrop, three to five years
was simply too long to wait for a solution. It would have to be
speeded up.

There followed a drastic reorganization of the emigration apparatus in Germany. On January 24, all agencies for emigration were concentrated in the Central Office for German Jewry (soon to be renamed *Reichsvereinigung der Juden in Deutschland*) and placed in the hands of Reinhard Heydrich, Minister of Security. The Central Organization for Germany Jewry, which had absolute authority over all Jewish activities, became within the next three months little more than an instrument of the Gestapo. At the same time Schacht's earlier mandate, to solve the Jewish problem by emigration, was canceled and Heydrich was charged with a new mission, to solve the Jewish question either by emigration or "evacuation," depending on "the way that is most favourable under the conditions prevailing." [32] The ominous use of the term "evacuation" in the Göring order could mean only that the radicals were prepared to use any means to make the Reich *Judenrein*. The order was so encompassing that it later became the enabling order for the Final Solution.

A clue to what was to come was given in a Foreign Office circular cabled to all German missions abroad on January 31. It again raised the argument that the negotiations were part of a conspiracy against the Reich, the purpose of which "was to force Germany, through international pressure, to release Jewish assets to the greatest possible extent." "It is doubtful," the circular went on, "whether international Jewry seriously desires the mass immigration of its fellow Jews from Germany without the equivalent of a Jewish State." Since the Jews are resisting immigration and the Reich cannot possibly support an independent Jewish state, "Germany will therefore herself take the initiative in finding ways and means and the destination for the emigration of the Jews from Germany." [33] Göring had, in fact, cited Madagascar as a resettlement possibility at an interministerial conference on November 12, 1938, and even earlier a special committee headed by Eichmann had been established to study the possibility of using the island to intern the Jews. The government was more anxious than ever to get rid of Jews, and would take the search for resettlement areas into its own hands because, "Germany has a major interest in seeing that Jews continue to be dispersed." [34] The Foreign Office circular still dealt in terms of emigration but Hitler had, one day prior to its distribution, mentioned the possibility of more drastic action. In a rambling address on January 30 he bemoaned the fact that all the democratic world had for Jews was "tears of pity," not resettlement havens. "If international finance Jewry should succeed once more in plunging nations into another world war, the consequence will not be the Bolshevization of the earth and thereby the victory of Jewry, but the annihilation of the Jewish race in Europe." [35] It was the first public warning that the alternative to resettling German Jewry was liquidation. Had refugee advocates outside the Reich known that war was only nine months away, more effort might have been exerted to extricate German Jewry.

THE RUBLEE-WOHLTHAT NEGOTIATIONS

The dismissal of Schacht, then, did not mean that the Nazi hierarchy had given up on the idea of working with the IGC, but neither would Berlin depend on the negotiations exclusively. The change in Berlin interrupted but did not halt the negotiations. When the talks were suddenly terminated, the "Statement of Agreement," scheduled to be discussed by the officers of the IGC in Paris on January 23, was ready for signing. What would happen now? Would the Germans demand changes? Prentice Gilbert, the American chargé, visited the Wilhelm-strasse in an attempt to find out about the status of the negotiations. Soon after, Rublee was invited to visit Göring at his country estate. There he was informed that the Reichsminister, who was responsible for the talks, was anxious to have them continue. Schacht's place would be taken by Helmut Wohlthat, a foreign exchange expert in the Ministry of Economic Affairs and recently attached to Göring's Special Tasks Committee for the Four Year Plan.

On January 25, after a brief sojourn in Paris, where he reported to the officers of the IGC, Rublee found himself back in Berlin, once again to take up the talks. The dismissal of Schacht, the tough pronouncements on emigration, and the centralization of all emigration administration in the hands of the Security Ministry could only mean that the hopes for a workable solution to the refugee problem had lessened. Indeed, with the moderates no longer a controlling influence, Wohlthat had little of Schacht's maneuverability. The talks were interrupted frequently so that he could consult with his superiors. Rublee found Wohlthat well-meaning but uncertain about the concessions he could make. In one sense he resembled Schacht. He was inclined to give the impression that matters would be worse if a less sympathetic negotiator replaced him.[36]

In the following week nine long negotiation sessions took place. Fear of underwriting an act of confiscation had led the State Department to suggest that Rublee press for the right of German Jews to retain title to their property in the trust fund. Wohlthat rejected the suggestion. Eichmann's example in Vienna had shown that the fastest way to get poor Jews to emigrate was to have wealthy Jews subsidize them. "The problem," as Heydrich saw it, "was not to make the rich Jews leave but to get rid of the Jewish mob." [37] Nor could Wohlthat agree to having a portion of the trust fund transferred outside of the sales system previously outlined and paid in foreign exchange. In return for such a concession Rublee offered to lift the international boycott. The result would have been an increase in German exports but the "new men" were less concerned with such advantages. In keeping with the Foreign Ministry's mandate, Wohlthat would no longer guarantee absolute security for the 200,000 Jews scheduled to remain in the Reich. That would depend on the international situation but Jews who had been forcibly detained after *Krystallnacht* would be released and a retraining program begun. No concession could be made on extending the agreement to non-Jews. This failure caused some discomfort in the Roosevelt Administration where a delineation between political refugees and Jewish refugees had been avoided. Among the first questions asked by Roosevelt, when Rublee visited the White House in early February to present his final report, concerned the reason for limiting the agreement to Jewish refugees. It took some doing to convince the President that Berlin only recognized a Jewish problem and refused to negotiate on anything else.[38]

With the abandonment of the idea of forced loans based on bonds backed by the collateral of Jewish property in the trust fund, the implementation of the "Statement of Agreement" had become relatively simple. The two sides would be able to work independently. The Germans would establish the trust fund and the IGC would organize a corporation representing international Jewry. Contact would be established directly between the head of the corporation and the German government, since technically the Germans did not recognize the IGC as a legal body. Each side would carry out its part of the agreement unilaterally but nothing would be done by Berlin until it had iron-clad assurances that resettlement havens were available. Schacht had not insisted on such a requirement and its inclusion marked a significant departure, since Nazi authorities were fully aware that the receiving nations were no closer to solving the resettlement dilemma in February 1939 than they had been in July 1938.

The "Statement of Agreement" was completed on February 2 after which Wohlthat insisted that the signing be delayed to allow for proper translation. The period was used for a careful final scrutiny of the memorandum. On February 7 Rublee appeared in Paris ready to report on the surprising concessions he had won. He told Hull that he was "convinced . . . that the document represented the maximum contribution that the Germans are prepared to make at this time. It represented substantial departure from the previous policies and an entirely new attitude toward the Jewish problem." [39]

Rublee's optimism was not fully shared by refugee advocates. The Administrative Committee of the World Jewish Congress passed a resolution "that no solution of the German refugee problem can be acceptable to the Jewish people if it rewards the Nazi regime with economic advantages in return for a policy of expropriation and expulsion directed against the Jews." [40] But Stephen Wise and Dorothy Thompson urged that judgment be withheld until the proposal could be studied. Miss Thompson then counseled that it be accepted. [41]

Official reaction to Rublee's work in Berlin was also more favorable. As soon as the talks were completed and the results known, Welles suggested to Roosevelt that Hugh Wilson be returned to Berlin because "Germany has at least in principle recognized our treaty rights and has offered a plan for the orderly emigration of Jews which was better than we hoped for." [42] Myron Taylor wanted to seize the opportunity to extricate the Administration from a situation which had become embarrassing. "The time has come to place a greater share of the responsibility for the actual direction of the Committee on British shoulders. Britain is the greatest colonial power and has the land available for settlement." [43] Two weeks later, Roosevelt, who had at first opposed the idea of such a *quid pro quo*, expressed a similar point of view. Washington, despite much discouragement, had sponsored an agreement which few thought could be made, now it was time for London to make its contribution.

Hull, still bothered by legal and free trade questions, did not get caught up in the general enthusiasm. He cautioned that although the program represented "a new and more favorable attitude toward the problem of Jewish emigration," there were certain features to which the United States could not agree and therefore "as a basis of agreement it would be definitely unacceptable." [44] There was, for example, the danger that German insistence on communicating directly with receiving countries would lead to dictation of numbers and types of refugees to be admitted. Nor was he satisfied that the agreement avoided our government underwriting the Reich's confiscation of Jewish property. The refusal to consider non-Jewish refugees also rankled with Hull, who staunchly upheld the Administration's policy of finding a solution to the problem of political refugees rather than relieving the Reich of its Jews. But the fact that the agreement was not acceptable, Hull maintained, did not necessitate rejection by the Administration. Since the agreement stated that each side would carry out its share of the agreement independent of the other, no signed document was required. Uncertain whether this would be understood, Hull explained: "The distinction between raising no objection to, and actively accepting a project may be a fine one, but it is nonetheless real." [45] He suggested that "active acceptance" be avoided and that instead the parties to the negotiations simply present each other with a "statement of cognizance." [46] Hull's legal distinction appeared on the surface to be chimerical, but the IGC accepted it wholeheartedly since it offered a way of avoiding association with a scheme that retained the basic characteristics of a ransom proposal. Thereafter the plan was simply called a "Statement of Agreement."

For different reasons the officers of the IGC could not muster much enthusiasm for the plan. Henry Bérenger, the French vice-chairman, apprehensive lest France receive more refugees, refused to commit France to the agreement. The Latin-American nations, aware that success of the scheme was predicated on finding resettlement in their area, protested vehemently. Dirksen, who had an inside line on the private proceedings, reported to Berlin that "the most difficult participants were the South Americans, who merely made fine speeches to the empty galleries, with the tendency to represent the German offer as inadequate and incompatible with the dignity of the Evian Committee." [47] A discussion of resettlement havens produced nothing except a long catalogue of possibilities. The repeated mention of the one resettlement project that appeared to be making progress, the Sosua project in the Dominican Republic, made the absence of other concrete offers seem all the more conspicuous.

Rublee, along with his report and his optimistic appraisal of it, submitted his resignation. As far as he could see he had successfully completed the mission to which the President had assigned him. His resignation would clear the deck for the resolution of a long-standing dispute between London and Washington over the status of the IGC and the High Commission for Refugees from Germany. Herbert Emerson, an Englishman who held the position of League High Commissioner, was given the position of director, and Robert Pell, Rublee's assistant, would be the vice-director who would carry on the negotiations. Both sides, the IGC and the Germans, had agreed that there was now a basis for periodic meetings. On April 15 Pell proceeded to Berlin for further consultation.

Wohlthat inquired about the meaning of the replacement of Rublee with Emerson. Pell hastened to assure him that the two agencies remained independent of each other. Any hint that the League was involved in the workings of the IGC was enough to endanger the agreement. Wohlthat chose not to question Pell's honesty but did caution that Emerson should not appear in Berlin. The IGC's awareness of Berlin's sensitivity on this point had been the reason for appointing Pell to the position of vice-director.[48]

Pell was aware that Wohlthat's chief interest would be resettlement and in this area he could offer little. In early March he had requested the State Department to forward to him all offers already in hand. Soon the answer reached him; the information he requested was "not yet available." Instead he was furnished with an accounting of what the United States had thus far done in the immigration area and statistics on the number of immigrants who entered the country in 1938.[49] Apparently the Department was still fighting the battle of Evian, where such arguments were used to prove good faith. When Pell arrived in Berlin, therefore, he could only offer Wohlthat a list of areas being considered. Wohlthat was distressed; a meeting with the Fuehrer was scheduled for April 28 and he now had little to show for weeks of discussion. The situation was embarrassing. Indeed a rumor carried by the German Delegation which visited London at Heydrich's behest in May reported that Wohlthat's meeting with Hitler had been stormy and Hitler had ordered that all cooperation with the IGC cease and that the memorandum not be made public until there was a better showing from the IGC and the international corporation then being organized. Heydrich's security police boasted that they could rid Germany of Jews in twenty-four hours; why could not the IGC act faster? The agency was obviously dragging its feet. Hitler was not aware of a second difficulty, Jewish opposition to the formation of an international corporation.

Meanwhile, Wohlthat informed Pell of Berlin's plans to conduct a census to determine precisely how many German Jews would be involved in the transfer of population and how much wealth they possessed. Pell, in his turn, nominated Professor Paul Bruni of The Hague as the third trustee. On March 4 Germany did, in fact, fulfill a small part of the agreement by issuing a labor conscription decree which put many Jews to manual labor. The agreement had promised Jews gainful employment and a training program. Technically the hard physical labor to which they were put fulfilled the promise.

Rublee had in the meantime sent his optimistic tidings to the White House amidst growing concern about the worsening situation in Germany. On February 24 the Ministry for Economic Affairs ordered all Jews to deliver their remaining gold, jewels, and other valuables to the government. Clearly the move violated the spirit of the agreement but diplomatic intercession at the Foreign Ministry brought no response. Within the next two days the Central Organization for German Jews was required to furnish the names of two hundred persons who would be forced to leave Germany within two weeks. It was an adaptation of the coercive policy that had worked so successfully for Eichmann in Vienna. The new wave of depredations did not discourage Rublee. "Despite recent press reports which at first sight appear discouraging . . . orderly emigration can be carried out and that persons awaiting emigration will receive much better treatment than has heretofore been the case." [50] The Jewish community could not share Rublee's optimism. The resettlement problem was nowhere near solution and the Nazis were in the process of breaking the agreement by coercing emigration. Myron Taylor would have a difficult time winning Jewish cooperation in organizing the corporation.

THE INVASION OF CZECHOSLOVAKIA AND THE DETERIORATION
OF THE JEWISH POSITION IN GERMANY

Those who hoped against hope that Rublee's optimistic evaluation of the agreement was accurate were dealt a sharp blow by Hitler's march into the remainder of Czechoslovakia on March 15. The "Statement of Agreement" reached after months of difficult negotiations created a way of removing 250,000 Jews from the Reich. Now in one day 350,000 Czech Jews were added to the refugee pool and the agreement was in danger of breaking down. London and Paris wanted to inform Berlin that the Rublee plan was no longer in existence because of the events in Czechoslovakia. The crisis offered an opportunity to bring to a halt a movement which only threatened to saddle them with more refugees. But Welles, sensing their mood, sent word that the Administration believed that the "basis of the program continued to exist despite events in Czechoslovakia." [51] He suggested that rather than relax the negotiations it was desirable to push them more energetically than ever. But to refugee enthusiasts such words had an empty ring. Even as Welles was encouraging the negotiations, the American quota for Germany became exhausted and with it one of the last hopes of escape for many German Jews. The Administration contributed further to the chaos by halting the issuance of visitors' visas at this juncture. Visitors' visas could only be issued if the immigrant could guarantee that he could return to his country of origin. Despite the Administration's efforts on behalf of refugees, its visa procedure was slowing down much of the momentum built up by the successful negotiations.

For those in the Nazi hierarchy concerned with ridding the Reich of Jews the occupation of Czechoslovakia proved a dubious victory. The movement eastward was solving the problem of living space but it was also bringing more Jews under German authority. Efforts were therefore multiplied to rid Germany of Jews. Ignoring the provision of the "Statement of Agreement" which provided that each side would be independent of the other, Heydrich sent a delegation of leading Jews from the Central Organization to London. The frightened emissaries tried desperately to communicate to the officers of the IGC the perilous situation faced by the Jews. They carried with them Heydrich's threat of dire consequences if the IGC did not come up with resettlement havens soon: Germany "would return to the shock tactics which were so successful in ridding Germany of Jews in the past." [52] The delegation begged to be given some sort of plan, even a hypothetical one, which might convince the Nazi authorities that the intentions of the IGC were serious. Emerson staunchly refused to participate in such fraud nor would he enlist the aid of leading British Jews to produce such evidence. The distressed delegation returned to report its failure to Heydrich. [53]

Heydrich proved true to his word. The heavy hand of the Gestapo which had cleared Vienna and Prague of Jews in record-breaking time was extended to Germany proper. Jews were picked up at random on the street and told they must leave Germany within a prescribed period of time or face life in a concentration camp. [54] The brisk business of selling visas and landing permits, flagrant among certain Latin-American consuls, was encouraged by the Gestapo. The going price for such documents was $500 to $600. [55] Winterton noted bitterly that "big money [is] being made in certain countries in Europe with the connivance of certain authorities in this crudest traffic—illegal immigration." [56] Ugly as such illegal trafficking may have been, it offered those who could afford the price a way out of an untenable life in Germany. That was more than the IGC was doing.

The sale of visas was behind the bizarre episodes which marked the refugee crisis between May and July 1939. By mid-May, Heydrich's drastic new measures resulted in several ships loaded with refugees, many of them possessing illegal documents, making their way to various ports in the Caribbean and Latin America. Among them was the S.S. *St. Louis* of the Hamburg-American line which left Germany bound for Havana with 930 Jewish refugees. All possessed landing permits signed by Colonel Manuel Benites, the director general of immigration, which the company had purchased wholesale and resold to the refugees at $150 each. On May 27 she arrived in Havana only to be denied landing rights. The Cuban government had a week earlier invalidated the refugees' landing permits and established a stricter procedure for accepting them. The line, proceeding with a business-as-usual policy, had simply failed to advise the passengers of the new regulations. No amount of pleading by the State Department and by Jewish private rescue agencies was able to move President Federico Raredo Bru. Even the offer of a $500 bond for each passenger made by the American Jewish Joint Distribution Committee fell on deaf ears. An additional bribe of $350,000 was demanded. Aboard the ship, Captain Gustav Schroeder was faced with the prospect of a rash of suicides should the ship leave the harbor. Two attempts actually succeeded. On June 6, Schroeder was forced to recross the Atlantic. His passengers were finally distributed among Britain, France, Holland, and Belgium.[57] The S.S. *Ordina*, S.S. *Quanza*, and the S.S. *Flanders* went through similar ordeals. As the push to rid Germany of Jews was moved into high gear by Heydrich, such ships would travel the high seas with their hapless cargoes, searching vainly for a port where they could be deposited.

At the same time the activities in the Reich continued apace. The Gestapo became specialists in smuggling hundreds of Jewish children over the border, often with the connivance of their parents. A day after the *St. Louis* was forced to leave Cuban waters the Security Police again picked up hundreds of Jews of Polish derivation and dumped them unceremoniously in the no man's land near the Polish border town of Sbonszyn. It appeared as if in the hands of the Nazi radicals the Statement of Agreement had become a dead letter.

AN EVALUATION OF THE SCHACHT-RUBLEE PLAN

Whether the Schacht proposal offered real hope for the rescue of German Jewry precipitated a bitter controversy among Jews at the time it was made. The passage of time has hardly dimmed its relevance. The argument first raised by Joseph Tenenbaum, when he cautioned Wise that victims ought not to cooperate with their persecutors, became a crucial issue in the postwar dialogue on the Holocaust although it was then primarily concerned with the posture of Jews under Nazi hegemony rather than Jews in the receiving countries. Less well known is the point raised by Schacht's defense counsel, at Nuremberg, where he was the only major defendant acquitted. The defense claimed that no German Jew would have lost his life had Schacht's proposal been speedily acted upon.[58] The Tenenbaum argument will probably remain controversial for some time to come since its emotional component is related to Jewish self-esteem, which remains a sensitive issue among Jews. The argument made by the Schacht defense can be examined with more certainty.

Nazi moderates such as Schacht, although primarily concerned with shoring up the German economy, were not totally insensitive to the moral question involved in the extrusion policy and even the impropriety of using the pressure by the Nazi radicals to attempt what appeared to be a simple case of extortion. Unfortunately, it was possible even at the time to disguise the extortion attempt as an effort to help the Jews of Germany. "If it were possible to realize it [the Schacht proposal]," states a moderate official in the Ministry of Economic Affairs, "we would in any case have contributed something." [59] Doubtless Schacht and other moderates were convinced that helping the Reich's economy in this case also allowed for helping the Jews. Under the special circumstances created by extremist Nazis, with whom they were not associated, the taking of Jewish property was not robbery. The blame, according to Schacht, must be sought among the receiving nations which did not accept his proposal with alacrity.

The role played by the receiving nations was bleak enough, but it is doubtful whether they can be blamed for hesitating in carrying out the agreement. It is true that Schacht's proposal and the subsequent negotiations marked the high point of Nazi cooperation to solve the Jewish problem by means other than the death camp. But Schacht could no more guarantee the safety and orderly exodus of German Jewry over a three-year period than the receiving countries were able to furnish suitable places for them to go. The internal political situation in the Reich was simply too unstable to offer any assurances. Prentice Gilbert, the American chargé, observed as much when he noted that "the Jewish question is so wrapped up with National Socialist politics that I do not believe anyone in Germany can give insurances regarding either Jewish emigration or the treatment which would be accorded the Jews remaining in Germany." [60] The events in the Reich during 1939 fully bore out Gilbert's contention. The precipitous dismissal of Schacht, the man who gave the guarantees, in the midst of the negotiations, the adoption of drastic extrusion methods even while the negotiations continued, the invasion of Czechoslovakia and the addition of thousands of additional Jews to the refugee stream were evidence enough that no guarantees about the future of anything, much less Jews, could be given in Germany in 1939.

Then why did the State Department take the talks so seriously? Why was Rublee so optimistic about the "Statement of Agreement"? There is some evidence to suggest that for Rublee and Welles and other State Department officials the issue by 1939 was not so much the extrication of the Jews from Germany, but rather the extrication of the Roosevelt Administration from the embarrassing position created by the Evian initiative. Jewish leadership, we shall see, did not share their enthusiasm for the proposal.

4

The Coordinating Foundation: A Rescue Prospect Fails

To those familiar with the elaborate murder apparatus conceived by Nazis in 1942, it seems incredible that barely two years before the Nazi regime was party to an agreement for an orderly exodus of the Jews of Germany. Yet such an agreement existed and Berlin appeared most anxious to carry it out. It conceived of the Final Solution only after it seemed clear that emigration was no longer feasible. How the fast-moving events of the several months preceding the outbreak of war, Jewish hostility, and the conflicting approaches of Washington and London, prevented an implementation of the agreement is an interesting story in its own right.

OPPOSITION TO ORGANIZING THE CORPORATION

Organizing the American part of the International corporation fell to the PACPR and particularly one individual, Myron Taylor. Almost immediately Taylor discovered considerable opposition among Jewish leaders who had not been able to reconcile themselves to the role of a development agency for their would-be destroyers. Roosevelt, who viewed the offer as distasteful but practical, received word of Jewish opposition via Welles.[1] Taken aback by the extent of hostility, the State Department assumed that it was directed by Lewis Strauss, Hoover's former assistant and a leading Republican and Arthur Sulzberger, owner of a major interest in the *New York Times*.

These men, it was thought, were motivated by their continued hostility to the New Deal and a "defeatist attitude." It was suggested that George Rublee be put in touch with the publisher of the *Times* and other leading opponents to "straighten them out." [2] The Department would soon discover that it had seriously underestimated the opposition in the Jewish community which, rather than being confined to a few leaders, was widespread and not easily overcome.

Almost daily there was new evidence that the threat against the Jews of Germany and Czechoslovakia was real. Jewish leaders called upon to establish the corporation had to make "the most agonizing decisions ever faced," wrote Lewis Strauss.[3] Ultimately they offered a token compliance with the agreement but even such collaboration was difficult. "Those who might criticize us for going even that far in so onerous a program," wrote Strauss in its defense, "should not forget that there were scores of thousands of innocent people held for ransom by a government of desperate and criminal misanthropes." [4]

Jewish opposition to implementing the agreement was tempered by the need to consider the fate of the hostages. No such considerations were detectable in the clamor raised by restrictionists against the proposal. Jews did not warrant such special consideration, claimed J. H. Patten, head of the Order of United American Mechanics, while testifying against a resolution to admit refugee children. "The plan is nothing but trying to export Jews to balance Hitler's trade by having them ransomed," and if allowed to do so, Patten argued, the Nazis will use other minority groups to shore up their economy. Where would the process stop and would it not lead to irresistible pressure to admit more refugees? [5]

The problem of implementation was also a difficult one. Leading Jews like Paul Baerwald, chairman of the most important nonpartisan private Jewish relief agency, the American Jewish Joint Distribution Committee (AJJDC), pointed out that the IGC had committed the private organizations to an agreement which they had no role in fashioning. The anomalous situation in which Jews now found themselves would have never existed had they been allowed to participate in the negotiations.[6] The negotiators might have been reminded that the concept of international finance Jewry was a figment of the Nazi central to the agreement, or more precisely, the anti-Semitic imagination.

Such were the circumstances under which Taylor finally brought together a group of seventy of America's most prominent Jews for the purpose of establishing the American section of the proposed international corporation. Samuel I. Rosenman, Roosevelt's well-known speech writer, who had already expressed some reservations about mass resettlement, was chosen chairman of the group. It was planned to send Lewis Strauss to London where he would join Paul Baerwald and his assistant Harold Linder to help coordinate the American and British efforts.

Such coordination would require some common ground on which they could operate. That proved to be uncommonly difficult since the group could find little in the Rublee plan to recommend it. At the outset the project was nearly derailed by the aforementioned untimely arrival on May 18 of a delegation of German Jews in London bearing a threat from Heydrich. Nazi moderates too attempted an intrusion in the delicate meetings in London with even more drastic effects.

On May 10, Helmut Wohlthat, who had conducted the negotiations with Rublee and Pell after the dismissal of Schacht, appeared in London to determine what was delaying the fulfillment of the agreement. The meeting was catastrophic. Despite his credentials as a moderate Nazi, Wohlthat seemed unable to fathom the full implication of his role. A spiritual obtuseness allowed him to convince himself that he was helping German Jewry while the committee saw him as a smooth blackmailer. When he spoke he urged speed in organizing the corporation and warned that the sum being considered was too small. He inquired whether the "outside people" were prepared to invest $230,000,000 in the agreed-upon program. It was too much for Viscount Bearsted, a prominent member of the British Committee, who lost his temper and answered with a flat No.[7] Dumbfounded, Wohlthat rose and told Pell that there was no longer any basis for the discussion; he would ask to be relieved when he returned to Berlin. It took some effort by Pell to smooth his ruffled feathers. The Jews, he explained, were working in a highly charged atmosphere. They were reluctant to make such a high investment in an arrangement which to them smacked of blackmail. Despite what was being said in Berlin, British and American Jews felt no direct responsibility for the Jews of Germany. Bearsted's view, moreover, was not that of the committee, which had not yet arrived at a capitalization figure. It would be better, Pell explained, if Berlin adhered strictly to the agreement which ruled out interference by one side in the affairs of the other. The agreement, he reminded Wohlthat, called for independent action by each side. Nor should the IGC be rushed when such astronomical figures were involved.[8] We shall see presently that Bearsted's refusal was based on something more than an emotionally overwrought condition.

ANGLO-AMERICAN DIFFERENCES ON THE CHARACTER
OF THE CORPORATION

Berlin's untimely interference occurred while yet another rift between the State Department and the British Foreign Office was developing over the organization of the Coordinating Foundation, the name applied to the international corporation.

Washington had from the outset conceived of the Coordinating Foundation as an independent, self supporting organization which would eventually deal directly with Berlin. The agenda and the final resolutions of the Evian Conference had specifically ruled out government financing. Once the Foundation was organized, the IGC would be disbanded and the road would be clear for the Roosevelt Administration to extricate itself from a situation which was proving daily more embarrassing. London's plans, on the other hand, proved far more embracing and eventually called for governments to assume at least a part of the financial burden. The corporation would act as a huge holding company, with separate *ad hoc* corporations for each small resettlement venture. It seemed a minor matter, but behind it was a difference in the approach to resettlement itself. The Administration envisaged one or two massive resettlement schemes which would give new homes to millions. London aimed at dozens of small ventures to resettle thousands. It seemed merely a matter of scale but again it generated much heat. "From time to time we have had many discouragements," wrote Taylor to Pell, "none greater than the failure of the British group so far to cooperate wholeheartedly with the American group." [9]

In June the conflict was exacerbated when a group headed by Paul Baerwald offered a plan to establish the Coordinating Foundation with token financing and to request that all governments involved contribute funds for the projected resettlement ventures. It was hoped that the token funding would pass the initiative back to Berlin so that the exodus of German Jews might begin. The plan's long-range objective was to capitalize the Coordinating Foundation at $100 million over a five-year period. That was $130 million less than the figure suggested by Wohlthat. For the immediate emergency Baerwald proposed to transfer $1 million from the AJJDC's account to the Coordinating Foundation. Jewish philantropy, already burdened by the need to support thousands of penniless Jewish refugees, could not assume financial responsibility for resettlement as well. The latest estimate of the cost of resettling one family was $10,000 or approximately $250 million to resettle a mere 2,500 families.[10] Baerwald therefore suggested that the resettlement ventures be financed on a one-to-one matching basis with the governments involved and that repayment be arranged from the proceeds of the resettlement projects. The mythical profits suggested by Schacht and accepted by Rublee and Pell now came back to haunt the Administration. The Baerwald scheme, which required only a small initial expenditure, would allow the Jewish leaders to determine how sincere was the will to save the refugees, not only in Berlin, but Washington and London.

The plea of poverty by the Jewish organizations told only part of the story. The question of financing the Coordinating Foundation threatened to renew conflicts that had been settled in 1939 in the formation of the United Jewish Appeal. Zionist and other "downtown" elements were opposed to paying ransom especially if it would draw away funds from their own pet schemes. In the case of Zionist opposition there was the additional fear that funds poured into resettlement ventures outside Palestine would result in fewer dollars for their pioneering efforts, besides giving their old rivals, the Jewish territorialists, a new lease on life. (Territorialists believed in the resettlement of the Jews, but did not focus on Palestine.) Stephen Wise informed Judge Joseph Proskauer in January of the developing opposition to the Rublee plan. But Proskauer, who was soon to head the American Jewish Committee, jokingly addressing his rival as "dear Pope," requested that he not open old wounds.[11] Four months later Wise's warning proved prophetic when Rabbi Abba Hillel Silver, head of the 1939 UJA fund drive, informed Wise that no money would be contributed to the Coordinating Foundation because it would be illegal since it is not a recognized Jewish organization.

Undoubtedly the more important reason was recalled by Silver at the conclusion of his letter to Wise—it would result in Palestine getting the "short end of the bargain." [12]

The lack of agreement among American Jewish leaders on how to respond forced Strauss to delay his mission to London until July. The State Department became concerned that the talks would collapse without a concrete offer by American Jewry. Suspecting again that Strauss was behind the delay, Proskauer was urged to proceed to London to help bring the talks to a successful conclusion. [13] But little happened until Roosevelt, acting on a suggestion by Myron Taylor, called Jewish leaders together on May 4 and virtually extorted a pledge of cooperation.

Four days later a preliminary agreement between the British and American Jewish leaders was concluded which followed roughly along the lines suggested by Baerwald. London showed its support by promising to sponsor an experimental resettlement venture in British Guiana. It would offer several thousand acres of land at nominal cost. [14]

Even so modest a commitment did not still the voices of opposition in the Jewish community. A resolution, sponsored by Joseph Tenenbaum and Dr. Samuel Margoshes, editor of the influential Yiddish daily, *The Day*, attempted to prohibit the Coordinating Foundation from using its funds to purchase German goods. [15] Paul Baerwald, the moving spirit behind the talks, confessed to Wise that he was hesitant about taking responsibility for the venture, especially if non-Jews and non-Jewish money would be invited to join the Foundation. Continued pressure in the Jewish community might force a total withdrawal from the enterprise. [16]

The Administration was unhappy about developments. Pell reminded Baerwald that Congress could not legally appropriate money for resettlement and even should such ventures become commercially viable—an unlikely possibility—the Administration was legally prohibited from backing its securities on the open market. He reminded Baerwald that the invitation to the Evian Conference and the final resolutions contained guarantees that the responsibility for financing would be borne, as usual, by the private organizations. In reply Baerwald could only cite the feeling in the Jewish community. [17]

More distressing than the maneuvers of the Jewish group was the change in British policy. Pell attributed the change to a cynical plot by the Foreign Office. "British private and government circles, believing that Congress would never authorize participation by our government, wished to evade all responsibility and place upon us the onus, before American Jewry and international public opinion, for eventual failure of the plan." [18] Like Rublee, Pell was preoccupied with appearances, but in his explanation of the British shift he need not have tried so hard for justification. There was nothing devious about London's move. The White Paper, which was to take effect in May 1939, restricted immigration to Palestine at a critical juncture and placed the British in a bad light. It was hoped that by offering support and a specific resettlement offer in British Guiana, they could undo some of the unfavorable publicity being generated by the Zionists. Moreover, no actual transfer of money would have to be involved since London's idea of support meant cheap land rather than British pounds sterling. The offer proved doubly embarrassing to the Administration since its efforts to develop Alaska and the Virgin Islands in a similar manner had run into serious opposition. The British offer could therefore not be matched.

If the British proved too tractable for Washington's taste, the French were inclined to view the idea of any agreement with the Reich with a jaundiced eye. Henry Bérenger simply threatened to resign if French Jews participated in the ransom deal. He had little fear that they would do so: "The French Jews were not stupit little fish," he informed Pell, "Robert de Rothschild was not a stupit little fish. Mr. Taylor could have his trap. He could put his head in it. . . ." He, Bérenger, would not allow French honor to be soiled by the "gaunt prophet" (Rublee) and the "romantic acolyte" (Pell) whose "fonction" was "apparently to go to Berlin every week or so and salute Hitler's—or is it Göring's behind." [19] It took some doing to gain French cooperation. Ambassador William C. Bullitt planned to show an affidavit of support from Dr. Otto Hirsch, executive director of the Jewish Council in Berlin, to Daladier. Perhaps Hirsch's plea for quick action might generate the needed sympathy. Ultimately Bérenger, whose anger had first been aroused by failure to translate the Statement of Agreement into French, agreed to give "symbolic," if not actual, support to the Coordinating Foundation.

For Pell, the British offer of a specific resettlement haven in British

Guiana and a subsequent request to the Administration to finance it "placed them in a strong moral position of which they plan to make full use in the international press and to place the responsibility for any failure to extend the work on behalf of refugees, both as regards financing and resettlement, on the other governments." [20] Such a challenge, if left unanswered, would again place the Administration in an unenviable position. He urged the Department to make a matching commitment in the Philippine Province of Mindanao which was rumored to be ideal for resettlement.[21] Such a move would go far in restoring the Administration's position vis à vis London.

Eventually an investigation commission was sent to Mindanao but its favorable report came too late to right the balance. At the time the State Department considered sending a "caustic note" to the British Foreign Office protesting the wide publicity given the British Guiana scheme. Particularly nettling was the fact that the offer involved only two small experimental schemes of two hundred and fifty persons each which would be carried out "provided the Americans finance it." [22] Like Pell, Pierrepont Moffat, chief of the State Department's Division of European Affairs, was convinced that the British were trying to create a "cross current" to prevent the organization of the Coordinating Foundation. It was part of "the old British game of all get and no give." [23] Like other middle echelon officials in the Department, Pell and Moffat tended to assign extraordinary wiliness and duplicity to the British Foreign Office. But by July Moffat thought he detected the real motive behind the British offer. London, he felt, was trying to make a compensatory gesture for the catastrophic effects of the White Paper.[24] The gesture, if such was intended, had little effect. Wise, writing to James McDonald, confessed to having the "profoundest doubts" about the Guiana project. He was "heart sick" about the White Paper. Formerly an admirer of things British, he now felt that they were insincere. "I begin to understand," he told McDonald, "the doubts that you and my family have long had with regard to the sincerity of a certain government." [25]

The British pressed the Administration to change its position on financing. If the United States could not agree to some government assistance, Britain would "be obliged to reconsider its attitude toward the Intergovernmental Committee. . . ." [26] Pell's plea that the British delay their request until the next official meeting of the IGC was rejected by Winterton, who had grown increasingly disenchanted with the American initiative and particularly the position on mass resettlement ventures. He was irked by the State Department's visionary schemes and talk of a supplemental national home. Thinking that Myron Taylor supported such ideas, he teased him about being haunted by the "dream of Angola" which the Roosevelt Administration was then investigating for resettlement possibilities.[27] Had he known that Taylor rejected the idea of a "new Palestine" in Angola and had told Roosevelt "their [the Jews'] real objective is to get into settled countries where they can set up their lives in existing communities and in professional, commercial, and industrial activities," Winterton might have been less irritated.[28] An outburst by Sir Herbert Emerson, the new chairman of the IGC, ironically showed that he harbored a strong distaste for the Jewish refugees he was supposed to be helping. "The trouble with the whole refugee affair was the trouble of the Jews and most eastern people," he told his fellow officers, "there was always some other scheme in the background for which they were prepared to sacrifice schemes which were already in hand."[29] Emerson's exasperation was caused by Jewish reluctance to consider British Guiana as a resettlement alternative to Palestine.

In mid-June the executive committee of the IGC met again. The heated discussion was focused on two basic sources of conflict: the question of government aid in financing the resettlement havens and the issue of scale of resettlement. The Administration relented on the question of government financing provided London would "apply it to a project which by its extent could bring about a major solution."[30] Perhaps then Congress might be induced to make such an appropriation. Three weeks later on July 17, James Dunn, State Department Adviser on Political Relations, phoned Taylor in London to instruct him again on the *quid pro quo* which the Department desired. The Administration would try to get an appropriation for resettlement but there was little probability of getting such money for small British-sponsored resettlement schemes. The British delegation should abandon their piecemeal approach to resettlement in favor of the large nation-building concept favored by the Administration.[31]

When the executive committee of the IGC met again on July 20, Wohlthat was again present, this time under the guise of attending a whaling conference. He had already been entrusted by Chamberlain to carry an urgent message offering Hitler a nonaggression pact or a "world political partnership," when he appeared at the meeting. He heard in silence the wrangling between the British and the American delegations and the token offer made by Baerwald. A year had passed since the Evian Conference and virtually nothing had been accomplished. War was less than two months away. The Administration marked the anniversary of its first initiative by extending a new invitation to the executive committee of the IGC to come to Washington on October 19, 1939 as guests of the President.

On July 20 the Coordinating Foundation was finally established. Its outlines approximated the Baerwald scheme but for the State Department's sake, simply omitted the essential question of financing until more information could be garnered from the commission sent to investigate the resettlement possibilities in British Guiana. No side conceded anything, little was contributed; only the potential refugees in Germany might have complained and they were not represented at the talks. Using the $1 million granted by the AJJDC the Coordinating Foundation set up shop. It would be administered by a management council composed of twenty members, at least ten of whom would be Americans, and the remainder British and French.[32] Not until August were the finishing touches applied. Lewis Strauss invited Paul van Zeeland, former Prime Minister of Belgium, to become its executive head. A charter was granted by the British Board of Trade. Emerson advised the new director not to communicate with Berlin until they demonstrated willingness to fulfill their side of the agreement.[33] He need hardly have bothered; the Nazi authorities would never have the opportunity to meet the director of the long-awaited Coordinating Foundation nor were they waiting patiently for the IGC to solve their Jewish problem.

THE EFFECT OF THE WAR ON THE ADMINISTRATION'S
REFUGEE THINKING

Roosevelt observed from a distance how his initiative, taken in good faith, became involved in a morass of argument. Dispatches from his ambassadors informed him that time to solve the problem was running out. If Germany and her new-found ally, the Soviet Union, tore Poland apart, more millions of uprooted people would become a permanent part of the world's social landscape. When that happened small resettlement schemes, such as suggested by the British, would barely scratch the surface. Something dramatic would have to be done. But in June Roosevelt saw only the possibility of extricating his Administration as soon as the Coordinating Foundation was established. "The IGC," he wrote to Taylor, "would continue in existence though in inactive form." [34] Paradoxically the plan, if carried out, would bring the Administration full circle to the position held by the British and French at Evian even while the British, with their offer to contribute funds for resettlement, seemed prepared to spur a more active refugee effort. That, of course, was the position originally held by Washington. But Roosevelt's position was not yet fixed. There would be ample time to change his mind again.

Meanwhile, the Administration prepared for the forthcoming conference of the executive committee of the IGC in Washington. A smoldering feud between "Pa" Watson, the President's secretary, and Myron Taylor broke into the open and Taylor had difficulty in seeing the President. But his suggestion that the President have a formal luncheon with the delegates was accepted. Welles' suggestion that the delegates discuss the extension of the activities of the IGC was rejected by Roosevelt, who planned to push for a large-scale resettlement plan.

This is where things stood when on September 1 Hitler's panzer divisions rolled into Poland. The invasion found Berlin and the IGC still waiting for some sign of movement from the other side. By September 21, almost before it began, Warsaw surrendered. At one stroke, Germany, which had waged a relentless campaign to rid herself of Jews, inherited as part of its victory most of Europe's largest Jewish community.[35] But Roosevelt's vision of a refugee population of 10,000,000 would never materialize. The Nazi regime had other plans for the Jews of Poland.

The war marked a turning point in the refugee crisis. Heretofore the receiving countries addressed themselves primarily to helping those unfortunate people who had to find new homes. This problem of refugees was to continue throughout the war on a smaller scale since there were always some channels through which refugees could trickle out of occupied Europe. After 1942 the refugee problem was supplemented and then overshadowed by the problem of rescue, which was concerned with those millions in the Nazi death trap who were never able to become refugees. Until 1944 the State Department recognized only the refugee problem, while it actively sought to suppress information of those in the death camps.

In mid-1939, Roosevelt's assumption that the refugee problem would grow to massive proportions was a natural one. No one could foresee that Berlin would plan a mass killing operation for the Jews of eastern Europe. His first reaction was to change his mind about retiring the IGC. That agency would now be more important than ever. When he caught a sentence in a State Department memorandum which suggested that "when the war broke out the principal justification for this consultative body [IGC] ceased to exist," he berated the Division of European Affairs for its lack of vision: "It is worthwhile keeping this committee very definitely alive," Roosevelt insisted, "it will be time enough later on to consider the question of transferring certain of its activities." [36] Hull too was overruled when he pointed out that "it is impractical for the Intergovernmental Committee to continue to facilitate direct emigration from Germany." [37] The Administration would continue to support the IGC and would press ahead with plans to hold a meeting of the officers of that organization in Washington.

The press release announcing Roosevelt's decision to go ahead with the October meeting did not still the voices calling for postponement. James G. McDonald argued in a closely reasoned memorandum that "the implementation of the Wohlthat memorandum is impractical." [38] The refugee stream had been reduced to a trickle by the war, and its movement was virtually halted since transit countries like Spain and Switzerland had sealed their borders. The IGC, argued McDonald, not conspicuously successful in dealing with the existing refugee problem, was not inclined to take on a larger one. The United States, moreover, as the only major receiving nation still able to deal with Berlin, ran the risk of accepting all the refugees. According to McDonald, there existed a subtle danger that an exclusive effort for refugees, now undeniably preponderantly Jewish, would stimulate domestic anti-Semitism. Moreover, in case of failure, the moral onus would now be primarily on the United States. Roosevelt remained unconvinced and dismissed McDonald's memorandum with a curt marginal note, "the meeting will be held." [39]

McDonald's reluctance to go ahead with the agreement was shared by London and the executive committee of the IGC. The outbreak of war seemed to be a natural point in time to close the books on the agreement and on the IGC itself. A curtain of fire had been rung down on those thousands of unfortunates still in Germany.

A day after the German assault the Foreign Office inquired about the future plans of the IGC. Winterton and Emerson, who led the refugee effort on the British side, were preparing to resign and take on more important duties. Washington's reply left little room for doubt, the meeting would be held as planned. Ambassador Kennedy was instructed to exert every effort to induce the government to keep Emerson and Winterton at their posts at least until after the Washington meeting when new officers might be chosen. Ironically, it was precisely at this point that the PACPR had ready for the President's eye a mixed report on the possibilities of resettlement of British Guiana.

The British did not share Roosevelt's enthusiasm for pushing ahead with the refugee effort. They pointed out that all potential refugees from Germany would now be classified as enemy aliens. France was already preparing to intern all refugees from Germany between the ages of sixteen and thirty-five. Moreover, Britain could no longer make funds available for resettlement ventures. The Foundation and the IGC, they felt, would have to be adapted to the limited role that the war imposed.[40] Winterton was particularly concerned about the possibility of enemy agents being planted among the refugees. Britain could no longer accept them.

The developments on the German side after the outbreak of war seemed to bear out Roosevelt's assumption that the IGC's mission might yet be fulfilled. On September 26 the State Department received a message from Berlin through London. "The Government of the German Reich is willing to continue to cooperate with the Intergovernmental Committee with respect to emigration of Jews from Germany." [41] Berlin would even allow them to take their personal effects, if not their capital, with them, with the exception of articles of which there was a shortage in the Reich. Nor could Germany provide transportation. Some of the agreement could no longer be carried out but Berlin was willing to maintain the trust: "Property left in Germany by Jews will be put at the disposal of the Reich Committee for German Jews [Jewish Council] for support of needy persons of that race in Germany." [42] Wohlthat's message was confirmed when appeals arrived from the *Hilfsverein* (self-help division of the Jewish Council), that emigration was indeed still possible and was urgently requested. There were many emigrants with valid immigration visas and passage on neutral lines was still available.[43] So conciliatory was Berlin that Weizsäcker suggested that Hans Dieckhoff be sent back to Washington even without reciprocation.[44]

Berlin's continued enthusiasm for emigration was not shared in London. When Whitehall received word of Germany's willingness to carry out the agreement, Winterton, never a proponent of the agreement, called foul. "Wohlthat's offer was a negation of the whole program," exclaimed Winterton, it represents "a return to the policy of forcing out penniless refugees." [45] Winterton had a point, since German Jews could not now hope to get out even the 25 percent of the trust fund earmarked for emigration. Inability to fully fathom the depth of Nazi anti-Semitism made Berlin's offer suspect. Why would the Nazis try to rid themselves of a particularly rich pool of skilled labor during wartime if not for the purpose of infiltrating agents into the receiving countries? This line of reasoning, first heard in London in September 1939, was soon echoed in France, and became, in 1940, the rallying cry of all those opposed to a more active rescue effort.

Interest in emigration of Jews was thus maintained, at least by the moderates in the Nazi hierarchy, until the final months of 1941. Although special SS killer groups were already active behind German lines in the Soviet Union, the formal decision for the Final Solution was taken in January 1942. The chronological sequence indicates that the decision to liquidate the Jews in an organized way came only after possibilities for extrusion were exhausted.

ROOSEVELT AND A NEW APPROACH TO REFUGEE-RESCUE

In June 1939, before the discussions to establish the Coordinating Foundation were consummated, a discouraged Roosevelt confided to Taylor that "In the absence of drastic changes in the government and attitudes, if not human nature, in Europe, the problem in its larger aspects appears almost insoluble except through a basic solution such as the development of a suitable area to which refugees would be admitted in almost unlimited numbers. . . . I am convinced, nevertheless, that every effort must continue to be made to attain a practical solution along these lines." [46] If a breakthrough was to be made on the refugee front something dramatic had to be done. The President was mulling over such a dramatic idea and would be ready to announce it at the forthcoming Washington conference. Meanwhile, the moral aspect of the refugee problem must be publicized so that the good will of the American people could be mobilized. A publicity program had worked with infantile paralysis, why not with refugees? One had to enlist an agency that embodies the spirit of human concern or Christian ethics, and what better body than the Vatican? It had a vast international following throughout the western world and the Pope's word still carried enormous weight. If he could be encouraged to speak out on the agony of the refugees and the moral obligation of the Christian world to help, even the resettlement block, especially in Catholic Latin America, might be dissolved. Early in October, Roosevelt confided this "wholly original thought" to Hull. He would send an "Ambassador on Special Mission to the Vatican" to establish direct communication on the matter of Catholic refugees. The Administration's concern with Catholic refugees, would, it was hoped, capture the interest of the Vatican, and then be extended to other refugees. "The whole refugee problem," thought Roosevelt, could be placed "on a broad religious basis, thereby making it possible to gain the kind of world-wide support that a mere Jewish relief set-up would not evoke." [47] The President seemed convinced that little more could be done until there was a basic change in public opinion. In December 1939, Myron C. Taylor, who had gained some renown for his work with refugees, was appointed Roosevelt's personal representative to the Vatican.

Undoubtedly Roosevelt believed that the Holy See, as a true neutral, could become an important intermediary in dealing with Berlin on the refugee and other outstanding problems. Over 43 percent of Germany's population was Catholic and the Pope maintained important links to the German Church and the Nazi government dating back to his long tenure as the Vatican's emissary in Berlin. Unknown to Roosevelt was the Vatican's reluctance to do anything that might increase the peril of the Catholic Church in the Reich. Moreover, the Vatican faced a serious dilemma in assuming the role of intermediary for the humane cause which Roosevelt envisaged for it. The Catholic population of the Reich was not immune to the virus of anti-Semitism. It may, in fact, have been more susceptible to it because of the influence of traditional Catholic dogma. Despite pressure to leave the Church, 22.7 percent of the storm troops were confessional Catholics, some of whom were later involved in the Final Solution. The now well-known crisis of conscience of Kurt Gerstein, the SS *Obersturm-führer* responsible for supplying the Zyklon B gas to the murder factories, was counterbalanced by the role of former Catholics like Heinrich Himmler and Adolf Eichmann, who, far from feeling pangs of conscience, chose to play leading roles in carrying out the Final Solution.[48] The moralization of the refugee problem which Roosevelt hoped for never materialized, nor did the Church officially play the role of an active rescue agent.

THE WASHINGTON MEETING OF THE OFFICERS OF THE IGC

A second suggestion for placing the refugee issue on a grander scale so that public opinion could be mobilized was presented by Roosevelt personally at the October meeting of the officers of the IGC. The conditions under which the meeting was held were not hopeful. Six weeks of war had demonstrated that the German Army was formidable. The delegates could no longer be certain whether their own nations would survive; they might themselves soon join the refugees, whose tragedy was now overshadowed by the larger tragedy of war. The delegates arrived in Washington on October 16, in an atmosphere of pronounced futility. A year's experience with the refugee problem had taught them that it would not easily be resolved. Most nations agreed that the conference should be postponed and the IGC itself allowed to expire.[49] But on Roosevelt's insistence neither of these notions had prevailed.

Dutifully the delegates went through their now familiar charade. Winterton and Emerson again reminded the delegates of the initiative Britain had shown before the war broke out. The war had unfortunately changed the situation; Britain would reluctantly have to withdraw the generous offer it had made in British Guiana. Taylor hastened to acknowledge Britain's contribution, and that of the other members as well, and urged them to seize the opportunity to complete the job that had been started. What had been intended by the British as an epitaph was converted by Taylor's adroitness into a starting point for new discussions. Hull pushed Taylor's effort by invoking the muse of history. "It would be most unfortunate," he cautioned the delegates, "if future historians should be called upon to say that civilized man confessed his inability to cope with this harrowing problem and let the undertaking die at its most critical period." [50] No one would have guessed that barely two weeks before the meeting he had advised the President that the British were perhaps on solid ground in thinking that the work of the IGC was over.

At the climax of the meeting the President delivered his long-awaited address. He began by cordially welcoming the delegates and then plunged directly into an analysis of the situation. The delegates must have been somewhat startled by Roosevelt's pessimistic prognosis. The current refugee problem was nothing compared to what the world was about to experience. If present trends continued there would be from ten to twenty million homeless refugees in the postwar world. This, Roosevelt stressed, is the real problem, not the few thousand refugees who now remain unprovided for. The private organizations have been working "on too small a scale" and had "failed to apply modern engineering" to the task. The IGC, Roosevelt suggested, should "clear the decks" of the old problem which was of comparatively "small magnitude." What was needed was a massive resettlement project in one of the "many vacant spaces of the earth's surface," a venture in nation building which by its magnitude would capture the imagination of the world and make a real contribution to a permanent resolution of the problem of the refugee. He concluded what was doubtless intended to be a stirring address by adapting a quote from Emma Lazarus, the poet laureate of the American immigration movement: "let us lift a lamp beside new golden doors and build new refuges for the tired, for the poor, for the huddled masses yearning to be free." [51]

Difficulty with the Jewish community, which had become very pronounced during the meetings called to establish the Coordinating Foundation, had convinced Roosevelt that a new approach was needed. Jews were reluctant to finance the foundation. The Zionist movement had the preponderant influence and resettlement in British Guiana simply did not gain support. Something had to be done to gain Jewish support and yet not interfere with London's Palestine policy. Roosevelt, a good catalyst of other people's ideas, incorporated elements of the Zionist idea and suggestions made at various times by Sumner Welles and Myron Taylor, packaged it in a new wrapping which he called a "supplemental national home," and hoped to sell it as a new approach to the refugee problem. When finally completed it bore remarkable resemblance to the old idea of the Jewish territorialist. Roosevelt knew he had to ignite the imagination of the Jews and thought that an alternate Palestine might work. It would be done on a massive scale so that it might draw the resources of the entire Jewish community. The Administration began a search for such an area.

Neither the officers of the IGC nor the Jewish community mustered much enthusiasm for Roosevelt's plan. The delegates must have been taken aback by the President's long-range view of a postwar problem. They were not certain that such considerations were relevant when their own national survival was at stake. The plan included no concrete proposal. It was difficult to determine whether this was more rhetoric to soothe the American Jewish community or a serious suggestion. The delegates decided to establish a committee to "study" the speech. They would go through the motions of giving it serious consideration. They extended their visits to the United States for one week, asked their home governments for instructions, but in the end decided not to act on the Roosevelt proposal.[52]

In the American Jewish community, where Zionism now clearly held the upper hand, the idea of a "supplemental national home" was the last in a series of body blows. In February a round-table conference with the Arabs, on which much hope had been based, failed. In May the White Paper went into effect and as if to convince the Jews that its policy of restricted entrance would be enforced, three unseaworthy Danubian freighters, overloaded with refugees, were turned back from Palestinian shores between May and September. The Administration's "supplemental national home" idea was simply too much. "Why not Palestine?" asked the editors of *New Palestine*, an organ of the Zionist Organization of America, "Why is Palestine . . . consistently and persistently kept off the agenda of the Intergovernmental Committee, called into service for the expressed purpose of serving refugee needs?"[53]

For Zionists the disappointment in the Administration's proposal was all the greater since they hoped to use the Washington conference to press their demand for Palestine. Wise had persistently urged consideration of the Palestine rescue alternative from within the PACPR.[54] Zionist organizations made known their willingness to finance the resettlement of 2,800,000 Jews in Palestine. The American Jewish Congress had submitted a formal proposal that the IGC sponsor an experimental resettlement project in Palestine.[55] Wise had even hoped to convince Roosevelt that the presence of Winterton and Emerson in Washington offered a good opportunity for the Administration to make a formal announcement of its opposition to the White Paper. In turn, Wise would not mention the issue of unlimited immigration into Palestine at the conference.[56] Instead he asked Felix Frankfurter to arrange a private interview between representatives of the Zionist organizations and the British delegation.[57] For the Zionists the situation had become especially urgent since Sir Malcolm McDonald, head of the Colonial Office, had announced his intention of considering all refugees coming from Germany as enemy aliens and to treat them accordingly. If that were allowed to happen, the small trickle of Jewish refugees to British possessions would be cut off.

Roosevelt might have thought twice about introducing the concept of a supplemental national home had he been aware of the psychological state of American Jewry. Nazi depredations against their religious brethren combined with a marked increase in domestic anti-Semitism had by mid-1939 so sensitized American Jews that few things escaped their perusal for possible anti-Semitic content. Some thought they detected in Roosevelt's term, "Jewish race," in his address before the delegates an indication that he too had succumbed to the Nazi doctrine. A projection of ten to twenty million refugees in the post-war world was in itself an admission that racism would win the day. The United States had never been a signatory to the Minority Treaty of 1919 which sought to grant protection to minorities where they resided and therefore was more prone to think in terms of movement of populations. This was behind Roosevelt's visionary scheme. Winterton argued along these lines at the conference. If the President's logic were accepted every unpopular minority would eventually have to be resettled. For once the Zionists and representatives of the British government found themselves united in their opposition to the scheme. But whereas the British feared anything smacking of resettlement, Zionists objected only to the fact that the President's plan did not focus on Palestine.

For Myron Taylor, sitting on the subcommittee formed to consider the President's proposal, there was a special dilemma. After a year of involvement with the refugee problem he sensed that Roosevelt's scheme was visionary. The Jews simply would not support resettlement outside Palestine and the receiving nations, if they ever had an interest in solving the refugee problem, were now preoccupied with the war. The President must be told of the difficulties involved in such a proposal and of the unlikelihood of it ever gaining support. But the continued enmity of "Pa" Watson and the pressure of problems relating to the war made it improbable that the President could grant him time for an interview on what was, after all, a peripheral matter. He therefore took his problem to Hull. The delegates were inclined to reject the President's scheme and Hull understood and even agreed with their view. Yet it would not do for the President's proposal to be rejected out of hand. Did Hull have any advice? The Secretary could muster little affection for outsiders, appointed directly by the President, who picked off choice department positions and whose policy was often in direct opposition to the Department's. Hull was not anxious to get Taylor off the hook. Instead he "hedged beautifully" and told Taylor that he would personally try to get him an interview with the President. As the incident is recounted in the Moffat diary, Taylor, sensing that he was being given a run-around, became furious at the Department's recalcitrance. He was determined to bring his complaint to the President. "The President soothed him down, covered him with compliments and then told him . . . that the reference to the long-term plans should be put back into the pending resolutions." [58]

Taylor was forced to return to the subcommittee with the Administration's refusal to reconsider. The delegates pointed out that the IGC's mandate did not authorize an extension of its scope even if the delegates were serious in proposing it. Including Roosevelt's proposal in the final resolution would be meaningless, but that did not appear to bother the Administration.

Even while the President was asking the IGC to address itself to the larger problem of the postwar refugee, the immediate problem of "small magnitude" which he had dismissed as all but solved, showed stubborn signs of life. The clamor from within the Reich to leave while there was still time, rather than decreasing because of the war, actually increased and would continue to do so until 1941.[59] The Nazi authorities, despairing of any help from the IGC, had in October 1939 attempted a resettlement venture of their own in Nisko, Poland. The project was poorly planned, and under the brutal supervision of Adolf Eichmann resulted in many deaths and much suffering. In that month too, Paul van Zeeland, the director of the Coordinating Foundation, made it known that the Foundation was obsolete since it could no longer communicate with Berlin. He proposed that the Foundation join the growing number of organizations seeking, usually unsuccessfully, resettlement havens.[60]

Although Roosevelt cast a statesmanlike eye on the future refugee problem, there seemed little that the Administration was willing to do to relieve immediate distress.

5

Rescue Through Resettlement: Illusion and Reality

By 1942 it was clear that neither side, Allied or Nazi, had much to show for its efforts at resettlement. For the Nazis the failure cleared the decks for the Final Solution. That decision, made at the Wannsee Conference in January 1942, was carried out in the next three years, using the terminology of resettlement. Thousands of Jews entered the cattle cars bound for Auschwitz, under the impression that they were being resettled in the East.

Both sides involved in the refugee crisis viewed resettlement as an ideal solution and spoke of it continually, until the victims themselves, not wanting to believe the unbelievable, chose, in their agony, to believe that this was what fate had in store. Nazi camouflage terminology was effective because of its credibility. For the victim, it offered an escape from a man-made hell, for others involved with refugees it offered an opportunity to tuck away a particularly troublesome minority in some remote corner of the world. Totalitarian nations seem particularly attracted by the allure of mass resettlement. The degraded concept of the individual allows him to be moved at will much like cattle. Moreover, no accommodation by the national community need be made since the degraded group simply vanishes from the scene almost as if it had been buried. In fact, the Nazi failure at coerced resettlement and the decision to annihilate the Jews is not an accidental sequential pattern. Both had the same objective; the decision to murder followed directly from the failure to resettle.

DEFINITION AND RECEPTIVITY TO RESETTLEMENT IN AMERICA

Resettlement and infiltration are two distinct forms of population movement. The former refers to the movement of communities or ethnic, social, or political groups to unsettled areas, where rerooting and pioneering occur. The movement of the Mormons to Utah or the Zionists to Palestine are good examples of voluntary resettlement. The mass migration to the United States in the post-1890 period serves as a good example of infiltration—that is, the movement of immigrants to established communities where a process of acculturation begins. On the scale favored by Roosevelt, mass resettlement leads naturally to the establishment of a new nation. The smaller projects, preferred by the British, may result in an alien enclave within an established nation. Resettlement and infiltration can take place simultaneously, as in the development of the United States during the colonial period.

During the refugee crisis, the United States, perhaps more than other nations, placed a great deal of faith in the efficacy of resettlement, undoubtedly because the existence of a restrictive immigration law made it impossible to think in terms of infiltration. But beyond that was the idealization by American historians of the Pilgrim Fathers as the victims of religious persecution and the pioneering or frontier experience as explaining much of American development and character. The Bernard Baruch–Herbert Hoover scheme to establish a "United States of Africa" where the oppressed people of Europe would "build in Africa a new country like America," is a good example of the pervading influence of the American experience on the thinking of American leaders.[1]

The Roosevelt Administration was not alone in its interest in resettlement. It was partly the hope held forth by the Evian idea of ridding themselves of their refugee burden which induced England and France to cooperate with the Administration. The invitation to the Conference had promised that they would not be expected to accept refugees beyond the number prescribed in their immigration laws and the agenda gave high priority to finding areas of resettlement. We shall see presently that Germany too displayed considerable interest in resettlement, albeit of a different character.

The Administration's keenness on the resettlement solution was reflected in the organization of the PACPR. It became the fulcrum of the resettlement effort and collected files of the most promising colonization possibilities. At the outset, however, there was little formal organization of the Administration's efforts. All departments, as well as friends of the Administration, were involved.

Roosevelt's wide correspondence was a fertile source of suggestions for resettlement havens. A letter from Antonio González, former Venezuelan Minister to Washington, led to an inquiry regarding the Orinoco River valley in which Roosevelt maintained an abiding interest.[2] Leo Sack, a former American Minister to Costa Rica, suggested to the President that certain areas in that country near the border of Panama were superbly suited for colonization, besides offering the advantage of increased security for the Canal Zone.[3] Apparently Sack was unaware that the State Department considered the refugees themselves the most likely source of danger for American security. A Dr. Stolper, perhaps a former refugee himself, forwarded a detailed plan for a commercial approach to resettlement which foreshadowed the idea behind the Coordinating Foundation. Paul Baerwald, the leading organizer of the Foundation, was attracted to the idea because of its "willingness to gamble for profit."[4] Frederick Cox, former British consul for Costa Rica and something of an amateur geographer, interested James G. McDonald in Lower California.[5] Someone suggested sending Dwight Morrow to Mexico again to repeat his performance in soothing ruffled Mexican feelings and to use his influence with General Cárdenas to loosen the Mexican stand on admitting refugees.[6] A proposal that Haiti be considered for resettlement caused some consternation in the State Department but Anthony de Rothschild, prominent in the British effort to find resettlement havens, was attracted by the idea and investigated. In general the State Department downgraded resettlement in the Caribbean, where so many of the suggestions seemed to focus, because of its assumption that spies planted among the refugees would pose a threat in this traditional area of American concern.[7]

Some of the suggestions were implausible, not because of the area which they recommended for colonization but because they originated with unlikely sources. In March 1941, Henry Ford, known for his anti-Semitic sentiments, offered to make part of his property in Brazil available for the resettlement of Jews. Brazil, which had always been a Department favorite as a resettlement possibility, rejected the idea.[8] Another prominent American who was not previously known as a philo-Semite, William Randolph Hearst, suggested in a speech that the Belgian Congo be sold to the Jews. The suggestion brought an immediate reply from Leopoldville that the Congo was not for sale and would not welcome refugees because of unemployment.[9] By December 1938 PACPR had screened fifty resettlement suggestions and was daily receiving more than its small staff could handle.[10]

The Administration's resettlement search brought with it some embarrassment. The United States was requesting of other countries what it could not offer itself. It seemed useless to explain the complexities of the American immigration law. Instead the Administration relied on the line of argument developed at Evian—the United States was admitting more refugees than any other area. Technically the claim could not be refuted. In the year 1939, the United States had admitted approximately 90,000 immigrants while Latin America admitted 84,000, Palestine 60,000, France, 38,000, and Britain and her colonies, 48,000.[11] Nevertheless, anxious eyes turned to the interior of the United States as a likely area for resettlement. The United States had, after all, taken the lead in trying to find a solution to the refugee problem, yet judged on the potential to absorb refugees she had barely pulled her weight, despite Department of State statistics. Paul Baerwald suggested at one point that refugees be resettled in the interior of the United States and even assigned a retraining role to the Rotary and the YMCA.[12] Antonio Salazar, Benito Mussolini, and Josef Beck were soon to make similar suggestions.

The Baerwald idea for Jewish resettlement in the United States had in fact the precedent of a plan proposed by Mordecai E. Noah in 1826. Noah was the American minister to Tunis, who after observing the misery and squalor in which his fellow Jews lived, determined to establish a Jewish settlement to be known as Ararat on Grand Island near Buffalo. In 1900, Baron de Hirsch and the United Hebrew Charities became concerned about the unnatural congestion of Jews in the eastern cities of the United States and established the colony of Woodbine in New Jersey. Three colonies, Alliance, Carmel, and

Rosenhayn were established in New Jersey in the 1880's. Russian Jews established an agricultural settlement in Sicily Island, Louisiana, Cremieux, South Dakota, and New Odessa, Oregon, in the same period and HIAS resettled several hundred families in Catopaxi, Colorado.[13] Whether the purpose of such schemes was to renew Jewish life by contact with the soil, or simply to relieve the congestion of the cities, the precedent was not followed by the majority of the Jewish community. None of the experiments endured for more than a generation and most of them for less.

The failure of earlier resettlement did not prevent new endeavors during the refugee crisis of 1938. The Refugee Economic Corporation, a private agency interested in resettlement, tried to establish a small colony at Van Eden, North Carolina, and sponsored numerous individual efforts of refugees at farming and other enterprises.[14] But such cases were the exception rather than the rule. Few refugee advocates seriously considered resettlement in the United States, aware, as they were, that a direct assault on the immigration law would prove counterproductive. But the prospect of resettlement in American possessions such as Alaska, the Virgin Islands, and the Philippines aroused considerable interest.

RESETTLEMENT SCHEMES: ALASKA AND MINDANAO

Many eyes turned as a matter of course to empty spaces in Alaska where the Federal Emergency Relief Administration had already done the preliminary engineering study for a colonization venture in the Matanuska Valley. In June the proposal to consider Alaska for resettlement made its debut before the fifth meeting of the newly organized PACPR. George Brandt, who served as the Department's liaison with PACPR, counseled against the idea, pointing out that Alaska could not legally serve as a back door around the immigration law.[15] By November 1938, when Charles A. Buckley, Democratic representative of a strongly Jewish constituency in the Bronx, wrote to Roosevelt offering to introduce a measure for refugee settlement in Alaska, a negative reply couched in State Department terms came from the White House.[16]

Despite such unpromising beginnings the idea of combining Alaskan development with the imperative need for resettlement picked up momentum, especially within the Department of Interior. Alaska, starved for population, especially population with entrepreneurial skills and capital, and the thousands of Jewish refugees, many of whom, it was fancied, had such assets, seemed made for each other. In August 1939 the Department of Interior released a report, prepared by one of its Undersecretaries, Harry Slattery, entitled *The Problem of Alaskan Development*, which emphasized this imagined confluence of needs. The report found the lack in growth due, in part, to under-population and suggested that an increase would go far to eliminate economic stagnation. It called for the establishment of public-purpose corporations, privately financed and federally chartered and regulated, to undertake development of the lumber, minerals, fur, and fish industries. The labor supply would be drawn from the United States and supplemented where necessary by other labor sources. Naturally there would have to be suitable modifications of the quota system to allow such special needs to be met.[17] Almost immediately a small group within the Interior Department, led by Slattery and Felix Cohen, an Assistant Solicitor in the Department, began to draw up legislation encompassing the ideas of the Slattery report. In February 1940, the Alaskan Development Bill was introduced by Senator William H. King, a Democrat of Utah, and Representative Frank Havenner, a Democrat of California.

Opposition to the proposal was widespread, not from the restrictionists, who viewed the legislation as an ill-concealed attempt to smuggle refugees in by the back door, but unexpectedly, from the top officials of Alaska. Included in this group was Anthony J. Dimond, the delegate from Alaska to the United States Congress, Ernest Gruening, director of the Interior Department's Division of Territories and Island Possessions, who would later become governor of Alaska, and Don Carlos Brownell, mayor of Seward and senator-elect of the Alaska legislature. Their arguments ran the gamut from disagreement with the economics of the Slattery report, charges that the territory would be turned into a concentration camp, and opposition to Jewish refugees, the resettlement of whom it was felt was the real purpose of the King-Havenner bill, rather than the development of Alaska. Sponsors of the King-Havenner bill had tried to forestall such criticism by including a provision that at least 50 percent of the jobs generated by the new developments had to go to American citizens. Moreover, a refugee who entered Alaska had to stay for a minimum of five years and then, if he wanted to enter the United States, he had to go through the normal visa procedure as if he were coming from his native country. The provision however, did not appear to satisfy those who were convinced that the King-Havenner bill's real motive was to rescue refugees rather than develop Alaska.

On the other side were aligned the rescue advocates and those officials in the Department of Interior who were convinced that the King-Havenner measure, if passed into law, could solve the problem of Alaskan development and at the same time make a contribution toward solving the refugee problem. Soon after the Slattery report was submitted they had formed a new group called the Alaskan Development Committee. The names associated with it, Frank Kingdon, Paul Tillich, Josef Chamberlain, and Harry Slattery were all drawn from the refugee effort. Significantly, no prominent names associated with Alaska appeared on the Committee's roster. The Committee's primary argument would be that the refugees and the refugee agencies would be a prime source of capital needed for development.

Much depended on whether Roosevelt would favor the proposal, and the circumstances were good. The officers of the IGC were in Washington and the President was scheduled to address them on October 19. Harold Ickes, whose appetite for the venture seemed to be stimulated by opposition, forwarded the report with a covering letter approving the report and suggesting that it be placed before the officers of the IGC as an American contribution.[18] Roosevelt was in a quandary; the proposal was attractive and would make a significant American contribution to the refugee dilemma. Undecided, he asked Sumner Welles, "Do you think I should sign this?" (the letter Ickes composed to be placed before the IGC meeting).[19] Welles counseled against the idea, pointing out that such a scheme "would lead to a breakdown in our whole system of protective immigration laws." To be effective there would have to be new laws restricting immigration from Alaska. This, cautioned Welles, "would in effect make Alaska a foreign territory for immigration purposes. . . ." The Welles reply was forwarded to Ickes.[20] Despite the fact that the King-Havenner bill made provision for this contingency, State Department opposition remained adamant.

The juxtaposition of Roosevelt's address to the officers of the IGC on October 19, in which he stressed the need to think in terms of resettlement havens for millions and urged the delegates to "clear the decks" of the puny ventures they had been thinking of, and the rejection of the Alaska proposal raises the question of the sincerity of Roosevelt's desire to solve the refugee crisis. Very soon thereafter the Administration's hopes were shifted from the Western Hemisphere to Africa, which offered the attraction of having no political risks.

For Roosevelt those risks appear to have been twofold: the risk of a direct confrontation with the powerful restrictionists in Congress and what some of the Administration's critics felt was an overclose association with the American Jewish community. When Ickes saw Roosevelt in November and the Alaskan scheme came up for discussion he was amazed at Roosevelt's detailed knowledge of the Slattery report and of the plan he had in mind for Alaskan development. But Roosevelt thought that Jewish immigrants should be limited to 10 percent to avoid the criticism that would arise "if there were an undue proportion of Jews." [21] The President's sensitive political antennae had picked up the theme that would be frequently heard during the May 1940 hearings. In April 1944 a parallel proposal for a haven in Oswego brought forth the same response from Roosevelt.

Without the Administration's support the King-Havenner bill lost any chance it might have had of becoming law. It was never reported out of the subcommittee of the Senate Committee on Territories and Insular Affairs. In December Rep. Samuel Dickstein (Democrat), introduced a new Alaska proposal to sell the idea of a refugee haven by highlighting its asset to the national defense and as a potential market for surplus production. The unused quotas of the previous six years which Dickstein, as Chairman of the House Immigration and Naturalization Committee, was continuously exercised about, would be used by refugees settling in Alaska. Technically this overcame Sumner Welles' fears about placing Alaska outside the purview of American immigration laws but it did not adequately respond to the many other reasons for opposition that had risen among the opponents of the idea. Like the previous measure, the Dickstein resolution died in the subcommittee.

The plan to establish a colony in the Philippines, in contrast to the Alaskan scheme, lived a happier if shorter life and had the support of the Administration. The idea originated within the Administration in mid-1938, at the same time as the Alaska scheme. In August, Roosevelt inquired of Paul V. McNutt, the Commissioner of the Islands, whether the Philippines could admit two hundred Jewish refugee families.[22] By December McNutt had made a preliminary survey and replied optimistically to the inquiry: "We think it would be possible for them to absorb . . . 2,000 families and possibly 5,000 more families thereafter." [23] The best place, McNutt thought, would be the island of Mindanoa where an influx of European refugees would go far to counteract the influence of that island's 30,000 Japanese. Manuel Quezon soon confirmed his willingness, under certain conditions, to settle one thousand refugees on the island and the PACPR rapidly organized a survey commission of engineers and agriculturists to make a study and find a specific location. The State Department ordered a minimum of publicity lest the price of the land be raised and needless domestic opposition aroused.[24] Already the venerable old independence fighter, Emilio Aguinaldo, had publicly stated that needy Philippinos, rather than Jewish refugees, should be resettled on Mindanao.[25]

As in the Alaska case, the rise of domestic opposition was not long in coming. The figure of 10,000 refugees, suggested by the survey commission, seemed extraordinarily high. There was fear that the introduction of European agricultural techniques would result in glutting the hemp and coconut markets. The Philippine legislature urged that production in the new settlements be limited to citrus fruits, rubber, and vegetables.

The survey commission, which was finally sponsored by the Refugee Economic Corporation, produced its report in October 1939, in time for the meeting of the officers of the IGC in Washington and as an alternate to the ill-fated Alaska proposal. The commission suggested that the Bukedon plateau in Mindanao was highly suitable for resettlement purposes and would eventually be able to support 10,000 people. A start should be made by purchasing 100,000 acres immediately to forestall land speculation. It also took care to follow the recommendation of the Philippine legislature by suggesting that noncompetitive crops be raised.[26]

Mindanao showed promise of becoming the most successful of the resettlement ventures and would besides be a specific American contribution which had none of the political liabilities of schemes

that focused on Alaska or the Virgin Islands. As a voluntarily associated area, scheduled to receive its independence in 1946, it was not
covered by the immigration law. Charles Liebman, an expert in
resettlement, was selected as director of the project and a start was
made in selecting and retraining and settling the first contingent of
refugees. But various problems soon arose to delay the project.
Selection and retraining of pioneer types took an inordinate amount
of time and the shipping problem made it impossible to get the project
off the ground until the Spring of 1941. The outbreak of war in the
Pacific and the subsequent occupation of the Philippines ended all
hope of resettlement there.

LATIN AMERICA

At the time of the Evian invitation and conference, between March
and July 1938, and for some months thereafter, the Administration's
primary hope for resettlement was centered in Latin America. It was
reasoned that a large influx of immigrants of European descent would
do for Latin America what it had supposedly done for the United
States. Domingo Faustino Sarmiento, the Argentinian statesman and
educator, had counseled the same course for his country at the turn
of the century.

But it had already become apparent at Evian that the Latin-
American republics did not share the Administration's conception of
their role as a primary area of resettlement. With the exception of
the Dominican Republic, Latin-American delegates expressed reluctance to accept refugees either by infiltration or resettlement. By 1939
most of the republics had imposed some restriction on immigration
which limited immigrants to a category called agriculturists. In
February 1939, Argentina, Uruguay and Paraguay, meeting for talks
on reducing trade barriers, signed a convention which included a
provision to place stronger restriction on immigration and promised
cooperation among themselves to keep out undesirables.[27]

The culmination of the State Department's efforts to make the
republics available for resettlement was reached at the Lima Conference in December 1938. Following Helio Lobo's advice, that the
Conference would be a suitable place to discuss Latin America's role
in the refugee crisis, Hull obliquely brought up the subject by
attaching a rider favoring a liberal immigration policy to a Cuban

resolution condemning persecution of minorities.[28] The tactic back-
fired when the Conference instead passed a resolution declaring
incompatible with the sovereignty of the American nations any
attempt to colonize racial or national groups within any country.
That may have referred to the various plans to bring refugees to the
Caribbean and the remaining colonies in the hemisphere. Much of
the apprehension of the republics was generated by concern regarding
the loyalty of the cohesive German minorities in Brazil, Chile, and
Argentina. Jews of German origin, it was thought, would hardly
improve the situation. Before his departure for the Havana Conference
in July 1940, Roosevelt again reminded Hull that he "might consider
the possibility of saying something at Havana in regard to the ancient
principle of political asylum." [29] The meeting did produce a Mexican
proposal for an inter-American committee to aid refugees. But such
resolutions were intended primarily as a gesture and had little effect
on the immigration policies of the individual republics.

Despite its reluctance to accept refugees, Latin America remained
the best hope of rescue advocates. This was especially true for non-
Jewish refugees, who were more likely to be accepted on an individual
basis. Mexico was generous to Spanish loyalist refugees from Vichy
France and for the remnants of the Polish Army from Iran. Brazil
proposed to accept thousands of refugees from Finland should they
materialize, and was more generous to non-Aryan Catholics. Non-
Aryan Catholics who were considered of Jewish blood in Germany
according to the Nuremberg laws were sometimes able to take
advantage of Latin America's affinity for Catholic refugees. A group
of these refugees formed an association of baptized Jews and half-Jews
and petitioned Ecuador, one of the most devoutly Catholic of the
republics, to accept them.[30]

A second reason for the continued focus on Latin America by
rescue advocates was the important role Latin-American papers, visas,
passports, citizenship papers, were to play in occupied Europe as a
rescue device.[31] Moreover, while Latin America was reluctant to
accept mass resettlement projects, many Jewish refugees had succeeded in reaching the hemisphere through normal infiltration or
immigration. Despite a considerable falling off after 1939, 10,000
Jews were still able to enter Latin-American countries in 1939 and

perhaps as many as 84,000 Jews had found refuge there between 1933 and 1939, especially in Brazil and Argentina.[32]

Undoubtedly the failure of Latin America to fulfill its promise as a refuge for Jews is partly related to a distaste for Jews. We have seen that non-Aryan Catholics found it easier to find havens in the area as did Spanish and Polish Catholics. This attitude had been apparent in the speeches of the Latin-American delegates at Evian, and eventually the State Department came around to the realization that Latin-American reluctance was focused specifically on Jews. Stephen Wise and Dr. Nahum Goldmann, a representative of the Jewish Agency in the Western Hemisphere, consulted with the State Department regarding a trip they planned in Latin America in December 1940, for the purpose of bringing the Jewish communities of the area into the rescue effort and attempting to loosen the restrictive immigration policies. They were cautioned by Adolf Berle that their activities "might energize the anti-Semitic feelings" of the natives.[33] Berle, then an Assistant Secretary of State, was not exaggerating. Anti-Jewish disturbances had broken out in Mexico and the Federation of Mexican Farmers urged stricter immigration laws against Jews because "almost all of them came in under false pretenses and did not engage in work as they promised. They have all become merchants and gangsters." [34] The Bolivian legislature entertained a resolution which would have prohibited Jews, Mongols, and Negroes from entering the country.[35]

Supplementing the traditional anti-Semitism was the fear of the indigenous merchant class that Jews, whose reputation for sharp business dealings preceded them, would create keen competition for the local market. Few Jews became gangsters, but many of them did become merchants. Much of the hostility was stimulated by a "drift back" phenomenon which saw refugees who had entered the country as farmers move into the cities to take up their old way of life. The reason given by the Brazilian Ministry of Interior for not accepting the Ford offer to resettle Jews on his rubber plantations was that there was strong feeling that Jews "would never remain there and we would have endless difficulties with them." [36] In the political arena the reluctance to take refugees was aggravated by the widespread knowledge in Chile, Ecuador, Bolivia, and Paraguay that certain consuls and government officials had grown wealthy by the illegal sale of

visas and landing permits. In Ecuador the Foreign Minister was forced
to resign after having signed a resettlement contract with a German-
Jewish group known as The New World Resettlement Fund.[37] The
willingness of certain Cuban officials to accept huge bribes to let the
passengers of the *St. Louis* land is fully documented by Arthur
Morse.[38]

The prospect for resettlement in Latin America was finally put to
rest, not in the capitals of the republics, but in the halls of the State
Department. The issue was closed for the same reason that all rescue
opportunities were thwarted between 1940 and 1942: the hysteria
regarding spies. By 1942 the United States was receiving "untrust-
worthy" aliens from Latin America and other areas for internment in
the United States.[39] The existence of large German minorities, often
imbued with Nazi-inspired race theories, also contributed to the
hostility toward Jewish refugees and the apprehension regarding
internal security.

RESETTLEMENT IN AFRICA AND THE
"SUPPLEMENTAL JEWISH HOMELAND" IDEA

One of the early resettlement schemes that won Roosevelt's interest
was conceived by Herbert Hoover and Bernard Baruch. The President
fondly called it the "big idea" and spent time poring over maps to
find a location for the "United States of Africa."

The scheme was deceptively simple in its outlines. It called for all
Jews to tithe themselves so that $300 million could be raised to
establish the republic. From there the plan was virtually a reenactment
of the American experience. The new state would be open to all
discontented and persecuted in Europe but would remain a British
protectorate. Baruch envisaged the new nation as eventually settling
ten million of "the strongest and the most courageous people because
they are anxious to get away from these over-regulated, goose-stepping
civilians of Russia, Germany, and Italy." [40] The scheme was forwarded
to London for consideration by the committee organizing the Coordinating Foundation in July 1939. Baruch foresaw that there would
be difficulty with London, since it refocused American resettlement
hopes in a largely British sphere of influence but there was little he
cared to do about it. "If Mr. Chamberlain and Mr. Baldwin want to
fully solve the problem there it is. . . ." [41] Samuel Rosenman, who

transmitted the plan to Roosevelt, agreed with Baruch's insistence that the new nation should not be restricted to Jews since he too had doubts about creating resettlement projects composed exclusively of Jews. "It is no solution," Rosenman told Roosevelt, "to create a world ghetto instead of many local ones." [42] It was perhaps Rosenman's influence that contributed to Roosevelt's belief that such projects should have only a limited number of Jews.

Roosevelt's enthusiasm for the "big idea" was not shared by Isaiah Bowman, president of Johns Hopkins University, who was generally considered America's leading expert on resettlement. He had examined over three million square miles of the earth's surface with a view to finding such havens. Discounting resettlement as a solution to economic and social strain, Bowman cautioned against the Administration's commitment to it because he felt it would "surely involve us in the rightness or wrongness of acts of the governments of the states of Central Europe." [43]

With the help of Morgenthau, Bowman was enlisted in the Administration's search for resettlement areas, and soon flooded the White House with reports on various possibilities. Despite his generally negative attitude toward mass resettlement, his opinion on specific areas showed considerable variation. He, for example, discounted every country in Latin America as a resettlement possibility except Costa Rica. On the other hand, he was fairly optimistic about Angola, which might account for Roosevelt's interest in that area.[44] Although Roosevelt held Bowman in high esteem, his warnings of the futility of involvement in resettlement were disregarded. There was no other practical solution on the horizon and at least the search for resettlement lessened the imagined pressure for modifying the immigration law. Even restrictionists could agree with the Administration that resettlement elsewhere was the most practical solution to the refugee problem. After *Krystallnacht* and Rublee's urgent pleas from London for lists of available havens to bring to Berlin for the impending negotiations with Schacht, the Administration could not abandon the search without negating the initiative it had taken with the Evian invitation.

In November 1938, Roosevelt invited William Phillips, Ambassador to Italy, George Messersmith, temporarily an Assistant Secretary of State, and Hugh Wilson, who had been recalled for consultation from his Berlin post as part of the Administration's response to *Krystall-nacht*, to his Warm Springs retreat for a discussion of the resettlement issue. Before he left Washington Roosevelt informed newsmen, in response to a question, that he had given a great deal of thought to resettlement but the time was not yet ripe to make his thinking known. The *New York Times* urged the Administration to start a massive resettlement program because the "self respect" of the democracies was at stake.[45] Welles, at Roosevelt's request, forwarded to him all the Department's data on the resettlement issue.[46]

From these discussions there emerged a clear shift in the Administration's focus from Latin America to Africa. William Phillips was instructed to sound out Mussolini on the possibility of resettlement in Ethiopia, while Roosevelt himself would make an inquiry regarding Angola.

It was Angola which soon became the center of the Administration's interest. Through the efforts of Sumner Welles the "United States of Africa" scheme, which was vaguely envisaged to encompass parts of Rhodesia, Kenya, and Tanganyika, was transferred to Angola, which Welles considered a more likely area. In October 1938 the Baruch group had taken its first step by sending Hamilton Fish, Jr., a New York congressman who headed the Interparliamentary Union, on a world tour to drum up support for the Africa idea. Roosevelt was annoyed at Fish's stealing the Administration's thunder and promptly informed Baruch that he did not think Fish reliable. "I wish this great Pooh-Bah would go back to Harvard and play tackle for the football team. He is qualified for that job." [47] Predictably Fish's trip did not generate enthusiasm among the receiving nations.

The prospects for resettlement in Africa, as in Latin America, were less than hopeful. At Evian the British had not displayed much enthusiasm for using British possessions in Africa for resettlement. George Rublee, while waiting in London for word from Berlin, reported that the position of the Foreign Office remained unchanged. Rublee felt that this was so partly because "Ambassador Kennedy was not disposed to a strong line." [48] The situation seemed to improve momentarily after *Krystallnacht*, when Chamberlain suggested before Parliament that the former German colonies such as Tanganyika might lend themselves to resettlement. But that hope faded when it became apparent that Berlin was adamant in opposing the idea and had in fact hopes of rejoining these areas with the Reich. Zionists too were opposed to such a scheme.[49] London's ability to make areas available in Africa was circumscribed by the opposition of the white residents, who much like the merchant class of Latin America, opposed the importation of a group of middlemen. Moreover, within a year London focused on its possession in the Western Hemisphere, British Guiana for resettlement, much the way Washington had focused on the British sphere in Africa. Both sides seemed to wax enthusiastic when the projected haven was in the sphere of the other nation.

It was Welles' early realization of London's opposition to all schemes involving its possessions in Africa that convinced him that the best opportunity to realize the United States of Africa idea lay in Angola. "The possibilities of Angola appear of such importance," he wrote to Roosevelt in January 1939, "as to warrant heroic efforts to overcome political obstacles." [50] The primary political obstacle was the approval of the Portuguese government and particularly its Prime Minister, Antonio Salazar. By an oversight, Portugal had not been invited to the Evian conference and was not a member of the IGC. The Department hastened to correct the error as soon as it realized the importance Angola was assuming in the scheme of things, but Portugal, aware of what was behind the sudden cordiality, proved reluctant.[51]

Early in January Roosevelt, having incorporated a series of ideas in a memorandum which Taylor was to present to Chamberlain, began his approach to Lisbon through London, Portugal's traditional great-nation mentor. "I cannot emphasize too strongly," he wrote, "the importance which I attach to the creation of a supplemental Jewish homeland as a step essential to the solution of the Jewish problem or my belief that Angola offers the most favorable facilities for its creation." [52] Although the idea of a "supplemental Jewish homeland," a product of Sumner Welles' fertile imagination ran counter to the basic outlines of the Baruch scheme for the establishment of a new nonsectarian nation, it caught Roosevelt's fancy as a way to enlist the full efforts of the Jewish community, where the idea of a national home had taken firm root. "Even if the political difficulties could be overcome," he acknowledged to Chamberlain, "it is doubtful whether Palestine could absorb and maintain the necessary influx of population. . . ." [53] To sell the idea to Lisbon, Roosevelt held out the prospect of increased prosperity for Angola as well as the mother country. Dr. Salazar "would become the greatest figure in the history of his country and of our time." [54]

For the Jewish refugees the idea of a national home in Angola was hardly original. In 1900 the Boers had actually established a settlement in Angola, and the territorialists had eyed it hopefully in 1912. With the onset of the Nazi racial depredations, Angola had again become the focus of resettlement interest. In 1931 a group of German Jews inquired about establishing a colony there but received a discouraging reply from Lisbon. Various inquiries from Warsaw and Bucharest evoked similar responses. It was upon the 1912 precedent that Roosevelt based his hopes. He apparently was unaware that in the intervening twenty-seven years the fortunes of the territorialists had ebbed while that of the Zionists had risen.

Predictably, the British were not impressed with the "dream of Angola." At the Washington conference of the officers of the IGC in October 1939, Herbert Emerson berated the idea as "utopian" and "unrealistic" and under the impression that Myron Taylor supported the idea (he did not) labeled him a visionary too.[55] Lord Halifax, Britain's Ambassador in Washington, found that the Angola scheme "would serve no useful purpose . . . but might on the contrary . . . cause serious embarrassment to relations between Portugal and countries interested in a solution of the refugee problem." [56] London's reluctance was partly explained by the unseemliness of asking Lisbon to offer her colony when Britain was unwilling to offer hers. Moreover, there was the question of immigration to Palestine, which might have considerably relieved the refugee problem. Understandably sensitive about her Palestine policy, the British Foreign Office had no desire to deal with a project that was being packaged as a "supplemental Jewish homeland." Chamberlain briskly refused to carry out the White House request and suggested that normal diplomatic channels directly to Lisbon be used. Taylor was instructed again to make clear to the British "the great importance" the Administration placed on Angola. "The possibility of successful mass settlement . . . appears so great," stated the note, "that we have no intention of letting the matter drop." [57] To this London could only reply that there was no objection to other governments approaching the Portuguese government although it was advisable that the matter be handled through private organizations which could guarantee financing. Meanwhile, the Portuguese Ambassador in Washington confirmed that Lisbon did not welcome an official approach.[58]

The private probings suggested by the British were, in fact, already in progress by a British group headed by Anthony de Rothschild. Jacques Politis, a cousin from the French branch of the Rothschild family, was dispatched to Lisbon and after five months of negotiations he obtained an option to buy land and a tentative agreement to accept refugees.[59] The Baruch group, working with the British group, sent a team to Angola to investigate and find a suitable area. The State Department, annoyed at Baruch's leaking the "Washington secret" and not yet prepared to give up an official government approach, decided next to establish contact with Lisbon through Paul van Zeeland, who was a good friend of Salazar. But by the time van Zeeland, the director of the Coordinating Foundation, came on the scene, he found that the private organizations had already begun their dealings with the Portuguese government. He cautioned the State Department not to "indulge in subterfuge when dealing with the Portuguese authorities." [60] But it was not subterfuge that marked the demise of the Angola scheme. The outbreak of the war, the change of Berlin's focus of resettlement to the east, the insurmountable transportation problem, and certain problems within the Jewish community all contributed to bringing the Angola project to a halt. It did not come to the fore again until the Agudath Israel, an Orthodox Jewish organization, began negotiations with Lisbon in 1943.[61]

The effort to find a resettlement haven in Ethiopia was the less serious alternative that grew out of the Warm Springs conference. The idea originated in Rome soon after Italy was placed under considerable pressure by Berlin to impose racial restrictions, similar to the Nuremberg laws, on its small Jewish community. The laws were not accepted with enthusiasm by the Italian people and the resettlement of Italy's Jews in Ethiopia was conceived by the Fascist Grand Council as an alternative. Italian Jews were actively encouraged to resettle in Ethiopia but according to Ambassador Phillips were extremely reluctant to do so.[62] The Fascist Grand Council also encouraged Italian Jews to seek resettlement in Palestine. Italy was invited to Evian because she was considered a receiving nation. She, of course, refused to attend.

But Roosevelt's inquiry regarding possible resettlement in Ethiopia, made through Ambassador Phillips and executed jointly with the British, received a cool reception. Mussolini suggested that Brazil, Russia, and even the United States offered better opportunity for resettlement.[63]

As in the case of Angola, the failure of the government was the signal for private groups to step into the breech. Frank van Gildmeester, a Dutch Protestant minister, heading a group calling itself the International Committee to Aid Jewish Refugees, negotiated with the authorities in Rome during August 1939. But Gildmeester's hope to establish the world's greatest Jewish city on the shores of Lake Tana failed.[64] Financial difficulties, rumors that Gildmeester was a Gestapo agent, and the opposition of Italian Jewry were factors in its demise.

In 1943 resettlement hopes were revived by unfounded rumors that Mussolini was planning to cede Harar, a province of Ethiopia, for an independent Jewish state if sections of British and French Somaliland could be annexed to Ethiopia. The denunciation of the scheme as a "rat trap" by the World Jewish Congress did not prevent Erwin Kraft, a German refugee, from organizing the "Harar Council for the Autonomous Jewish Province in Harar." [65] In the end, however, the plans for resettlement in Ethiopia, as in Angola, Alaska, British Guiana and Mindanao, proved chimerical.

By early 1939, while Rublee's critical negotiations with Schacht and Wohlthat were taking place, it had become clear that the lack of resettlement havens rather than German recalcitrance would be the chief stumbling block to extricating the Jews from Germany. Havens were not being made available and infiltration of individual refugees was too slow and uncertain. Moreover, the negotiations to establish a Coordinating Foundation, the international corporation which the agreement with Berlin called for to bail out German Jewry, ran into the problem of financing. The cost went far beyond the capacity of the private organizations and moreover was not subject to normal considerations of profit, as the organizers of the Foundation had planned. The Jewish Agency, probably the most experienced colonizers in the twentieth century, calculated that it cost £1,200 to resettle one person and that commercial viability could not be expected in less than a decade.[66] Not only would receiving governments have to make land available, but they would also have to contribute some financial aid. By mid-1939 refugees had become a more onerous burden than ever.

BRITISH GUIANA

We have seen that during the negotiations to establish the Coordinating Foundation, the British, partly to offset the effects of the White Paper of May 1939, recognized the financial limitations of the private organizations and, to the dismay of the State Department, made an offer of a haven in British Guiana at a nominal cost. The State Department interpreted the move as part of an effort by the British Foreign Office to embarrass the United States, which could not match the offer of cheap land and could not hope to get an appropriation of money, especially for small projects that contributed little to the solution of the total problem. Ultimately the Administration turned to Angola and the idea of a supplemental national homeland as its model for a solution by resettlement. It was hoped that such a project "which by its extent could bring a major solution" to the refugee problem "might unloosen the purse strings." The Administration might grant some financial aid "when practical plans emerge." [67] What galled the State Department was that London had captured the headlines, passed the onus to the United States despite the White Paper, but unbeknown to most, financing of the British scheme would still come largely from American sources.

American Jewry would be called upon to furnish the money for the British project and it was apparent from the outset that they could muster little enthusiasm for it. For the Zionists, British Guiana hardly represented a suitable substitute for Palestine and for others an area only five degrees from the equator did not seem suitable for a European population. Refugee advocates, moreover, had learned that the attempt by the League of Nations Refugee Commission to resettle 20,000 Syrians in the area during the twenties had been a dismal failure. The prognosis of the experts was not hopeful. Isaiah Bowman, for example, felt that resettlement in the hinterland of British Guiana "would be like a city in the South Pole. Civilization could maintain it, but the cost would be prohibitive." [68]

Undeterred by the poor reception of her offer, the British authorities insisted that a start be made. Anthony Rothschild established
contact with George Warren, the executive secretary of the PACPR
and urged him to organize an Anglo-American Survey Commission
as rapidly as possible. "The essential point," wrote Rothschild to
Warren, remains . . . that for political and other reasons we must
take the necessary steps to get some schemes working if only on an
experimental scale." [69] The Rothschild-Bearsted group had no more
fondness for the British plan than the American group but, under
pressure from Malcolm MacDonald, Minister for Colonial Affairs,
they acceded to the wishes of the government.[70] But the Zionists, represented by Stephen Wise, were not so easily mollified. Wise had already been informed by Abba Hillel Silver that it would be unthinkable to divert funds from Palestine to British Guiana and that the
United Jewish Appeal drive which he headed could not legally do so,
even if it wanted to. When Josef Rosen, a resettlement expert for
the Jewish Colonization Society, was chosen to serve on the survey
commission, Wise protested vehemently that his views would be
partisan and Isaiah Bowman agreed "that it would be rather easy to
forecast what he [Josef Rosen] would say on Palestine or British
Guiana." [71]

Reluctantly the PACPR organized the commission, borrowing an
Army engineer and two airplanes for that purpose, and surveyed the
area during February and March 1939. In May a report, predictably
optimistic about the area, but hedging on the actual resettlement possibilities was released. Resettlement was "feasible," climate, tropical
diseases, and transportation (there was only a trail to the coast which
was 250 miles away) presented "no insurmountable difficulties." But
actual possibilities would only be determined by a trial settlement of
three to five thousand settlers at a cost of $3 million.[72]

The Zionists ripped into the report as being too optimistic. Josef
Rosen, whose advocacy of a territorial solution made him anathema,
was forced to admit publicly that British Guiana was, in fact, not
ideal for refugees from Central European countries. But he hastened
to add that in the situation in which Jews found themselves, no opportunity should be overlooked.[73]

Meanwhile, London pressed ahead with its plans. As soon as the
commission's report was made public, Prime Minister Chamberlain

appeared before Parliament to announce the generous terms under which the land would be leased. The settlers would even be given a measure of autonomy.[74] But at the Washington conference of the executive committee of the IGC, held in October 1939, it was apparent that the opposition was intractable, and it included not only Zionists but the Administration as well, albeit for different reasons. Threats of British withdrawal from the IGC had little effect. The war soon forced London to direct its attention elsewhere; there were more important things to do than worry about what to do with unwanted Jews. All promise of financial support was withdrawn.

The British Guiana scheme appears to have been primarily a tactic of the British Foreign and Colonial Offices, intended to quiet the agitation caused by the White Paper. It consumed an incredible amount of time and energy which might better have been devoted to more viable schemes. Moreover, neither side foresaw that a by-product would be suspicion and hostility between Washington and London at a critical juncture. Even after London lost interest, the project clung to life. Settlers were selected and retrained and by mid-1940 a contingent of 500 settlers was ready to begin. A small nucleus of pioneer refugees was actually brought to Guiana before the project expired. We shall see presently that the burden of blame for the failure of the British Guiana scheme does not belong exclusively to the British, who pressed ahead with it despite the advice of experts. There were factors inherent in the idea of resettling Jews which seemed to foredoom even the most promising resettlement schemes. One such was the colony at Sosua in the Dominican Republic.

THE DOMINICAN REPUBLIC SETTLEMENT ASSOCIATION

The failure of the resettlement plans in Mindanao and British Guiana and the schemes for Angola and Ethiopia and the dozens of others that did not even leave the drawing boards, made it especially urgent that the project in the Dominican Republic be a success. The Roosevelt Administration's early skepticism gave way to a contrived enthusiasm as it became apparent that this venture would be the only one to be implemented.

Under the experienced hand of James Rosenberg, Chairman of Agro-Joint, the resettlement agency of the AJJDC, the Dominican

Republic Settlement Association (DORSA), was established, and in 1940 it appeared as if it might actually succeed.

The Dominican offer, first made unofficially at Evian, was confirmed by the Trujillo government in August 1939. The area, part of General Trujillo's personal estate, would, according to Dominican officials, accommodate 50,000 to 100,000 settlers. In March 1939 a survey commission sponsored by the Refugee Economic Corporation and directed by the PACPR investigated the proposed area and returned a favorable report.

Sosua was an area of improved land consisting of a tract of 26,000 acres, located in the northern part of the island east of Puerta Plata. The State Department, suspecting Trujillo's motives and racial theories concerning the better quality of European blood, continued to urge caution, especially about the figure of 100,000 cited by Virgilio Trujillo Molina, the Dominican delegate to the IGC.[75] In January 1940 the PACPR, following the publication of the survey commission's report, scaled the figure down to 28,000. As in the case of Mindanao, the State Department wanted as little publicity as possible until the project was underway. But partly to play down other abortive projects and partly to herald a good precedent, the Administration was forced to reverse itself and cast the full limelight on DORSA's Sosua. When Roosevelt addressed the executive committee of the IGC on October 17, 1939, he expressed the hope that the venture would become the "forerunner of many similar projects in other countries." [76] This, despite the fact that the theme of the address was the preferability of large resettlement projects such as the "United States of Africa" idea. Nevertheless, the Administration cooperated closely with James Rosenberg and assured him of complete support. On January 1, 1940, the DORSA corporation was formed and a contract with the Dominican Republic signed. The signing of the contract, which guaranteed the settlers full economic and civil rights and a tax-exempt status for the corporation, was the occasion of a special meeting of the IGC on the island. The occasion, designed to focus publicity on the one successful resettlement venture, was almost marred by the attempt of the Vichy delegate to impose plans for the dumping of 60,000 French Jews on the project.

In March 1940 about fifty refugees, the first contingent of a projected 500 settlers, arrived at Sosua. Transportation difficulties arose almost immediately. The entry of Italy into the war on June 10, 1940, cut the transportation route and many of those selected and trained were not able to reach the Dominican Republic. By mid-1942 it was apparent that the project would not go beyond the first phase of 500 settlers. Too much of the early optimism had worn thin as the project became enmeshed in a series of administrative, financial, and social difficulties that cast further doubt on whether it would survive.[77]

ROOSEVELT AS RESETTLEMENT VISIONARY

Shortly before the outbreak of war, Roosevelt's enthusiasm for resettlement temporarily waned. In June he "reluctantly" acknowledged to Myron Taylor that the "Government effort to stimulate concrete action by other Governments to meet the problem have been met at best by a lukewarm attitude." [78] He decided to follow Taylor's advice and let the IGC, the symbol of the Administration's rescue initiative, gradually die out.

The war, however, caused a dramatic change in the President's thinking. His concern for the refugee cause, and especially resettlement, was renewed. The Washington conference of the executive committee of the IGC was held at Roosevelt's insistence, as scheduled, despite the reluctance of the delegates who were convinced that the war had changed the situation. The President used the meeting as a platform to express the Administration's preference for large-scale resettlement ventures.

With the establishment of the Coordinating Foundation, the resettlement quest became institutionalized. All ventures would be organized under its sponsorship. Its director, Paul van Zeeland, soon was forced to work out a resettlement strategy based on small ventures, since the grandiose schemes outlined by Roosevelt had simply not materialized. On December 1, 1939, the plan was forwarded to the White House. It was designed to maximize rescue possibility at minimum cost. Small industrial as well as agricultural projects would be encouraged and financing would be arranged on a "strictly business basis . . . as investors not as dispensers of charity." Following the British model, the plan called for the chartering of subsidiary companies held together by a central holding company. Each subsidiary would be expected to show a profit after an initial period of dependence on the parent company.[79]

Roosevelt's devastating critique of van Zeeland's strategy gives some insight into how attached he had become to the idea of a massive resettlement solution. The plan did not "stimulate the imagination . . . of the average individual of the civilized world." It "missed the psychology which is necessary to success." "This is not the time," insisted Roosevelt, "to speak of small settlements . . . the picture should be in terms of a million square miles occupied by a coordinated self-sustaining civilization . . . I could raise money on that far quicker than if I talked in terms of individual communities . . . overall planning on an enormous scale is essential." The President had some new thoughts on financing such projects; he no longer believed that resettlement could be handled on a "strictly business basis," as van Zeeland had suggested.[80]

Where such territory was to be found and who would supply the money, Roosevelt, as usual, did not say. The critique was a further spelling out of the idea in his October 17 address, and emphasizing the necessity of getting public opinion behind the resettlement idea. It was visionary, long-range, already projecting into the postwar situation, and totally impractical as far as the immediate problem was concerned. Like everyone else, Roosevelt knew what had to be done, but when it came to practical plans like Alaska, he had no inclination to take the political risk involved. He fell easily into the role of elder statesman poised above the battle.

In one sense, however, Roosevelt's critique displayed a keen insight. No real support from governments could be expected until the issue had been dramatized and captured the public imagination. Nor could such ventures be commercialized. Van Zeeland soon experienced difficulty in attracting capital to the "business" of resettlement. Nor would the backers of Roosevelt's favorite scheme, the "United States of Africa," switch their allegiance. Lessing Rosenwald, a Jewish philanthropist, had promised to subscribe to several million dollars worth of bonds in the Coordinating Foundation, providing others followed his lead. But no such support developed. Van Zeeland asked Roosevelt's help to give the "necessary impulse" for fund raising. On July 8, Lewis Strauss, who continued to work closely with van Zeeland, followed up this request by inquiring whether the President wished to continue with the plans for the Foundation in light of the situation in Europe and the poor response from potential supporters.[81] Welles, apprised beforehand of Strauss's suspicion of Roosevelt's motives, hastened to assure him that "the President maintains unabated his interest in a practical solution to the refugee problem . . . ," but the President's meeting with a group of philanthropists, designed to loosen their purse strings, would have to be postponed.[82]

In 1940, while Breckinridge Long was moving to tighten the visa procedure, questions naturally arose in the Department about whether the Administration's charade concerning its interest in the refugee problem should not be abandoned. The assumption that such an interest existed was subjecting the Department to constant pressure from refugee advocates. The symbol of the Administration's interest was the IGC and its elimination would go far to bring rhetoric and practice into line. In February Robert Pell, who had done much of the negotiating behind the Statement of Agreement, suggested that the IGC be "put quietly to sleep." Included in the memo were some realistic appraisals of the men who were involved with the agency and their activities: "These gentlemen, as in the past, will make pretty speeches or in most cases will not speak at all. Mr. Taylor will offer a large banquet . . . the hope of the unfortunate refugees will be raised by the announcement that a meeting is to be held . . . and will be dashed to lower depths after the session."[83] Pell felt that the refugee problem could be best handled by removing it from politics and giving it over to a neutral agency like the International Labor Organization for management on a scientific basis. It was a popular but simplistic approach since anti-Semitism in the Reich, which had brought the problem into being, was at the very heart of what passed for politics and ideology among the Nazis. The Department simply wanted to get rid of a problem that seemed to them insoluble. It may have been Roosevelt's realization that the Department could not muster a real enthusiasm that caused his angry reply: "Even if this proposed meeting [of the IGC] makes 'pretty speeches,'" Roosevelt lectured the Department, "it is worthwhile keeping this committee very definitely alive. . . . The Division, I fear, is thinking in terms of immediate needs . . . and fails to appreciate the enormous importance of the long range view. . . . I am not quite ready to put the IGC 'quietly to sleep.'"[84] It was the same line the President had used at the Washington conference. Times had changed, the refugee problem would grow to tremendous proportions, Roosevelt expected, and a political safety valve might yet prove useful. It was in this way that the IGC remained, at least nominally, in existence to clutter and confound the rescue effort until, in the hands of the State Department, it became an instrument to thwart a more active effort. Ultimately the IGC became precisely what Roosevelt intended, the seed of the International Refugee Organization, a United Nations agency which handled the postwar refugee problem.

Meanwhile, the war seemed further to stimulate Roosevelt's imagination. When Eleanor Roosevelt inquired again about the prospects for using French and British Guiana as havens, the President confided a new idea for a "Pan American Trusteeship" to her. The trusteeship, composed of all European colonies in the hemisphere whose mother countries could no longer guarantee their security, would have a double purpose. It would forestall apprehension about the security of the hemisphere and at the same time avoid the bickering and antagonism among the jealous Latin-American republics.[85] Roosevelt, undoubtedly influenced by the pessimistic dispatches of the diplomatic corps, especially Joseph P. Kennedy, appeared to share their assumption that a Nazi victory in Europe was inevitable. The problem of the disposition of European territories in Latin America was naturally coupled in Roosevelt's mind with the refugee problem to produce the idea of a "Pan American Trusteeship." It was the same preoccupation and association with the disposition of these territories that was the genesis of the destroyer bases deal in September 1940. Stephen Wise's thinking ran along the same lines. In June 1940 he submitted a suggestion to the PACPR that the British and French make available their possessions in the Caribbean for temporary reception of refugees.[86]

Additional evidence of Roosevelt's abiding interest in a resettlement solution to the refugee problem can be gleaned from a secret project initiated by him in 1940 to organize a survey of all settlement possibilities. For that purpose he brought Henry Field, an archeologist and anthropologist from the Chicago Museum of Natural History, to work on the secret "M" project. Before the staff for the "M" project was disbanded in 1945 they had produced 666 studies of possible resettlement havens. But nothing was ever done with the material they compiled.[87] Dr. Aleš Hrdlička of the Smithsonian Institute also stimulated Roosevelt's interest in the general problem of population movement and settlement. In contrast to Isaiah Bowman, Hrdlička offered an optimistic view of the possibilities in Latin America and suggested that the State Department's thinking on race mixture and demography was outdated. To Roosevelt he recommended the creation of a central "immigration nucleus" to scientifically control population movements.[88] Roosevelt referred the memo to the State Department where it was promptly reasoned to death. To Hrdlička's suggestion that new resettlement activity be commenced in Latin America Long replied, "it is probably not a propitious moment to approach Central and South American countries." According to Long they were having a good deal of trouble digesting what they had already taken in.[89] Moreover, "recent history shows plainly," claimed Long, "that settlement there is not desired by Europeans." [90] Breckinridge Long was convinced that all the refugees wanted to enter the United States, and he was planning to do something about it. For whatever cause, the State Department closed the books on resettlement far earlier than did Roosevelt.

By 1942 rescue advocates undoubtedly were aware that despite a great deal of talk and activity, resettlement played virtually no role in actually rescuing refugees. The overwhelming number of Jews who did succeed in leaving the Nazi inferno did so by infiltrating rather than resettling. The exceptions were those Jews who were enlisted in the Zionist Pioneering movement or those who became involved in Sosua or the British Guiana project. A small group of experts led by Isaiah Bowman had consistently cautioned the Administration that resettlement was at best a dubious proposition in the twentieth century.[91]

NAZI RESETTLEMENT CONCEPTS AND THE FINAL SOLUTION

Paradoxically, the closest match one can find for Roosevelt's enthusiasm for resettlement is among Nazi officialdom in Berlin. Of course the Nazi resettlement concept was a lethal one: either a movement preceding annihilation or in itself a form of annihilation. But all forms of imposed resettlement, whether originating in the humane environment of Washington or the depraved one of Berlin, had in it this germ of a permanent solution of a minority problem by making the minority vanish. Bowman warned that resettlement notions were naturally closer to Berlin's view of the world: "Talk of empty spaces in Africa and Latin America is fundamentally misleading . . . [and] belongs to the species of thinking we call geopolitical." [92] Doubtless he was referring to the ease with which the notion of uprooting people, and shipping them elsewhere like so many cattle, entered the Nazi mentality. The objective of radical and moderate Nazis alike was not to help Jews but get rid of them. Carl Goerdler, a leading member of the July 20 movement to assassinate Hitler, nevertheless advocated the resettlement of Jews in some colonial country.[93] So did Schacht and most other moderate Nazis, so, in fact, did all Nazis before the Wannsee Conference.

But while the Nazi government favored resettlement or at least ridding Germany of Jews, it also looked hungrily at Jewish-owned assets. By not permitting Jews to transfer their property, the Nazi authorities created the principal barrier to the realization of their fondest hope, making the Reich *Judenrein*. Of course, the radical Nazis eventually wanted something more than simply cleansing Germany of Jews but in 1940 they could not make up their minds what it was. Should Jews be locked up in some vast concentration camp to prevent contamination or should they be dispersed to receiving countries to spread anti-Semitism or as the Berlin authorities put it, to "heighten political consciousness?" "The poorer the immigrant Jew" reads a Foreign Office circular, "the greater the burden he is on the host country and the more desirable will be the effect in the interest of German propaganda." [94]

Ultimately the Nazi government chose to lock Jews in a reserve in Lublin—the Nazi version of resettlement. But that was not done until it became apparent that rather than ridding itself of Jews, Germany's movement eastward was increasing the number of Jews in the Nazi sphere. At the same time, evidence accumulated during the negotiations with Rublee and Pell and the subsequent period of organizing the Coordinating Foundation and finally with the outbreak of the war, that the "host" countries were unable or unwilling to provide living space for refugees.

In January 1939, the Wilhelmstrasse, exasperated with the failure of other nations to take the Jews, announced that the Reich would itself "take the initiative in finding ways and means and destination for the emigration of Jews from Germany." [95] The location most frequently mentioned by Nazi officials was the island of Madagascar. Oswald Pirow, the pro-Nazi defense Minister of the Union of South Africa, learned of an attempt to approach the French on use of the island in December 1938 but a general strike and cabinet crisis delayed the meeting.[96] On February 7, 1939, Alfred Rosenberg, the official theoretician of the Nazi party, announced at a news conference Nazi plans to settle 15,000,000 Jews in Guiana or Madagascar.[97] Doubtless such talk was triggered by Göring's mention of it during the inter-ministerial conference held on November 12, 1938, to discuss the adverse effects of *Krystallnacht*.

Madagascar had long been a focus of resettlement thinking. The Japanese did preliminary engineering studies in 1929 and subsequently rejected the island as a prospect. A Nazi publicist, Egon von Winghene, recommended it for resettlement of Jews as early as 1931. In 1937, a Polish survey commission investigated it for the same purpose and returned a controversial report.[98] France was thinking of resettling 10,000 Jews in Madagascar in November 1938.[99]

Soon after the Compiègne armistice, Adolf Eichmann, a captain in Reinhard Heydrich's Security Ministry who had earned a reputation as something of an expert on Jews, and Theodor Dannecker, a captain in the SS, were asked to work out a complete plan to transfer the Jews to Madagascar. After almost a year's work Eichmann and his partner produced a plan which was little more than a thinly disguised scheme for a giant concentration camp. "There is no question of a Jewish state," warned Alfred Rosenberg in speaking of the Madagascar plan, "but only a Jewish reserve."[100] Nazi authorities displayed a certain sympathy for Zionists as fellow dissimilationists, but the idea of giving Jews a new national home which might become a power base for the Jewish world conspiracy was unthinkable.

Simultaneously with the Madagascar scheme, Berlin tried to implement a resettlement program in the Lublin area of Poland. During October 1939, hard upon the occupation of Poland, the Nazi press began drumming up the idea of a special Jewish reservation in the East. Typical was the observation of a Nazi political commentator, Hermann Erich Seifert: "From time to time there is talk of a Jewish settlement area in the district of Lublin, a sort of Jewish reservation, in which the Jews would live among themselves and, for the first time in their existence, would have to organize their lives in every

detail. . . . Since February 1940 they [Nazi officials] are tackling
the Jewish question, especially in Lublin, not with the 'humanitarian'
nonsense you find in democracies, or with soulful appeals, but according to new methods, with order and work." [101]

The Nazi authorities were already demonstrating the "new
methods." In October 1939 a transport of 1,672 Viennese Jews were
dumped in the district. They were followed by thousands of other
Jews including a contingent of Jewish war prisoners from the Polish
Army. By January 20, 1940, approximately 78,000 Jews had been
shipped to the Lublin reservation and plans were afoot to ship 400,000
more. The conditions were so chaotic and unplanned that the population movement became an atrocity in its own right. By March 1940,
clamor in the press forced the Nazis to abandon the Lublin plan.[102]
But the label of the plan, "resettlement in the East" remained and
became the euphemism for the destruction of European Jewry. It
made the link between resettlement and genocide crystal clear.

EVALUATION OF THE RESETTLEMENT FAILURE

The Reich was no more successful than the Allied powers in finding
a solution to the refugee or Jewish problem by resettlement. The
failure had ominous consequences. Whether resettlement might have
saved the Jews of Europe is difficult to tell since neither side gave the
experiment a fair chance.

Most of the areas under consideration were in the tropics, where
soils were quickly exhausted and tropical diseases made talk of "biological optimums" commonplace. Most experienced colonizers agreed
that Europeans could not work efficiently in such areas.[103] Moreover,
a cheap labor supply and depressed market conditions made mass
employment of refugees unlikely. Transportation to the interior was
poor and the market, where goods produced by the settlers might
have been sold, was not developed. There was therefore little hope
that such colonies could ever pay for themselves. Planning on the
basis of producing a profit, as Paul van Zeeland did, was simply unrealistic. When it became clear that there was little possibility of
producing a profit, the problem of raising capital was compounded.
Government aid, upon which such projects might have depended,
was virtually ruled out by the war and there was little likelihood of

proper financing from any other source. Underfinancing had been a basic cause of the failure of many previous colonization schemes.

In the one example of successful resettlement the motives of the receiving country, the Dominican Republic, were as suspect as those of the refugees who had become "agriculturists." The State Department suspicion of the Trujillo offer was bolstered by the common knowledge that he was anxious to gain favor in Washington and believed that an infusion of "European blood" would invigorate the Dominican people.[104]

By 1941 an unforeseen problem made the possibility of finding resettlement havens even more remote. The Latin-American Republics, never anxious to accept the refugees, found in the security hysteria a ready instrument to withstand Washington's pressure to offer refuge. An insight into the extent of the security hysteria can be gleaned from an FBI report on DORSA's Sosua project, based on "confidential and reliable" sources, the Cuban federal police. The report discovered active espionage in the Colony consisting of shore-to-sea signals, supplying of enemy submarines, and short-wave signals.[105] A later investigation revealed that the shore-to-sea lights were actually made by flashlights carried by the settlers in going about their chores. The Department became particularly distressed about illegal infiltration into the hemisphere "because of the possibility that such clandestine activities may embrace subversive elements." [106] Dozens of dispatches forwarded by the American diplomatic mission, usually originating with local police authorities, flooded the Department with reports of refugee spies working either for the Nazis or the Communists, whichever seemed more suitable.[107]

There were not many encouraging examples in the history of resettlement, while the list of failures in the twentieth century was impressive. A group of Irish settlers failed to reestablish themselves in Peru in the 1920s; a Boer group failed in Argentina; Italian Waldenesians failed in Uruguay; Mennonites failed in the Chaco; the much-heralded Biro Bidjan project in the Soviet Union appeared to be on the road to failure and heretofore successful Agro-Joint colonies in Argentina showed few signs of growth. The Zionist colonization experiment in Palestine seemed the one exception.

In the case of European Jews, moreover, the resettlement problem was even more difficult. We have already noted that in Latin

America opposition to Jewish immigrants per se was an important factor in determining the generally hostile attitude of the governments. Undoubtedly this factor also played a role in Africa, especially among the Boers and the English farmers of Kenya and Rhodesia.[108] The distaste for Jewish settlers was based on more than sociohistorical factors. The demographic and psychological characteristic of European Jewry reinforced the general doubt about the feasibility of resettling them. We have no overall statistical description of European Jewry but we can be fairly certain that at least in Western Europe it followed fairly closely the general character of German Jewry. This meant that European Jewry was highly urbanized, with almost no representation in agriculture, and slightly older than the general population (73.7 percent of German Jews were over the age of forty in 1939).[109]

Older people do not, as a rule, make good raw material for pioneering endeavors and in the case of the Jews many of the best prospects for pioneering had already been recruited for Palestine. To be successful, pioneering resettlement required zeal, faith in ultimate success, and a willingness to uproot oneself. Because such qualities must come from within, it is unlikely that colonization schemes can be imposed by one community on another. The successful Mormon and Zionist experiments are remarkably similar in their search for Zion. They both possessed a sense of mission and were voluntary. Between 1935 and 1941 the average Jewish refugee had no such enthusiasm. He did not welcome the cut in his standard of living or the insecurity of pioneering life. His goal was not to build a new world but to survive in a world which gave him no quarter. After observing the refugees for several months in 1939, Myron Taylor was convinced that the objective of Jewish refugees was "to get into settled countries where they can set up their lives in existing communities . . . in commercial and industrial activities." [110] Dr. Munoz, Brazil's chief of Immigration Bureau, confirmed Taylor's conviction. He observed that "the principal difficulty in admitting Jews was their unwillingness to [follow] a pioneering life." [111] An FBI observer of the Sosua project in the Dominican Republic who harbored deep-seated prejudices against the refugees reported that "[he] had observed no refugees at work, a few employed Dominicans tilling the soil, the homesteads adorned by healthy looking refugees in athletic shorts, naked to the waist, lounging in comfortable chairs." [112] The settlers are described as being "allergic to work" and interested only in improving their already luxurious private quarters. The report probably tells us more about the hostility of agencies like the FBI to refugees whom they fancied to be security risks than it does about Sosua, but there may be a residue of accuracy in depicting the nonpioneering mood of the settlers.[113] The observation of their attitude was confirmed by Isaiah Bowman who wrote, "the migrant in 1937 wants civilization to follow him because the homeland is comparatively rich and safe in contrast to the meagerness and limited security of life on the frontier." [114]

ZIONISM AND RESETTLEMENT

Even if European Jewry had been able to furnish good raw material for resettlement, the success of Jewish resettlement ventures outside Palestine was still dubious. Not only were individual Jewish refugees resistant to resettlement imposed by hostile communities, but a growing segment of the community, where Zionist sentiment had become strong, considered resettlement outside Palestine something in the nature of a betrayal. Territorialism, the traditional term used in the Jewish community to describe settlement outside Palestine, had considerable influence in the early 1900s. The territorialists were, however, losing ground steadily to the Zionists. But the refugee crisis placed a high priority on finding any resettlement haven. Palestine could not absorb all Jews who needed to find a new home and the British White Paper of May 1939 planned to limit immigration. To the dismay of the Zionists, these factors infused new life into a virtually dormant movement. The Freeland League for Jewish Territorial Organization, a successor to ITO, was organized in Poland in 1935 and rapidly gained a following. In 1938 a new organization, the International Colonization Society, coordinated the efforts of all territorialist groups. In addition, many smaller groups dedicated to a specific colonization project were organized. In the United States, Agro-Joint, the colonization arm of the AJJDC, occupied originally with organizing and financing colonization projects in Russia and Argentina, attracted some of the most prominent Jewish philanthropists. While territorialism was showing new vigor, the world Zionist movement became hopelessly enmeshed in a political problem. Its success depended on the availability of Palestine for colonization and that, in turn, depended on the benevolence of the British government. The promulgation of the White Paper signified that British good will, on which Chaim Weizmann had depended, could no longer be counted on.

The White Paper placed the Zionists in a quandary. To acknowledge that Palestine had, by London's fiat, become the "impossible solution" and to place their financial and organizational resources as well as their pioneering experience at the service of the IGC, would have meant the end of their movement. Convinced that a Jewish state in Palestine offered the best hope of saving the Jews, they could point with some pride to their success in pioneering. If Palestine had been made unavailable by a political decision, then that decision could be undone by politics. The agitation for a homeland in Palestine became the primary thrust of the movement and it was supplemented eventually by an illegal immigration known as Aliyah Beth.

Nevertheless, the idea of a supplemental Jewish homeland, advocated by Roosevelt, was not totally ignored by Stephen Wise despite its territorialist flavor. "Being a Semite," he wrote, "I would be willing to do a little bargaining with Britain if we get two things." [115] He had Kenya and Uganda in mind. When the question of partition came up in 1938, Wise confided to a prominent fellow Zionist, Pesach Rosenblatt, that "if we must have a limited Palestine [then give the Jews] . . . some great additional English colony." [116] But the Zionists were generally distressed at the areas chosen. Wise thought very little of the Alaska scheme and even less of British Guiana. Chaim Weizmann observed that of all the territories being considered "none could be found in the temperate zone." [117] When Chamberlain suggested the former German colony of Tanganyika, the bitterness of Wise's reaction outdid Berlin's: "I would rather have my fellow Jews die in Germany than live somehow, anyhow, in the lands which bear the imprint of yesterday's occupation by Germany, in lands which may tomorrow be yielded back . . . to Germany." [118] Zionists were reluctant to see any competition to their Palestine enterprise. The distress felt by Wise on learning of Roosevelt's support of the United States of Africa scheme, is a good case in point.

The Zionist attitude toward resettlement outside Palestine became more flexible as the crisis intensified. The World Jewish Congress proposal at Evian made no mention of resettlement in Palestine. In 1943, when news of the Final Solution had been confirmed, Wise urged that the Allies prepare "temporary refuge and even permanent asylum" for those who may not wish to return the lands of "famine and slaughter" after the war.[119] At the Bermuda Conference, the World Jewish Congress requested simply the setting aside of "uncultivated areas . . . with a view toward Jewish agricultural settlement." [120] Agitation to revoke the White Paper continued but the immensity of the disaster and the realization that all of Europe's Jews needed immediate havens changed the situation. In May 1942, the *Jewish Forum*, a popular Anglo-Jewish monthly, argued that it would be "folly to think of establishing 100,000 Jews a year in Palestine and ignore the crying needs of millions of other Jews." [121] In June the magazine sponsored a discussion on "Palestine and Auxiliary Immigration Stations."

But the Zionists never forgot what they considered the first order of business—support of the Yishuv in Palestine. During the period of negotiation for the Coordinating Foundation, Dr. Abba Hillel Silver would not pledge a dollar to the new agency lest Palestine get the "short end of the bargain." [122] What might have happened had the Zionists been able to transfer momentarily their zeal, energy, and pioneering skill to the effort to resettle Jews elsewhere is a moot question.

The tragedy of the effort to rescue Jews by resettling them was that in order to be successful it required extreme efforts, a passion to achieve it even under the most dismal circumstances and that neither the nations involved nor the Jews seemed able to muster.

In the difference between the energy expended to establish an Auschwitz as compard to a Sosua may lie a good part of the reason for the failure of rescue between 1938 and 1942.

6

The Struggle over Refugee Policy

In the three years between the Evian Conference and the outbreak of war much rhetoric emanated from the Administration but little concrete achievement. The U.S. immigration law limited the number of immigrants to 153,774 annually. A national origins formula assigned a specific quota to countries other than Canada, Mexico, and the independent nations of Central and South America. But if one considers those European nations eventually to fall under Nazi hegemony, the number of spaces actually available to refugees came to approximately 53,000.[1] Between 1938 and 1941 approximately 212,000 refugees might have entered the United States but only 150,000 were actually able to do so.[2]

The battle to save the refugees was waged not so much in attempting to change the Immigration Act of 1924 and its amendment of 1929. Most agreed that such an effort would have been futile. It was rather in the area of the administration of that law and other regulations by the State Department. At stake was not only the fate of the approximately 62,000 additional refugees who might have come here between 1938 and 1941 but that of the many thousands more who might have entered on other grounds on temporary visas which did not fall under the Immigration Act. Between 1938 and 1941 refugee advocates could not effectively counter the State Department's rigid administration of immigration regulations. The cost of that defeat was not only the many thousands of lives but the antirescue precedent which lasted until 1944.

126

The first reminder that much more might be achieved by a more liberal interpretation of the law was given by James G. McDonald. In 1935 he had reminded the Administration that "just as President Hoover, by administrative interpretation, in effect instructed consuls to block immigration, so now President Roosevelt could, by relaxing further the requirements in the case of refugees, make easier the admission of a few thousand additional Germans a year." [3] McDonald had reference to "soft" areas in the Immigration Act which could be interpreted either broadly or strictly. Thus Hoover's interpretation of the LPC provision in September 1930 was on the rigid end of the spectrum, whereas Roosevelt's extension of visitor's visas in November 1938 was a liberal interpretation. There were other ways in which the law might have been liberalized without changing it. The Treaty-Merchant provision which permitted businessmen who showed promise of being able to generate employment to come here was especially pertinent since many refugees were skilled businessmen and some had already displayed considerable talent in this area. [4] Temporary immigrants might have been taken into the Virgin Islands without breaking the immigration law, a suggestion later made by Harold Ickes. Greater use might have been made of visitors' visas and other nonquota devices for Rabbis and professors. Other proposals included were redistribution of unused portions of the quota to needy refugees, mortgaging future quotas, making current use of previously unused quotas, excepting children outside the quota system and the use by refugee agencies of the mass or corporate affidavits procedure. Most interesting was the idea of "temporary havens" or "free ports" which would have allowed refugees to be interned here for the duration with the status of goods awaiting transshipment or prisoners of war. The idea was finally put into effect in mid-1944 when it was all but too late.

The struggle over refugee policy was precipitated by an opportunity to save a portion of Europe's cultural community, its scientists, writers, artists, intellectuals, and labor leaders as well as a sizable number of ordinary people, including children. In no case was a wholesale departure from the restrictionist intent of the law intended. Refugee advocates addressed themselves to the humanitarian instincts of the Roosevelt Administration, arguing that America's tradition of offering a haven for the oppressed should be kept intact. On a practical level they could point to the fact that Europe's loss could be America's gain. The refugees could be an economic asset since they must be clothed, housed and fed, and would stimulate rather than depress the economy.

THE DEVELOPMENT OF THE SECURITY ARGUMENT

On the opposing side were the restrictionists who came to rely chiefly on the argument that admission of refugees would endanger the national security. It was an argument that rescue advocates were hard put to answer without compromising their own credentials as loyal Americans. The restrictionist argument was reinforced by the fact that the Nazi authorities had already attempted to use the refugees to shore up their economy. What would prevent them from using them to plant espionage agents? Stories of the exploits of the "fifth column" in Spain were abetted by the film industry, which discovered that heavily accented German spies made good box office. Roosevelt echoed the hysteria in his fireside chat in May 1940: "Today's threat to our national security is not a matter of military weapons alone. We know of new methods of attack, the Trojan horse, the fifth column that betrays a nation unprepared for treachery. Spies, saboteurs and traitors are the actors in this new strategy. With all that we must and will deal vigorously." [5] The Trojan horse analogy echoed the rhetoric of the Dies Committee hearings and was also used by Leland Stowe, columnist for the Washington *Evening Star*.

It did not take long to discover that the security could be played upon for political ends. Restrictionists developed a security gambit, and ultimately they were able to sponsor ever tighter visa regulations. The security gambit was not exclusively an American discovery. Earl Winterton cited the fear of spies in his speech before the Washington conference of the IGC to put that agency out of business. When Anthony Eden, Britain's Foreign Minister, was told in 1942 of the possibility of rescuing 70,000 Bulgarian Jews he fell back on the security gambit: "Hitler," he claimed, "might well take us up on any such offer . . . [and] would be sure to put a number of agents in the group." [6] The Latin-American republics too, found that citing a security problem could counter Washington's persistent requests for resettlement havens. They flooded the Department with intelligence about refugee spies.[7] Reports from Cuba that German-Jewish refugees remained loyal to Germany were received by State Department officials and passed on to Breckinridge Long, who was always in search of such "evidence." [8] By June 1940 the Latin-American Division was actually discouraging the acceptance of refugees in the Caribbean and Central America on the ground that spies had infiltrated the refugee stream.

Some of the psychosis about security was generated by a still amateur American intelligence service. The activities of the chief cable censor in producing confirming intelligence to prove that HICEM, the oldest and most respected rescue agency in the American Jewish community, was actually an espionage agency, may serve as an example. After examining the outgoing and incoming cables of the agency the censor arrived at an "inescapable conclusion." "The Nazi have utilized HICEM to their advantage" and the rescue and relief organization "either does not know or does not care—and the record indicates the latter to be more nearly the truth." [9] Based on a fleeting knowledge of the Jewish agencies, such reports were passed on to State Department officials who, if they suspected their sheer absurdity, did not hesitate to use them.

William C. Bullitt, former Ambassador to France, passed on such an unconfirmed story in a speech in Philadelphia in August 1940. He asserted that "more than one half the spies captured doing actual military spy work against the French Army were refugees from Germany." [10] *The Nation* tried to refute Bullitt's widely circulated story by publishing a letter from Heinz Pol, a refugee journalist familiar with the French scene. He pointed out that not a single refugee was involved in espionage in France and that there was no need to use them since the French government including the Bonnet group itself had already been penetrated by German intelligence. The German intelligence service, moreover, shunned the use of refugees and preferred to use tourists or businessmen because they could be trained and were more reliable. Refugees in France lived such harassed lives, Pol pointed out, that it was difficult to imagine how they could take time for espionage, especially for a nation that had treated them so shabbily. [11] Pol's contention was confirmed after the war when it became general knowledge that Admiral Canaris, chief of the German intelligence service, made good use of alienated minorities such as the Irish and Welsh in Britain or German-American Bundists in the

United States rather than refugees.[12] The main effort of German intelligence against the United States, for example, made against Canaris' advice, was the landing of a group of agents on Long Island in May 1942. When they were apprehended it was discovered that the group consisted entirely of German-Americans who had returned to the Fatherland and English-speaking Germans. But it remained difficult to challenge the contention that Berlin relied on the refugees to garner intelligence because the drama of the spy stories had captured the public imagination and were continually supplemented in the press.

Isolated instances of espionage, real and imagined, fed the public appetite. The most dramatic was the case of Lili Stein, a Viennese refugee, who had been rescued by Canaris after her parents committed suicide. Others referred to rumors of seven Jewish *Abwehr* agents sent to Latin America. Samuel Lubell's article in the *Saturday Evening Post*, "War by Refugee" was based on special access to the State Department files. He claimed that the Nazis were using the refugee stream to plant their agents "all over the world" and had established a special school in Prague where Gestapo agents learned to pass as Jews.[13] In a similar vein was the sensational testimony of Richard Krebs, author of *Out of the Night*, who claimed before the House Committee of Un-American activities that agents in the guise of refugees were being infiltrated in the United States.

There was an irony in the spy stories. In the case of the Dies Committee, for example, it was the urging of two Jewish congressmen, Samuel Dickstein and Adolph Sabath, who wanted the Nazi front organizations investigated, which gave Martin Dies his start in the summer of 1938. Dies soon turned his attention to the conspiracy from Moscow and ignored the Nazi fifth column until the security psychosis provided an opportunity to gain the national limelight. Breckinridge Long seems to have taken the Dies files at face value and worked closely with him throughout the refugee crisis. A second irony was that although stories of refugee spies became popular currency, no mention was made of the use which was being made of refugees in counterintelligence. Britain found refugees well equipped to make a significant contribution here.[14] The State Department showed scant interest in material that refuted the spy story. Karl Lowenstein, a well-known scholar, prepared a carefully reasoned memorandum which pointed out that planting spies among the refugees was by no means a simple task because of the unique ethnicity and cohesiveness of the refugees "conditioned by the requirements of mutual help" would make agents relatively conspicuous.[15] The most dangerous place for a spy to be was in the refugee stream, according to Lowenstein. But such revelations were heard reluctantly by the Department and not at all by the Seventy-Sixth Congress, which saw the introduction of over sixty measures designed to restrict the activities of aliens. The security gambit had become part of the political dialogue, according to Senator Lewis B. Schwellenbach, who observed that the introduction of such measures was "perhaps the best vote-getting argument in present day politics."[16] The efforts of Dr. Frank Kingdon, director of the Emergency Rescue Committee, and other refugee proponents to refute spy stories met with little success. Few government officials, according to Alfred Wagg, a prominent refugee reporter, were able to see the refugee as a potentially good American. " 'Refugee' in Washington means 'alien' to the bureaucrat and 'secret agent' to the military man."[17]

For the Jewish rescue organizations the security gambit posed a special quandary. Opposition to the ever stricter visa regulations put forth by the State Department could be made to appear that the rescue of their religious brethren was closer to their hearts than the security of the United States. Few Jewish leaders cared to tamper with the question of loyalty. The Nazi depredations and the rise of domestic anti-Semitism had made them sensitive on that point. Stephen Wise must have been chagrined when he received a congratulatory letter from Breckinridge Long for his support of the "close relatives" edict of June 1941 which made it virtually impossible for any refugees with relatives remaining under Nazi control to come to the United States.[18]

BRECKINRIDGE LONG

The war faced the State Department with a host of new problems. American citizens abroad had to be brought home from the war zone, diplomatic duties of the belligerents had to be assumed, and missing American citizens traced. To meet this emergency a Special War Problems Division was created within the State Department. Breckinridge Long, the former Ambassador to Rome, became its head, assuming the position of Assistant Secretary held temporarily by George

Messersmith. Included in the new division, established in January 1940, was the Department's visa section. That placed Long in a position where his decisions would be crucial on refugee matters.[19] Ultimately Long's influence would reach even further. By 1943 he supervised twenty-three of the Department's forty-two divisions.

Ironically, Long's appointment to head the Special Problems Division was accidental. After his precipitous resignation as Ambassador, Long hoped that Roosevelt, with whom he maintained a regular correspondence, would appoint him to a Cabinet position. He was disappointed, and he viewed with mixed emotions the prospect of becoming Ambassador either in London or Berlin. Despite the influence of Joseph P. Kennedy, George Messersmith, and James Roosevelt, Long was passed over for these positions. More anxious than ever to get back into government, Long was growing impatient when the Assistant Secretaryship was offered him in mid-December 1939. He jumped at the opportunity and imagined that he finally had a position that would allow him to be in on policy-making. But except for the decisions Long made on the refugee rescue problem, the critical importance of which few realized at the time, Long was again disappointed. He continued to maneuver for a better position in the Department.

Like Roosevelt, Long had begun his career in national politics during the Wilson Administration. A substantial contribution to the Wilson campaign in Missouri in 1916 resulted in an appointment as Third Assistant Secretary of State. He shared with Wilson a connection with Princeton University, on whose board of trustees Long served until the end of his life. He frankly enjoyed public life. The State Department was composed of a small cohesive group, largely people of his own social background, the social elite who wished to serve and play in the capital cities of the world. When Long later found himself in the storm center of the rescue of refugees, he was inclined to look back at his relatively peaceful tenure in the State Department with nostalgia. "It is different from last time," he confided in his diary in 1942, "Washington then was gay and confident. Now it is sober. Then it had many aspects of social as well as intellectual leadership. Now it is intellectual without the social setting." [20]

In June 1920, Long resigned his post. Among its unforeseen advantages was the opportunity to make the acquaintance of young

Franklin D. Roosevelt, then an Assistant Secretary of the Navy, and a salty tongued Congressman from Tennessee named Cordell Hull. Both contacts were to prove useful in his later career.

Long's exposure to politics on the periphery of the Wilson-House circle whetted his appetite for elective politics. He tried his wings by running, unsuccessfully, for the Senate seat from Missouri on the Democratic ticket in the election of 1920. The loss of the election was attributed to a split in the party for which Long was at least partly responsible, and his untimely support of the League of Nations.

The experience seemed to have cooled his desire for elective office. He never again was to run for office but he remained active in Missouri politics throughout the twenties, at the same time establishing a reputation as an international lawyer. Long did not appear to muster much enthusiasm for the law. His mind, heart, and fortune were committed to politics. When Roosevelt, now Governor of New York, was being groomed for the Democratic nomination in 1932, Long became a floor manager at the Democratic convention and made a sizable contribution to the campaign fund. His reward for service was not long in coming. In April he assumed the coveted post of Ambassador to Italy.

From the moment King Victor Emanuel sent his special royal carriage for the elaborate presentation-of-credentials ceremony, the Fascist regime seemed to have captured his heart. "The head of the government [Mussolini] is one of the most remarkable persons," he wrote to his friend Joseph E. Davies, the soon-to-be Ambassador to Belgium, "and he is surrounded by interesting men. And they are doing a unique work in an original manner, so I am enjoying it all." [21] He admired the energy and precision of the Fascist regime. "The trains are punctual, well-equipped, and fast," he wrote to Roosevelt, echoing a frequently heard characterization.[22] His initial admiration, which was to extend to support of Mussolini's foreign adventures, was tempered two years later. But in the early months of his tenure his admiration knew no bounds and he confided it to his many friends in Washington. To Attorney General Homer Cummings he suggested a careful study of the corporate state devised by the Fascist regime for any lessons that might be applied to the National Recovery Administration.[23] Roosevelt was urged not to oppose Italian designs on Al-

bania, whose annexation to Italy Long viewed as a foregone conclusion.[24] How much his admiration had clouded his vision became
apparent in 1935, when Mussolini was preparing for his adventure in
Ethiopia. Long's dispatches observed with assurance that Il Duce was
simply too smart to allow himself to be sucked into a war over a
worthless piece of real estate. He soon changed his mind and when
Mussolini did invade Ethiopia, Long's prediction proved uncannily
accurate but when the League of Nations proved unable to impose
oil sanctions, he counseled against a unilateral oil blockade by the
United States because "it is not consonant with the status of neutrality as fixed in the principle of international law." [25]

By 1935 his admiration for the Fascists had turned to a gloomy pessimism for the future of Europe. Only Joseph P. Kennedy matched
him in discouragement. Both men harbored a distrust of the motives
of the British and the French; both ultimately turned to a sophisticated brand of isolationism, and both hinted that an accommodation
with Berlin would be necessary.

Health reasons were given for Long's resignation in the Spring of
1936. Undoubtedly his sharp attacks of ulcers were triggered by a
State Department reprimand for an attempt to act as a neutral mediator
in the Ethiopian conflict without first informing the Department.[26]

In the course of time Long's initial admiration for the dictators
turned to deep distrust. He hoped the United States would be able
to remain out of the war he was certain was coming. But a deeply
conservative vein in his political thinking continued to cause an
ambivalence in his approach to the authoritarian regimes in Italy
and Germany. Hitler and Mussolini may have been "obdurate, ruthless and vicious," but they were also admirable for their ability to
mobilize their people. Their national aspirations were not without
some justification. Thus the Anschluss was acceptable because the
Germans were the only people "with intelligence, courage and obe-
dience sufficient to bring order, system and comparative peace in that
whole country lying between the Rhine and the Black Sea." [27] After
1938, his political thinking bore a strong similarity to that of the
Cliveden set, a segment of the British establishment led by Lady
Astor, whose advocacy of appeasement was nurtured by the hope
that Hitler could be turned eastward against Moscow. In 1939, for
example, Long mused regretfully in his diary that the United States

seemed to be drifting into war with Germany. It "seemed so un-
necessary" since "Hitler [was] not looking West. He is moving East
and no one is going to fight him there . . . he is not going to risk
a war in France." [28] The fall of Paris required a change in tune but
no change was discernible in Long's fear that the United States would
somehow antagonize Berlin and ruin the possibility of accommodation
after the Nazi victory, of which he was certain. "If we are not very
careful," he cautioned, "we are going to find ourselves champions of
a defeated cause." [29] Even worse "we may have a war thrust upon us
if we antagonize the military machine which is about to assume control of the whole continent of Europe." [30]

Although Long's anti-Semitism was not as crude as that of the
Nazis, it held many of their assumptions. Like most Nazis, Long
somehow linked communism and Jewish internationalism. Like many
Nazis, Long harbored a hysterical anxiety about communism which he
also linked to Jews. A typical string of epithets from his diary refers to his opponents as "the communists, extreme radicals, Jewish
professional agitators, refugee enthusiasts." [31] He felt that he possessed
a special insight into Hitler's Jewish phobia. His impression after
reading *Mein Kampf* was that it was "eloquent in opposition to Jewry
and to Jews as exponents of Communism and chaos." [32] The refugee
issue caused Long considerable nervous tension. Entries in his diary
often revealed a paranoic tone. Since these refugee enthusiasts with
their "inadmissible" or "peculiar" ideals were often Jewish they were
lumped together as "radical boys" or "Frankfurter's boys" because,
as Long saw it, they were "representative of his racial group and
philosophy." [33] The radical boys tended to be prolabor and exces-
sively humanitarian in their thinking. They were "bleeding hearts"
who harbored "wild theories" about admitting refugees to the United
States. In talking of liberal support for de Gaulle in June 1944, he
observed that "as usual, they (the radicals) espouse some foreign cause
to champion rather than advocate the AMERICAN point of view or
propose some practice in our own interest." [34] It was not long before
he detected a conspiracy. "The attacks in the newspapers still seem
to continue against me little by little and indicate that the wild-eyed
elements have marked me out as their objective." [35] Nine months later,
in September 1941, he refers to the "wolves" who were trying to ruin
his political career.[36]

By 1942 Long seemed to be suffering from the kind of nervous exhaustion he had experienced in Rome. He viewed himself locked in battles with enemies against whom he won "victories." People hated him, he knew it, but he would carry on to victory. "Each of these men [refugee advocates, radicals, etc.] hate me," he wrote in his diary, "I am to them the embodiment of a nemesis. They each and all believe every person, everywhere, has a RIGHT to come to the United States. I believe NOBODY anywhere has a RIGHT to enter the United States unless the United States desires." [37] For Long it was people like himself, with a long lineage (he proudly traced his roots to the Breckinridges of Kentucky and the Longs of North Carolina), who were America, not the people around New York City who welcomed un-American ideas.

On the refugee issue Long viewed himself as the "policy making officer and the executive agent of the Government." [38] The policy Long devised was to halt, as soon as possible, the trickle of refugees to the United States. Long was a restrictionist for social as well as economic reasons. He brought to his position a singleness of purpose and a formidable arsenal of political weapons. He had a keen knowledge of the inner workings of government and a wide circle of friends, especially among the conservative leaders of Congress. One of these was Martin Dies, Chairman of the House Committee on Un-American activities. Long was given access to the Committee's files and cited them frequently as the reason for a particular antirefugee action. His contacts in Congress were also called upon to sponsor legislation on aliens or refugees.

A disarming charm and grace of manner belied the intensity of Long's feelings. These were poured into his diary, when time permitted, with unabashed vitriol. Unquestionably his belief that the acceptance of refugees posed a threat to the security of the United States was genuine during the first months of his tenure. Thereafter it is not difficult to detect in the frequent citing in his diary of spies among the refugees, a note of personal pique and prejudice against refugees and their supporters. The security argument was used capriciously and with little concern for the lives of thousands which hung in the balance. Just as his own motivation became highly personal, he viewed those opposing him as motivated by personal animosity rather than a concern for the lives of refugees. The struggle over the admission of refugees became for Long a test of his ability to exercise power, a game he had to win. In September 1943, the Visa Division was transferred from his own to the Undersecretary's office. Long wrote in his diary: "I took it to the Secretary, told him I had decided I had won all the battles and the war in the immigration fight, that it was in smooth systematic order, that all the vilification and abuse that had been heaped on me by the radicals was on account of my fair administration of the issues involved and while I would not quit in a fight I felt that having won I would take this instant to be relieved of that work." [39] It was not an idle boast. During the first phase of the refugee effort, Long was everywhere successful. It took four years to remove him. They were the most crucial years of the rescue effort.

THE STRUGGLE TO RESCUE EUROPE'S CULTURAL ELITE

The rescue problem was sharply highlighted during the "phony war" period between September 1939 and April 1940, when it became imperative to rescue the remainder of Europe's cultural and scientific elite who would not be able to fit into Hitler's "New Order." Prominent refugees were already well known to the American public. The professor with a thick German accent had become a stock Hollywood character. But in real life the nation had no more desire to be inundated by intellectuals than by ordinary refugees, perhaps less so. American intellectuals, as a group, had never captured the popular imagination. Congressional sentiment continued to be strongly opposed to the admission of refugees. In April 1940, Roosevelt was forced to veto the Starnes Bill (HR 6724) which called for the deportation of certain categories of aliens. Time was essential if these elite were to get out of Europe; pressure to do something for them had reached a high point.

Many prominent men in Washington were being prevailed upon to act as conduits for special visa requests to the Administration. Ironically, Breckinridge Long, who appeared to be especially hostile to the intellectuals, was the recipient of a visa request from one of the most suspect of these refugees, a former Jewish mistress and advisor to Mussolini, Madame Sarfatti. She had come to know Long during his tenure as Ambassador in Rome. Now, after having idealized *Il Duce* in a biography, she had been turned out, penniless, and was in danger of being jailed. Long referred her to Anne O'Hare McCormick, the columnist for the *New York Times*.[40] Roosevelt, naturally, was the object of many such requests. In January 1940 he forwarded a list of two hundred names to the State Department with instructions that they be given special treatment, which meant emergency visas. Thus Roosevelt established the precedent of by-passing the visa hurdles established by the Department.

Soon dozens of special committees sprang up, each with clientele in need of special consideration. In the case of refugee scholars, two institutions trace their origins to special programs to rescue them. The Institute of Advanced Study at Princeton was established early in the refugee crisis by Abraham Flexner, who modeled the Institute after All Souls college at Oxford. It soon became famous as the new home of the most eminent of the refugee scholars, Albert Einstein. Later the Emergency Committee in Aid of Displaced Scholars, which functioned for twelve years, established the University in Exile. Led by Dr. Alvin Johnson, Director of the New School for Social Research, the new university became the graduate faculty of that institution.[41] Hundreds of scholars were placed by the committee in existing American institutions.

Other rescue committees were operated by organized labor, doctors, artists, writers, and scientists. Jewish organizations of all political and religious types ran their own rescue committees. There were committees for each national group under Nazi occupation or threat, and committees for Catholics and Protestants as well as committees whose existence grew up outside the Jewish refugee crisis, such as those concerned with the various elements of the Spanish loyalist cause. By June 1940 so many rescue committees existed that Dr. Frank Kingdon moved to the next logical step by establishing the Emergency Rescue Committee to coordinate the various efforts.

The committees' requests for "special treatment" proved particularly troublesome to the Special Problems Division of the State Department. "There is a constant pressure from Congressional and organized groups in this country to have us proceed on behalf of non-Americans," Long wrote in his diary, adding that, "so far I have been able to resist the pressure." [42] The committees, representing every shade of the political spectrum, soon allowed themselves the luxury of resuming their old-world conflicts. "Committees were springing up on every hand," explained George Warren, executive secretary of the PACPR, "each committee with a list of candidates for admission to the United States and already they were beginning to fight among themselves and accuse the government of favoring one side or the other." [43] Before the war the organizations involved with Spanish refugees had complained that Jews were getting favored treatment. Now a right-wing group headed by Prince Otto, whose candidates were Austrian Catholics and whose supporters included Archbishop Spellman, accused the Jay Allen Kingborn Committee of favoring left-leaning Spanish loyalists. Bitter recriminations concerning the selection of only secular Jews came from the Aguda Chasidei Chabad, an organization representing Orthodox Jews. The Aguda had submitted a list of 10,000 names representing what they thought was the "cream" of Europe's Jewry.[44] The committee to rescue refugees from France split into separate political factions which mirrored the prewar political factionalism of France. Dutch, Belgian, Czech, and Italian committees were "all contending for favorable treatment for their respective candidates and most of them panning this government either for doing nothing or for favoring political opponents." [45]

The fall of France on June 22 lent a special urgency to the business of compiling lists. Rumors that Article Nineteen of the armistice agreement which compelled the Vichy government to return on demand "all Germans named by the German Government" was being put into effect, threw the rescue committees into a panic, since thousands of political refugees had found a precarious safety in that area. Prominent refugees such as Count Carlo Sforza, Italian opponent of Mussolini, Dr. Juan Negrin, and Manuel Azaña y Diez, Prime Minister and President of Spain during the years 1937 and 1939, respectively, were the special concern of the refugee advocates.[46]

The PACPR, whose original function was to search for resettlement havens, became, at the suggestion of James G. McDonald, the official agency through which the names of prominent refugees would be submitted to the State Department.[47] In june it presented a list of 600 names which was to become the source of much contention within the Department. The Department procrastinated, and its reasons were made clear at a special meeting held with the PACPR. There seemed to be no way to distinguish clients for emergency

treatment from ordinary visa applicants. The Department had discovered that in some cases persons applying for admission were not
desirable while others were on the list only because they were for-
tunate enough to have friends in high places.

The PACPR also complained that although the committees furnished adequate affidavits, the candidates were not receiving visas.
Was the Department stalling in the knowledge that time would solve
the problem in Vichy France? The dozens of separate regulations
created chaos among the refugees. The Department's increased
stringency was difficult to understand in the face of a much worsened
crisis. Moreover, the consuls remained a principal obstacle. It was
for these reasons that the PACPR suggested that the special lists be
centralized in Washington and that all names be forwarded to the
State and Justice Departments for review. The names would then
be cabled to the consuls who would be compelled to issue the visa.
The State Department agreed to the new procedure but the hope
that the consul road block could be by-passed, was short lived. A
movement to further tighten the visa procedure was already under
way in the State Department.

In June 1940 the Immigration and Naturalization Service was removed from the Department of Labor and placed in the Department
of Justice. The reason for the change, according to Secretary of
Labor Frances Perkins, was the realization within the Administration
that immigration had become primarily a security rather than an economic matter.[48] At the same time regulations for visitors' and transit
visas were tightened. In the case of the former, the applicant would
have to furnish conclusive evidence of his ability to return to the
country of origin, and in the case of the latter, evidence of ability to
move on to a third country. Two important means of extricating
refugees from immediate danger were thus closed. There would be
stricter supervision of regulations governing the movements of foreign seamen. The FBI was concerned lest agents be smuggled into
the country by this means. Visitors' visas would henceforth be issued for a four- rather than a six-month period. Most important of
all, visas already issued and all forthcoming visas would be examined
for legitimate purpose. "Special care" was to be taken in issuing all
visas even if it reduced the number of visas issued and lengthened
the waiting period.

A few weeks after the new regulations were put into effect, the Administration further tightened the procedure by implementing the Alien Registration Act (HR 5138). This Act was an omnibus measure requiring registration and fingerprinting of all aliens above the age of fourteen. A public opinion poll indicated that 95 percent of the public approved the measure and would have favored even more stringent controls.[49] The advocates of more liberal immigration procedures were in full retreat. The price of their defeat was paid by the hundreds of refugees with valid visas and ship tickets, whose qualifications were suddenly reexamined and found wanting. Those on visitors' visas could, after all, no longer guarantee that they would have a place to return to, and the new regulations converted an opportunity to live into internment and sometimes death.

By August it appeared that a showdown between PACPR, now playing the role of coordinator for the private rescue effort, and the State Department was inevitable. The refugee organizations were left in the dark about the new regulations, which represented administrative fiat rather than new legislation. Of the list of 567 names submitted for special visa consideration in June, only fifteen visas had been issued by August. There had been ample time for the State and Justice Departments to screen the list which originally contained 600 names. Moreover, the consuls continued to hamper the rescue effort.

George Messersmith, for example, passed on complaints to Long regarding the "inflexibility and lack of understanding" of Consul Young in Lisbon, an important point of departure for refugees.[50] In July 1941, *The New Republic* called attention to the mistreatment of Jewish refugees by Consuls Leland Morris in Berlin and James Stewart in Zürich.[51] The consuls at Nice and Stuttgart were requiring a police report of good conduct. Such documents were almost impossible to get from the unsympathetic police. Consul Young refused to issue replacement visas to applicants whose visas had expired because they could not get to an American consulate in time. Delay was the order of the day, as consuls, aware of the unsympathetic attitude of their superiors toward refugees, outdid themselves in an effort to build up a good record. "To this day," complained the editors of the *Nation*, "not a single anti-fascist trapped in France has escaped except through his own efforts or the efforts of his fellow refugees." [52] James McDonald and other leaders of the refugee efforts became convinced that labor leaders, Spanish loyalists, and refugee intellectuals were being signaled out by the Department for more rigid screening than others.[53]

In July Long capped his own program for restriction by issuing a directive to the consuls to issue no more visitors' or transit visas to persons who did not possess exit permits. Such permits were difficult to come by, epecially for German refugees who now resided in Vichy or the occupied low countries. Long had thereby cancelled out the entire rescue program by a series of administrative devices, precisely as he had suggested could be done to Adolf A. Berle, Jr., and James C. Dunn: "We can delay and effectively stop for a temporary period of indefinite length the number of immigrants into the United States. We could do this by simply advising our consuls to put every obstacle in the way and to resort to various administrative advices which would postpone and postpone the granting of the visas." [54]

The effect of the new regulations was most keenly felt in Vichy, where thousands of refugees had found a tenuous sanctuary. One of the first steps of the Vichy government was to request Washington's assistance in removing the Jewish refugees so that a more "equitable distribution" could be obtained. The note suggested that the interior of the United States or Latin America could serve as a suitable haven.[55] The offer was rejected by the Department on the reasoning that if the Vichy government was willing to release these refugees it was doing so at the behest of the Gestapo which had undoubtedly planted its agents among them. Moreover, the Vichy dispatch spoke of Jews and the Department did not recognize a specific category of Jewish refugees. They must be political refugees. The Department went on to suggest that Vichy issue exit permits to all possessing valid visas so that the State Department could proceed under its new regulations. Although the Portuguese and Spanish authorities were liberal in granting transit permits in the late months of 1940, it proved uncommonly difficult to obtain the exit permits required by the new regulations. One of the first acts of the new Vichy government was to close its borders to departures. The refugees were caught in a net created by a combination of State Department and Vichy regulations. If the State Department relented on the exit permits, refugees might make their way to Lisbon and from there out of Europe. In January 1941, after the refugees had been screened, Vichy began to issue the exit permits and for the next four months a trickle of refugees was able to escape. But in June 1941 a new series of State Department regulations stopped all refugee movement. The thousands remaining in Vichy were eventually forced to board the cattle cars which took them to their destruction.

THE STATE DEPARTMENT AND THE PACPR

The hardness of the State Department's visa policy was demonstrated further in the unfortunate case of the S.S. *Quanza*, which exacerbated the already bitter quarrel between those who favored and those who opposed a more humanitarian rescue policy.

In September 1940, the S.S. *Quanza*, a Portuguese freighter, approached Norfolk with eighty-three refugees on board. She had left Portugal on August 9 destined for Latin America, where the captain hoped to discharge his passengers at a tidy profit. But when the ship reached Nicaragua she was refused permission to dock. The same thing happened at Vera Cruz, Mexico. The *Quanza* then proceeded to Norfolk where she would take on fuel for the voyage back to Portugal. Officials in the State Department, ever vigilant about attempted refugee smuggling, surmised that the refugees on board planned to organize their transshipment to other havens or to secure visas to remain in the United States. Many of the passengers had purchased visas from Latin-American consuls which permitted them to go anywhere except to the country that had issued the visa.

The arrival of the *Quanza* was a signal for refugee advocates to try all manner of legal ploys to keep the ship at Norfolk until pressure could be brought to bear on the Administration to get the refugees temporarily admitted to the United States. Such a request was submitted by Patrick Malin, representing the PACPR. Meanwhile, Solicitor General Francis Biddle, Assistant United States Attorney David Hart, and Edward Prichard, chief attorney for the Office of Economic Stabilization, examined the legal aspects of the case. They became convinced that under the Executive Orders issued in June 1940, which put the Department's new visa regulations into effect, it was perfectly legal to land and to be screened in the normal manner to determine whether they qualified for visas. But Long was convinced that this was an attempt to circumvent the regulations and a direct challenge to his authority, and refused to accept their legal reasoning. Not until Long received a call from Eleanor Roosevelt, requesting that he call the President, did he become more flexible. It would hardly do to trigger another *St. Louis* episode, with all the adverse publicity that it would entail. He agreed to accept a compromise suggested by James McDonald and Marshall Field, who had assumed a prominent role in the rescue effort. The PACPR would determine those who were in imminent danger, those who qualified for special visas such as prominent intellectuals, children who qualified for normal immigration visas, and those who possessed authentic transit visas. In this manner Patrick Malin was able to select forty of the eighty-three passengers to set foot on American soil. But when Long was informed that almost half of the refugee group qualified, he became furious because it was far in excess of the number he had anticipated.

I remonstrated violently; said that I thought it was a violation of the Law; that it was not in accord with my understanding with them; that it was not a proper interpretation of my agreement; that I would not be party to it; that I would not give my consent; that I would have no responsibility for it; and that if they did that that I would have to take the matter up in some other way.[56]

The "other way" which occurred to Long was to gain the President's personal intercession on the Department's side. Hull arranged an interview for October 3. Long's objectives were confided in his diary: "The list of Rabbis has been closed and the list of labor leaders has been closed and now it remains for the President's Committee to be curbed." [57] Long was anxious to put the PACPR out of business.

One of the immediate consequences of Long's temper tantrum was that he was identified as the official most responsible for the Department's hostility toward refugees. Long worried about it: "McDonald . . . has developed a very definite and violent antagonism to me, he thinks I have been non-cooperative and obstructive. . . ." [58] But if Long had his way, McDonald would experience some difficulty in apprising Roosevelt of his sabotage of the rescue effort. "Pa" Watson, a good friend of Long's, would keep him informed of the activities of the rescue advocates and would delay in granting McDonald's request for an interview with the President until Long gave his prior approval. The result was that while Long had ready access to the White House, leaders in the refugee effort, such as Myron C. Taylor, James G. McDonald and Stephen Wise, were experiencing serious difficulties in bringing their case to the President. Rescue leaders were compelled to find another way of getting a line to the President through the First Lady but even then a State Department official was usually able to get to Roosevelt before such an interview and brief him. The result was that until 1944 Roosevelt viewed the refugee-rescue problem almost entirely through the eyes of the State Department. Not until Secretary of the Treasury Henry Morgenthau, Jr., was activated in the rescue effort was a countervailing source of information made available to him from within the Administration.

In the case of the special visa procedure, however, Roosevelt had other sources of information directly on the scene. Herbert (Birdie) Pell, Minister to Portugal, where the activities of Consul Young had become well known to the rescue advocates, was one of the many officials who maintained a personal correspondence with the President. He attributed the trouble in Lisbon to the fact that many deserving people had no organization pressing their case in Washington. He cited several cases of persons whom he considered suspect being placed on the list for special visas.[59] Similar complaints were produced from the Department's files and the dispatches of Laurence Steinhardt, the American Ambassador in the Soviet Union. The State Department, citing the security risk in accepting prominent refugees, requested that the PACPR halt the compilation of special visa lists. Sufficient time had elapsed, claimed Long, for the presentation of the most urgent cases.

Thus, when Long saw the President, he had little trouble in making his case for leaving the final decisions for issuing visas with the consuls instead of in Washington. The consuls were on the scene and had complete files and knew who the subversive refugees were and were therefore able to make better judgments. Long then played his trump card. He paraded before Roosevelt the case of two World Jewish Congress officials whose sponsor for special visa consideration was Stephen Wise, the well-known leader of the rescue effort in the Jewish community. "They were a man and his wife who had represented the Rabbi's organization but who professed to a long series of political activities in Europe and an intention to follow a course in the United States irrespective of the desires of the American Government but to take orders from the World Jewish Congress. They professed to have been responsible for the overthrow of one Rumanian government and to have been very active in politics in Europe for years." [60] Despite the difficulty in believing that people who wanted admittance to the United States would deliberately portray themselves as potentially poor citizens and Long's assumption that people who were politically active automatically were potential threats to American security, Roosevelt "agreed that those persons ought not to be admitted to the United States in spite of the fact that Rabbi Wise in all sincerity desired them here." [61] In fact, Long felt that he was completely successful in getting Roosevelt to see his point of view. "I found that he [Roosevelt] was 100% in accord with my ideas. . . . The President expressed himself as in entire accord with the policy which would exclude persons about whom there was any suspicion that they would be inimical to the welfare of the United States no matter who had vouchsafed for them and irrespective of their financial or other standing." [62] Roosevelt, only peripherally interested in the problem, appeared unwilling to question the security gambit.

On October 7, six days after Long's discussion with Roosevelt, a group of rescue advocates were finally able to see the President. But they were hard pressed to present the kind of response which would allow Roosevelt to act without risking the ire of those who were making political capital out of the security psychosis. Moreover, they did not seem to be able to shake Roosevelt's belief that the refugees represented a potential fifth column. McDonald maintained that the Department was cynically using the security gambit to block the admission of prominent refugees. "[I] cannot believe," he suggested, "that those still without visas present threats to the national interest." [63] He was referring to the fact that of the 567 names screened and submitted to the State Department only forty received visas and, of the forty intellectuals on the list, whose credentials had been guaranteed by Dr. Alvin Johnson, founder of the University in Exile, only two had received visas. McDonald impressed on Roosevelt that the critical situation in Vichy was being exacerbated by the negative attitude of the consuls. [64]

Faced on the one hand with Long's contentions regarding the threat to security, which he backed by frequent references to the Dies files, and on the other by McDonald's plea for a more humane attitude, Roosevelt avoided a clear-cut decision. He urged that the two sides get together and iron out their difficulties using as a guideline the rule that only bona fide refugees in extreme danger, whose activities were not inimical to the United States, should be allowed special consideration.[65] That of course settled nothing, since refugee advocates maintained that all persons on the lists were in extreme danger and none would partake in activity "inimical to the interest of the United States." There was, however, little agreement with the State Department on what constituted such activity. Long, too, was encouraged; the President's guidelines clearly followed his own suggestions. Moreover Roosevelt had referred to McDonald's plea as "sob stuff" and added that he rejected any plan which would allow anyone "whether it be Rabbi Wise or McDonald or William Green to have final say on who should be admitted to this country."[66]

An important outcome of the meeting of State Department and PACPR officials was an agreement on a new screening procedure which broadened the responsibility for making the final decision in the special cases. A committee composed of representatives of the State Department, Justice Department, the FBI, Military Intelligence, and the Office of Naval Intelligence would make the final recommendation to the consuls. If the consul then rejected the application, it would then go back to the screening committee for review and a final binding recommendation. Long seemed happy with the decision. The FBI and the intelligence agencies would probably be more sensitive to security than the State Department. The plight of the refugees "excites the sympathy of all of us," he wrote to Robert Jackson, "unfortunately the real solution is not in sight."[67]

Long's jubilation over what he considered a clear-cut victory was soon tempered by trouble from a new source, the Justice Department. Long had become interested in curtailing any political activity of newly arrived refugees, and especially their right to speak freely. A bill which his division had drawn up to be introduced in Congress proposed to give these refugees the same legal status as those on visitors' visas, who did not enjoy the right of freedom of speech. In November 1940, the Justice Department advised that such a measure was unconstitutional. Refugees, like citizens, were immediately protected by the Constitution and were therefore entitled to all the rights and privileges of citizenship. Long was understandably disheartened. He reasoned that the growing crescendo of criticism of the Department, and his own role in it, emanated from refugees who were motivated by their desire to subvert American institutions. The people in the Justice Department, he complained, "have peculiar ideas and radical tendencies and sympathies toward forces which are inadmissible . . . it is these persons . . . whom Dies has investigated and about whom he has files." [68] He persuaded Rep. Dies, with whom he worked closely, to forward his information to the Justice Department. The effect was negative. Robert Jackson and Francis Biddle were never able to muster much enthusiasm for surveying refugee activity.

The new interdepartmental screening committee did, however, succeed in further slowing down the already cumbersome visa procedure. Of the 1,137 names submitted to the State Department between August 5 and December 18, 1940, only 238 received visas. [69] All of which prompted one of the most persistent critics of the State Department, Freda Kirchway, editor of the *Nation*, to observe that "the Department does not refuse visas. It merely sets up a line of obstacles stretching from Washington to Lisbon to Shanghai." [70]

Two additional issues arose to fuel the smoldering conflict between the State Department and the Departments of Interior and Justice and the PACPR. The first was the renewal of the refugee children issue and the second concerned the use of the Virgin Islands for a certain type of rescue operation.

REFUGEE CHILDREN

Refugee children were to a degree exempt from the general anti-refugee sentiment. Long, disturbed by the sympathy, characterized the concern for children as "an enormous psychosis" which he attributed to "repressed emotions about the war." "We have had to handle the thing very delicately and carefully," he wrote in his diary, "and deal with a great many of emotional people—people temporarily emotional and who ordinarily are hard-headed, common-sensed individuals." [71] Labeling such sympathy as mental illness may reveal more about Long's emotional health than that of those who favored the admission of children, in contrast to the strong popular opposition to the admission of their parents. The United States Committee for the Care of European Children (U.S.C.), headed by Clarence Pickett, attracted the most prominent names in the country in its drive to bring refugee children to the United States. So encouraging was the support, that after *Krystallnacht*, on November 9, a gradual belief grew up among refugee advocates that the public benevolence toward refugee children offered a good opportunity to neutralize restrictionist sentiment.

On February 9, Senator Robert Wagner of New York and Rep. Edith Rogers, of Massachusetts introduced identical bills in their respective houses. It was the culmination of a public effort, the creating of the Non-Sectarian Committee for German Refugee Children, which conceived the actual legislation. The proposal called for the admission of 10,000 refugee children under the age of fourteen in each of two years, 1939 and 1940. Provision would be made for the children either by individuals or by the private agencies.

As expected, the introduction of the measure set off a strong restrictionist reaction. One of the sixty antialien proposals introduced into the Seventy-Sixth Congress by Rep. Stephen Pace of Georgia (HR 9999), suggested simply that "every Alien in the United States shall be forthwith deported." They were supported by the American Legion, the Daughters of the American Revolution, and a slew of organizations opposed to any liberalization of the Reed-Johnson Law.

Refugee advocates mobilized in favor of the Wagner-Rogers measure. Clarence E. Pickett, executive secretary of the American Friends Service Committee was made head of a nonsectarian committee to push the bill through Congress. By the end of April refugee organizations had in hand 5,000 offers from American families to open their homes to refugee children. Although the majority of German children in need of homes were Jewish, support was strongly interdenominational. The executive committee of the powerful National Council of Churches called on the American government to do more for refugees. "It was not enough to call upon other nations to help . . . but some such practical step as the one contemplated is imperative. . . ."[72]

By the time the hearings began on April 20, the two sides were facing each other squarely and a great deal of bitter vituperation had already been heard. Some of the most renowned names in the nation had become associated with the Wagner-Rogers bill. Within the Administration Eleanor Roosevelt, Harold Ickes, Frances Perkins, Francis Biddle, and numerous lesser lights had expressed support for the measure. The names of Herbert Hoover, Alf Landon, Joe E. Brown, Eddie Cantor and Helen Hayes were prominently involved.

Despite the support of some newspapers in the South, Clarence Pickett, who fashioned the political strategy by which it was hoped to steer the bill through a hostile Congress, recognized that the main thrust of the opposition came from the South. By calling on as many prominent southern supporters as possible, he hoped to disarm some of the southern congressmen and create the impression that support for the measure was nationwide. Frank Graham, the president of the University of North Carolina, was chosen to lead off for the measure.

On the opposite side, an impressive group of ultrapatriotic organizations were arrayed. Typical of the sentiments expressed was that of Mrs. Agnes Waters, who represented an organization of war widows. She began by presenting the committee with an impeccable American lineage which she used subsequently to launch a vitriolic attack on foreigners whom she felt were ruining the country. "Let us not be maudlin in our sympathies," she exhorted, "as charity begins at home." [73] More sophisticated was the view expressed by Mrs. James H. Houghteling, wife of the Commissioner of Immigration, who confided to Pierrepont Moffat at a Washington cocktail party that the trouble with the Wagner-Rogers bill was "that 20,000 children would all too soon grow up into 20,000 ugly adults." [74]

Notwithstanding the restrictionist cry that there were still many American children who needed homes and the more subtle argument that the bill would make the American government a party to breaking up families who would be better off if they stayed together, the bill did receive favorable consideration by each subcommittee. But now it ran into trouble. Prompted by pressure of the American Legion, the House Committee on Immigration and Naturalization called for new hearings. The new hearings, held in late May and early June, were more hostile to the measure. An amendment was introduced which suggested that rather than allowing the children to enter outside of the quota, the children be given preference within the regular quota. This Senator Wagner would not accept since it meant that adults who had patiently gone through the complex process prescribed by the visa regulations would be replaced. When the Senate committe reported the bill favorably with the amendment, it signified that restrictionists had hit upon a successful tactic; they would amend the bill to death.

As the showdown neared, much depended on the degree of Administration support. It soon became evident that Roosevelt would follow the line of least political risk suggested by the State Department, rather than the humanitarian prompting of his wife. Hull had communicated to the Committee that the "present phraseology [of the Wagner-Rogers Bill] would raise difficult administrative problems." [75] The Department had argued in January that the measure would stimulate anti-Semitism and more antialien legislation in Congress. [76] Although no outright rejection came from the White House, it was clear that the Administration had decided that it was an inappropriate time to antagonize the many southern congressmen whose votes would be needed for the bigger defense allocations soon to be necessary. When Caroline O'Day, a Democratic congresswoman from New York, inquired about Roosevelt's position on the bill, the President scribbled in the margin of the memo forwarded by his secretary, "File—No action, FDR." [77] The 1939 proposal thus died in committee when Senator Wagner refused to accept the amendment suggested by restrictionists, but the "psychosis" regarding refugee children was not yet cured.

Under normal conditions the failure of the Wagner-Rogers bill to emerge from committee would have been enough to temper any further enthusiasm for refugee children. But mid-1940 could hardly be considered normal times. The fall of France and the battle of Britain did much to refocus public attention on the plight of refugee children, especially British children. Pressure to admit children again began to mount. A Gallup poll taken in late June 1940 showed 58 percent of Americans favoring the admission of English and French children for the duration of the war and 25 percent indicated to the pollsters that they would be willing to open their homes to such a child. [78]

But Breckinridge Long was troubled:

The Secretary asked me to handle the evacuation of children out of England to this country. Under our laws we are limited. The British quota is 6,500 a month for ten months and has not been filled. . . . The British want to send all the children here, and of course that cannot be done, as there are estimated between one and two hundred thousand of them. They could send them to Canada, and we could take up to our quota limit from Canada each month. There is a lot of sentiment about it and sentimentality, but the enthusiasm is liable to wane at the end of a long period. . . .[79]

James G. McDonald and Joseph Chamberlain, director of the National Refugee Service, the coordinating arm for the private refugee agencies, had in the meantime entered the fray. Pointing out to Roosevelt that the State Department's plan to use the British quota would barely make a dent in the estimated 200,000 children who needed to be evacuated, they offered financial guarantees to meet the requirement of the public charge provision and urged that the children be admitted immediately outside the quota.[80] Such guarantees could be given because the public response to the plight of the children surpassed that of 1939. The newly formed United States Committee for the Care of European Children, whose honorary head was Eleanor Roosevelt, had in its possession, by early July, 15,000 offers to accept refugee children from Britain. In 1941, Francis Biddle, assisted by James Rowe, Jr., a former adviser to Roosevelt, succeeded in getting a token sum of $125,000 added to the Emergency Relief Appropriation Act of 1941, so that the Department of Labor's Children's Bureau could, if needed, defray the expense of transportation and upkeep for the refugee children.

The hopes of the children's sponsors were dashed by problems of shipping and safe passage. What if a ship carrying refugee children were sunk? "The very surest way to get America into this war would be to send an American ship to England and put 2,000 babies on it and then have it sunk by a German torpedo. That would shove us right in the middle of the war," argued Long.[81] It was a difficult argument to refute and figured prominently in Roosevelt's reluctance to give full support. At a news conference on July 26, Roosevelt echoed Long's words almost verbatim.[82] Indeed the argument became almost a prophecy after the Berlin authorities refused to assure safe passage.[83] In August a German submarine sank the *City of Benares* with the loss of 260 lives, among them seventy-nine refugee children.[84] But such factors hardly deterred the determined members of the USC who were now thinking in terms of mercy ships, sailing under the American flag, to solve the safe passage problem. Raymond Clapper of the Washington *Daily News* tried to spur the Administration into action in a taunting column entitled, "Lets Save the Children." Citing the traditional State Department sabotage of every rescue effort, Clapper pointedly questioned the sincerity of Roosevelt's humanitarianism: "Why doesn't Roosevelt, great humanitarian, do something?" [85] The barb succeeded in drawing Roosevelt out. He retorted sharply through his Secretary Stephen Early, "A little less politics and a little more thought" might have led Clapper to the conclusion that children can "be given visas infinitely faster than . . . [they] can be brought to this country on ships." [86] Apparently it was the continued fear of the possible sinking of a ship carrying refugee children which concerned Roosevelt. In Congress an amendment to the neutrality law called the Hennings Bill, after Congressman Thomas C. Hennings, of Missouri, was making some progress. It would permit unarmed and unescorted American mercy ships to evacuate refugee children, provided safe conduct was granted by all belligerents. Roosevelt was concerned lest the Hennings proposal leave to the White House responsibility for the sailings and possible sinking of such ships. He assured Caroline O'Day, who was steering the measure through the House, that he fully supported the measure but would prefer that the ships sail under the auspices of the International Red Cross, rather than the United States; no safe conduct would then be needed.[87] Mrs. O'Day assured Roosevelt that the onus would not fall on the Administration in case of a sinking, but the safe-conduct clause could not be removed because doing so would cost the measure considerable support.[88] After some token opposition the Hennings Bill became law on August 27. The rescue advocates had won the first victory, but significantly the children to be admitted were not strictly speaking refugees, nor were they Jewish. They were simply British children living in the war zone. The passage of the Hennings Bill stands in sharp contrast to the defeat of the Wagner-Rogers bill of the previous year which had concerned German-Jewish refugee children.[89]

The fruits of all the efforts invested by the private organizations to get the bill through Congress were meager indeed. Only 835 children were admitted when, in the early months of 1941, the measure became a dead letter because of a shortage of ships, a letup in the Battle of

Britain, and a breakdown in the precarious safe-conduct procedure which the law required.

The Administration's handling of the problem of refugee children, largely Jewish, stranded in Vichy, was hardly characterized by the generosity extended to British children. In the years when rescue of this group was possible, June 1940 to November 1942, the Administration, reflecting the sentiment of Congress, did little. Between March 1941 and August 1942, the USC was able to bring only 309 refugee children out of Vichy and these were all furnished with regular immigration visas from the practically unused French and German quotas. In August 1942 it came the turn for German Jews living in Vichy to be deported to Auschwitz. Thousands of parentless children were stranded and living in the most squalid conditions imaginable. As many as 8,000 children faced death by disease and starvation.

At this juncture the State Department granted the USC authority to bring 1,000 of these children to the United States. The figure was raised to 5,000 at the behest of Eleanor Roosevelt. Predictably Breckinridge Long was wary of the proposal. On September 12, he wrote in his diary of the Vichy children:

> The appeal for asylum is irresistible to any human instinct and the act of barbarity just as repulsive as the result is appalling. But we cannot receive into our own midst ALL—or even a large fraction of the oppressed—and no other country will receive them or even a few thousand, except that the President of Santo Domingo offers to receive and care for 3,500 children. . . . My personal reaction to that is that Trujillo was trying to embarrass Warren [Avra Warren, formerly Long's assistant].[90]

But Long's opposition was tempered by Hull's insistence that sometimes "humanitarianism makes good politics." [91] Scalding attacks by the liberal press on the Department's refugee policy had created a keen sensitivity to the issue. Nevertheless the Department remained cautious about publicizing the number to be admitted lest fire be drawn from the restrictionists.[92] Preparations were made to bring the children out and the AJJDC appropriated $1 million for that purpose. But the plan was aborted by the Allied invasion of North Africa on November 8, three days later. One day before the first contingent of refugee children was scheduled to depart for Lisbon, the Germans occupied Vichy France and put an end to the effort.

The effort of the private agencies to rescue the children continued well into 1943 and many of the children involved were ultimately smuggled out of southern France by an underground rescue apparatus organized by the World Jewish Congress, the Jewish Agency, and the AJJDC, which financed the operation. The failure to rescue the Jewish refugee children of Vichy in 1942 was marked as a separate tragedy in the history of the Holocaust. If it had been started a few months earlier it might have succeeded.

THE VIRGIN ISLAND EMBROGLIO

The attempt to utilize the Virgin Islands as a rescue way station expanded the controversy over rescue policy within the Administration. The voice of Harold Ickes was to add spice to the dispute.

After the fall of France had intensified the urgency of the rescue problem, David Hart and Nathan Margold, solicitors in the Justice and Interior Departments respectively, hatched a scheme to use the Virgin Islands as a rescue way station. The aim was to provide in a relatively secure area a temporary haven for refugees awaiting visas. They reasoned that a special Executive Order issued in 1938 gave the governor of the Islands special authority to admit visitors without visas in emergency cases. It seemed like a foolproof method to aid certain categories of refugees and might even result in giving the economy of the Islands a boost since refugees would have to guarantee self-support and would be prohibited from gainful employment. In August, the Islands' legislature passed a resolution supporting the proposal, and on November 12 Governor Lawrence W. Cramer issued a decree permitting the entrance of such visitors. The State Department, alerted to what was about to happen because of its negotiations with the Interior Department over some of the legal aspects of the scheme, acted quickly to put a stop to the operation. Long predictably sensed a conspiracy "to siphon refugees out of Portugal into the United States without the precautionary steps of investigation and checking . . . [it] is part of a program which Mr. Hart has indulged in in connection with the President's Advisory Committee." [93] A hasty call to Roosevelt assured him of the President's support. He was referred back to Ickes to iron out the difficulty.

The meeting was an unhappy one for Long. Ickes responded sarcastically to his description of the security danger posed by the refugees. Long patiently explained his intention to plug up the holes in the immigration regulations only to have Ickes reply tartly that he thought the holes already too small. "The inference was quite plain," Long angrily confided to his diary that night, "he was trying to take into the United States persons whom he thought the Department of State would not admit. He was rather obdurate and a little sarcastic." [94] Ickes refused to budge from the position that Cramer was within his legal rights in acting on his discretionary power to waive visa requirements for nonimmigrants during an emergency. While Long again appealed to Roosevelt, Ickes made public his support of the scheme.

Despite the President's full support, which was given to him in writing on December 18, and a direct order to Ickes requesting that he drop the scheme, Long was throughout the episode in an extremely agitated state.[95] He betrayed some anxiety regarding his position in the Administration. He imagined that the uproar in the liberal press was directed against him rather than the Department: "The opposition is using me as a fulcrum to pry open the door," he complained in his diary.[96] He knew where the criticism originated. It was among the interventionists and "those persons are largely concentrated along the Atlantic seaboard, and principally around New York." [97] He feared that he had antagonized Ickes "irreparably" and that he would now join "certain persons in the Department of Justice and in other branches of the Government in an effort to unseat me officially." [98]

Indeed, Ickes' anger had been aroused. He was convinced that the Virgin Island plan was legal as long as the refugees remained nonimmigrants, and that the State Department's contention that the immigration code covered all American possessions was incorrect. Like McDonald before him, he suggested to Roosevelt that the State Department had developed a security gambit, which it was using to counter all arguments in favor of refugees. But the President remained unconvinced and in no mood to tangle with Martin Dies. He had suggested to Ickes that he find less controversial solutions. "Tell Margold," Roosevelt added, trying to soften the blow, "I have sympathy. I cannot, however, do anything which would conceivably hurt the future of present American citizens." [99] Such sympathy had not softened the bitter reaction of the Jewish Press before. "Be careful by all means," wrote the Anglo-Jewish monthly, *The American Hebrew*, "check the record of every refugee . . . but in the name of humanity let us open the gates of the Virgin Islands and bring a new ray of hope to the victims of totalitarian terror." [100]

Ickes, despite Roosevelt's disapproval, continued agitating for the Virgin Islands. He enlisted the aid of the PACPR to help screen the incoming refugees, 2,000 of whom had already been selected for removal from Portugal. The PACPR petitioned Roosevelt at least to make the Islands available to a limited number of deserving cases. That idea too was rejected by Roosevelt. Long's timely presentation of evidence that several of the special cases presented by Ickes, and accepted by the PACPR were, according to the consul in Lisbon, Trotskyists, erased any doubts the President may have had. [101] Finally, in April 1941, Attorney General Robert Jackson ruled that the immigration code did, in fact, rule out any exception to the visitors' visa procedure used by the State Department. Ickes was now ready to give up the idea.

Even then, to make doubly sure, Long called upon Admiral Alan G. Kirk, Chief of Naval Intelligence, and suggested that the Navy could play a role in resolving the dispute. "If the Navy could declare it a restricted area for strictly naval reasons," Long explained, "[that would] prevent the raising of the political questions involved in this refugee and undesirable citizens traffic which is going on. . . . [Then] we would have no more trouble." [102]

Could rescue advocates hope to counter such shrewdness? Though the Virgin Islands proposal was lost, it contributed, together with the visa debacle and the case of refugee children, to the growing awareness among refugee advocates of the identity of the officials who were blocking a more humane response to the crisis. But their chief tactic, the security gambit, continued to present insurmountable difficulties.

ANTI-SEMITISM OR FEAR OF ESPIONAGE

It took little to convince American Jews that the State Department's antirefugee stance was based as much on anti-Semitism as it was on a concern for national security. Jewish sons were not groomed for positions in the Foreign Service because the possibility of attaining such positions was considered too remote. Undoubtedly such sensitivity to anti-Semitism had been somewhat aggravated by Nazi persecution of Jews in Europe and the strident voices of domestic anti-Semites. The Owen Norem case went far to confirm that the State Department was hopelessly anti-Semitic.

Norem was the American Minister to Lithuania, where many thousands of Jews, including a group of prominent rabbis, had found a precarious asylum in 1939. Returning to the United States in April 1940, Norem delivered an anti-Semitic address in Minneapolis which drew the fire of Jewish leaders. The Department was embarrassed. Hull's marriage to a Jewess made him personally immune to charges of anti-Semitism, but that immunity did not extend to officials in the Department. Sol Bloom, chairman of the House Foreign Affairs Committee, was prevailed upon by the Department to try to convince leading Jews that Norem's utterances did not represent official policy. Norem was ordered to see Bloom to straighten the matter but he simply ignored Hull's order. Ultimately Roosevelt's intercession and Norem's removal from the Foreign Service gave the Jews some satisfaction.

The incident left a residue of bad feeling and suspicion because it supplemented numerous reports that the consuls were, if not outright anti-Semites, basically unsympathetic to Jewish refugees. The same observation could be made of the American Congress, which while refusing to admit Jewish refugees outside the quota system, appeared willing to do so in the case of British refugee children. In mid-1941, just as the State Department was phasing-in an even more stringent visa procedure, the liberal press began to examine the charge of State Department anti-Semitism.

In July 1941, Alfred Wagg, who had been forced to resign from the State Department under mysterious circumstances after his involvement with the Dominican Republic Settlement Association, began a series of articles in the *New Republic* in which he called for an investigation of the prevalence of anti-Semitism among Department officials.[103] Wagg's charges corroborated what many Jews had long suspected, there was "widespread anti-Semitism in the foreign service." [104] In June the magazine challenged the security gambit: "[The] motive for this action comes not from any genuine concern about Nazi spies but from the same little nest of anti-Semites . . . in the State Department." [105]

Attacks on the Department in 1940 caused Hull some anxiety. He eagerly accepted Long's suggestion that a counteroffensive be initiated by a press release from the White House, which would detail all that the Department had done for refugees. The release was duly prepared by Long and forwarded with a covering letter to Roosevelt.[106] It presented such a reasonable explanation of the Department's delays and inaction that the public no doubt wondered how the Department achieved the miracles of rescue which it did. But one of the most outspoken critics of the Department, the *Nation*, dismissed the attempt at good public relations as "patently disingenuous."[107]

Although Breckinridge Long, the principal official involved, counted among his pet animosities his distaste for Jews, he also harbored antipathy for Catholics, people who lived around New York City, liberals, in fact everybody who was not of his own particular background. Most important, Long had also became anti-Nazi, and sincerely believed that somehow refugees would be made to serve the Nazi cause. It is probably impossible to separate the two strands in Long's thinking. Somehow, for Long, it was possible for Jews, who were Hitler's principal victims, to become at the same time, his principal weapon against the United States.

1941, LOCKING THE GATES

In the early months of 1941, Long renewed the drive to cut off completely the trickle of refugees still able to reach American shores. He spoke to his friends, Senator Richard B. Russell (Democrat, Georgia) and Rep. Hatton Sumners (Democrat, Texas) about the possibility of enacting a law which would at one stroke exclude all immigrants "inimical to the public welfare."[108] In June such legislation was introduced. It was almost as encompassing as Long had suggested. It would permit consuls to deny any type of visa to any immigrant whom they felt would "endanger the public safety of the United States." The State Department might review such cases but the consul retained the last word. When the Russell bill was passed into law in June, Long succeeded in one stroke in getting back for the State Department the visa authority which had been shared with the PACPR and the screening committees.

"There has to be a sieve or screen somewhere," Long testified when requesting an appropriation to enlarge the visa division, "through which can be filtered persons acceptable to the United States, thereby excluding persons who might be sent into the United States by interested governments in the guise of refugees." [109]

For some time, too, Long had been anxious to get rid of the meddlesome PACPR, which was partly dependent on the Department for operating funds. An attempt to ease the agency out of the visa business in December 1940 had been countermanded by the President.[110] Long's neglect in requesting an appropriation for the agency may have been a simple oversight, but few in the PACPR thought so. Long was known to forget to appropriate funds for departments and agencies he did not like.[111] Aware of what might happen, James McDonald inquired about the 1941 appropriation and was told that the unspent portion of the 1940 appropriation would be available in the 1941 budget. But McDonald made further inquiries and confirmed what he had suspected—no appropriation for the PACPR had been made. He immediately informed Eleanor Roosevelt, who had become a kind of mother hen for all rescue agencies, and she apprised the President of what had happened. When the omission was discovered, Long apologized profusely and made certain to correct his oversight.[112] Other methods for emasculating the agency would soon be available.

His desire to tighten the visa procedure was spurred by the revelation, stemming from the Alien Registration Law of June 1940, that there were 4,200,000 aliens rather than the 3,600,000 estimated in the country.[113] There must be a system, Long thought, to give the President absolute control of entrance to and egress from the country. Such a law, he recalled, was in effect during his first tenure in the State Department during the Wilson Administration. Sol Bloom was prevailed upon to introduce such a measure. The Bloom-Van Nuys law was passed on June 21, 1940.

These laws marked the inception of new visa regulations to take effect on July 1. In early June the Department had begun preparation of a regulation which would deny a visa to any immigrant who had "close relatives" in occupied Europe. According to the Department, there was evidence that refugees were being coerced to become agents for Germany by holding relatives as hostages. For Long the "close relatives" regulation was a substitute for what he really wanted, the exclusion of "all persons whether they had relatives in Germany or not and to deny visas to any immigrant in Germany, Russia, Italy or any of their occupied territories." [114] The effect of the "close relatives" edict would be virtually the same since there were few refugees who did not have some relative in Nazi hands. For Jews, of course, no exception was made if the relative was starving to death in a concentration camp. In addition Long was successful in extending the screening procedure, reserved for the special visa list cases, to all refugees who desired to enter the United States.

The new regulations hardly seemed necessary. In mid-June the American consulates in occupied Europe had virtually ceased functioning and on July 15 were closed down. The refugee stream would be shut off at its source. There were, of course, many thousands of refugees in the neutral nations who could still get to an American consulate but those who had hoped to get out of the Reich itself or France, Holland, or Belgium would no longer be able to do so. The most pitiful cases were those who possessed visas, valid for four months, who would be left stranded once the consulate was no longer operating. On August 15, Berlin stopped issuing exit permits. The Reich was developing different plans.

The sudden closing of the consulates and the new regulations caused a last-minute spurt to get in under the line. "The immigration problem is very hot," Long wrote in his diary, "the consulates close July 15 . . . everyone wants their friends out *now*. Pressure is *very* bad and Germany sees her last chance to get her agents out and our inspection is very austere." [115]

Austere was hardly the word. Even for those who could reach neutral countries, there remained a series of hurdles which few could surmount. The interpretation of the "close relatives" regulation was surprisingly liberal considering its source. It would be used only as supplementary evidence to deny a visa, rather than a cause in its own right. But other regulations filled the gap nicely. It now took six months to process applications for visas. The screening now required for all applicants required a biographical statement and two financial affidavits, to be supported by two letters of reference by American citizens. The applicant and the affiant would then be investigated and finally the application was screened by the Interdepartmental Committee to determine purpose of entry and attitude toward the United States. Even if the screening committee made an affirmative recommendation, the consul retained the right to overrule it. For such cases an appeal board composed of two prominent outside presidential appointees was later established, which could reverse the decision of the Interdepartmental Committee.[116] The procedure proved so restrictive that of the 985 applications received by September 1941, only 121 were approved while 800 were rejected.[117]

The reaction to the "close relative" regulation and the cumbersome screening procedure set the stage for the squabble between the State Department and the Department of Justice. Although their differences had been germinating for two years, it was the appointment of Francis Biddle to head the Justice Department that set off the controversy. Biddle was more prone to question the stringent regulations concerning aliens and more favorable to refugee admission in general. Long was understandably apprehensive about the appointment. "In case Biddle is appointed," he confided in his diary, "it will make a decided difference in the cooperation between the Department of State and Justice on matters of refugees." Things could always be straightened out with Jackson, "but with Biddle and his subordinates . . . I have nothing but difficulty." [118]

Long did not have to wait for the difficulty to materialize. Upon taking office, Biddle informed the Department of his dissatisfaction with the screening procedure, especially the question of appeals. He informed Long that in cases where the appeals board could not arrive at a decision he reserved for the Department of Justice the right to do so. The Justice Department would thus have last word on certain visa cases. It was too much for Long, who had spent many months reassembling the visa authority in the State Department. Moreover, he suspected that Biddle intended to liberalize the screening procedure. He could not agree with Biddle's interpretation and told him so "in the spirit of friendly cooperation." [119]

In the meantime, Roosevelt was alerted to what was happening by a rash of criticism in the liberal press. James McDonald also informed him that if the new regulations were allowed to stand the Administration's refugee program would be virtually cancelled. He asked for an interview with the President to examine the situation.[120]

The *Nation* and the *New Republic* maintained a steady barrage of criticism of the Department's refugee policy. The *New Republic* aimed its barbs directly at Long, revealing that he had, in 1938, been actively involved as a lobbyist for Franco.[121] Long was stung by the disclosure and Hull was anxious to put an end to criticism of the State Department. "Hull somewhat uneasy about policy which puts through a careful scrutiny all prospective immigrants who have close relatives in Germany or Russia," Long wrote in his diary, "There is a recrudescence of criticism from radical elements and organizations interested in getting persons into the United States from doubtful territory." [122] He welcomed Welles' advice to see the President, convinced as he was that the President would see things his way.

With the help of his assistant Avra Warren, Long dictated a long memorandum which played strongly on the theme of security. The Department now had new classified information on the prevalence of agents among the refugees. As usual the memorandum was sweet and reasonable. The Department understood the consternation of McDonald and the members of the PACPR. Their opposition to the "close relatives" edict was "a natural and wholesome development" but the Department's latest measures were a "hold" order mandated by the Bloom-Van Nuys law which required careful scrutiny of all people entering and leaving the country. The President might arrange an interview with the PACPR so these facts could be made clear to them.[123] "Pa" Watson was informed of the possibility of an interview between McDonald and the President. Could he sneak "Breck" in to see him fifteen minutes before the scheduled interview? On August 27, Long again saw Roosevelt and found him "thoroughly in accord with our policies and practices." [124]

Long's shock must have been awesome when, eight days later, he witnessed Roosevelt agreeing to the modifications of the "close relative" edict and the screening procedure suggested by Macdonald and Biddle. Those suggestions concerned better protection of the civil rights of refugees in the review procedure which would now become official. The suppliers of affidavits, for example, would now be permitted to testify before the appeals board. McDonald presented evidence that at the rate of screening applicants by the committees, 1,126 per month, not even half the former German annual quota, would be filled, not to speak of the quotas for the remainder of occupied Europe.[125] What the Department was doing, it was clear, was keeping refugees out by administrative fiat. That, of course, was irrefutable.

Long vented his spleen in his diary:

At the request of the President attended a conference with him, McDonald's Refugee Committee and Attorney General Biddle. They are critical of the Department's policy—consequently of me. Biddle is their advocate. Rabbi Wise and the Archbishop of New Orleans were their principal spokesmen. Various amendments to procedure were proposed. Wise always assumes such a sanctimonious air and pleads for the "intellectuals and brave spirits, refugees from the tortures of the dictators" or words to that effect. Of course an infinitesimal fraction of the immigrants are of that category—and some are certainly German agents and others are sympathizers, the last named coming here because it is away from the scene of combat and looks like a safe place. I got a little mad and I fear I betrayed it. . . .

The exclusion of any person is objectionable to these eminent gentlemen and my system of selection is anathema to them. They would throw me to the wolves in their eagerness to destroy me—and will try in the future as they have in the past to ruin my political status.[126]

Long considered the security procedure his own and therefore any attack on it an attack on himself and his political career. Time of course was on his side. The President had not scrapped the "close relatives" edict but simply improved the appeals procedure. In June 1941, war between Germany and Russia broke out, endangering millions of Jews and cutting off the Shanghai escape route. Biddle's suggestion that the review and investigation function in the screening procedure be separated in the interest of good legal procedure, was only slowly implemented. Of the approximately 9,500 visa applications submitted by October 1941, only 4,800 had been cleared. The rate of rejection, however, was reduced by 15 percent.[127] But the process was painfully slow. The Justice and the State Departments remained at odds. Biddle insisted that the review boards be independent of all government agencies but Long was reluctant to part with any of his hard-won power. Finally, in November Biddle suggested a compromise which Long found acceptable. The President would appoint two outsiders but the Secretary of State could reverse the review board's decision in exceptional cases. Long was jubilant. His principal objective, control of the visa procedure in the Department, had been obtained. He quickly prepared a list of names from which Roosevelt would select the independent outsiders. "Thanksgiving Day," he wrote in his diary, "came at an appropriate time as far as I am concerned." [128]

Indeed, Long had much to be thankful for. Singlehanded, he had halted the flow of refugees to the United States. A soul-chilling account by Varian Fry, European director of the Emergency Rescue Committee, on the effects of the "close relatives" edict in Lisbon told of the kidnapping of prominent anti-Nazi refugees by the Gestapo and the stranding of hundreds of other refugees.[129] Paradoxically, had Long been able to see into the future, he might have saved himself a great deal of trouble. The Japanese attack on Pearl Harbor and the entrance of the United States into the war achieved at one stroke what Long had wanted all along. It created a situation in which it became well-nigh impossible for refugees to reach American shores. It also activated Berlin again. In January 1942, the Nazi regime, perhaps because it was now convinced that there no longer existed an opportunity to rid itself of Jews by emigration, made the decision to solve its Jewish problem by liquidation.

If Long imagined that the four years of rancor generated by the refugee question would now come to an end, he would be disappointed. Already Biddle had expressed opposition to the internment of the Nisei which Long predictably favored. Long regretted that a man of Biddle's background who possessed "reserve courage and determination" was in the camp of those with "tender hearts." [130]

Momentarily the war had actually created more than the ordinary danger for the refugees stranded in Vichy. . . . The deportation of non-French Jews in Vichy was the Nazis first order of business. Under pressure from rescue advocates, the Department made representations to the Vichy government concerning the deportations which began on April 29, 1942. In September a rumor that Pierre Laval, who had been reinstated in April as the Foreign Minister of the Vichy government, had repeated an earlier offer to release the refugees if the United States would accept them swept through the refugee agencies.[131] Hull hastened to deny the rumor.[132] Under pressure from Congressman Celler, Roosevelt requested information from the State Department. Welles' replied to the inquiry; he did not hold out much hope but perhaps intercession by the Vatican or the International Red Cross might yet redeem the situation. Stronger pressure on the Vichy authorities might endanger the program to save the refugee children. "We have to face the disagreeable fact," Welles informed Celler, "that most of the damage has already been done." [133] The invasion of North Africa in November and the subsequent occupation of Vichy brought an end to this rescue opportunity.

After 1942, all concerned with the refugee-rescue effort were aware of the relation between the movement east sponsored by Berlin and the movement west which might have been sponsored by the receiving nations. For every cattle car that rolled eastward loaded with Jews, there was a corresponding decrease in the refugee burden. By liquidating Jews, Berlin was not only solving its "Jewish question," it was solving the State Department's refugee question as well. The Vichy episode illustrated that the two problems were really two sides of the same coin. All one had to do was wait, and refugees clamoring to come to the United States would be converted into silent corpses.

CONCLUSION

The cost in lives of the State Department's curtailment of the refugee inflow is difficult to determine. Perhaps as many as 62,000 to 75,000 additional refugees might have come here between 1938 and 1942. But such calculations do not take into account what might have been achieved between 1942 and 1944 had the precedent established in the first phase of the rescue effort been more humane. In a sense, the battle to save lives by bringing the United States into an active rescue role was lost during this first round. The precedents established by Breckinridge Long held until 1944 when the advocates of a more active rescue policy were able to break through. By then much of the killing was already history.

The Bermuda Conference:
Mock Rescue for Surplus People

In March 1940, six months after the mass deportation of Jews to Poland had begun, adverse publicity caused Göring to suspend it temporarily. The unorganized movement of people had caused such needless suffering that it seemed wiser to hold off the much desired goal of making the Reich *Judenrein* until more order and organization could be brought to the procedure. In the final months of 1941 new rumors of unspeakable depredations against Jews leaked out of occupied Europe. Again the atrocities were involved with deportation and ghettoization. In the ghettoization process there were stories of hardships, crowded conditions, and a few rumors of starvation. Even after the invasion of the Soviet Union in June 1941, there were few rumors that spoke of the activities of the *Einsatzgruppen*, who roamed behind the Wehrmacht lines with the specific function of killing Jews. Few suspected at the time that something more than deportation, ghettoization, and incidental killing was involved. A massive annihilation of Jews, using modern industrial processes, simply beggared the imagination.

THE ROOSEVELT ADMINISTRATION AND NEWS
OF THE FINAL SOLUTION

On January 30, 1939, Hitler warned that if war should come, it would see the liquidation of the Jews. He was, however, not ready to carry out that threat until the Soviet Union and the United States entered the war in the final months of 1941. The decision to do so was reached at a series of meetings of the highest officials of the Nazi regime beginning with a special meeting held at Grossen-Wannsee in the suburbs of Berlin on January 20, 1942, almost two and a half years after the war began. It was those years, between September 1939 and January 1942, that offered the best opportunity to save the Jews of Europe.

Berlin soon discovered that the mass production of death, like all industrial processes, entailed problems of efficiency and cost which were not easily solved. Moreover, the Nazi regime naturally wanted to keep the Final Solution secret. The use of Zyklon B gas, it was discovered after some experimentation, solved the problem of cost and efficiency but even the most painstaking efforts to camouflage the operation did not fully succeed. An operation in which thousands and ultimately millions of people vanished could not easily be kept secret. Ultimately, news of what the Nazis were doing leaked out and precipitated a new phase in the rescue effort.

The first unconfirmed reports of mass killing were made by Thomas Mann, the German novelist, in his BBC broadcasts in December 1941 and January 1942. In September 1942 he was among the first to report the gassing of Dutch Jews at Matthausen concentration camp.[1] Only the second report was related to the operation of the Final Solution and news of the gassing had been confirmed by two sources. In August, one month before Mann's Matthausen report, Washington received a report of the killing from the Polish Government in exile, which had word of successful smuggling of a member of the Polish underground, disguised as a policeman, into the Treblinka death camp. When enough information had been accumulated, Jan Ciechanowski, Ambassador of the Polish government in exile, joined by representatives of other governments in exile, presented a collective demarché to the White House which requested retaliation such as the bombing of German cities.[2] The State Department rejected the request on the ground that such retaliation would lead to an escalation of the terror since Berlin was unhampered by humanitarian considerations and in physical control of a vast number of captive people.[3] At the same time a public warning to Berlin was also rejected on the grounds that such statements, made while Germany was in a winning position, posed an empty threat. Prime Minister Wladyslaw Sikorsky pointed out in vain that protests coming from the victims exclusively, while the great powers remained silent, would create the impression of a rift between the nations occupied by Germany and those still actively belligerent. But the precedent of saying nothing, so perplexing to later observers, was firmly established in 1942. Its effects on the rescue effort, for the year and a half it remained in effect, would be devastating.

For Jewish rescue advocates Sikorsky's fight to wring a statement of concern from the Allied governments had a special irony. In January 1942, before hard news of mass killing was available, the eight governments in exile met at St. James's Palace, London, and issued a statement branding Germany guilty of atrocities against various national groups, but strangely omitted to mention that Jews were the principal victims. Sikorsky's explanation that such a specific reference "might be equivalent to an implicit recognition of the racial theories we all reject," came as something of a shock since the Poles were hardly known for their tolerance of Jews.[4] The World Jewish Congress requested that a specific statement about the crimes against Jews be issued lest the St. James's Declaration convince the Nazi hierarchy that the leadership in the democracies condoned the atrocities. The World Jewish Congress plea was rejected but time was to prove that its contention was accurate. On December 13, 1942, Josef Goebbels wrote in his diary: "The question of Jewish persecution in Europe is being given top news priority by the English and the Americans. . . . At bottom, however, I believe both the English and the Americans are happy that we are exterminating the Jewish riff-raff."[5]

The second source of information about the Final Solution was the agent of the World Jewish Congress in Bern, Switzerland. Dr. Gerhard Riegner, who was in communication with a German industrialist with close connections to the highest echelons of German officialdom. The informant presented Riegner with a detailed account of the Wannsee Conference and told of thousands of victims slaughtered by means of prussic acid, a prime ingredient in Zyklon B gas. Riegner transmitted his information to Samuel Silvermann, representative of the Congress in London, who forwarded it to Stephen Wise.[6] Wise hesitantly forwarded the unsubstantiated story to Welles, stating that he was "reduced to consternation by the cable" and requesting the Department to seek confirmation of the story and to inform the President so that a course of action might be considered.[7] Welles promised to do so and requested that Wise, in the interim, withhold the information until it could be confirmed. The Department now possessed two reports on the operation of death factories in addition to numerous reports of deportation from Paris and Holland. But the actual mass-killing operation was still in the experimental stage in July 1942 and the Department felt it needed more information.

Riegner had waited until August to send word to Wise, but now, convinced of the reliability of his source, he forwarded more details. In September Wise, still reeling from the impact of the first report, received these additional gruesome details from Jacob Rosenheim, a representative of the World Jewish Congress in Europe. It was more graphic than the original: "The corpses of the murdered victims are used for the manufacture of soap and artificial fertilizer. Please do best to arouse American intervention." [8]

Wise tried to do just that by informing Justice Felix Frankfurter, who had become an unofficial liaison between rescue advocates and the White House, and Henry Morgenthau, Jr., who was beginning to show signs of interest in the rescue program. But Frankfurter discovered only what Wise already knew. The Administration was reluctant to accept the reports of murder centers and discounted the idea of an organized attempt to liquidate the Jews. Roosevelt explained the deportations to Frankfurter; the deported Jews were simply being employed on the Soviet frontier to build fortifications.[9]

Such explanations would suffice for the moment only. Evidence that something quite different from fortification building was taking place was accumulating too quickly to permit the Administration to rationalize its inaction. Hitler had repeated his pledge to eradicate the Jews on September 30 and again in his New Years message. In October the Jewish Telegraphic Agency, without waiting for the go-ahead from Welles, broke the Riegner story so that the press was able to give wide circulation to the first reports of the Final Solution in operation.[10] Those in the Administration who remained skeptical were faced in November with four affidavits from eye witnesses which confirmed every gruesome detail of the original Riegner cable. No longer able to hold the story back, Welles informed Wise that the Government possessed information which "confirm and justify your deepest fears." [11] The original Riegner cables could be made public. The new information in the hands of the Administration was forwarded by Anthony J. Drexel Biddle, Jr., Ambassador to the governments in exile on August 26. It consisted of a report by Ernest Frischer, a former ranking official of the Czechoslovak government, reconfirming what was already known. Riegner too continued to forward confirming evidence through Consul Paul Chapin Squire. For American Jewry, Washington's official recognition came as an anticlimax; already the clamor for action had reached new heights. December 2 was set aside as a day of mourning.

THE JEWISH REACTION

The official confirmation of the Final Solution came at the end of a decade in which Jews in America heard increasingly gruesome stories of the martyrdom of the Jews of Europe. Among rescue advocates there was undoubtedly an awareness that the governments of the United States and Britain, despite the rhetoric of concern, were not truely concerned about the plight of the Jews. How could one explain the ever stricter visa procedure, the attitude towards Jewish refugee children as compared with British, the rejection of Alaska as a haven for refugees, and the Virgin Island debacle? For Britain the case was even clearer. The White Paper threatened to curtail immigration to Palestine at a critical juncture. The case of the *Struma* and the *Patria* went far to catalyze the feeling that Britain was hardly less hostile to Jews than the Nazi regime.

On February 24, 1942, the Danubian steamer *Struma*, a completely unseaworthy vessel, according to her captain's testimony, was towed out of the harbor at Istanbul after the British authorities refused to grant Palestine entrance certificates to the passengers on the grounds that there were spies among them. The ship sank outside Istanbul harbor with the loss of 767 lives. It was a rather transparent use of the security gambit, according to Stephen Wise, who informed Eleanor Roosevelt that "the fear that German agents might have been included on the passenger list of that ship is hardly convincing. The Nazis have no need for such precarious methods of transportation as was the *Struma*." [12] The *Patria*, like the *Struma*, was a refugee ship denied entrance into Palestine in the early months of 1942 and subsequently sank under mysterious circumstances with great loss of life.

Thus in the early months of 1943 it must have been readily apparent to rescue advocates that a change in rescue ground rules could not be achieved with the protest tactics that are normally employed. It would take too much time and the results were by no means assured. A movement was initiated to mobilize the entire Jewish community with as many other groups as could be mustered. The liberal press, especially the *Nation* and the *New Republic* began the aforementioned series of articles exposing the inactivity of the State Department. The *Nation* published Robert Bendiner's *The Riddle of the State Department*, a partisan but not wholly inaccurate account of the inner politics of the State Department which was especially unkind to the "career boys" around Hull. Long, who felt he had been singled out for special treatment, consulted counsel for possible libel action.[13] Meanwhile, protest rallies and memorial meetings were being organized in all major cities with large Jewish communities. Stephen Wise, who sometimes occupied the position of the Administration's spokesman to the Jews, found himself in an uncomfortable position. "I don't know whether I'm getting to be the J of Jude," he confided to Felix Frankfurter, "but I find that a good part of my work is to explain to my fellow Jews why our government cannot do all the things asked or expected of it." [14] In Berlin too, Goebbels took note of the growing protest: "The Jews are . . . talking again. Emil Ludwig Cohn, in an interview in the American press, demands the complete destruction of the German economy and the German war potential. The Jewish campaign against us is growing in volume. What won't the Jews do to discredit the Reich!" [15]

One of the earliest targets of the renewed agitation was the revival of the stalled project for creation of a war crimes commission. Such a commission would go far in breaking "the wall of silence" which surrounded news of the Holocaust. The suggestion for the commission came in June 1942 during a Roosevelt-Churchill meeting in Washington. The British, under growing pressure at home, accepted the suggestion with alacrity and set up a committee within the Cabinet which suggested that a provision should be included in the armistice agreement for the surrender of all major war criminals. Ambassador Winant, who was invited to take part in the meeting of the Cabinet discussing the judicial framework in which a war crimes commission might operate, became embarrassed when it became apparent that the State Department was stalling. He received no response between July and October and his request for guidance addressed directly to Roosevelt remained unanswered.[16] Beset by a public outcry, the London authorities were ready to proceed. Finally, in October the State Department consented to a war crimes commission but its purview would be limited to only top echelon Nazis.[17] The limitation tended to severely limit the usefulness of the commission. The precedent for men like Eichmann, who had actually operated the killing apparatus, to argue that they were bound to obey the orders of their superiors, was established in Washington.

Meanwhile the Administration, now acting as if the initiative for the commission came from within, proceeded with its plans. Roosevelt wanted his old friend Herbert C. (Birdie) Pell, the former American minister to Portugal, to head the commission.[18] But Pell was not appointed until June 1943, a full year after the original suggestion for the need for a commission had been made. But on December 17, 1942, a joint Anglo-American statement "insure[d] that those responsible for these crimes shall not escape retribution."[19] It was the first official recognition that something that went far beyond the usual war atrocities was occurring in Poland.

Despite the establishment of the War Crimes Commission there was little inclination by the Administration to do anything in the way of rescuing the victims. The thrust of the December 17 "solemn resolution" and the Commission itself showed clearly which way the Administration was heading. There would be punishment after victory but little effort to prevent the Final Solution while the war was in progress. The news of the slaughter of the Jews of Europe was received by an officialdom and public already saturated with atrocity stories. The Jews would be rescued, like everyone else in need of rescue, by beating the enemy as quickly as possible. There was in Washington little inclination to admit that the Jews had been marked for extinction. Special pleas for the rescue of Jews, especially if it could be argued that the steps suggested interfered with the war effort, were rejected. The State Department developed a new argument which proved as effective as the security gambit, "rescue through victory." Since virtually every step suggested by rescue advocates such as negotiating with Berlin through neutrals, accepting more refugees into the United States, relief shipments to the camps, diverting shipping for rescue, government financing of resettlement and retaliatory bombing, could be interpreted as interfering with the prosecution of the war, the new rationale for inaction was foolproof. When Harold W. Dodds, leader of the American delegation to the Bermuda Conference, was faced with such options by the rescue advocates, he maintained that they interfered with the war effort and therefore "would not only be foolish, it would be criminal." [20]

CONTINUED DIVISIONS WITHIN AMERICAN JEWRY

The knowledge of an organized attempt to liquidate their religious brethren in Europe did not noticeably quicken the movement for unity within American Jewry. Persistent bickering among a bewildering number of factions continued to forestall a full mobilization of the rescue forces. "The length it has gone to, the activities it has paralyzed and the personal antagonisms it has developed," observed Maurice Wertheim, acting President of the American Jewish Committee, "have brought us to a point where the real issues have been obscured if not almost forgotten." [21]

As soon as the news of the Final Solution was confirmed, the American Jewish Congress called for a meeting of the major Jewish organizations to plan a course of action. Such a call, coming from the American Jewish Congress, was likely to cause even greater divisiveness. Predictably, it was ignored, but when Henry Monsky, President of the middle-of-the-road B'nai B'rith, invited thirty-two organizations to meet in Pittsburgh during the month of January 1943, the stage was set finally to bring some unity among Jewish organizations. The conference established a temporary Emergency Committee for European Jewish Affairs which would function until a central organization or steering committee could be established by elections. Such a time, however, never arrived. Instead, even the nominal unity represented by the Emergency Committee did not survive the year.

Meanwhile, on the periphery of Jewish organizational life, almost unnoticed, a new group known variously as the American Friends of Jewish Palestine, The Committee for an Army of Stateless and Palestinian Jews, and the American league for a Free Palestine, began to emerge with a bold new approach to the rescue problem. Settling in July 1943 on the name, Emergency Committee to Save the Jewish People of Europe, it began filling the vacuum left by the bickering major organizations, and picking up support from the large number of unaffiliated Jews who were growing impatient with the inability of the regular organizations to take effective action. The organization displayed a special skill in mobilizing public opinion through the news media. Under the skillful direction of Peter Bergson it experienced little difficulty in raising funds. It was this skill as well as supposed attachment to Zionist revisionism, a more militant and less anglophile brand of Zionism, which made it anathema to Stephen Wise and the American Zionist movement. But focused exclusively on the rescue issue and unhampered by the disputes within the community, its influence grew. On February 16, 1943, it sponsored a full page ad in the *New York Times* featuring the first of a series of strident messages which became its hallmark and caused a good deal of anxiety for the officials of the State Department.

The flow of information regarding the operation of the Final Solution brought new support for the movement. Countless church groups, women's clubs, labor organizations and professional groups were drawn into the effort to bring pressure on the Administration. The public agitation culminated in a massive rally in Madison Square Garden on March 1, 1943, under the exhortation, "Stop Hitler Now." The rally, sponsored by the Church Peace Union, the A.F. of L., the C.I.O., and numerous other groups, was the largest of its kind ever held in the United States. Twenty-two thousand people crowded into the huge hall and at least 15,000 more waited outside to hear the impassioned speeches of the leaders of American Jewry. Their condemnation of the Roosevelt Administration gave no clue to the special popularity Roosevelt maintained among Jews. The rally seemed to have set the pattern for a regular protest ritual. On March 9, the Emergency Committee to Save the Jewish People of Europe sponsored a memorial meeting and on March 30 and April 14 huge demonstrations, following the New York City pattern, were held in Washington and Chicago. Virtually all rallies stressed the theme struck by Stephen Wise at the Madison Square Garden rally, which roundly condemned the State Department's "rescue through victory" policy. "We are told that the best way to save the Jews is to win the war," Wise told the rally, "but what hope is there that victory will come in time to mean survival of European Jews?" [22] The publicity-wise Bergson group initiated a new protest technique. On April 2, Ben Hecht, a noted dramatist and producer, presented a pageant entitled "We Will Never Die" starring the popular Paul Muni and Edward G. Robinson and directed by Moss Hart. It proved extremely effective and thereafter the leaders of the rescue effort frequently tapped the theatrical talent in the Jewish community to bring its message to the public.

The Madison Square Garden rally produced a twelve-point resolution embodying the new ground rules which became the crux of all rescue discussions for the next two years. The following steps were suggested:

(1) Negotiate with Germany and her satellites through neutral agencies and nations regarding the rescue of Jews.

(2) The United Nations should prepare sanctuaries for those who may be rescued through such negotiations.

(3) The United States should adjust the administration of its immigration laws to war conditions so that it does not act as a "deterrent and retardation of legal immigration under the established quotas."

(4) Britain should receive a "reasonable number" of refugees subject to the requirements of her national security.

(5) The United Nations should again explore resettlement possibilities in Africa, the Caribbean, Latin America, and the British Empire.

(6) England should open the doors of Palestine especially for refugees from Spain, Portugal, and the Balkan nations.

(7) The United States should urge Latin America to modify its immigration laws which rule out immigration to this area.

(8) The United Nations should establish a War Crimes Commission.

(9) An "appropriate intergovernmental agency" should be established with sufficient authority to implement the rescue program.

(10) The feeding of the victims under the auspices of neutral nations and agencies should be organized "with due regard for the economic warfare being waged against the aggressor states."

(11) The United Nations should provide a new identity passport, similar to the Nansen passport, for stateless refugees.

(12) The United Nations should guarantee postwar repatriation

of the refugees as well as assume financial responsibility for all escapees who make their way to neutral countries.[23]

On March 27, Wise received new reports detailing the mass killing of Jews in Treblinka and immediately cabled Myron Taylor requesting that special emphasis be given to Points 1 and 9, the establishment of a new rescue agency with special powers to negotiate with the Reich through neutral intermediaries.[24] These two points thereafter received priority. Other recommendations for action were soon added to the program. One suggested that Jews in the camps be considered *de facto* prisoners of war or civilian internees with all the legal benefits belonging to such a status such as the right of exchange. Another group of suggestions, originating primarily with the Bergson group, included psychological warfare such as threats of retribution and bombing. Prominent too was the suggestion that the Office of War Information broadcast vows to bring war criminals to justice and urge the people of occupied Europe to offer shelter and concealment to escapees.

The public agitation did not subside after the high point reached at the Madison Square Garden rally but, based on a concrete rescue program, reached the halls of Congress. On March 9 the Senate passed the Barkley resolution which advocated punishment for war crimes. The House followed suit on March 18. In Britain, where the public agitation was even more intense, the House of Commons gave its "fullest support for immediate measures on the most generous scale compatible with the requirements of military operations for providing help and temporary asylum for refugees." [25]

Despite growing public awareness of the urgency of rescue, the State Department's opposition proved difficult to overcome. Even after the operation of the Final Solution was fully confirmed, some middle echelon officials continued to view the news as exaggerations or worse, products of a mythical Jewish propaganda machine. The State Department could not fathom an order of priorities which placed the rescue of Jews above the winning of the war. Not until May 1943, almost a year after the first reports of the Final Solution, did Breckinridge Long inform the Department that "it may for present purposes be accepted as more than Jewish propaganda that a large number of Jews have been killed." [26] Statistics released by HIAS in March showed of the 460,000 visas available between 1938 and 1942 only 228,964 had been issued.[27] Long had not allowed humanitarian concern to interfere with his plans in the first phase of the rescue problem, he would be even less inclined to do so in the second.

Congressman Celler, aware that Long's success in establishing the interdepartmental visa screening procedure, had become the principal instrument to deny access to the United States, insisted that he and a committee of Jewish congressmen be allowed to see the President for an "off the record conference." On March 28 the committee saw Roosevelt and lodged a strong protest against the State Department's continued sabotage of the rescue effort.[28] But Roosevelt referred them back to the State Department and Breckinridge Long. The President was not yet prepared to remove the implementation of refugee and rescue policy from the Department, because it served as scapegoat for hostility generated by an unpopular policy. Roosevelt found little use for the Department in making foreign policy but in the domestic arena it could sometimes play a useful role.

THE STATE DEPARTMENT AND NEWS OF THE FINAL SOLUTION

To Cordell Hull the role that Roosevelt chose to assign to the State Department was a source of constant frustration. Sensitive to the fact that Roosevelt often bypassed the Department's slow-moving machinery by the use of personal emissaries, and convinced that the War and Treasury Departments were ever ready to intrude into the Department's domain, Hull seemed to be waging a holding action to prevent further erosion of the Department's position within the Administration. The refugee problem threatened to further denigrate the State Department's influence, since it was the focus of bitter comments in the liberal press. Doubtless there was the realization in the Department that it was the flow of information from Europe on the effect of the rigid screening procedure, and now on the operation of the Final Solution which provided the liberal critics of the Department with ammunition. It was probably Breckinridge Long who conceived the idea of diminishing the protest by halting at its source the flow of information on which it fed. That was within the realm of possibility, because much of the data was transmitted by the Department's diplomatic pouch and cable, the use of which had been extended to men like Riegner. Suppression of unwelcome information was not unprecedented. In January 1940, two years before the

Wannsee Conference, Pat Frank, a syndicated columnist, complained that the Department was deliberately suppressing stories of depredations in Poland and Rumania on the grounds that such stories were not verifiable.[29] Frank's complaint was fully confirmed by the Department's handling of the dispatches of Franklin Mott Gunther, the American minister in Bucharest. Gunther forwarded detailed dispatches describing the atrocities committed during the Horia Sim Iron Guard putsch in January 1941. When later Rumania began prematurely to deport Jews to the East, Gunther again informed the Department and warned of the request for intercession which could be expected from Jewish leaders. The dispatch, which duplicated a private letter to Roosevelt, even gave unsolicited advice for resettlement in Africa and informed the Department of an apparent willingness by the Bucharest authorities to enter into negotiations with receiving countries regarding the disposition of Rumanian Jews.[30] But the last bit of information proved highly unwelcome and if it were known it would surely arouse a storm. Cavendish Canon, of the Department's European Division, replied that "endorsing of such a plan is likely to bring about a new pressure for an asylum in the Western Hemisphere."[31] How could we intercede on behalf of Rumanian Jewry, reasoned Canon, when the precedent would then be applied to all countries where Jews were persecuted? "So far as I know," Canon observed, "we are not ready to tackle the whole Jewish problem."[32] Relieving pressure clearly took precedence over saving lives. The Department was no more ready to negotiate for the lives of Rumanian Jews in 1943 than it had been in 1941 when Gunther informed the Administration that such an opportunity existed. Gunther was never given a specific reply to his suggestion and he soon decided "not [to] seek further to trouble an already uncertain atmosphere by direct or specific representations."[33] Gunther uncannily sensed the Department's policy on information regarding rescue opportunities and information regarding anti-Jewish depredations. From that position it was but a small jump to an attempt to suppress such news at the source.

For Long, who viewed himself as being in a virtual state of war with rescue advocates, there was little realization of the ethics involved in curtailing a source of news. Long had in fact been responsible for managing some news for the Department since 1940 and had several times planted articles in the press to project a certain story or counter something not in the interest of the Department.[34] Long doubtless felt that the Department had no need to transmit news over its facilities which might ultimately result in an increase of pressure or the castigation of the Department. Thus on January 27, 1943, when another of Riegner's reports on the Final Solution was included in the dispatch forwarded by Leland Harrison, minister at the Bern legation, instructions were cabled to him on February 10 not to transmit such reports: "In the future," read the cable, "we would suggest that you do not accept reports submitted to you to be transmitted to private persons in the United States unless such action is advisable because of extraordinary circumstances."[35] It was the second suppression of a Riegner report. His first report to Wise was not forwarded because of the "apparently unsubstantiated nature of the information."[36] Unknown to the State Department, Riegner had taken the precaution of also sending the report to Jacob Rosenheim of the British branch of the World Jewish Congress with instructions to inform New York. Wise received the report and forwarded it to Welles. The ostensible reason for the odd request to Harrison was that such private messages circumvented Swiss censorship, thereby endangering official communication. Harrison was puzzled. The Swiss government had shown no inclination to complain, much less to intrude upon the sanctity of diplomatic correspondence. Moreover, the report, as the Department well knew, was reliable. Sumner Welles was unaware that his signature followed the unusual cable requesting Harrison not to forward private communications. He had probably signed it as a matter of routine. Two months later Welles had the opportunity to inquire about the Rumanian offer, about which Wise had apprised him. Naturally, Riegner had the fullest information, so the inquiry went to Harrison, who must have been more perplexed than ever, since he had been told two months before not to forward Riegner's information. He cabled Welles: "May I suggest that messages of this character should not—repeat not—be subjected to the restriction imposed by your 354, February 10, and that I be permitted to transmit messages from Riegner more particularly in view of the helpful information which they frequently contain."[37]

The scheme to cut off news of the Final Solution worked for two months. In April two alert Treasury Department officials discovered a reference to cable 354, when Harrison's April 20 reply was inadvertently forwarded to the Treasury Department, which, as general practice, monitored all pertinent diplomatic correspondence. But when the Treasury Department attempted to get hold of the original cable (354) they ran into incredible difficulties. The Department maintained that the cable did not concern the Treasury Department. After much bickering Long was forced to comply with Morgenthau's request but rather than delivering the original cable intact, which would have revealed the Department's subterfuge, he composed a summary of it which carefully omitted all references to the suggestion made to Harrison. The ruse worked until January 1944 when a true copy of the original cable fell into Morgenthau's hands. It gave the Secretary the evidence to prove that the Department had contrived to suppress news of the Final Solution and that the principal official responsible for such matters, Breckinridge Long, was not above falsifying cables. Roosevelt was finally persuaded to remove the State Department and Breckinridge Long from exclusive control of the Administration's rescue activity.[38]

The suppression of Riegner's reports was uncovered by Welles when he was tracking down a ransom offer made by the Rumanians. Such offers to ransom Jews, either individually or in groups, were not uncommon. Plans for personal enrichment or for filling the coffers of the Nazi treasury had been an integral part of the anti-Jewish depredations from their inception. The most recent instance of this commercial aspect of the Final Solution occurred in October 1942 when the Gestapo accepted ransom for George Born, a wealthy partner of the German firm of Binge and Born.[39] In November 1942 there were rumors of an offer to ransom Dutch Jews.[40] The State Department had warned against such ransom negotiations in November but after the surrender of the German Sixth Army at Stalingrad in February 1943 and the initiation of large-scale bombing of German cities in May, the Nazi client states such as Rumania began seeking ways to disassociate themselves from the Final Solution.

THE RUMANIAN AND BULGARIAN RESCUE OPPORTUNITIES

Paradoxically Rumania, where the sheer ferocity of the early anti-Jewish depredations outpaced even those of Nazi Germany, was at the same time a sensitive barometer of how the war was going for the Axis powers. Rumanian susceptibility to "business" deals had always been greater than other satellites and it was for this reason that the World Jewish Congress revived a plan to ransom 60,000 to 70,000 Rumanian Jews. Predictably, the business-minded dictator of Rumania, Ion Antonescu, quickly approved the plan offered by the World Jewish Congress and ordered the Central Organization of Rumanian Jewry to make its own selection for the expected Palestine visas.[41] No trouble was expected from Berlin since Hitler was anxious to placate Bucharest after a loss of part of the Rumanian Army in Russia.

In February 1943, Arthur Hays Sulzberger revealed details of the ransom plan in the *New York Times*.[42] The Jews would be released from camps in Transnistria in turn for a "tax" of 20,000 lei per inmate. The Bishop of Bucharest and the Papal Nuncio would arrange for transportation and Antonescu would even make two Rumanian ships available to transport the "cargo" to its destination in Palestine. They would travel under the flag of the Vatican. Since the State Department had ignored Gunther's earlier information on the opportunity for rescue from Rumania, the new attempt was managed through Morgenthau, who passed the information on to the Administration. It was at this juncture that Welles requested additional information from Bern and inadvertently uncovered the attempt to suppress information regarding the Final Solution.[43] The money would be placed in blocked accounts in Switzerland. In the meantime, Nazi authorities, also aware that Soviet armies might ultimately break into Rumania, ordered a speeding up of the deportation of the Jews. Rumania must be made *Judenrein* by May 1, 1943. That gave the rescue opportunity a special urgency.

We have seen that the State Department's first reaction to the offer was to squelch news of it. Not until Herbert Feis, the Department's economic advisor, appealed personally to Welles was an inquiry made.[44] Full details of the offer were not in the Department's hands until mid-June. Incredibly, the Department now began to echo the economic warfare argument used by the British Foreign Office to counter similar requests from British rescue agencies. Such funds, ran the argument, would fall into enemy hands but more important, it would relieve them of the burden of supporting a part of the population for which they were legally responsible. This argument had a double irony. It was well known that Rumania was not supporting the Jews of Transnistria but simply letting them starve. Moreover on March 23, 1943, the Department was in possession of a secret peace feeler from Bucharest.[45] Rumania was beginning to withdraw her remaining troops from the Russian front and there were rumors of internal difficulties in the Antonescu regime. If anything, there was a golden opportunity to separate Rumania from the Axis. Under the circumstances, the Department's concern that such funds would be of use to the enemy, even in the unlikely case that it could get hold of them, seemed unwarranted. Moreover the Treasury Department, which had transmitted the Rumanian offer, must have found the economic warfare argument especially amusing, since for years the State Department discredited the same argument when used by the Treasury.

Without waiting for a formal State Department request, the Treasury's Foreign Funds Control Division offered to make the required license available. Stephen Wise had already received Roosevelt's personal approval of the transaction. Nevertheless, the license was not issued until September, two months after the Treasury Department had approved it and ten months after Rumania had made its proposal. For rescue advocates such delays emphasized the necessity of removing the official rescue operation from the Department of State. Nor was there clear sailing once the Department gave its consent in September. Ambassador Winant ran into difficulties with the British authorities who had to consent to the transaction and provide the necessary Palestine certificates. Anthony Eden incidentally remarked that the real reason for not grasping at this rescue opportunity concerned the "difficulties of disposing of a considerable number of Jews." [46] Rarely has a death sentence for thousands been more casually delivered.

On December 20, Morgenthau and John Pehle, then head of the Foreign Funds Control Division, went to see Hull and explained that the British objection went well beyond the requirements of economic warfare policy. They urged that it would be more humane, if the transaction fell through, to accept the Jews in the United States as POW's rather than allowing them to die. Hull, expecting Morgenthau's protest, had already replied to Eden that he had read his comments "with astonishment" and was "unable to agree with the point of view set forth" because it was "incompatible with the policy as it has been understood by us." [47] Rescue advocates were probably as surprised as the officers of the British Foreign Office at the State Department's sudden solicitude.

The foiling of a parallel rescue opportunity in Bulgaria, in which both the Foreign Office and the State Department participated, was more typical of the cooperation of these two Departments. Although the Bulgarian government had gone through the motions of accepting the Final Solution it had never been popular with the Bulgarian people, among whom there were only some 30,000 Jews. While Sofia had allowed itself to be coerced by Berlin into deporting the Jews of the Bulgarian-occupied section of Greece, the Jews of Bulgaria proper were relatively safe. Much like Rumania, the Bulgarian government became anxious to disassociate itself from the Final Solution when the tide of war seemed to be turning in favor of the Allies in the early months of 1943. The most practical haven for Bulgaria's Jews, as Rumania's, was Palestine.

The State Department learned of the opportunity to save the Jews of Bulgaria in the final months of 1942 but did little to expedite matters. Finally, when Eden visited the United States in March of 1943, Hull brought up the matter of the Bulgarian Jews for discussion.[48] (Both Hull and Eden appeared to be ill-informed and may have confused the rescue opportunity in Rumania with the one in Bulgaria. They cited Bulgaria but used figures applying to Rumania.[49]) Eden's response to Hull's inquiry about the possibility of extricating Jews was predictable. "If we do that then the Jews of the world will be wanting us to make a similar offer in Poland and Germany. Hitler might well take us up on such an offer and there simply are not enough ships . . . in the world to handle them." Eden did not fail to mention the ever-reliable security argument: "Hitler would be sure to sneak his agents into the group." [50] The British government might be able to accommodate some of the victims but, cautioned Eden, the State Department ought not to make any extravagant promises that could not be kept. In April, Joseph Proskauer, the new leader of the American Jewish Committee and Chaim Weizmann, head of the World Zionist movement, joined by Stephen Wise, inquired at the State Department as to the disposition of the case. Time was passing and the opportunity, they stressed, must not be allowed to slip by. But they received only a vague reply from Welles that "active consideration [was] being given to the possible measures for saving them [Bulgarian Jews]. Certain definite steps have been taken toward this end. . . ." [51] Turkish government officials were in fact approached concerning through passage, but without the guarantee of Palestine certificates which were controlled by the British Foreign Office little would be achieved.[52] Already Berlin, alerted to the trickle of Jews making their way to safety via Turkey, had alerted their Ambassador, Franz von Papen, to do all in his power to halt the flow. H. Shoemaker, former United States Minister to Bulgaria, was prevailed upon to broadcast a strong appeal to the Bulgarian people and a protest against the impending deportations were beamed to Bulgaria from the Bulgarian-American Committee in New York.[53] In April an *aide-mémoire* from the British Embassy told of increasing difficulties with Turkish authorities and the opposition of General Giraud and Robert Murphy, Roosevelt's special emissary in North Africa, to having Jews of Bulgaria and Spain in special camps in North Africa.[54] Such a move would have placated the Foreign Office, which was above all anxious to prevent more Jews entering Palestine. On June 21, the State Department informed the World Jewish Congress that it had taken all possible steps on behalf of Bulgarian Jewry. The effort was at least partially successful. On June 30 Dr. Marcus Ehrenpreis, formerly chief rabbi of Sofia, informed the private agencies that the situation had momentarily eased.[55]

THE STATE DEPARTMENT AND THE VATICAN

After the entrance of the United States into the war in December 1941, the Vatican, because of its representation on both sides and its claim to some moral preeminence in the western world, occupied a strategic position for rescue. We have seen that the State Department's reluctance to take advantage of rescue opportunities did not prevent it from encouraging others to do what it would not. But in the case of the Vatican it was dealing with an institution whose reluctance to become officially involved more than matched its own. We have seen that Roosevelt's appointment of Myron Taylor in December 1940 as Special Emissary to the Holy See was partly designed to add a moral dimension to the refugee crisis.

The Administration's approach to the Vatican proved unproductive. Concerned lest an intrusion on the refugee scene compromise its tenuous neutrality, the Vatican hesitated to play the role of spiritual guardian of western morality which Roosevelt had in mind for it. In December 1942 it rejected an opportunity to join the Allies in a "solemn resolution" condemning Nazi war crimes.[56] Thereafter the Vatican's statements on war atrocities were kept very general despite the fact that it was probably the best informed international institution on the actual workings of the Final Solution. A mass of information to the contrary could not convince Pius XII that stories of mass murder which circulated throughout Europe in 1942 were not exaggerations. When Harold H. Tittman, Jr., Taylor's assistant, and former American consul general at Geneva, suggested that the moral posture of the Church was being seriously compromised by not speaking out, the Pope could only reply that he would in full conscience be forced to speak out against Communist depredations as well.[57] On an unofficial level, some sections of the Church and many individual bishops were in fact carrying out an important rescue mission but Church officials preferred not to publicize these steps lest Berlin retaliate. Not even the deportation of the Jews of Italy in February 1943 could provoke the Vatican to act. Nor would the Bishop of Rome go as far as some of the Bishops in Vichy France and Holland who did speak out against the atrocities. When Stephen Wise, for example, was informed of the deportations of the Jews of Rome, he communicated with Myron Taylor in a last attempt to activate the Vatican. Acting through the Vatican's Apostolic Delegate in Washington, Archbishop Amleto Giovanni Cicognani, Taylor urged the Vatican to act before it was too late.[58] But the last plea proved futile. Even Ernst Weizsäcker, now the Nazi Ambassador to the Vatican, was surprised at the silence of the Church on October 16–17 while Jews were being hunted down "under the windows of the Pope." [59]

THE RELIEF QUESTION

In the early months of 1943 the State Department was confronted with a new suggestion. Rescue advocates, concerned about keeping victims from mass starvation, pushed for a program to bring food and medical aid into the camps and ghettos under Nazi control. This was openly suggested in the Madison Square Garden rally of March 1, 1943, although the framers of the resolution were careful to suggest that relief should be provided through neutral intermediaries and "with due regard for the economic warfare being waged against the aggressor state." [60]

The Department's policy was deceptively simple: "The responsibility and manifest duty to supply relief rests with the occupying authorities." [61] No consideration was given to the fact that these particular authorities starved their victims to death as part of the mass murder program. In the Warsaw ghetto, for example, the death rate among Jewish children was thirty times as high as among other Polish children. [62] Opposition was not confined to the State Department. There was a widespread notion that Germany would intercept such relief shipments and utilize them to sustain her own population. The Unitarian Service Committee, usually in the forefront of the rescue effort, opposed the sending of relief supplies. A group of Catholic laymen declared that "any attempt to force the British blockade and feed the conquered population of Europe, is contrary to the best interest of Christianity and America." [63] As early as March 9, 1941, London, which as a result of its success in World War I considered the blockade a crucial weapon in its arsenal, warned "that no form of relief can be devised which would not directly or indirectly assist the enemy's war effort." [64]

Before such relief could be dispatched to occupied Europe a formidable barrier of blockade regulations would have to be breeched. In 1941 private organizations had partly circumvented the blockade by procuring licenses to purchase food in neutral countries such as Portugal and shipping it to the ghettos. But in 1943 such a procedure proved difficult because of the limited amount of food available and increasing difficulty in transferring funds to Lisbon. Nevertheless, the AJJDC was granted a license by the Treasury Department in May 1943 to send food parcels to the inmates of Theresienstadt, but it was clear that the Allied governments would also have to lend their support. The natural agency for such a program was the International Committee of the Red Cross (ICRC). The ICRC was reluctant to extend its food parcel service to the camps, claiming that it had no authority except through whatever good will as individual belligerents might show. Nor did it have enough funds. On September 16, Nahum Goldmann spoke to Long and suggested that the United States and Britain make such funds available to the ICRC.

For the State Department, relief shipments posed a special dilemma. Although considerable opposition to relief to occupied Europe existed there was at the same time a strong American tradition of providing food to the starving. In 1940 Herbert Hoover again became vitally concerned with such a program, and clashed with the British Ambassador who would have preferred such a program to be focused exclusively on Britain.[65] The massive "bundles for Britain" campaign had created a strong public interest but the public had not yet shown a concern for aid to people under Nazi hegemony, much less Jews in the ghettos. The Department's answer was to steer a middle course; relief shipments to Spain and Vichy France would be encouraged.[66] Relief shipments to occupied Europe were ruled out on September 25, 1941. That meant that relief shipments destined for Jews, who were signaled out for starvation, would be treated like all other people of occupied Europe.

A year later, when word of the Final Solution had leaked out of Europe, Jonah Wise of the AJJDC and Nahum Goldmann, agent of the Jewish Agency in America, saw Breckinridge Long to request a change in this policy. Specifically they wanted to ship food to the Jews in the Warsaw ghetto.[67] They had already received approval for a small relief operation from the Board of Economic Warfare. Surprisingly, Long agreed to change the policy slightly. Hull had for some time been concerned about the attacks against the Department which had in the final months of 1942 become more outspoken. He impressed on Long the need for some political consideration on the relief shipment issue. Long, who unlike Hull had never held elective office, was insensitive to the political aspects of the rescue and relief problem. Long complied, after discussing with Hull "the necessity for us to take into consideration the POLITICAL CONSEQUENCES if we are just to say 'no' for military reasons and oppose the humanitarian decisions of large groups of our citizens, etc." [68] The Department therefore agreed to approve a license for the transfer of $12,000 per month to Lisbon for the purchase of food parcels. Long even helped enlist the aid of Norman H. Davis, Chairman of the American Red Cross, to help expedite the matter of sending relief supplies. "The decision," he confided in his diary, "[was taken] on purely political grounds. The total amount of food involved is infinitesimal. But I did not want that policy along with others to serve as the basis for antagonisms toward us after this war. . . . So that is our policy." [69] That is where the matter stood when Nahum Goldmann requested government funding of the project on September 16, 1943. In November, the Department decided to honor the request at least nominally by granting the ICRC $4,000,000.[70] But such funds were not extended to the ICRC until August 1944. A host of new problems arose to block implementation of the program.

The ICRC remained hesitant about involvement because of its fear of breaking the tenuous link to Berlin which permitted it to carry on some relief programs in Axis Europe. A possible solution to the ICRC was suggested by the Rescue Commission of the American Jewish Conference. It called for the ICRC to use its influence to change the status of concentration camp inmates to that of civilian internees. Such a change in status would have automatically extended the food parcel program to camp inmates. Moreover, the ICRC's program for periodic inspection of POW and civilian internee camps might then have been included at least to the work camps where Jews were kept. Berlin's peculiar concern for certain legal niceties, in the midst of its murderous operation, were well known and might have been used. A Leon Kubowitzki, who was deeply involved in the effort to get relief to the camps, made the following observation in 1948:

The battle for the Red Cross food parcels was another episode in the tragic lack of understanding by the Gentile world of the peculiarity of the Jewish plight. The British and American Red Cross standard parcels were, by the terms of the directions given by the blockade authorities, reserved exclusively for recognized prisoners of war and civilian internees. Yet, while the Germans refused to consider officially the segregated Jews as civilian internees, they would sometimes permit food parcels to be delivered in certain camps. The Congress requested in vain that full advantage be taken of this de facto situation. Its pleas could not shatter the fetish of Economic Warfare primacy.[71]

A food parcel program was ultimately financed by the War Refugee Board in August 1944, using the facilities of the ICRC. But by that time it was too late.

PREPARATIONS FOR THE BERMUDA CONFERENCE

Doubtless the Department's policy on the rescue opportunities in Rumania and Bulgaria, its unseemly attempt to stem the flow of information concerning the Final Solution, and its policy on relief shipments can be made understandable if they are viewed as part of a general policy to avoid a commitment to rescue. The most impressive effort to quiet the growing agitation for new rescue ground rules was made in mid-1943 in calling a new refugee conference. Its purpose, as it turned out, was not so much to help the victims of the Nazi terror, but the governments of Britain and the United States.

The idea originated in the British Foreign Office. On January 20, 1943, Lord Halifax delivered a carefully worded *aide-mémoire* to the Department. It spoke of the Foreign Office's concern with the growing clamor for more concrete rescue action and prescribed "some kind of private conference of Allied representatives" as the most "expeditious procedure" for handling the situation.[72] London was particularly anxious that no publicity attend the planning of the conference and, repeating the stipulation made first at the Evian Conference, ruled out any consideration of Palestine as a refugee haven.[73] London proposed, and Washington quickly agreed, that the purpose of the conference should be to "assist those who make their way to countries beyond German control."[74] The two powers, in so many words, intended to limit the discussion to those who were already safe. When the conditions became known, rescue advocates charged that the conference was a "hollow mockery." It was, they would argue, those who could not make their way to a neutral country who needed rescue. The British *aide-mémoire* was amazingly candid. The conference would allay pressure rather than speed rescue. It cautioned Washington about "raising false hopes." Palestine was ruled out because Germany and its satellites might "change from a policy of extermination to one of extrusion . . . [and] aim as they did before the war, at embarrassing other countries by flooding them with immigrants."[75] The Foreign Office maintained a rather cold-blooded preference for the first alternative. The *aide-mémoire* also attempted to pass the initiative to Washington by including a request for a reexamination of the American immigration law with a view to admitting more refugees.[76] The answer to such requests was known beforehand by Whitehall. The Roosevelt Administration was no more willing to open up the question of its immigration law and visa administration than London was to consider the Palestine question. But by posing such requests or requesting that Washington give guarantees to neutrals that any refugees they accepted would be repatriated at the war's end tended to create the illusion that London was willing to go further than Washington. By 1943 the game of "whose got the moral onus now?" which Robert Pell and Pierrepont Moffat complained about in 1939 had become a ritual. London, in fact, had requested a "preliminary conference" to make certain that the proceedings would not get out of hand. Washington responded to the British gambit by making news of the impending conference public without informing London, thereby creating the impression that the credit for the new initiative belonged in Washington. When the Foreign Office protested the Department replied that it had been "regretfully forced to the conclusion . . . that the British government was permitting the impression to be created that it was the great outstanding champion of the Jewish people . . . and that it was being held back in its desire to undertake practical steps to protect the Jews in Europe." [77] The Department was particularly incensed by the *aide-mémoire's* characterization of the Administration's rescue measures a mere "words and gestures." The dispatch which, although signed by Welles, bears the earmark of Long's keen resentment of the British, ended with the charge that "It is well known to us that a campaign to undermine our foreign policy has been pursued by certain elements in the British Government." [78]

The Department did not formally reply to the British *aide-mémoire* for a full month despite London's request for speedy action. Only after the Department had again been warned by Richard Law, the Parliamentary Undersecretary for Foreign Affairs, that "public opinion in Britain had been rising to such a degree that the British government can no longer remain dead to it," did the Department make its reply. [79] It was prefaced by the traditional litany of good deeds committed in the cause of rescue, including things that might nudge Whitehall, such as the acceptance by the United States of many thousands of German POW's captured by the British. But Long probably went too far when he listed, as part of the American refugee burden, the internment of thousands of Japanese, most of whom were American citizens. [80] Under such circumstances, argued Long, the

United States could hardly be expected to contribute more. Nevertheless, the United States was not averse to a conference which promised to relieve some public pressure, providing it required no additional commitment. The most significant aspect of Long's reply was
the suggestion, made before the conference began, that its conclusion
should be the revival of the virtually defunct IGC. If the requirements could be agreed upon, the conference on political refugees
would take place, preferably in Ottawa.[81] (Long preferred to maintain the fiction that the rescue problem concerned political refugees
rather than Jews.)

When Anthony Eden, heading a British delegation, arrived in
Washington in March 1943, it was apparent that the *aide-mémoire*
detailing British concern with public pressure was not exaggerated.
The delegation seemed preoccupied with the public clamor at home
and Eden voiced his desire to bring back some plan of action which
might silence the Archbishop of Canterbury, whose inquiries in Parliament were proving embarrassing to the Churchill government. But
Eden rejected Long's idea of holding the conference in Ottawa and
Canada did not favor it either. Long immediately suspected that
Eden's pressing for an American location for the conference had an
ulterior purpose—to move the spotlight from London to Washington.
He alerted Hull and Roosevelt on his plans to counter the British
move. He would seek an area for the conference which was at once
in the British sphere and away from the prying eyes of the press.
Bermuda fitted these requirements and thus became the agreed-upon
site of the conference. Eden, Long wrote in his diary, had made a
transparent attempt to place "responsibility and embarrassment in our
laps, now they have the baby again." [82] His inordinate suspicion of
Eden dated back to 1935 when Eden proposed a strong stand against
Mussolini's Ethiopian adventure, while Long, then American Ambassador to Rome, opposed American oil sanctions. He feared that Eden
would recall past antagonisms and would not want to see him.[83] But
Eden was more intent on relieving public pressure on the British government than on fighting with an underling in the State Department.
He suggested a joint statement on the rescue question that might at
least temporarily conciliate the critics of the Foreign Office. At the
same time, Eden informed Hull, the British government would
announce its readiness to admit 30,000 refugee children to Palestine.

Could the American government, Eden inquired, make some equivalent contribution? [84] The Department had the baby again. Hull could only suggest that Ray Atherton, chief of the European Affairs Division, William Strang, the British Assistant Undersecretary for Foreign Affairs, and Breckinridge Long confer and prepare a joint statement.[85]

The meeting was a stormy one. Long entered the meeting certain that Whitehall was trying to denigrate the Department's efforts on behalf of refugees and to humiliate him personally.[86] When Strang reopened the question of location of the conference, a victory which Long felt he had already won, Long blew up.[87] He then composed a statement "designed to push the conversation away from Washington." [88] The highly emotional account retold the story of how he, Long, had personally foiled an attempt to compromise the security of the United States through planting spies among the refugees. Hardly in keeping with the formality of diplomatic exchange, the statement must have surprised the cool, somewhat reserved Strang.[89] It may have been that Long's belligerence and apparent paranoia was caused by nervous exhaustion. He tells us in his diary six days later that he suffered a physical collapse and that his "reserves of nervous and physical energies are lacking." [90] Long's statement, in any case, did not impress Strang, who strenuously objected to Long's idea of reviving the IGC. He insisted that all references to the agency be stricken from the final memorandum. Long was forced to agree but not before he had obtained an agreement that the omission would not be taken as a precedent that would prohibit the consideration of the IGC at some future time. The memorandum divided the Nazi victims into two groups: those under German control and those in neutral countries. For the second group some new efforts would be made but for the first "no steps to relieve them other than military steps can be taken." [91] The planners of the conference thus went on record beforehand as not favoring any significant action for the overwhelming majority of the people who were either in camps or ghettos. The hoax of calling a conference to do nothing but assuage the sensibilities of the growing number of concerned people did not escape the rescue advocates.

A day after the meeting in Long's office, Roosevelt was informed of the Department's plans to counteract the "deep sentiments on the part of the Jewish elements of our population." [92] For Long, who composed the memorandum, only Jews were interested in saving their brethren. Long lost no time in gathering a properly responsive delegation. A member of the House and a Senator were chosen, Long explained to Roosevelt, to maintain proper congressional liaison. The delegation consisted of Sol Bloom, Chairman of the House Foreign Affairs Committee, Senator Scott Lucas, Democrat of Illinois, and Supreme Court Justice Owen J. Roberts, who was to head the delegation. Shrewdly chosen, the delegates could be relied upon to be in sympathy with the Department's point of view. The delegation's support personnel, Robert Borden Reams, George Warren, and Robert Alexander of the Visa Division, were men who had proved their absolute loyalty to Long on the rescue issue.

But from the outset Long's carefully laid plans ran into trouble. London had at Hull's suggestion chosen a fairly high-ranking delegation headed by Richard Kidston Law, the Parliamentary Undersecretary for Foreign Affairs. The American delegation, it was felt, should be of equivalent rank. More important, the situation in London had become so urgent that Foreign Office officials were beginning to doubt whether they could wait for the American preparations to be completed. The conference must be held forthwith. To comply with the British request for speed, Long was forced to cancel the appointment of Justice Roberts, who could not immediately leave the bench, and substitute his old friend, Harold W. Dodds, president of Princeton University. The delegation's rank was now lower, to the dismay of the British. The private organizations, who witnessed the activities of the Department with a jaundiced eye, were suspicious of Long's plans. There was no provision for these groups to be represented directly in the delegation or even to get to the conference. How would their views be heard? Not even the entire press corps would be available at Bermuda since the Department, perhaps aware that a hostile press would defeat the purpose of the conference, arranged to have only select reporters from the news services present. No one could attend the conference on his own since Bermuda could be reached only by military aircraft. Long had the advantage of a perfectly controlled environment.

Predictably, requests for changing the arrangements and the makeup of the delegation were not long in coming. Representative Samuel Dickstein, Chairman of the House Immigration and Naturalization

Committee, would have been a natural candidate for the delegation but his views did not correspond with those of the State Department and he could not be handled. Dickstein did not base his request to be on the delegation, made directly to Roosevelt, on his unquestionably superior background on rescue and refugee matters, but on the fact that he "was very much favored by the Orthodox branch of the Jewish faith and [he] knew that [his] appointment would please that group immensely." [93] The request was, as a matter of course, forwarded to Long who was not interested in the intricacies of Jewish community politics and probably knew quite well why he did not select Dickstein. Long had selected Sol Bloom, Chairman of the House Foreign Affairs Committee, who also claimed to represent "Orthodox Jewry." Moreover Bloom offered the advantage of being "easy to handle" and "terribly ambitious for publicity." [94] Wise's inquiry about the composition of the delegation had to be carefully handled. Long replied that he was confident that "the composition of the group as a whole is such as to justify the thought that any matter which comes before them will be intelligently considered." [95] Wise refused to be put off by such double talk and protested against Bloom, whose reputation as the "State Department's Jew" would be complete after the conference, as not being representative of American Jewry. It was an unfortunate choice of words, for it enabled Long to reply righteously that Bloom "was representative of America." [96]

The rift between the State Department and the British Foreign Office was, strangely enough, not based on differences in intent. Both organizations were unenthusiastic about rescue and the British feared what might happen should mass rescue actually be accomplished. The Foreign Office, always opposed to the organization of the IGC, had not changed its mind in 1943. They were aware, moreover, that it would be extremely difficult to "sell" a farce like the reactivation of the IGC to the leaders of the British rescue effort. They would have preferred, for appearances' sake, to organize an entirely new agency in compliance with the request of the private organizations on both sides of the Atlantic. The debate over the status of the IGC was part of a continuing series of differences on virtually every wartime issue. Some portion of the conflict might be attributed to a species of anglophobia among the middle echelon officials in the State Department. Men like Pierrepont Moffat, James Dunn, Robert Pell, and Breckinridge Long attributed an extraordinary degree of wiliness to the older and more experienced Foreign Office apparatus. Like novices they were constantly on guard lest they be taken in. On the refugee issue differences had already arisen concerned primarily with the question of why the other side was not doing more. In 1942 these were supplemented by the question of acceptance of certain groups of refugees. Hull, for example, was compelled to rescind an order admitting five hundred workers from the Czech shoe factory of Bata because the firm was on the British blacklist. Long clashed with the Foreign Office when he blocked the entrance of 7,000 aliens from Canada whom Eden was interested in bringing into the United States.[97]

Meanwhile, Long proceeded with preparations for the conference. On March 29 he rejected a last-minute British request to be allowed to bring representatives of the central organization for British Jewry, the British Jewish Board of Deputies, to the conference. He reminded the British that the American position was that the refugee-rescue problem was not an exclusively Jewish one and that the impending conference was concerned with refugees, not Jews. Any exception to the "no visitors" rule might prove embarrassing.[98]

Long's response to the Foreign Office's urgency might have been accelerated had he been able to foresee the storm brewing in his own bailiwick. His choice of delegates and conference site had aroused suspicion. Stephen Wise had already registered a personal complaint with the White House. He was concerned about Long's passing reference to the conference as "primarily exploratory." With so many confirmed Jewish dead, explained Wise to Welles, it was utterly cynical to have yet more exploration.[99] A letter from Philip Murray, president of the C.I.O., warned the Department not to repeat the "futile" Evian Conference at this late date.[100] The Department published a strong denial of the charges that the conference site had been chosen for its inaccessibility.[101] The private organizations which had been excluded from the conference flooded the delegation with suggestions for the more active rescue policy outlined in the twelve-point rescue resolution drawn up by the American Jewish Congress for the March 1 Madison Square Garden rally. Receiving priority was the demand for a new agency which might negotiate with the enemy through neutrals. Long predictably found such suggestions "unrealistic" and counseled the delegation to ignore them.[102]

But as the agitation continued even to the day that the conference was to begin, Long became apprehensive:

One Jewish faction under the leadership of Rabbi Stephen Wise has been so assiduous in pushing their particular cause—in letters and telegrams to the President, the Secretary and Welles—in public meetings to arouse emotions—in full page newspaper advertisements—in resolutions to be presented to the conference—that they are apt to produce a reaction against their interest. Many public men have signed their broadsides and [Senator Edwin C.] Johnson of Colorado introduced their resolution into the Senate.[103]

Long feared that Berlin would get the impression that the Allies were in fact concerned about the Final Solution.

One danger in it all [he reveals in the same entry] is that their activities may lend color to the charges of Hitler that we are fighting this war on account of and at the instigation and direction of our Jewish citizens, for it is only necessary for Nazi propaganda to republish in the press of neutral countries the resolution introduced in the United States Senate and broadsides bearing the names of high Government officials in order to substantiate their charges in the eyes of doubting neutrals. In Turkey the impression grows—and Spain it is being circulated—and in Palestine's hinterland and in North Africa the Moslem population will be easy believers in such charges. It might easily be a definite detriment to our war effort.[104]

No matter what the rescue advocates did, whether it was pressure for more liberal visa procedures, admission of refugee children from Vichy, or attempts to deal with the major problem of rescue rather than the minor refugee problem, Long inevitably found their efforts detrimental to the war effort or compromising the security of the United States. Somehow the attempt to change policy was subversive.

THE BERMUDA CONFERENCE

Once in Bermuda, the American delegation, concerned about the "unrealistic" suggestions of the rescue advocates, called a press conference in which the strategy of the delegation was revealed. The fastest route to rescue, it was maintained, was a victory in the war. Nothing would be considered by the Conference that would in the remotest way interfere with that goal.[105] It was implied that everything suggested by the rescue advocates would have this effect. By casting suspicion on suggestions for a more active rescue program the Depart-

ment initiated a new angle to the highly successful security gambit.
Now the rescue advocates' commitment to winning the war was held
up to doubt. To question the slogan "rescue through victory," in the
words of Harold W. Dodds, "would not only be foolish, it would be
criminal." [106] In the same vein, Borden Reams, Long's hand-picked
secretary of the American delegation, attacked the proposal for establishing a new rescue agency, negotiating with Berlin through neutral
intermediaries, and sending relief supplies into the camps as either
being "not honest or foolish." [107] When George Backer, president of
the American ORT, and member of the Executive Committee of the
Refugee Economic Corporation, warned the delegates that "at least
125,000 people have to be gotten out of Eastern Europe if this conference is to yield results," Senator Lucas dismissed the warning because it "would entangle the United Nations in commitments which
could only be fulfilled at the expense of the war effort." [108] As it
developed, the Conference's principle appeared to be to reject virtually every proposal made by the rescue organizations. Yet the public
clamor in both Britain and the United States made it clear that the
delegates could not simply return home empty-handed. Despite the
rigid ground rules laid down by Long, the delegates became involved
in a discussion of the forbidden rescue schemes.

The breakthrough was inadvertently created by Sol Bloom, whose
behavior at the Conference reflected his discomfort at being labeled
the Administration's lackey by certain sections of the Jewish community. Bloom had associated himself with the Vaad Hahatzala, which
became the principal rescue committee of the Union of Orthodox
Rabbis and indirectly of the Orthodox community. Its claim to special
rescue priority often threatened the delicately balanced peace within
the Jewish community. Early in the Conference Bloom, doubtless
anxious to prove himself a staunch rescue advocate, brought to the
attention of the delegates a very personal rescue project which
involved bringing to the United States a group of rabbis who had
found refuge in the Soviet Union. Although compared to the situation
of most European Jews, the rabbis were relatively safe where they
were, their fate was a primary concern of Rabbi Kalmanowitz's
group and therefore of Sol Bloom.[109] But soon Bloom broadened his
scope by suggesting that negotiations with Berlin, through a neutral
intermediary, might, after all, not be so far-fetched. Dodds im-

mediately reminded Bloom that there was no place to put them, whereupon Bloom suggested that their exodus might be staggered for infiltration purposes. Dodds, exasperated, reminded the congressman that such a suggestion violated the delegation's instructions. He was then able to inform Long after reporting the conflict, "Bloom then began to recede from his former position." [110] Probably only token opposition was intended by Bloom.

But on the following day Bloom again mentioned the forbidden issue of Palestine. Dodds promptly reminded him that Palestine "was after all a British Government matter" and Bloom's initiative collapsed like a deflated balloon. He obediently replied, "All right, I understand." [111] Formerly an actor on the Yiddish stage, Bloom seemed content to go through the motions of the role of rescue advocate. Clearly Long had chosen well. Only when Bloom returned home was he made to understand the meaning of his play-acting.

In the long run Bloom's posturing made little difference. The British delegation was remarkably candid. Richard Law held back nothing when he argued against attempts at negotiation with Berlin. Law feared that such negotiations might succeed and that "would be relieving Hitler of an obligation to take care of these useless people." [112] This way the "useless people" made some contribution to the winning of the war for even the killing of millions required some expenditure of resources.

Both delegations were adamant in their refusal to consider any program to rescue Jews in occupied Europe. When George Backer, for example, mentioned the possibility of rescuing large numbers of children by accepting a long-standing Rumanian and Bulgarian offer to negotiate, he was informed that negotiations are simply not in the realm of possibility even if lives could be saved. [113] The final report of the Conference held out the hope that such negotiations might take place "some time in the future" but in the meantime the refurbished IGC, which had begun its inglorious career with dramatic negotiations in Berlin, would be confined to negotiating only with other Allied nations and neutrals. [114]

The delegates did not arrive at a decision about reviving the IGC without some conflict. Although the British delegation could agree heartily about ruling out any attempt to negotiate with Berlin, they were not convinced that a revival of the IGC would not agitate the rescue advocates rather than calm them. They reminded the American delegation that the IGC had, in fact, depended for financing and information on the private organizations, who could now easily refuse to assume this obligation. Moreover, the mandate and scope of the IGC, which was too narrow in 1939, was even less suitable in 1943, and would need extensive revision. Its membership still reflected the prewar situation when the continental members were sovereign. France, now occupied by the Nazis, remained a member of the executive committee of the IGC as was the pro-Axis neutral, Argentina. The new governments in exile would not be able to make any substantial contributions to the upkeep of the organization, and the Latin-American nations, who formed the largest bloc, were being expressly discouraged by the State Department from accepting refugees because of the fear of spies among them. A replacement would have to be found for Sir Herbert Emerson, the director of the IGC, who would no longer be able to serve. Under such circumstances, argued the British, would it not be wiser to establish a new agency with a clean record? "World opinion," argued the British, "would be bitterly disappointed if all future action was relegated to the IGC." [115]

When Dodds informed the Department of continued British opposition to resurrecting the IGC, Long became furious and hurriedly cabled back that the British had already agreed to accept the agency, which was after all "the ready made logical and natural instrument" for the work to be done.[116] The British reluctantly conceded the point. The strategy of the American delegation then became clear. Every subsequent recommendation for a more active rescue policy which could not be disposed of by arguing that it was outside the purview of the Conference or would help the enemy, was referred to the IGC. So perfect was the holding action that at midpoint of the Conference it became apparent that with the circumscribed instructions and the assiduousness of the American blocking action there would be nothing to show for the week of discussion. It was at this point that the British delegation realized that, after having led rescue advocates to expect some new move, they would have nothing to show for the Conference except the idea of bringing the IGC back to life.

The absence of any specific new steps and the division between the two delegations was therefore not allowed to reach the news media.

In a bland press release on the second day of the Conference, Richard Law confidently proclaimed, "we are starting from the basis that every human life that can be saved is something to the good . . . we are getting into the heart of the problem now, after an analysis to decide what is practicable." [117] It was not revealed, of course, that the "analysis" had ruled out virtually all rescue alternatives and the Conference stood in danger of producing nothing.

If Long's desire to refurbish the IGC was shortsighted, it did offer a certain continuity to American rescue policy. Roosevelt had requested in October 1939, against the advice of the State Department, that the IGC be kept alive so that it might handle the long-range refugee problems which would follow the war. He hoped ultimately to combine it with the League Commission for Refugees and extricate his Administration from the problem. From the outset Britain and France had opposed the agency. The State Department, while seeming to comply with what it considered Roosevelt's whimsey, was, in practice, allowing the agency to die a natural death. After Earl Winterton's plan to hold a meeting in Paris in March 1940 had been given up as impractical, the agency had expired in all but name. Now three years later, Breckinridge Long reversed the Department's policy and seized upon the agency as a ready instrument to go through the motions of doing something about rescue without actually doing anything. Dodds informed his delegation of the centrality of the IGC plan. "The Bermuda Conference," he said, "will depend almost exclusively upon the degree of life and authority which can be injected into the Intergovernmental Committee and upon the speed with which the machinery of the Committee can be set in motion." [118] The revitalizing of the IGC, which might have been done without a conference, became at the insistence of the State Department the basis of a new rescue program.

The final report of the Conference recommended that the IGC be invited to broaden its scope, increase its membership and revise its mandate. It would now be able to negotiate with neutrals and allied states "to preserve, maintain and transport refugees," [119] but not to negotiate with the enemy via intermediaries. The revitalized committee could receive and disburse public and private funds. Clearly private support was still envisaged. France's position was considered vacant. The staff would be increased so that a management committee could be created within the executive committee to actually run the organization. There would also be a salaried vice-chairman, a director, and a secretary.[120]

At the Bermuda Conference a good deal of time was also spent on the question of whether a special refugee camp should be established in North Africa. Although this was a relatively minor issue, the delegates tackled it as though it were a crucial one. Doubtless they came to view it as a substitute for confronting the more vital twelve steps suggested by the rescue advocates.

The plan was to relieve Spain and perhaps some other nations of their refugee population, thus converting these countries into conduits which might siphon refugees out of Europe. The idea was first suggested by the Zionist organizations, who hoped that the ultimate goal of these refugees would be Palestine. Predictably, London was reluctant to accept such a proposal.[121] The British therefore came to Bermuda armed with an alternate scheme of creating a refugee camp in Cyrenaica in the newly won territory of Lybia.

The idea was not accepted with enthusiasm. George Backer, spokesman for the private agencies at Bermuda, pointed out the difficulties of establishing a camp in such an inhospitable area and suggested that a Cuban site would be more suitable.[122] Sol Bloom opposed the idea because it smacked too much of another concentration camp.[123] But the principal opposition came from the State Department, which showed a high sensitivity to concentrating a largely Jewish group among Moslems.

The Bermuda delegates [Long wrote in his diary] are sending us some difficult questions to answer. I worked late this evening with Dunn, Atherton, Murray and Brandt outlining our reply to the use of North African territory for an internment camp for German, Czech, and stateless Jews now in Spain. To put them in Moslem countries raises political questions which immediately assume a paramount military importance—considering that of the population of 18 million behind our lines 14 million are Mohammedans. The whole Mohammedan world is tending to flare up at the indications that the Allied forces are trying to locate Jewish people under their protection in Moslem territory. . . . Altogether it is a bad tendency.[124]

The concern for Moslem sensibilities seemed strange coming from the State Department rather than the Foreign Office, which had based its Middle East policy on it. That did not prevent Roosevelt from reiterating Long's apprehension when Hull inquired about the possibility of such a camp in North Africa. Roosevelt agreed to the camp but stressed that it should not be permanent and that all authorities should first approve it.[125] But the American delegation was first instructed to discourage the camp idea. When the British proved adamant a compromise was worked out. There would be a camp but it would be administered by the IGC.[126] Even then Hull, in communicating the results to the President, spoke deprecatingly of "the unknown cost of moving an undetermined number of persons from an undisclosed place to an unknown destination, a scheme advocated by certain pressure groups is, of course, out of the question." [127]

The problem of refugees in Spain originated well before the Conference when Carlton J. Hayes, the American Ambassador to Spain, informed the Department of the terrible conditions in the camps and the lack of cooperation of the Spanish Ministry of Interior. Hayes, anxious to be rid of the refugees, overestimated the number of refugees in Spain and the urgency of the situation.[128] Hull discussed the problem of the Spanish refugees on January 5, confiding that there might be an opportunity to bring these refugees to Mexico.[129] Some money to relieve the conditions which Hayes described in his dispatches was made available from the President's emergency fund but a suggestion that the refugees be redistributed to Palestine and Jamaica was rejected by London.[130]

Now with the Bermuda agreement, which entailed the sharing of the cost of transportation but American responsibility for the cost of running the camp, Long was forced to go ahead with the preparations for the camp. General Henri Giraud was approached through Robert Murphy and the Joint Chiefs of Staff were petitioned for consent. But by June Long was backing out of the agreement. "The British have misunderstood us," he wrote in his diary, "and have got firmly fixed in their minds that we had agreed to a considerable refugee camp in North Africa which we would build and maintain. It seems hard to correct the impression, and I am unable to ascertain the origin of their understanding." [131] Long, exasperated with "impractical" notions, could muster little enthusiasm for any of the recommendations of the Bermuda Conference or for that matter any step to help rescue the victims of the Holocaust. "The truth of the whole thing" wrote Long, "is that there is no authority in this

Government that can make commitments to take refugees in groups and that there are no funds out of which the expenses of refugees could be paid for safe keeping in other localities." [132] After incredibly complex negotiations, Camp Marshall Lyantey was eventually established and refugees were found to fill it up.

Another excuse used by the State Department to avoid movement on the rescue issue was the shipping shortage. So persuasive was Avra Warren, former chief of the Department's Visa Division, in detailing the shortage, that the ingenuous Bloom inquired why the shortage had not been given more publicity. [133] In that way the meager results of the Conference could be rationalized. But George Backer's equally persuasive examination of the shipping situation before the American delegation cast some doubt on the existence of a shipping problem. Backer, for example, reminded the delegates, who had probably never heard of it, that the Rumanian government had actually offered to lease two of her own vessels to carry Rumanian Jews to Palestine. [134] Bucharest was even willing to arrange safe passage. Private agencies, Backer explained to the uninformed delegates, had been in the business of leasing ships since the beginning of the crisis. Backer might have cited the illegal Zionist rescue operation, Aliyah Beth, which had been able to find skippers and ships to smuggle Jews into Palestine. Moreover, what of the empty cargo vessels making their way back to American ports? Why could not these ships fill their holds with refugees on the return trip? Backer's comments, which are preserved in Long's papers, were among the most penetrating critiques of State Department action on rescue. He uncovered the fact that the shipping dilemma, cited as a cause for inaction since 1940, was at least to some degree part of rationale devised by the Department to prevent a more active rescue policy.

One of the most interesting episodes of the Conference was Backer's report to the American delegation of the little known facts behind the Latin-American refugee block. Backer carefully explained how the State Department itself, because of its inordinate fear of spies, was behind Latin America's refusal to accept refugees. Congressman Bloom was nonplussed. The British, early in the Conference, had raised the issue of Latin America. A spokesman for the British delegation stated that he viewed the closing of the Western Hemisphere as the "initial failure of the conference." [135] The British delegation requested that the State Department change the policy. Avra Warren, who responded for the American delegation, fell back on the security gambit. Under ordinary circumstances this would have been enough to silence all opposition, but George Backer possessed an interesting bit of information which he revealed to the delegates. He pointed out that the "British [were] in a somewhat more dangerous position and yet the logic of their security [did] not drive them to a point where they [were] one hundred percent exclusive." [136] Bloom, whose career in the theater may have given him a sixth sense about a good retort, immediately chimed in, "I argued practically the same as Mr. Backer." [137] But when Senator Lucas proposed a resolution that the State Department review its refugee policy in the case of Latin America with a view toward lifting the security ban, Backer reneged. He did not want to do away with the security precaution but rather to make them more realistic and human. He maintained that Cuba and other Latin-American republics were anxious to resume "the profitable business of rescuing refugees." [138] Backer's reservation was based on good reason. Like so many people involved in the rescue effort, he must have realized that to confront the security gambit head-on would be to invite disaster. It would allow Long to picture the entire rescue effort as part of a conspiracy against a quick American victory.

But Backer did succeed in presenting the case for a more active rescue effort. He was the only person in Bermuda who dared remind the delegates that the alternative to rescue was annihilation, and that far from being unrealistic, the suggestion made by the Jewish community, while "born of despair," were the only way to achieve rescue. He suggested that the Conference at least urge the Vatican to rescue the children. "This step," he implored the delegates, "must be taken and that in the refusal which may come to you from them— it is history which must bring the account." [139] They were prophetic words.

When Senator Lucas raised the British point that there was simply no place to settle large numbers of Jews should that become possible, Backer replied that "if 100,000 Germans would offer to surrender we would find some way to get them out." [140] The point was well taken since the United States had taken in thousands of POW's, yet the proposal to bring in the victims under similar terms, heard as early as 1941, were rejected out of hand. There was, as Backer pointed out, no passionate concern for human life. An old rabbi who visited Representative Emanuel Celler to plead the cause of rescue made a similar observation: "If 6,000,000 cattle had been slaughtered," he observed, "there would have been more interest. A way would have been found. These are people . . . , people." [141]

In 1965 Richard Law, now Lord Coleraine, was asked to recall the events of Bermuda. "It was a conflict of self-justification, a facade for inaction. We said the results of the conference were confidential, but in fact there were no results that I can recall." [142] It was the same Richard Law who had referred to the refugees as "useless people" during the Conference.

Aware that to report that nothing was achieved would contribute to heightening tension, rather than lessening it, which was, after all, the reason for calling the Conference, Dodds suggested to Secretary Hull that both delegations announce that no report would be forthcoming "until delegates can consult their respective governments." [143] It was hoped that the press outcry would be forestalled until emotions cooled. Hull agreed and Long sent Howard K. Travers, chief of the Visa Division and one of his trusted underlings, to help with the tricky business of writing a report which had little to say.

The tactic of withholding the report boomeranged. The State Department miscalculated the degree of interest in the Conference and the agony of the rescue advocates who were willing to hope against hope that something had after all been achieved. Withholding the report actually seemed to whet their appetite for news. The solution for the Department was to try to cloak the report in military secrecy. Three weeks after the Conference a "preliminary" report was released which stated little except that the delegates were working "harmoniously" on a final report whose details could not be divulged "so long as a knowledge of the recommendations contained therein would be of aid or comfort to our enemies or might adversely affect the refugees." [144] This rather cynical tactic also boomeranged. The curiosity about what happened at Bermuda grew apace. The preliminary report that the delegates had considered only what was in the realm of the possible and would not interfere with the war effort, hinted at the bad news which was to come. [145]

In the five months between the end of the Conference and the release of the final report on November 19, 1943, public agitation was fed by the suspicion that a fraud was being perpetrated by the Department. In London the sole Jewish representative of the Polish government in exile, Szmul Zygielbojm, distressed by the suppression of the Warsaw ghetto uprising and the farce of the Bermuda Conference, committed suicide.

The one unforeseen result of the Bermuda Conference was that it set the stage for the removal of Breckinridge Long and his coterie from the levers that controlled rescue policy. Less than two months after the report was released virtually the entire rescue program advocated at the Madison Square Garden rally of March 1, 1943, became the policy of the Roosevelt Administration. It was about that rally that Long wrote excitedly in an interdepartmental referendum that the "hot headed masses" in their desire to save Jews "would take the burden and the curse off Hitler." [146]

8

The Changing of the Old Order:
A Bermuda Postscript

The Bermuda Conference marked the fifth year of frustration experienced by rescue advocates in their effort to redirect the Administration's rescue effort. The Conference was the last in a long series of dilatory tactics employed by the State Department in response to pressure to change rescue ground rules. In the second half of 1943, however, the details of the mass murder operation were well known and the idea of yet another simulation at rescue appeared a particularly cruel hoax. The Conference, which was intended as a public relations gesture, instead set off a series of events which finally wrested the rescue effort from the hands of the State Department.

"You can't imagine," Long fretfully wrote to Carlton J. Hayes, who shared his aversion to refugees, "the flood of correspondence that has poured in from all over the country." [1] Representative Celler, who had advance knowledge of the Bermuda proceedings through Department leaks, did not wait for the final report to denounce the Conference. In July he called it "a diplomatic mockery of compassionate sentiments and a betrayal of human interests and ideals." [2] In May he had spoken of it as another "bloomin' fiasco like the Evian Conference." [3] Armed with the same information, Stephen Wise requested a meeting with Roosevelt so that he might learn the reason for the "inexplicable absence of active measures to save those who can still be saved." [4] Rabbi Israel Goldstein, president of the Synagogue

208

Council of America, shrewdly surmised that "the job of the Bermuda Conference apparently was not to rescue victims of the Nazi terror but to rescue our State Department and the British Foreign Office from possible embarrassment." [5]

Had Stephen Wise been able to see the President to express his protest in person he might not have found a sympathetic ear. By mid-1943, the pressure of the war effort had pushed the question of refugees and rescue of Jews further into the background. Roosevelt was more than ever dependent on State Department briefing, which were supplied by Breckinridge Long and delivered by memorandum or in person by Hull. Hull in his memorandum to the President on the Bermuda Conference viewed with a jaundiced eye even the meager suggestions made by the delegates. In his justification he cited America's generosity in admitting refugees using the figure 580,000 as the number actually admitted between 1933 and 1943.[6] This figure was almost triple the number actually admitted but no one could know that it had been furnished to the White House until Breckinridge Long again cited it, under different circumstances, in November. The erroneous figure was fed several times to the White House during 1943 according to Breckinridge Long, who either deliberately or inadvertently made the initial miscalculation.[7] Roosevelt therefore received an exaggerated account of what had actually been done. Until the end of 1943 the ability of the Department to get the President's ear was a crucial advantage. Not until a countervailing source of information from within the Administration could be mobilized would rescue advocates be able to correct the impression created by the Department.

In Britain, where the furor created by the farcical Conference was greater than in the United States, Anthony Eden tried to head off the expected sharp questioning in Parliament by declaring at the outset that he, not wishing to raise false hopes, did not believe that rescue of more than a few was possible.[8] But Eleanor Rathbone challenged Eden's contention. An M.P., she headed the National Committee for Rescue from Nazi Terror and had written a pamphlet, *Rescue the Perishing*, in which she outlined a practical rescue program that Britain might follow.[9]

The despair in the Jewish community at the results of the Conference may be best illustrated by the rough handling reserved for Sol

Bloom, the sole Jewish member of American delegation. A particularly vitriolic attack, sponsored by the Bergson group, accused Bloom of allowing himself to be used as the State Department's "shabbas goy," a Yiddish expression referring to non-Jews retained to perform chores forbidden to Jews on the Sabbath.[10] The Zionists, who had protested Bloom's appointment to the delegation, joined the attack. At the Conference Bloom had been skilfully managed by Harold Dodds, who made allowances for Bloom's verbal gymnastics, knowing that Bloom would comply in the end with the wishes of the Department. Dodds extended the sympathy Bloom craved and assured him that he was aware of the difficulty of his position as an intermediary between the State Department and the Jewish community.[11] But once back in the United States, Bloom was vulnerable to attack and had to justify his behavior. In May he attempted to explain his position in an address before the convention of the Hebrew Immigrant Aid Society, but became so overwrought that he was barely able to plead that Jews withhold judgment until the results of the Bermuda Conference became known. In June, he had in fact joined in a plea to Long to avoid further embarrassment and publicise the results of the Conference.[12] Long did not agree. Bloom was able to point to his unsurpassed record of rescuing individuals as evidence of his good faith. He had in fact aided hundreds of refugees to enter the United States, including rabbis from the Soviet Union and Shanghai. In the S.S. *Quanza* case he had personally given affidavits for some of the refugees. His personal papers, housed in the Manuscript Division of the New York Public Library, contain dozens of touching thank-you letters from refugees.[13] Had he handled himself differently, the anger over his activities might have subsided. But he felt compelled to defend his reputation by defending the Conference. On May 24 he stated that "as a Jew" he was "perfectly happy" with the results of the Bermuda Conference.[14] In July he was again tearfully explaining his action to a group of journalists from the Yiddish press.[15] But Bloom remained under a cloud of suspicion; he was never considered a member of that group of legislators, Guy M. Gillette, Will Rogers, Jr., Emanuel Celler, and Samuel Dickstein, who pressed the rescue effort in Congress. In January 1944 a rumor spread through Bloom's congressional district that he disapproved the establishment of the long sought new rescue agency and had said that it would come into being "only over his dead body." [16] Bloom vigorously denied the story and succeeded as usual in being reelected.

THE BERGSON GROUP

The campaign to discredit the Bermuda Conference and establish new rescue ground rules was spearheaded by the Bergson group, which now called itself the Emergency Committee to Save the Jewish People of Europe. Disregarding the advice of the Joint Emergency Council, the rescue agency for the dominant national organizations, to withhold its campaign until the results were available, the militant group, perhaps sensing that the State Department had no intention of ever making the results public, began a campaign to smoke out the Department. It placed a full-page ad in the *New York Times:* "TO 5,000,000 JEWS IN THE NAZI DEATH TRAP BERMUDA WAS A CRUEL MOCKERY." [17] Calling for "action, not pity" the advertisement drew attention to the State Department's lack of will to embark on a genuine rescue program. It called for the enactment of a ten-point rescue program which bore some significant departures from the program drawn up for the Madison Square Garden rally. The publicity campaign received unexpected attention when Senators Lucas, Truman, and Chandler rose on the floor of the Senate to disassociate themselves from the ad and the use of the names of thirty-three senators without their authorization.

The opposition of the major national organizations did not deter the Emergency Committee, which proceeded to constitute itself a permanent organization at a well-staged conference held at the Hotel Commodore in New York between July 20 and 26, 1943. The new rescue program of the Emergency Committee, although it bore a surface resemblance to that of the Emergency Conference, gave far greater emphasis to the specific Jewish nature of the rescue problem and was more insistent that some kind of action be taken despite the war. Most significant was the omission of any reference to a Jewish national home in Palestine, something that had become *de rigueur* in any rescue program.[18] Congressman Will Rogers, Jr., explained the omission in his testimony before a congressional subcommittee: "This resolution was specifically drawn up to eliminate Palestine. Anytime you inject that into the refugee situation it reacts to the harm of the refugees." [19] It was this judgment, one which must have taken considerable courage for a Zionist, albeit revisionist, group to make, which in part was behind the hostility directed by Zionists against the new organization.

For Breckinridge Long, the Emergency Committee's "action not pity" campaign was particularly unnerving. He displayed more than the usual hysteria. He was certain that there was a connection between the committee's slogan and one used by Goebbels' propaganda ministry in 1935, while he was Ambassador in Rome. He formulated a confidential memorandum to his colleagues in the Department informing them of his suspicion that the rescue agencies were really in the employ of the Axis: "This idea [action not pity] has been a favorite capital item of the Gestapo and Axis propagandists who have created and instigated the creation of certain refugee organizations for their ulterior motives. . . . We must not let Hitler get away with it. We must not let the emotionalists who are misled by Hitler, mislead us. . . . We must prevent Hitler from using the refugees once more to break through our defenses and prolong the war. . . ." [20] There is no recorded response from Long's colleagues to his contention that rescue organizations were "created and instigated" by the Gestapo, nor is it known whether Long's grasp of reality was ever seriously questioned by the Department after the memorandum left his desk.

Long's memorandum went on to suggest that "in some indirect manner it may be desirable to explore the myth of the slogan 'action not pity' which has become the watchword of the pressure groups who are interested only in a particular class of refugees. . . . The Department might instigate a story, for instance in *Collier's* which would give a picture of the Department of State in the refugee movement." [21] Long was harking back to a tactic he had employed before, the planting of articles in the press to create or counteract a particular impression.

Meanwhile, the tactic of withholding the final report of the Bermuda Conference was causing some unforeseen complications. We have seen that Sol Bloom and Harold Dodds, who were busily parrying questions and counseling a "wait and see" policy, were under increasing pressure. In June Dodds informed Long of his unhappy situation: "You told me that the difficulty was across the water, but that doesn't obscure the fact that we shall soon be charged with misleading the public." [22]

Bloom had already faced such an accusation. But Long still hesitated; he needed more time to refurbish the IGC so that rescue agencies could be faced with a *fait accompli* and, it was hoped, abandon their agitation for a new rescue agency. It proved a difficult task.

The revival of the dormant organization without the support of London and the private rescue agencies was enough to give Long second thoughts.[23] His plea of helplessness stood in sharp contrast to the enthusiasm he had shown for the idea in February and March. Weeks were consumed in preparing the IGC for its new mission but at every turn Long ran into British opposition. The British insisted on a full-scale plenary session whereas Long, apprehensive about the publicity that might attend such a meeting, favored only a meeting of the executive committee. Winterton again raised the specter that had plagued the IGC in 1938: relations with the League High Commission for Refugees. Moreover Long encountered difficulty in attracting anyone to head a venture of such dubious value. Myron Taylor, former leader of the American delegation at the Evian Conference turned down the State Department's offer of the post, despite a personal appeal by Roosevelt. He took the occasion to remind Hull that "the Bermuda Conference was wholly ineffective, as I view it, and we knew it would be." [24] James G. McDonald, always anxious for public service, would nevertheless reject the offer of the vice-directorship. It was a symptom of the rejection of Long's plan to bring the IGC back to life by prominent men traditionally associated with the rescue effort. Because of the difficulty of finding a suitable American to head the IGC it became necessary for Lord Herbert Emerson to remain director, even though he carried other wartime duties and had candidly confessed his distaste for "eastern people" at the Washington Conference in October 1939. Almost immediately Emerson suggested that the private rescue organizations, who he knew had the zeal and the financial support for rescue, be welcomed to joint a technical subcommittee of the IGC. But Long adamantly opposed such a move.[25] The idea was to simulate action without allowing oneself to be pushed into a position that might hurt the war effort by persons who, according to Long, were not fully loyal to the United States. Significantly, after a particularly fruitless meeting of the IGC's executive committee, Long frantically cabled John Winant to remind the officials of the IGC to publicize the meeting.[26] Undoubtedly Long felt that such publicity would help counter-act the continued opposition of rescue advocates to the refurbishing of the IGC.

That meeting was held on August 4 and it was only a meeting of the executive committee because London soon discovered that there was so little enthusiasm for reconstituting the agency that it was virtually impossible to call together a full plenary session. Neverthe-less, plans were drawn up to officially revise the mandate and invite new members.[27] Meanwhile, the State Department had already referred the problem of government-financed relief shipments and the estab-lishment of a refugee camp in North Africa to the IGC. It appeared as if the State Department planned to use the IGC to rid itself of the rescue problem in much the same way that the Roosevelt Adminis-tration used the Department to absorb the pressure of the rescue advocates.

By November the IGC was finally fully constituted but continued to be plagued by the paradox that it was a rescue organization whose mandate specifically ruled out actual rescue. The committee's pro-gram consisted of giving relief to those already rescued. In the area of relief, however, it could not hope to compete with the newly organized United Nations Relief and Rehabilitation Administration (UNRRA); it lacked the financial resources and the far-flung appa-ratus. A network of branch offices was established but Washington and Ankara, two important rescue posts, were unaccountably left without an IGC office. The vagueness of the new IGC mandate was revealed by Long's untimely testimony, hastily denied by Emerson, that the IGC possessed authority to negotiate with the enemy. That unexpected contention further confused and weakened the agency. Any doubts that the IGC ought not to have been reconstituted were dissipated by the post-Bermuda developments.

PALESTINE, AMERICAN JEWRY, AND THE STATE DEPARTMENT

In May 1943 Breckinridge Long momentarily felt that he had over-come the opposition. The illusion was caused by a commendatory cable from a dissident rabbi praising the Department's rescue effort. Long hastened to inform Sir Ronald Campbell, the British chargé, of what he thought was a hopeful development.[28] But Long was soon rudely awakened. The Zionist influence in the Jewish community continued to grow rapidly throughout 1943 and that could only mean that rescue agitation, particularly rescue conceived through the medium of establishing a Jewish commonwealth in Palestine, would increase. The difficulty was compounded, in the case of the Zionist demand, by the Department's inability to maneuver lest it arouse Arab hostility.

The Department had, in fact, already received representations from Arab nations concerned with the increased Zionist pressure for a Jewish commonwealth in Palestine. In February 1943 the Egyptian Minister, Mahmoud Hassan Bey, called at the Department to warn of possible repercussions if Zionist agitation continued. He expressly ruled out the rescue operation from Rumania and Bulgaria by settlement in Palestine. Sumner Welles assured him that the likelihood of such refugees ever reaching Palestine was remote because of the shipping shortage.[29] The steady flow of resolutions from the state and federal legislatures alarmed Ibn Saud, monarch of Saudi Arabia, who also apprised the State Department of his concern.[30] Such representations traded on the continued need for good relations with the Arab nations.

The State Department proved far more sensitive than the Foreign Office to interning Jewish refugees in North Africa, a largely Moslem area. The Department was less concerned about the threat to the Black Sea rescue operation, by which small groups were filtered out of Rumania across the Black Sea through Turkey to Palestine, than it was about the prospect of renewed Jewish-Arab hostility, which might adversely affect the war effort. Moreover, there was always inherent in Zionist agitation in the United States the chance that it might actually succeed in creating a rift between Britain and the United States. There were some portents that even outside the Zionist-Arab polarization there existed other grounds for conflict with London in the Middle East. In Saudi Arabia, where the United States had opened a legation in 1942, the feeling that London was trying to squeeze out American oil interests led, in February 1943, to a move to funnel lend-lease aid directly to Jidda rather than indirectly subsidizing the cash grant which Britain gave annually to Saud. In February 1942 Long complained bitterly that Britain's policy was "to suck the United States dry" when he learned that lend-lease supplies included oil pipe for British development of Iranian oil in the postwar period. He felt that the United States should have been cut in on the oil deal.[31]

The Administration, while adhering to the line that the Middle East was a British sphere in which the United States should not intervene, nevertheless reserved the right to criticize and occasionally make diplomatic representations. In October 1942, at Roosevelt's behest, the Administration dispatched Colonel Harold B. Hoskins to the area to determine whether some *modus vivendi* between Arabs and Jews was realizable. The mission was undertaken against the advice of the British Foreign Office. But when Hoskins delivered his report it was not optimistic on the possibility of friendly cooperation between Arab and Jew. Instead it recommended putting the conflict in cold storage until a better moment arrived for solution. Until that time the Administration, advised Hoskins, should make it clear to both sides that no final decision regarding Palestine would be made until after the war and not without consultation with all parties concerned.[32] For rescue advocates, the most noteworthy section of the Hoskins report was his contention that Zionist insistence on linking the objective of a Jewish commonwealth with the objective of rescue of Europe's Jews was working to the detriment of both.[33] It was precisely the same point made by the Emergency Committee and would not pass unchallenged by Zionist elements.

Hoskins' advice, to freeze the Palestine problem until after the war, proved difficult to follow in view of the increasing Zionist influence among American Jews. In May 1943 the Jewish Agency for Palestine, a quasi-sovereign agency established by the Mandate, established an official mission in Washington, against the advice of the State Department. Meanwhile amidst alarming reports of growing Arab-Jewish tensions, Chaim Weizmann succeeded, with the help of Sumner Welles, in getting an appointment with Roosevelt.[34] Weizmann, fearing that the Palestine situation would simply be allowed to drift, pleaded eloquently for an immediate establishment of a Jewish state. If the Allies were firm in their resolve, he maintained, there would be no Arab uprising.[35] On his part, Roosevelt told Weizmann of plans that he and Churchill had discussed to try to bring Arabs and Jews together after the war. But to declare in favor of a Jewish state during the war was not in the realm of possibility. Roosevelt tried to detail some of the difficulties involved in the area, the continued fear of

Axis incursion in Iraq and the difficulty of finding responsible Arab leaders to deal with. Nevertheless, Roosevelt would attempt to arrange a meeting between Saud and the Zionist leader. Perhaps they could iron out the difficulties by themselves.[36] But Hoskins, who was dispatched to arrange the meeting, was unsuccessful in gaining approval from Saud, who viewed the Weizmann mission as a gambit to win Palestine for the Jews. Saud informed Hoskins that he had no authority to speak for Palestine, much less to deliver it to the Jews.[37] No further effort to break the Arab-Jewish log jam was attempted. At the Quadrant Conference, held in Quebec on August 22, 1943, Roosevelt and Churchill agreed to follow the Hoskins line and hold the Palestine question in abeyance until after the war. The State Department followed along as a matter of course.

For the Zionists the inability to achieve a diplomatic breakthrough in 1943 was a tragedy. It meant that Palestine, which they viewed as the most logical rescue haven, would after the March 1944 White Paper deadline no longer be available. Moreover, the Arab nations had become more vocal in their opposition to using Palestine as a haven. Saudi Arabia, for example, suggested a scheme which would divide the refugees proportionately among the United Nations.[38] In addition, Roosevelt seemed to be returning to the visionary resettlement schemes which had marked his thinking between 1939 and 1941. He spoke again of the possibility of resettlement in the trans-Andean section of Colombia and seemed as fascinated with it as he had been with the Orinoco River Valley in 1940.[39]

The dream of finding some resettlement haven outside Palestine had, in fact, been largely abandoned in 1943. Palestine had by default become, even among non-Zionists, an essential cog in any successful rescue operation. The immediate goal for all involved in the rescue effort was to prevent the White Paper from becoming effective. The Jewish commonwealth goal, while still important, was linked to the campaign to have the White Paper revoked so that the Black Sea rescue route might remain open. In 1943 the campaign was at least partly successful when the Foreign Office informed the State Department, in confidence, that Jews who reach Turkey would be granted refuge in the Middle East provided they could pass a security check.[40] In the absence of Hull, Adolf A. Berle, Jr., hastened to reply that "such action would be of great assistance. . . ."[41] In addition, London made known its willingness to make 34,000 unused Palestine visas available after the White Paper went into effect. These concessions led Breckinridge Long, who had born the brunt of the criticism, to believe that the White Paper issue, the main cause for Zionist and general agitation, was really a "dead letter." [42] He was to be disappointed. The rescue issue, now strongly influenced by the activities of the Emergency Committee, had a life independent of Zionist goals and for Zionists too, the goal of a national home existed above and beyond the immediate issue of rescue.

If sheer will power could have unified American Jewry, then surely the Zionists would have been rewarded in 1943. But despite their commanding position, other Jewish organizations refused to accept Zionist leadership. Every effort to impose such unity failed. The American Jewish Conference, which met between August 29 and September 2, represented a last-ditch effort to achieve unity in 1943. The Conference grew out of an earlier initiative taken by the middle-of-the-road B'nai B'rith and had already produced a nominal unity on the rescue front by founding a new organization, the Joint Emergency Committee for European Jewish Affairs. The agenda of the Conference, however, gave a higher priority to "problems relating to the right and status of Jews in the post-war world," than the pressing rescue issue.[43] A forceful reminder by Stephen Wise corrected the situation.

Some 500 delegates representing 171,000 voting members of sixty-five Jewish nationwide organizations met at the Hotel Commodore in New York. Little had occurred between May 1943, when the Pittsburgh Conference was held, and August, to create a new basis for unity. Although those delegates favoring the Zionist position were in the majority there was no way to bring non-Zionist organizations into line. They were simply unwilling to vanish at Zionist behest and the Zionists seemed unable to broaden their platform so that all interests could live harmoniously in one coalition. Instead there occurred the now customary endless debates which seemed to be motivated more by personal rancor than by genuine issues. One British observer reminded American Jews that "ideological squabbles between Zionists and anti-Zionists . . . seem strangely lacking in a sense of realism and responsibility." [44] An American observer cautioned that "it is not necessary to wait for a situation like the one in which the Jews of

Warsaw found themselves before you learn to cooperate, to compromise, to form a united front for the common good." [45] Such warnings went unheeded as the organization continued to dissipate its energy in internecine conflict.

The disunity in American Jewry went beyond an immature leadership, however, and was not easily resolved because deeply felt principles were involved. For the Zionist-oriented American Jewish Congress, locked into the idea of the superiority of representative democracy, it was virtually impossible to abandon the idea of Jewish "peoplehood." Clearly the majority of American Jews leaned toward the Zionist position. For Zionists to abandon the leadership to which their numbers entitled them would have been, they felt, tantamount to betrayal. The American Jewish Congress thought in terms of an organized community in which the majority ruled, but other organizations like the American Jewish Committee, an elitist group which shunned mass membership, did not feel bound by such rules. Once they felt that American Jewry had granted them a mandate, Zionist-oriented organizations felt even less need to entertain rescue resolutions which did not include the Jewish commonwealth goal. The crisis was evidence of the basic correctness of their position. Had there been a national Jewish homeland, Zionists reasoned, the ordeal which Europe's Jews were going through need never have happened. For Zionists this was the basic lesson of the Holocaust and it compelled them to press strongly for a commonwealth resolution at the Conference. In 1943 most American Jews were inclined to concede the point and bothered little with the fine distinctions between the national home and commonwealth idea, presented by the non- or anti-Zionist organizations.

The leading non-Zionist organization, the American Jewish Committee, based its cooperation with the Conference on the assumption that the organizational integrity of the several groups would be maintained. Nevertheless, it rested uneasily in the newly unified central organization and observed warily as the Zionists, obsessed with the rightness of their position and armed with what they thought was a popular mandate, pressed the organizations to follow the Zionist lead. Judge Joseph Proskauer, the new leader of the American Jewish Committee, suggested to the delegates that diversity had always been the hallmark of the Jewish community. A program should be worked out to which all groups might adhere without losing their organizational integrity. "I suggest, my brethren, that the method should be in the first instance that we emphasize not our differences but our agreements," he declared in his opening address.[46] It was a good start but it did not deter the struggle over the commonwealth resolution from breaking out into the open. It proved to be the rock on which the conference foundered.

By August of 1943 two rescue programs had been generated by the Jewish community. They were alike in most respects, but the first, that of the Emergency Committee to Save the Jews of Europe, advocated the separation of the Palestine commonwealth idea from rescue question. The second, introduced by the American Jewish Conference, advocated rescue through the establishment of a Palestine commonwealth. Jews would face trying times before the divisions could be bridged and the operation to rescue the surviving Jews of Europe given its rightful priority.

Rabbi Stephen Wise and Henry Monsky, president of B'nai B'rith, were elected cochairmen of the new central organization and an interim committee was organized to put the resolutions into operation. The interim committee in turn organized three commissions: one to implement the commonwealth resolution, a second to plan postwar community reconstruction, and a third to coordinate all rescue activity in the community.

Almost before the Conference had become operational it began to disintegrate. On October 24, objecting to the attempt to make the commonwealth resolution morally binding on all Jewish organizations and the bulldozing through of the American Jewish Congress' concept of a "unified American Israel," the American Jewish Committee withdrew from the Conference. In the process the Committee fragmented its own organization. Two of its leading members, David de Sola Pool and Judge Louis Leventhal, objected to an act which they considered isolated the Committee from the overwhelming majority of American Jewry. But the trend toward organizational separateness had begun and soon the Jewish Labor Committee, smouldering because the conference had ignored the second-front issue, also left.[47] A movement that began on a note of hope was by October a lost cause.

While the abortive attempt to create a united front in the Jewish community was under way, the maverick Emergency Committee to Save the Jewish People of Europe was able to focus exclusively on its rescue objective. It planned to involve itself directly in rescue but when it attempted to place an agent in Ankara, it came up against the same bureaucratic block that others had experienced in dealing with the State Department. In October the Emergency Committee succeeded in winning intercession by the Treasury Department to send Ira Hirschmann, a New York department store executive, to begin an independent rescue operation.[48] An attempt to bring their case directly to Roosevelt and Churchill, then meeting in Quebec, was less successful. Steve Early, Roosevelt's press secretary, advised the delegation that such contact would be impossible in Quebec and a better opportunity to see the leaders would present itself in Washington.[49] The Emergency Committee then turned to the newspapers to bring their message to Roosevelt and Churchill. It took the form of a dramatic "open letter" written by Pierre van Paasen in a full-page ad in the *New York Times*, which detailed in highly emotional terms, the urgency of an effective rescue program.[50]

In early October, Peter Bergson, the energetic leader of the Emergency Committee, sustained the momentum by leading a group of rabbis to see the President in Washington. But Roosevelt was not in Washington and rabbis did not have the opportunity they were promised. The mishap was seized upon by the rival organizations to vent their fury about the independent course the Emergency Committee was following. Too many delegations were visiting Washington and the result was chaos. "The spectacle is enough to make the angels weep," cried the *American Hebrew*, "many people cannot but come to the conclusion that some of the groups are exploiting the situation for reasons of their own."[51] Exposed to full public view was the continued disunity of the American community of Jews.

The Emergency Committee's keen ear for publicity and its growing success in attracting prominent names to its roster proved particularly disturbing to the major organizations. It scored a brilliant publicity *coup* by inviting the Swedish envoy to a rally to honor Sweden for its role in the successful effort to rescue the Jews of Denmark. The envoy, after cautiously checking with the State De-

partment, attended the Conference on November 1.[52] Publicized by
a full-page ad in the *New York Times* entitled IT CAN BE DONE,
the rally drew large crowds and featured an address by Leon Hender-
son, Roosevelt's economic advisor and former member of the Securities and Exchange Commission, which roundly condemned the
Allies for moral cowardice and specifically charged Roosevelt and
Churchill with not doing enough.[53]

Meanwhile the Emergency Committee's unabated pressure on the
State Department caused renewed anxiety for Breckinridge Long. In
October he composed an intradepartmental memorandum warning
that "since Bermuda a number of new organizations have come into
being which are urging extreme measures which were rejected at
Bermuda." [54] They were of course rejected by Long well before
Bermuda, but the memorandum was a subtle confirmation that Long's
hope of stilling agitation had actually succeeded in calling to the
fore new elements in the Jewish community which were nowhere
bound by "proper decorum." Long soon acquired a healthy respect
for the power of the new group, especially its success in organizing
a group of articulate congressmen to press its cause. When the Emergency Committee was forced to consult Long regarding the placing
of their agent in Ankara, he took the opportunity to remind the
group that its newspaper broadsides "made it very difficult for the
Department and injured the cause for which they professed to have
so much at heart." [55] The group, which included Peter Bergson and
Henry Pringle, were well aware of Long's activities, and paid scarce
attention to Long's admonitions about what would help the cause of
rescue. When the Emergency Committee's suggestions came across
Long's desk, he naturally rejected them out of hand, especially the
demand for a new government rescue commission. "That," Long
explained, "would be an unwarranted duplication of effort of the
Intergovernmental Committee." [56] Nor would he reveal to the group
what precisely the Department was doing to speed rescue. That was
a military secret, as we have seen. But Long seriously underestimated
the determination of the Emergency Committee. The request was
taken over Long's head to Edward Stettinius, the new Undersecretary, and in Congress the Committee was planning an action that
would prove especially threatening to Long.[57]

THE NEW RESCUE INITIATIVE IN CONGRESS

On November 9, the fifth anniversary of *Krystallnacht*, Representatives Will Rogers, Jr., and Joseph B. Baldwin and Senator Guy M. Gillette introduced identical resolutions in the House and Senate. It was the same resolution which had been rejected by Breckinridge Long and it read:

Resolved, that the House of Representatives (Senate) recommends and urges the creation by the President of a commission of diplomatic, economic and military experts to formulate and effectuate a plan of action to save the surviving Jewish people of Europe from extinction at the hands of Nazi Germany.[58]

The resolution represented a direct confrontation with the State Department and specifically Breckinridge Long, who was committed to the refurbishing of the IGC. He prepared for the onslaught by informing London of his intention to make the "Final Report" of the Bermuda Conference public. Without waiting for a reply he did so on November 10, the day after the resolution was introduced in Congress. Apparently Long was obtuse enough to believe that the release of the meager recommendations would help his cause but the opposite was the case. The new conflict coincided with a shuffle in Department's top echelon personnel caused by the precipitous resignation of Sumner Welles. The resignation raised Long's hopes of attaining the Undersecretaryship. From such a vantage point he would be able to make short shrift of the rescue resolution and the numerous additional "enemies" who had been plaguing him. The appointment of Edward Stettinius to Welles' position on September 25 put an end to such hopes and marked a downturn in his fortunes. On September 13, the Visa Division was transferred to the Undersecretary's office. Long told Hull that he "had decided [he] had won all the battles and the war in the immigration fight, . . . and while [he] would not quit in a fight [he] felt that having won [he] would take this instant to be relieved of that work."[59] Long seemed tired. After his failure to win the Undersecretary's post he wrote in his diary that he was happy to be "rid of the executive details connected with supervision of the very active division." He was seeking "a field of work which will not carry with it the minutiae of executive supervision and direction."[60] Several times he complained

of inability to tolerate close work. Long seemed to be anxious to remove himself from the arena just when the rescue battle seemed to
be reaching a climax.

RESCUE ACTIVITY DURING POST-BERMUDA PERIOD

The quickened pace of rescue and relief activities already apparent
before the Bermuda Conference continued in the second half of
1943. The Department had a way of mauling these efforts so that
they amounted to little. A typical example is what happened to a
British suggestion made at the Quebec Conference. It was proposed
Emerson approach the neutrals to guarantee financial support for
refugees and promises of postwar repatriation in order to encourage
a more hospitable policy towards refugees.[61] The Department quickly
agreed, suggesting only, at the request of Ambassador Hayes in
Spain, that Spain be omitted from the project and that refugees be
removed forthwith. The Foreign Office was agreeable provided that
Ankara, the anchor point for the trickle of refugees entering Palestine,
also be left out. A procedure that might have considerably expanded
refugee havens in neutral nations was thus vitiated.

But in the case of rescue of over six thousand Jews from Denmark
in October 1943, the Department heeded the advice of Nahum Goldmann and Stephen Wise and encouraged the Swedish government to
accept the Danish Jews.[62] An early precedent for the work of Iver
Olsen, agent for the War Refugee Board, was established when at
the request of the IGC, the Department interceded with Sweden on
behalf of the rescue of children.[63]

The Department also renewed its pressure on the Vatican. Harold
Tittman made strong representations to the Holy See and the Badoglio
regime when Jews in the Italian-occupied portion of France suddenly
found themselves in great danger after the German take-over of Italy
in September 1943.[64]

The effort to pierce the Allied blockade to bring relief supplies
to the camps continued in the post-Bermuda period. Rescue advocates
were encouraged by the British precedent of sending such supplies to
Greece through Sweden. In the November hearings before a subcommittee of the Senate Committee on Foreign Relations on a resolution which looked towards extending relief to all starving people in
Europe, they were able to press for more action.[65] Dr. Howard

Kirschner, director of the International Committee for the Assistance of Child Refugees, urged Roosevelt "to refuse to take 'no' for an answer" from the British.[66] The Senate passed the resolution in February 1944 but before that time the State Department was beginning to show some flexibility on the matter of relief. We have seen that in September it consented to granting a license for special food shipments to the camp at Theresienstadt in Czechoslovakia. Even government financing, at least on a token basis, was approved. But after the refurbishing of the IGC Long's sudden benevolence came to an end. He referred the whole matter of relief shipments to the bankrupt, powerless agency. But Herbert Emerson informed him that the IGC had little experience in handling problems of such magnitude.[67] Next, Long revealed the projected government aid for the relief program in his testimony before the House Foreign Affairs Committee.[68] Immediately there was a charge from London that by making such a revelation and stating that there was Jewish money involved, Long was subtly trying to arouse opposition from the neutrals and Congress.[69] Long protested his innocence. He had been assured, at his insistence, that the testimony would be held in strictest confidence. Moreover, he felt he had a right to defend the Department by any means when it came under such bitter criticism.

The rescue opportunity in Rumania, too, continued to cling to life in the post-Bermuda period. Turkey remained a road block by insisting that for every Jew brought into Turkey one would have to leave so that the number of Jews in Turkey did not rise. Moreover, London's reluctance to issue Palestine certificates hampered the effort. The Department attempted to pressure Bucharest through Spain and Sweden to reaccept the surviving Jews in the Transnistria area.[70] Sweden was urged to intercede with the Rumanian authorities and to "leave no doubt as to the depth of the American feeling of revulsion to and abhorence of such disregard of the elemental laws of humanity . . . which the failure to stop the slaughter represents." [71] In mid-1944 the policy of protecting the Jews of Transnistria where they languished finally bore fruit.

Under continuing pressure, the State Department also moved to safeguard those Jews who clung to life by means of passports and visas from neutral nations. Until the final months of 1943 the possession of papers could make the difference between life and death.

Such papers would be passed from hand to hand after the death of the original owner. Through the efforts of Dr. Abraham Silberschein, head of the Relief Committee for Jewish War Victims who worked out of Geneva, hundreds of these life-saving documents were smuggled into Axis Europe. Sometimes the Gestapo itself trafficked in such papers.[72] In November 1943 the operation was placed in danger when the governments in exile began to acquire such papers for their own purposes with the result that their price rose to exorbitant levels and placed their continued usefulness in jeopardy. In December Berlin officials, who had honored such documents and interned their possessors in a special camp in Vittel, France, began to rescreen the documents. Apprehension for the safety of the Vittel inmates rose to a high pitch. Jacob Rosenheim, of the World Jewish Congress, "implored" the State Department to make inquiries and to use its influence especially with the government of Paraguay, where many of the papers originated, to affirm their legitimacy.[73] The Department complied. It informed the Latin-American governments involved that although it did not approve the sale of unauthorized documents, the situation was so critical that the governments ought at least to delay cancelling false passports so that the holders might remain alive.[74] But the Department became skittish when rescue advocates and the WRB suggested that the Swiss government be used as intermediary to transmit to Berlin the government's concern for the continued welfare of the internees at Vittel. Enough pressure had already been placed on the Swiss government and it was unseemly for the United States to be involved with the protection of people who held fraudulent documents.[75] After considerable pressure by the War Refugee Board the Department finally forwarded a toned-down request to the Swiss government in April 1944.[76] By that time 240 Vittel Jews had already been earmarked for Auschwitz. Only two were ever heard from again. In May, as suddenly as it had begun, the Nazi authorities reversed themselves and began again to honor Latin-American documents.[77]

A softening in the Department's strict adherence to a "no ransom" policy was perceptible in the closing months of 1943. We have seen that the Rumanian ransom proposal caused the Department to establish such guidelines, but when the Vaad Hahatzala found an opportunity to ransom scores of rabbis in Czechoslovakia, they made a special plea to the State Department. Adolph A. Berle, Jr., then acting Secretary of State, approved a license for the transfer of funds. The "no ransom" policy, Berle maintained, was no longer suitable to the times.[78] As in the case of relief shipments and validation of fraudulent documents, it was not until mid-1944 that the new policy became fully effective.

The same delay marked efforts to get the Office of War Information to modify its policy of silence on the Final Solution. That policy was based on the assumption that broadcasts informing the people of occupied Europe of what was really happening to the deported Jews would strike such terror into the hearts of people living under the Nazi yoke that the task for the Nazi occupation would actually be facilitated. Rescue advocates repeatedly pointed out that even in theory such thinking was not logical since the Nazi authorities, rather than painstakingly camouflaging their liquidation program, would have given it wide publicity in order to create submissiveness among the occupied peoples. The irony of the situation was not lost on the Emergency Committee and the World Jewish Congress. Both pointed out repeatedly that the OWI, by its silence, had virtually become an adjunct to Goebbels' propaganda machine whose goal was to conceal the operation of the Final Solution.[79] Finally, in September 1943 the OWI complied with the urgent requests of the private rescue agencies to utilize psychological warfare techniques, such as encouraging local populations to conceal the victims facing deportation by promises of reward and punishment. Thereafter, the OWI increased the time devoted to broadcasting carefully authenticated information on the systematic slaughter of the Jews. The effects were unexpected. In October 1943 and again in July 1944, the Reich Propaganda Ministry felt compelled to counter the OWI broadcasts by disseminating cover stories to explain the virtual disappearance of the Jews. "The Jews have been incorporated in the European production system," read one statement, "in accordance with their professional training." That could mean anything from the organization of Jewish slave labor in certain camps to the use of the bones of the Jewish dead to fertilize the fields. The episode is interesting because Goebbels' contingency plan to counteract charges of atrocities was to publish a spate of atrocity stories in the captive European press.[80] By the end of 1943 this was apparently no longer felt to be sufficient.

As with the policy of relief shipments and the use of fraudulent documents, the Administration was painfully slow in accepting change. The use of psychological warfare against the perpetrators of the Final Solution was not fully developed until 1944. Then John Pehle of the War Refugee Board developed an entire new rescue strategy. In May 1943, for example, the American Jewish Congress suggested that the best way to bring across the idea that criminals would be held accountable would be to begin some war crimes trials immediately. Such a procedure, it was pointed out, would go far in avoiding the recurrence of the "Leipzig Comedy," the name tagged on to the farcical attempt to try Germans accused of war crimes after World War I.[81] It was hoped that such a trial, employing the rules of evidence and protection of the defendants would help open up a dialogue on what was really happening in Europe, as well as seeing that justice was done. Moreover the rescue opportunities that had developed in Rumania and Bulgaria were, rescue advocates believed, related to the fear of retribution, especially bombing. Demonstrations in Sofia had led to delay by the Bulgarian authorities in the deportation procedure, which saved, for the moment at least, as many as fifty thousand Jews. The same could be said for the Finnish authorities, where a healthy respect for the United States played a significant role in protecting its few thousand Jews.[82]

In exerting pressure on the Administration to broadcast statements of retribution, Jewish rescue advocates found themselves in strange company, the Polish government in exile. Because the fear of escalating the terror remained uppermost in the minds of Allied leaders a Polish request for direct reprisals, such as bombing, was rejected at the Quebec Conference. But continued pressure by the governments in exile and the rescue advocates did convince the British that a statement of retribution might have some effect. The British delegation to the Moscow Conference recommended on October 18, 1943, a joint declaration of war crimes by the three Allied Supreme Commanders. The declaration was issued on November 1, 1943, and given the widest circulation. It sought to minimize the possibility of Berlin's murdering those who had evidence by deemphasizing past atrocities and concentrating on the crimes that might still be committed.[83] For the Jews, however the Joint Declaration on War Crimes proved to be a bitter disappointment, for while the Declaration vowed to bring back war criminals "to the scene of their crimes" to be "judged on the spot by the peoples whom they have outraged," like the St. James Declaration of the government in exile issued in 1942, it neglected to mention crimes against Jews. The Emergency Committee quickly pointed to the dangers of such a "fatal oversight" and argued that it would suggest to Nazi authorities "that the United Nations are indifferent to Hitler's proclaimed intention to proceed with the extermination of the entire Jewish people of Europe." [84] The American Jewish Congress sounded a similar note by citing the fact that even "Cretan peasants" had deserved mention as victims, but not Jews. It reminded Roosevelt that "the Germans are half convinced that it is relatively safe to murder Jews" and expressed the accumulated bitterness regarding the Allies' lack of concern to save Jewish lives:

To almost every plea for rescuing the Jews of Europe by feeding them, by evacuating them, by obtaining recognition of their status as war prisoners—it may have been possible to oppose arguments of practical difficulties. But a warning by the United Nations that Jews cannot be killed with impunity lies wholly within the discretion of the Allies. There could have been no conceivable practical difficulty in taking this step—and with all the world's attention centered on Moscow its effects would have been tremendous.[85]

In March 1944, after considerable pressure by the War Refugee Board, the White House released a statement aimed at undoing the harm mentioned in the Jewish protest. It specifically cited crimes against Jews and urged the people living under German occupation as well as neutral nations to exert every effort to help the Jews.[86]

On December 7 the patience of rescue advocates was rewarded with the announcement that the United Nations War Crimes Commission, for which they had been waiting for over a year, would finally hold its first plenary session. Repeated delays had prevented Herbert Pell, who was appointed to the Commission in June 1943, from leaving for London. Even after his arrival in December he was handicapped by the Department's reluctance to confront head on the question of mass murder.[87] The Commission also was to prove a disappointment to those who favored vigorous action against war criminals.

In the second half of 1943, a keen observer might have noted a slight quickening of pace in the State Department's actions on the rescue front, especially in the area of relief shipments, ransom offers, and use of fraudulent documents. It was not a vigorous, enthusiastic passion to save lives but rather a resigned surrender to pressure or political expediency. The action taken was not only insufficient to save large numbers of lives but was taken so slowly that the opportunities themselves tended to vanish. Time and again legalism and sheer bureaucratic viscosity put a brake on the action. Henry Morgenthau, Jr., from his vantage point in the Treasury, observed that the Department "dealt with human lives at the same bureaucratic tempo and with the same lofty manner [it] might deal with a not very urgent trade negotiation." [88] The problem of saving lives had a low priority in the Department not only because of anti-Semitism or restrictionist sentiment or the personal pathology of Breckinridge Long, but also because the appraisal of rescue opportunities by Department officials was inevitably negative. The best that could be done was to win the war as quickly as possible. It was a comfortable rationale for inaction. There is no recorded suggestion for rescue from within the Department. This attitude of hopelessness, that everything that could be done was being done, was the tenor of Long's testimony before the House Foreign Affairs Committee hearings. The battle in November 1943 was really concerned with the challenge that rescue advocates had to make over the Department's appraisal of the possibilities of rescue. They had to make it because if the Department's appraisal were allowed to stand in 1944 there would again be a rationale for inaction.

THE RESCUE RESOLUTION HEARINGS

The hearings before the House Committee on Foreign Affairs on November 10, 11, and 26 were based on the rescue resolution sponsored by the Emergency Committee entitled "Resolutions Providing for the Establishment . . . of a Commission of Diplomatic, Economic and Military Experts to Formulate and Effectuate a Plan of Immediate Action Designed to Save the Surviving Jewish People of Europe from Extinction at the Hands of Nazi Germany." At the outset the hearings gave no clue that they would mark a high point in the rescue effort. When they terminated, an instrument for changing the State Department's ground rules had been found.

Among the earliest to testify was Dean Alfange, vice-chairman of the Emergency Committee, who dramatically mustered the growing evidence that the Administration's "good" intentions on the rescue front had been persistently sabotaged by the State Department. He reminded the committee that the "doors of escape are bolted not from within but from without by ourselves and our allies." [89] The statement was read into the record and a duplicate was forwarded to the State Department. Similar accusations were echoed by Mrs. John Gunther and New York's Mayor Fiorello H. La Guardia, the fate of whose sister in the Ravensbruck concentration camp would concern the War Refugee Board in 1944.

The testimony revealed a startling similarity in the way the Nazi authorities and the Jewish rescue advocates viewed the Administration's rescue policy. A statement from the *Voelkischer Beobachter*, the official organ of the Nazi party, questioned the sincerity of the Allied rescue policy in almost the same tone as did Dean Alfange: "Through many years the democracies would have had time to give their professed love for Jewry practical expression by opening their frontiers to these Jews. Yet while on the one hand shedding crocodile tears for the Jews one made sure—as we have seen from straying Jewish refugee boats—that the door remained locked to all except those with a full purse." [90]

On November 26 Breckinridge Long was called to testify. At his own insistence he was heard in executive session, since he maintained that the revelations he would make might compromise rescue operations then in progress. Later, when pressure on the Department mounted, he would abandon such precautions. He came to the hearings convinced that the resolution seeking to establish a new rescue commission was a direct attack on himself, conducted by vindictive Jewish agitators. The Department, he felt, had tried its utmost, within legal limits, to effect rescue. Circumstances beyond its control had limited its success but he was certain no one could do better. He was determined to defend his good name and the Department's record. But a series of disturbing questions by the cosponsor of the resolution, Representative Will Rogers, Jr., caught Long off guard.

Long's testimony began with the familiar ritual of enumerating the various steps the Department had taken to facilitate rescue and then came to the heart of his story, the particular pride he took in being able to bring the IGC back into action. The revamping of that agency, he told the Committee, was a considerable achievement in wartime when military considerations had to be kept uppermost in the Department's consideration. Undoubtedly Long hoped to impress on the Committee the idea that no new agency was needed and to create one would repudiate the magnificent effort the Department had thus far made. Carefully he explained how the plan to disinter the IGC came about: "We decided that the thing to do since we already had a number of governments party to this, was to revitalize, reform it, reinvigorate it, hitch up the horses to the old surrey and go down the road with it. That was the best instrument we had at hand." [91] Long was the proud owner of a racing stable and naturally fell into the use of such metaphors.

Congressman Rogers' questions revealed that the IGC did not even maintain an office in the United States. Rogers' crucial question was whether the new IGC mandate would give the agency authority to negotiate with Berlin via a neutral intermediary. The question was designed to bring out the difference between the commission proposed by the Emergency Committee and the IGC. Everyone knew what Long's response had to be, since he had been the Department official most adamant in ruling out such negotiations. Rescue advocates sitting on the committee could not help but be startled when Long, rather than going into the customary argument about the war ruling out such negotiations, insisted that the IGC had such powers. It was an amazing turn of events and on December 10 the testimony was made public and the rescue community was able to read Long's assertion that the IGC was "given plenary authority to do whatever they can within and without Germany and the occupied territories." They undoubtedly were aware that a new day for rescue was finally dawning. [92]

The evidence that Long had opposed such a position was overwhelming. He had been instrumental in ruling out such a proposition from the agenda of the Bermuda Conference. Moreover the preliminary report of the Conference and the final report, which had come into the hands of the rescue community barely two weeks prior to his testimony, specifically rejected such negotiations. At the Conference itself Dodds had characterized the idea as bordering on the criminal while Borden Reams had found the notion foolish. Had Long lost his touch or had he decided on the spot to soften Department policy? Long's continuing testimony soon presented additional evidence that the former was more nearly the case.

As Long continued to catalogue the Department's achievements in rescue he came to the admission of refugees. He announced to the committee that the number of refugees admitted since 1933 amounted to 580,000.[93] There was an immediate reaction from both sides. Senator Karl E. Mundt (Republican, South Dakota) was visibly taken aback at the size of the figure and Long hastened to assure him that "except for the generous gestures . . . made with visitors and transit visas during the awful period, the immigration laws remained intact."[94]

The figure Long had cited was the same one that the Department had used several times in 1943 in briefing Roosevelt on the refugee issue.[95] The Rescue Commission of the American Jewish Conference immediately began calculating and estimated that for the years cited by Long, July 1, 1933 to June 30, 1944, only 166,843 had been admitted through normal channels and an additional 43,889 were admitted on emergency visas. According to the Commission, the number amounted to about 5.9 percent of those who could have been admitted if one considered the entire quota rather than the effective one.[96] Rescue advocates soon found how he had tripled the figure of the number admitted. He had been using a figure which approximated the number of visas issued in that period. It bore only a remote relation to the number of refugees actually admitted and even less to the number of Jews admitted. Long appeared genuinely unaware of his miscalculation, and he went on to imply that the motivation for the Rescue Commission was generated by a handful of agitators and that not only was there no reason for special consideration since the Department was doing "every legitimate thing [it] could" but such a commission would establish a bad precedent.[97] "The Department of State has kept the door open. It has been carefully screened but the door is open and the demands for a wider opening cannot be justified for the time being because there just is not any transportation."[98] Long seemed unaware that the shipping shortage argument had been challenged at Bermuda by George Backer and the Emergency Committee had published a well documented refutation of it.[99]

Long was too shrewd to recommend to the Committee that the

resolution be voted down. When Congressman Luther Johnson deduced from Long's testimony that "a new commission . . . would simply be two committees trying to do one and the same thing," Long, whose sentiments the Congressman captured precisely, hinted that he would nevertheless not recommend that the resolution be rejected out of hand.[100] "I think it would be very dangerous to vote it down," he replied to a direct inquiry. "I think this is a very important moment in the history of the refugee movement, and I think the Jewish people are looking forward to this action and the decision of the Committee and I think if an entirely negative action were taken here it would be misconstrued and might react against the Jewish people under German control." [101] The Committee was hard pressed to determine what Long wanted. On the one hand, he had stated that creation of the rescue commission would repudiate the State Department's policy and be a needless duplication of the function of the IGC, on the other, he counseled that the resolution ought not to be clearly rejected. Long could not tell them candidly that what he wanted was for the Committee to act with some finesse, to do something to kill the resolution but at the same time avoid bringing down an avalanche of protest. The answer was to shelve the resolution, which is what the Committee did. Ironically, they were unaware that Long's testimony had given the idea of a new rescue commission a new lease on life.

The State Department, unaware that Long's testimony contained serious flaws, gave it the widest domestic and foreign circulation.[102] On December 10, steadily mounting pressure in the rescue community caused Long, who remained unaware of the errors and contradictions in the testimony, to make it public. Almost immediately there was protest that he was sabotaging the relief program by revealing that Jewish money was involved.[103] He remained confident that his testimony would help the Department's position on the rescue issue. The first inquiries regarding his contention that the IGC had power to negotiate with the Axis through neutral intermediaries did not visibly shake this confidence.

The matter of claiming such power for the IGC was especially puzzling. The evidence that Long was in error was overwhelming and it seems inconceivable that after going through so much trouble to make certain that such negotiations were out of the question he should now admit that they were possible. But he would not change his position and matters took their own course. On December 21 the Jewish Telegraphic Agency, the principal news medium of the Jewish community, cabled an inquiry regarding Long's contention to the IGC in London. It brought a response from Herbert Emerson that Long was "absolutely incorrect" the IGC had no such power.[104] Congressman Emanuel Celler, to whom Emerson's reply was given, gave it wide circulation in the press and among his fellow congressmen. It was a perfect example of State Department duplicity. By the time Celler's evidence became known to him, Long undoubtedly realized that he had made a serious error in not backing down when there was time. Now it was too late. Long decided to make his testimony true by simply revising the mandate of the IGC. Desperately he cabled London requesting a reversal of Emerson's interpretation of the new mandate. "Your early reply will be appreciated, as you will understand that a direct challenge to good faith cannot permit of delay in treatment." [105] But Emerson's reply, delivered through Ambassador Winant, was disappointing. He was not aware of Long's problem when he replied to the inquiry by the Jewish Telegraphic Agency. Again Long pressed Emerson for an "authoritative interpretation," one which would show that "the mandate does not preclude indirect of direct negotiations by the Committee with any Government when and wherever such negotiations became necessary and promises success for rescue of persecuted persons." [106] The new inquiry precipitated some confusion in London. Finally, Herbert Emerson, still not fathoming that Long probably was requesting a change in the new mandate to correspond with the testimony he had given before the Committee, consulted with Anthony Eden and Patrick Malin, the new American vice-director, regarding Long's peculiar behavior. All agreed that Long's interpretation had no source in the new IGC mandate and they so informed him.[107] In a separate reply Emerson went as far as to point out to Long that the final communique of the Bermuda Conference specifically limited the activities of the IGC to aiding those who had escaped to neutral nations.[108] Long was destined to remain on the defensive. His correspondence with Judge Joseph Proskauer, one of the few leaders of the Jewish community with whom he remained on fairly cordial terms, yielded little satisfaction when Long explained the case to him. "Those of us who have studied the burning question of attempting presently to save as many human lives as possible," wrote Proskauer, "have been impressed with the fact that the efficiency of the Intergovernmental Committee on Refugees has been retarded because of its lack of adequate power to deal with the problem." [109] That, of course, had been the gist of the criticism of the IGC from its inception.

Finally, after New Year's Long let the matter rest. The whole mess, he insisted, was due to Jewish agitation. In explaining why he made certain details of the classified operations public, he told the Foreign Office, "we are confronted here by a serious internal pressure based on humanitarian impulses and surrounded with doubts, uncertainty, and suspicion on the part of high officials and a large part of the public including groups naturally interested on account of race and religion." [110] Doubtless the high official to whom Long was referring was Henry Morgenthau, Jr., whose staff was busily compiling a dossier on the State Department's mismanagement of the rescue effort.

Strangely enough, Long continued to be convinced that he had made an "enormously favorable" impression on the Committee.[111] The request to make the testimony public came from Sol Bloom, who, like Long, may have felt that the testimony would relieve the pressure on both of them. It must have come as something of a shock to them when, on the release of the testimony on December 10, a wave of protest swept the Jewish community. The initial complaint focused on Long's vastly exaggerated figures on the number of refugees admitted. Congressman Celler, never one to mince words and informed of other errors in the testimony, accused Long of shedding "crocodile tears" when he in fact was least sympathetic of all the State Department officials on the refugee issue. "I attribute to him," announced Celler, "the tragic bottleneck in the granting of visas." [112] Soon there was published and widely circulated a devastating point-by-point refutation of Long's testimony by the rescue commission of the American Jewish Conference. The report found "extremely disturbing" Long's refusal to acknowledge that the problem of the rescue of Jews was distinct from the problem of political refugees who had already found some security in neutral countries. Long had hinted in his testimony that it was somehow unfair to focus special attention on Jewish refugees at the expense of other refugees. "It is difficult to understand," read the Conference report, "Mr. Long's repeated implication that specific aid to Jews excludes help to other people, or that there is no distinction between the problem of rescuing Jews from Hitler Europe and aiding refugees in general." [113] Jews interned in Nazi Europe were not, of course, refugees and these Jews were the primary concern. Moreover, Jewish agencies had given considerable financial support to nonsectarian agencies like the National Refugee Service and the PACPR. The latter organization, no longer very active, had also challenged Long's testimony. The liberal press naturally joined in the clamor. The newspaper *PM* featured an article, "Justice Department's Immigration Figures Knock Long's Testimony into a Cocked Hat," and the *Nation* borrowed Congressman Celler's phrase "crocodile tears" to expose what it considered Long's hypocrisy. [114]

Most amazing was Long's reaction to the difficulties his erroneous testimony had imposed on himself. He refused to acknowledge that an error had been made and remained so convinced that his testimony was a *tour de force* that he proudly forwarded a copy of it to his former underling, Avra Warren. He received plaudits from Warren: "I marvel at the accuracy of your memory for detail of the many complicated situations." [115] No irony was intended. When the errors were revealed he confided all manner of rationalizations to his diary:

I made a statement to the Foreign Affairs Committee which was subsequently printed and in the course of a long four-hour inquisition made several statements which were not accurate—for I spoke without notes, from a memory of four years, without preparation and on one day's notice. It is remarkable I did not make more inaccurate statements. But the radical press, always prone to attack me, and the Jewish press have turned their barrage against me and made life somewhat uncomfortable. . . . Anyhow I have written to Bloom to straighten it out. The Jewish agitation depends on attacking some individual. Otherwise they would have no publicity. So for the time being I am the bull's eye. . . .[116]

The admission that he had made errors did not come until five weeks after the testimony was given and about four weeks after his testimony had been effectually refuted.

AMERICAN JEWISH DISUNITY ON THE BRINK
OF A RESCUE BREAKTHROUGH

For the Jewish community, the hearings on the rescue resolution proved to be a mixed blessing. On the one hand, the congressional hearings themselves gave the rescue effort a boost, and Long's testimony was in a sense an unforeseen dividend. On the other hand, the resolution, because it originated with the Emergency Committee and contained no reference to a national Jewish homeland in Palestine, exacerbated the divisions within American Jewry.

The American Jewish Conference, which represented most of the main-line organizations, might have tolerated a stealing of its thunder by the Emergency Committee if the failure to mention the national homeland in Palestine had been an oversight but, as we have seen, it was deliberate. The Emergency Committee thought it had good reason for the omission. Many of its members were in fact Palestinian Jews, strongly committed to Zionism, albeit of a revisionist stamp. They were aware that there had grown in the Arab community an intense fear that the Jewish population of Palestine would eventually surpass that of the Arabs. Every time the Zionists mentioned a Jewish national home in Palestine Arab resistance stiffened. Why arouse Arab fears by public pronunciamientoes, reasoned the leadership of the Emergency Committee, if the same objective could be achieved without endangering the rescue operation? By muting the national home appeal the rescue momentum might actually be improved since there existed considerable sensitivity to Arab feelings in the Allied camp. The Emergency Committee reasoned that there was almost no chance that the Allies would affront Arab sensibilities during wartime. They gave rescue priority.

For Zionists, however, no such division could be made. It was simply inconceivable that the goal of rescue and that of the national homeland might work at cross purposes. Both were part and parcel of the same objective, redemption of the Jewish people. One hardly had meaning without the other. By the time Rabbi Stephen Wise testified at the hearings the issue between the two groups had been joined. Wise refused to endorse the resolution outright, for although there was no divergence on the idea of having a rescue commission, he felt that the resolution was "inadequate" because of its failure to mention the opening of Palestine to unlimited immigration.[117]

In the weeks after the hearings, the conflict between the two groups broke out in the open. The American Jewish Conference, now representing primarily pro-Zionist organizations, cited persistent rumors of financial irregularities and urged the Emergency Committee to open its books. It condemned the Committee as a front group for the

Irgun Z'wai Leumi, a right-wing Zionist terrorist group. The Committee, claimed the Conference, was presuming to speak for American Jewry when it had no mandate. Most important, the activities of the Emergency Committee "caused discord resulting frequently in a disservice to the cause they had assumed to represent." Their clever press agentry misled people of good faith. A brief containing these arguments was published in the *New York Times* and forwarded by the Conference to the State Department.[118]

The Emergency Committee could do little more than label the public display of strife within the Jewish community a "tragic error." [119] On the threshold of a breakthrough on the rescue front, internal strife had reached a new peak. When the breakthrough was made, it was by neither the Zionists nor the Emergency Committee. It originated from within the Administration, from someone only remotely affiliated with Jewish organizational life and strife. Henry Morgenthau, Jr., succeeded finally in convincing Roosevelt that a change was in order.

THE MORGENTHAU FILE

In 1938 Morgenthau had taken only a peripheral interest in the refugee problem. He declined the White House offer of a seat on the PACPR and did not generally involve himself in the visa procedure issue or the rescue of refugee children. But the Treasury Department's responsibility for issuing licenses under the Trading with the Enemy Act, which was held jointly with the State Department, gave some officials in Treasury an opportunity to observe the workings of the State Department on the relief and ransom problem which came to prominence in 1943. It was in this way that the Treasury's Assistant General Counsel, Josiah E. DuBois, Jr., and the head of the Treasury's Foreign Fund Control Division, John Pehle, were alerted to the transmission of a cable from Gerhart Riegner in Bern to Leland Harrison, requesting that he not forward information on the operation of the Final Solution. They also learned how the Department had procrastinated on an opportunity to rescue seventy thousand Rumanian Jews. It did not take much to convince Morgenthau, whose Department was considered a model of efficient management, that the State Department was incompetent. That was generally known in the Roosevelt Administration. But when it became clear in 1943 that it was not only incompetence, but a deliberate attempt to sabotage the rescue operation, Morgenthau, who had been alerted by his assistants, began to take an active interest in the rescue question. His anger knew no bounds when after months of effort he still could not gain cooperation of the State Department in getting the original cable which had been sent to Leland Harrison. When definitive proof came into his hands that there existed in the State Department a surreptitious attempt at concealment of the cable and deliberate delay on the Rumanian rescue case, Morgenthau acted. Members of his staff, Randolph Paul, the general counsel of the Treasury, Josiah DuBois, and John Pehle began to prepare a file on the State Department's sabotage. Morgenthau visited Hull on December 10 to face him with the facts uncovered by his assistants.

The visit was not a happy one. Morgenthau could not help but notice that Hull seemed poorly briefed on refugee matters. When Morgenthau asked to be introduced to the new director of the Visa Division, Howard K. Travers, and the political advisor on refugees, Breckinridge Long, both of whom were in the room, Hull was bewildered and did not appear to know who they were.[120]

Soon after his visit Morgenthau put the finishing touches on a highly confidential report prepared by his assistants, now entitled "Personal Report to the President." Originally titled "Report to the Secretary on the Acquiescence of this Government in the Murder of the Jews," Morgenthau probably thought the title too inflammatory and changed it.[121] The original title, however, gave a more accurate picture of its contents. It was, in fact, a devastating documentation of the State Department's sabotage of the rescue effort.

Morgenthau personally composed the preface of the report, indicating that the activity documented in the report had all the earmarks of a nasty political scandal. That implication was probably not lost on the politically minded Roosevelt as he leafed through the document. What he saw was a carefully documented account not only of "gross procrastination" as in the visa debacle, the delay in authorization of licenses to transmit funds, but firm evidence of deliberate attempts to block the flow of information concerning the Final Solution and outright misrepresentation, as in the case of Long's testimony on November 26. Little was said about Cordell Hull and Sumner Welles, who was no longer with the Department, was specifically exempted from the charges, but Breckinridge Long was accused of master-minding the affair and attempting to cover up the evidence. The Department of State, the report stated, was neither psychologically nor administratively suited to carry out an operation which required commitment and compassion to succeed:

The matter of rescuing the Jews from extermination is a trust too great to remain in the hands of men who are indifferent, callous and perhaps even hostile. The task is filled with difficulties. Only a fervent will to accomplish, backed by persistent and untiring effort, can succeed where time is so precious.[122]

On January 17, 1944, a Sunday, Morgenthau, accompanied by Pehle and DuBois, presented their case to the President.

Roosevelt was doubtless aware, after reading the Morgenthau file, that the State Department's usefulness in handling the potentially explosive rescue question was at an end. Political pressure to do something for the rescue of Jews appeared to have broadened its base and was no longer confined to Jews and their sympathizers. Even the inmates of Lewisburg Penitentiary had sent a petition urging the President "to lend [his] influence in an effort to save the starving innocent children of Europe." [123] A formidable new pressure group, headed by Supreme Court Justice Frank Murphy and including Wendell Willkie, Vice-President Henry A. Wallace, and other prominent names associated with the Administration, had been organized. Calling itself the National Committee Against Nazi Persecution and Extermination of the Jews, it hoped "to rally the full force of the public conscience" in order to gain "sustained and vigorous action by our government and United Nations to rescue those who may yet be saved." [124] There appeared to be a new mood in the Administration.

Nevertheless, the State Department defended itself. Roosevelt could hardly ignore Hull's charge that Morgenthau had always possessed a hungry eye for State Department business and that in the case of rescue policy he had a special "racial sensitivity." [125] But opposing voices reaching the President's ears were dominant. Among them was Eleanor Roosevelt, whose memory of the Department's sabotage of the effort to rescue five thousand children in 1939 and 1940 had not faded. Roosevelt, in fact, needed few reminders that the administration of the unwieldy State Department left much to be desired. His low opinion of the Department was well known. He frequently by-passed it and selected his own people for critical missions in the foreign policy area. An undated memorandum, probably written in 1942 or 1943, to his closest advisors promised a thorough housecleaning of the State Department at an opportune time, because there was "a lot of dead-wood in the top three grades, that should never have got there." [126] But in the case of rescue such "deadwood" proved to be an asset to Roosevelt, because the referral of the rescue issue to the Department meant that little would be accomplished. Roosevelt did not desire precipitous action since he was simply not prepared to risk a con-frontation with congressional restrictionists. By the time the separate issue of rescue came to the fore in late 1942, Roosevelt was preoccu-pied with the war and simply left it to the State Department. The Department thus served to keep Roosevelt's humanitarian image intact even among American Jews, while the already unpopular State De-partment simply became more tarnished. Not until the mood visibly changed in the second half of 1943 and the whipping-boy role of the State Department was no longer useful did Roosevelt contemplate a change in rescue ground rules. That event was signaled by Mor-genthau's devastating evidence of sabotage which might easily have spilled over to tarnish Roosevelt's own image. Morgenthau was given the authority to create the new rescue commission which the House Committee on Foreign Affairs, heeding the hints of Breckinridge Long, had failed to report out. Roosevelt suggested only that the Secretary of War, Henry L. Stimson, and the soon to be appointed Secretary of State, Edward R. Stettinius, be incuded in the decision-making body of the commission.

Overjoyed, Morgenthau and Pehle met with Stettinius, and Pehle again recounted the unhappy story. Stettinius, charged with the unenviable task of reorganizing the Department, was not surprised. Things promised to be different under the new management. Mean-while, Samuel Rosenman, Roosevelt's principal speech writer, was assigned the delicate task of clearing the new agency with the sensitive Hull. He found the Secretary surprisingly cooperative, offering even to send "Breck" along to help organize the new agency. Rosenman, somewhat nonplussed at Hull's ignorance of the controversy around Long, quickly informed him that "[he] didn't think that would be helpful." [127]

Hull expressed strong feelings of relief at finally extricating the Department from a situation that seemed to have no satisfactory resolution, but Long's reaction contained a note of self-righteousness. To Joseph Proskauer, who questioned some of his decisions he wrote: "In the security of the years to come, it may appear that the screening process was too rigorous." But no one could deny that "it avoided incalculable damage to the refugee cause." [128] He had caught the new prorescue mood in the Administration. In the long run his actions enhanced the opportunity for rescue. He wondered where along the line he had lost the confidence of the President and characteristically came to the conclusion that it was Harry Hopkins who had undermined him.[129] Men of Long's political persuasion credited Hopkins with diabolical influence on the President, but on the rescue question Hopkins was not involved and he probably did not know Long. The more likely source of such a conspiracy, if a conspiracy existed at all, was the Treasury. Morgenthau was fully aware of Long's activities.[130]

Long attributed the creation of the new agency almost entirely to the pressure of the Jewish community.

I think it a good move—for local political reasons—for there are 4 million Jews in New York and its environs who feel themselves related to the refugees and because of the persecution of the Jews, and who have been demanding special attention and treatment. This will encourage them to think the persecuted may be saved and possibly satisfy them—politically—but in my opinion the Board will not save any persecuted people I could not save under my recent and long suffering administration. . . .[131]

For Long the creation of the new commission was simply a political gesture to the Jewish community, who were the only ones interested in rescue. There is no acknowledgment that something more than "persecution" was involved. To the end, in spite of the evidence in the Department's hands that a scientifically planned mass murder operation was in progress, Long remained convinced that it was all Jewish propaganda. Nor did he change his feeling that rescue was simply not possible. In his final months at the levers of policy-making on the rescue question he reveals himself as a brutishly ignorant, stubborn, often pathological official, who aspired to high office but had not the inner security and the insight to change when change was necessary. The years of battle against phantom enemies had left him exhausted. "I have lost the desire for the details of frantic executive responsibility which I once enjoyed," he confessed.[132] He would have been gratified if some consultive position had been proffered but, despite Hull's support, none materialized.[133]

ESTABLISHING THE WAR REFUGEE BOARD

On January 22, 1944, Executive Order 9417 was issued by the White House. It established the new agency known as the War Refugee Board (WRB). The order set an entirely new tone to rescue pronouncements. The Administration announced its intention "to take all measures within its power to rescue the victims of enemy oppression who are in imminent danger of death and otherwise afford such victims all possible relief and assistance consistent with successful prosecution of the war." [134] The largely Jewish character of the rescue problem was forthrightly acknowledged by giving the board broad powers to specifically forestall "Nazi plans to exterminate all the Jews." [135]

Three days later the State Department, having caught the new spirit, displayed fresh vigor in implementing the order. Instructions were cabled to all the involved missions ordering that the highest priority be given to cooperation with the WRB. They were told to apprise the governments to which they were assigned of the new direction of American rescue policy and the strong commitment which the Roosevelt Administration now had for the rescue objective.[136] The Treasury Department, now unofficially in control of the new agency, sent a similar cable to its agents overseas. Some of them would soon double as agents of the WRB. The White House received 850,000 letters supporting the Administration's new initiative.[137]

Much depended on the man chosen to carry out the new policy. Even the strongest commitment by Roosevelt had become ineffective in 1938, when it was given to the officials of the State Department to implement. Congressman Emanuel Celler cautioned the President in his congratulatory letter that "much will depend upon the personnel that will direct the operation." He urged Roosevelt to select men who were attuned to hear "the soft sad music of humanity." [138] But finding such types during wartime was no small challenge. Ultimately, the leaders of the new agency were selected from the energetic team which Morgenthau had gathered around him in the Treasury Department. Morgenthau, however, shared Roosevelt's inclination to find a "big name" to be director of the agency and hit upon Wendell Willkie as ideally suited for the post. His name was stricken when Roosevelt's close political advisors felt that Willkie's recent world tour had given him too much personal publicity and political build-up. Isador Lubin, a Roosevelt advisor, recommended the unemployed former Undersecretary of State, Sumner Welles, but there was still too much scandal attached to his name.[139] Roosevelt inquired about the possibility of Thomas K. Finletter or Aubrey Williams for the position but informed Hull that he remained undecided about filling the position.[140] In the interim John Pehle, Jr., the energetic Assistant Secretary of the Treasury, was made temporary director. It was from his vantage as chief of the Treasury's Foreign Funds Control Division that Pehle first was able to observe the State Department's undermining of relief operations. Pehle was thirty-one when he joined the Treasury Department in 1940 after an outstanding record at Yale Law School. Together with Josiah DuBois, assistant to the Treasury Department's general counsel Randolph Paul, he helped draw up the brief detailing the State Department's record of inactivity and sabotage. It was Pehle who explained the Treasury's findings to Roosevelt and Stettinius and he became deeply involved in the rescue question. For rescue advocates a more propitious appointment could hardly be imagined. Indeed, within a few weeks it became apparent to all that he had taken such a strong hold of the director's job that it would no longer be necessary to attract a "big name." John Pehle, Jr., became permanent director.

The mandate of the new agency was extraordinary for in some respects it gave the director more power than a Cabinet officer. The WRB was charged with the development of plans and programs for rescue, transportation and maintenance and relief of the victims of enemy oppression. It had specific authority to establish temporary refugee havens and the right "to enlist the cooperation of foreign governments and obtain their participation in the execution of such plans and programs." [141] Moreover, the Departments of State, War, and Treasury, who shared decision-making power on the Board, were mandated "to execute at the request of the Board the plans and programs so developed." [142] In theory, the Board could commandeer the facilities of these Departments to get its job done. But in practice, dependence on the administrative apparatus of the War and State Department was a disadvantage since both departments had over a decade demonstrated hostility towards refugees. In practice, the Board was dependent on the good will of the Treasury Department, the one agency within the Roosevelt Administration that was friendly to the endeavor to rescue Jews.

Nevertheless, new rescue ground rules and a new priority for rescue were spelled out in the executive order. Much would depend on how well the agency would be able to carve a niche for itself. For example, close liaison with the White House was seemingly assured by the specific charge in the executive order that the director should report to the President "at frequent intervals concerning the steps taken for the rescue and relief of war refugees." [143] In practice, however, such contacts would continue to depend on Morgenthau's ability to keep Roosevelt interested. The executive order was necessarily vague on how the mandate should be implemented. That gave the Board a relatively free hand in fashioning unorthodox but effective new rescue tactics. Its operations eventually included leasing boats in Sweden to smuggle refugees out of the Balkans, financing Hechalutz (Zionist pioneer) cadres to smuggle refugees from Hungary to Slovakia, sponsoring Red Cross relief packages to camps and the use of psychological warfare techniques and diplomatic channels to encourage rescue activity. Agents like Ira Hirschmann were instructed to avoid red tape. He did.[144]

The actual operation of the WRB was kept deliberately small and flexible. The staff never exceeded thirty-five people, among whom specialists in refugee and rescue affairs figured prominently. Full use was made of the State Department's wire service and diplomatic pouch and coding and decoding operations. In all cases except one, Carlton Hayes, the American Ambassador to Spain, WRB agents could depend on close support from the diplomatic missions. This was especially true in Turkey, Sweden, and Switzerland. Without such support the fulfillment of the Board's mission would hardly have been possible.

The factor most inclined to make the power of the WRB more illusory than real was the lack of provision for funding the new agency. Roosevelt granted the agency $1,000,000 from his emergency fund, but thereafter the Board was to be financed by the private rescue agencies, primarily the AJJDC. Morgenthau experienced some difficulty in explaining this oversight to rescue advocates. In May 1944 the WRB received an additional $4,000,000, which it had to share with the IGC. It proved to be more than enough. When the agency ceased operations in 1945 it was able to give some of this money back.

With these modest beginnings, a group of devoted men armed with little more than will and compassion, began finally to fashion a human response to the Final Solution. We shall see that it did not nearly balance the scales. It was a small operation which came relatively late. But it did mark a sharp departure from the previous policy of indifference and inadvertent collusion with the Nazis.

It took six years to change the ground rules of the rescue operations. The activities of the WRB in Hungary during 1944 and 1945 present a distressing glimpse of what might have been had the two sides, those for life and those for death, been more evenly matched.

The War Refugee Board

John Pehle did not have long to wait for the mettle of his new agency to be tried. Early in 1944 the Jewish community of Hungary, formerly third largest in Europe, was finally placed on Berlin's schedule for liquidation. The WRB barely had time to establish itself before the crisis was upon it.

There would be no problem in devising rescue techniques and tactics. The private agencies had, over a period of years, fashioned a full arsenal of rescue weapons; now all they needed was official government sanction and financing so that they might scent out rescue opportunities. How to communicate the newly felt urgency to the neutrals, on whose cooperation much depended, proved a more difficult task. The rescue operation in Hungary, although by no means the only WRB rescue project in 1944, offers an opportunity to view the new agency at work.

THE SITUATION OF HUNGARIAN JEWRY IN 1944

Within the larger tragedy which was the destruction of European Jewry, the liquidation of the Hungarian Jewish community has a special place. Hungarian Jewry almost survived to witness the downfall of the architects of the Final Solution. Its destruction was undertaken after it was clear that the war was lost for Germany. Moreover, in the case of Hungarian Jewry's liquidation there was no longer any doubt that the Reich intended to wipe out the Jews. In Hungary the Final Solution operated within full view of world opinion.

The survival of Hungarian Jewry until the last moment is partly attributable to the peculiar proprietary interest which the Budapest regime maintained in "its" Jews. Between 1941 and 1944, Admiral Miklos Horthy, Regent of Hungary, jealously guarded Hungary's sovereign right to handle its "Jewish problem." Its position as a cobelligerent, rather than an occupied area, gave Hungary the legal leverage to thwart Berlin's plans.

The Jewish question is being solved least satisfactorily in Hungary [wrote Josef Goebbels in his diary on May 8, 1943] the Hungarian state is permeated with Jews, and the Fuehrer did not succeed during his talk with Horthy in convincing the latter of the necessity of more stringent measures. Horthy himself, of course, is badly tangled up with the Jews through his family, and will continue to resist every effort to tackle the Jewish problem aggressively.[1]

The tangles to which Goebbels made reference referred to Horthy's Jewish wife. Such matters were given much weight in Berlin. Indeed, there was an element of truth in Goebbels' contention. When Hungarian Jews residing in France were forced to wear the yellow star, Döme Sztójay, Hungary's Minister in Berlin, registered an official protest. Such actions did not mean that Hungary loved its Jews. When the Horthy regime imposed its version of the Nuremberg Laws in 1940 they were in some cases harsher than those of the Reich. At least one reason for the concern for Hungarian Jews in German-occupied areas was the feeling that Hungary was the "rightful heir" to Jewish property rather than Germany.[2] Nor was the protection of the Hungarian government extended to Jews in the newly acquired areas of post-Trianon Hungary. There thousands of Jews were unceremoniously pushed into Nazi-occupied eastern Poland where they perished. The Hungarian government had even requested Berlin's aid in deporting "foreign Jews who infiltrated or found refuge" in Hungary.[3]

As it became apparent that the war was lost, the existence of nearly a million Jews in the heart of Europe was a source of frustration to Berlin. "The greatest enemies of the Nazis, the targets of their deepest hatred," wrote Miklos Kállay, Prime Minister of Hungary, in discussing the reasons for the German occupation of Hungary on March 19, 1944, "were living unmolested in the very heart of the German sphere of power—a million strong. Was one little country, one man, to hinder the execution of their totalitarian plans?" [4] Döme Sztójay also observed the high priority given the Final Solution by the Nazi authorities from his vantage point in Berlin. "They mark out Jewry as a more dangerous and greater enemy than any other adversary." It was, he wrote to Kállay, "a matter of life and death for Germany." [5] Hungarian Jews had become for them the one "enemy" from which they might still wring a victory. Waiting at the Mauthausen concentration camp was Adolf Eichmann and his well-trained killers who would make certain that the ovens of Auschwitz were never lacking fresh "Hungarian salami," the term used by the guards and inmates of Auschwitz for the new victims. Nowhere were the deportations fiercer and more swiftly executed and with less concern for the sensibilities of world opinion.

To the well-oiled Nazi liquidation machinery there would for the first time be some counterbalance. There was the new vigor of the American rescue effort, still to be proved, to be sure, and the hope that other rescue components, the neutrals, the CIRC, the Vatican, and the people in occupied Europe, would follow the American lead. The back of Nazi power, moreover, seemed to be broken in 1944, and there existed in Rumania and Yugoslavia two fairly accessible escape routes.

Despite the good prognosis, however, these favorable new conditions had almost no effect in the first phase of the rescue effort. The speed with which Eichmann was able to establish the destruction apparatus far outpaced the ability of the rescue agencies to respond. The WRB was barely in its eighth week of existence when the position of Hungarian Jewry worsened. On March 17 Horthy was again summoned to Klessheim where Hitler, half crazed with anger, demanded dismissal of the Kállay government, which he abhorred for its recalcitrance on the Jewish question and which he knew to be anxious to make a separate peace with the Allies. By the time Horthy returned to Budapest on March 19, German troops were firmly in control of the capital, bringing with them the Eichmann *Sondereinzatskommando*. Döme Sztójay, the former Minister to Berlin, became the new premier.

Rumors of the impending change of fortune for Hungarian Jewry were carried as early as February 1944 by the Jewish Telegraph Agency. [6] Although they were denied by rescue agents in Istanbul, apprehension persisted. Almost immediately upon the news of the fall of the Kállay regime the World Jewish Congress urged Pehle to broadcast warnings to the Jewish community of Hungary to destroy all community lists, and avoid special registration and the wearing of the tell-tale yellow star.[7] The suggestion embodied a wisdom dearly learned in the Netherlands, Poland, and other areas. Such steps inevitably preceded actual concentration and deportation.

Despite such warnings, Eichmann was able to organize the Jewish Council, a cog in the liquidation procedure, in record-breaking time.

WRB STRATEGY

Amidst calls for help from Hungarian Jewry and anguished pleas for action at home, Pehle and his small staff were forced to devise a practical rescue strategy. The insurmountable reality was that the WRB lacked a physical presence on the scene. The call to neutral nations to enlarge their diplomatic missions in Budapest was at best a poor substitute for such a presence. As long as the Jews of Hungary remained in Berlin's physical control there could be little hope of mass rescue. Moreover, even if Hungarian Jewry could be physically extricated, the problem of where to resettle such a large group was no closer to solution in 1944 than in 1939, 1940, and 1941. The only hope, rescue advocates believed, was in encouraging Hungarians, especially the government bureaucracy, to disassociate itself from the Nazi plans to eliminate European Jewry. Without the cooperation of the local people and government agencies, concentration and deportation would become infinitely more difficult, perhaps impossible. "A program of this character," Pehle explained to Stettinius, "offers the best potentialities for saving hundreds of thousands of lives. The number we can save by changing attitudes far exceeds the number by evacuation."[8]

A psychological warfare campaign was designed to cajole Hungarian officialdom into noncooperation with the Final Solution. It was hoped that continued Allied victories in the field would give the warnings of retribution the ring of authenticity. The Jewish Agency was requested to prepare a list of all Hungarian officials cooperating with the Eichmann *Sondereinzatskommando*. Soon after the German occupation a series of warnings were transmitted to Budapest and other satellites informing them of the Administration's determination to rescue the Jews of Hungary. It cautioned that the meaning of the ghettoization procedure, then taking place all over Hungary, was well understood as a preliminary to deportation. A solemn warning was included: "Any continuation by these governments of the execution of these policies of Hitlerite persecution is viewed with great seriousness by this Government and will be kept in mind." [9] When no visible effect was noted in three weeks and concentration continued, a new message with specific details on the fate in store for Hungarian Jews was transmitted to Budapest. It contained entire passages from Roosevelt's address promising retribution specifically for crimes against Jews. Roosevelt urged Hungarians to "record the evidence" and help Jews escape the Nazi noose. The United States would somehow "find the means of maintenance and support [of escapees] until the tyrant is driven from their homelands. . . ." Only let the neutrals open their gates. It would be a major tragedy, Roosevelt pointed out, if "these innocent people, who have already survived a decade of Hitler's fury, should perish on the very eve of triumph over the barbarians. . . ." [10] Widely distributed by printed tracts, and through the European underground and repeatedly broadcast to occupied Europe through OWI facilities, rescue advocates hoped it would turn the tide. [11] Roosevelt had, for the first time, been enlisted in the rescue effort and his prestige was at an all-time high.

The reinvolvement of Roosevelt was attributable to the activities of Morgenthau and Pehle. The President had preferred to make the declaration on retribution for war crimes jointly with the British government, but when London delayed Morgenthau urged him to make the gesture unilaterally. [12] Undoubtedly, Anne O'Hare McCormick, the *New York Times* columnist, hinted at one of the reasons for Roosevelt's sudden willingness to intercede personally when she observed that bitterness about the Administration's rescue policy has "become so vocal that the policy makers cannot ignore it." [13] Rescue advocates were in fact anxious to have Roosevelt compensate for the failure of the Moscow War Crimes Declaration to mention crimes against Jews and so informed Pehle. Opposition to such statements came from London where it was felt that such "war crime" rhetoric might do more harm than good. Pehle addressed a furious note to the Foreign Office pointing out that it was such reasoning that had convinced Berlin that the Allies did not oppose the Final Solution. So fiery was Pehle's message that the State

Department refused to send it until it was redrafted in a "more friendly and courteous manner." [14] The note prompted Roosevelt to speak out on March 24 and that in turn helped smoke out the British Foreign Office. On March 30, Anthony Eden rose in the House of Commons and appealed to all Quisling officials to redeem themselves by not cooperating further with Nazi plans for the liquidation of the Jews. He held out the hope of special consideration for such officials on the day of reckoning, which surely would come. [15]

More exasperating than the reluctance of Whitehall to catch the new enthusiasm for rescue was the continued rejection by the CIRC of an active rescue role. Arguing that such activities as inspection of the camps and intercession against ghettoization were "unrelated to the Committee's traditional and conventional competence" the Committee refused at the outset to send a special emissary to Budapest. [16] Not until further frantic appeals by Pehle did the CIRC agree to reconsider its decision. [17] The Red Cross emissary did not appear in Budapest until the first wave of deportations were virtually completed. The effort to have the CIRC extend its food package program to certain camps did not bear fruit until September 1944. Not until October did the agency risk approaching the German Foreign Office to request that foreign nationals in the camps be reclassified as civilian internees or prisoners of war, entitled to all the protection of such a classification. This suggestion had been made by rescue advocates in the early months of 1943.

The effort to enlist the Holy See in the rescue operation in 1944 continued to be a frustrating one. The Myron Taylor mission to the Vatican, dispatched by Roosevelt in December 1939, had not been noticeably successful. On an official level the Church proved more wary of being drawn into the Holocaust question than other neutral bodies. [18] Pehle's effort to enlist the Vatican's aid in the Hungarian crisis could not be viewed with much hope. Nevertheless, an approach to the Vatican was made through the Apostolic Delegate in Washington, Archbishop Amleto Giovanni Cicognani. The message, which tactfully suggested that "his Holiness may find it appropriate to express himself on this subject," [19] succeeded in wringing a highly generalized statement concerning war atrocities from the Vatican. It made no reference to the Final Solution.

Within Hungary the Church could not help but react to what was happening. On May 15, the day of the first mass deportations, Angelo Rotta, the Papal Nuncio, observed that "the whole world knows what the deportations mean in practice." Paradoxically, the protest to the Hungarian Foreign Office, Rotta hastened to add, was made "not from a false sense of compassion but on behalf of thousands of Christians." [20] While officially the Vatican remained reluctant to participate in the rescue offensive, local Church officers often sponsored such activity. Cardinal Angelo Roncalli, later Pope John XXIII, at the behest of WRB agent Ira Hirschmann, forwarded thousands of baptismal certificates to Rotta which were instrumental in saving lives. [21] The Catholic Primate of Hungary, Justin Cardinal Serédi, on the other hand, seemed more concerned for the thousands of converted members of his flock than for Jews per se. In April he requested the Sztójay regime to draw some distinction between baptized Christians of Jewish origin and Jews who had not converted. They were granted the right to wear a white cross in addition to the yellow star. Ultimately Seredi found means to limit the number of baptismal certificates. More important, he exerted no influence over those members of his flock who chose to be directly involved in the deportations and did little to arouse the humanitarian interests of Hungary's overwhelmingly Catholic population.

From Eichmann's point of view the first wave of deportations was highly successful. The first trial transports left the Carpatho-Ukraine destined for Auschwitz on April 27 and 28. The Hungarian bureaucracy and gendarmarie cooperated fully. Eichmann achieved a perfect *gleichaltung* despite the efforts to create a rift between the *Einzatsgruppe* and the Hungarian officials. The broadcasts of prominent Hungarians in America requesting noncooperation and a new warning that those involved in the deportations would be brought to account seemed to have had no effect. [22] Eichmann's deportation strategy demonstrated a diabolic cleverness learned from several years' experience. He planned to begin with the newly annexed areas closest to the advancing Soviet Army and save Budapest for last, thus avoiding any great crisis of conscience among Hungarian officials when it came to deportations from Hungary proper. The strategy worked smoothly. Pehle was informed of the amazing speed of the deportations by underground reports from Bratislava relayed through Bern. According to calculations of railroad workers who carefully counted the cattle cars enroute to Auschwitz, approximately 12,000 Jews a day were deported throughout the months of May and June.[23] So efficiently did the deportations proceed that the excitable Kommandant of Auschwitz, Rudolf Hoess, rushed to Budapest to complain personally to Eichmann about the severe overburdening of the crematoria facilities.[24] Before it was over somewhere between 400,000 and 437,000 Jews had been gassed in a forty-six-day period.[25]

When the news of the deportations reached the rescue advocates, Patrick Malin, executive director of the refurbished IGC, reflected sadly that "there is almost nothing one can do . . . it is a terrible and brutal fact." [26] Even so, the WRB continued its desperate effort to turn public opinion in Hungary. Roswell McClelland, the WRB agent in Switzerland, suggested that an effort be made to capitalize on the mortal fear many of the collaborators had of the Russians. Perhaps Moscow could be persuaded to issue a specific warning about atrocities against Jews? [27] But the Russians had ideas of their own on war atrocities. They preferred a policy of swift retribution at the scene of the crime with a minimum of legal technicalities. In June still another note was forwarded to the Hungarian government requesting that it state its "intentions with respect to the future treatment to be accorded to Jews in ghettos and concentration camps." [28]

Meanwhile, the WRB got into the business of actual physical rescue in a small way. Financing was arranged through the WRB for several small-scale rescue operations in Hungary. The Zionist Hechalutz group was paid through Nathan Schwartz, the representative of the Jewish Agency in Switzerland. Freies Deutschland, an anti-Nazi religious group, also received some financial aid from WRB.[29] It was hoped through these groups and others to send more than 2,000 Hungarian Jews into Rumania, which was now welcoming Jews with "open arms." Two hundred and fifty would be sheltered in Slovakia and 500 in Yugoslavia.[30]

The OWI continued to beam appeals and warnings to Hungary. Included was an appeal by Al Smith and a group of seventy-three prominent Americans, a broadcast of a special religious service by Hungarian-Americans, wearing the symbolic yellow star, while urging their countrymen not to participate in Nazi barbarities, a broadcast explaining the rescue resolutions passed by the House Foreign Affairs

Committee and the Senate Foreign Relations Committee in April, Hull's address supporting these resolutions, and Roosevelt's speech promising retribution for atrocities against Jews delivered on March 24.

THE CRY FOR RETRIBUTIVE BOMBING

Despite such activities, reports from the underground indicated that the efficiency of the liquidation operation was not diminished. Rescue agitation within the Jewish community assumed a vengeful tone. "Hungary," cried one Anglo-Jewish monthly, "must be taught a lesson similar to that of Berlin." [31] The lesson such rescue advocates had in mind was bombing, not only of Hungary, but of the rail lines leading to Auschwitz, the crematoria and the gas chambers themselves. Such requests, voiced as early as March 1943, were given fresh impetus during the crisis by a request from Jewish sources within Hungary for precision bombing of certain buildings in Budapest which were involved in the operation of the Final Solution as well as rail junctions on the line to Auschwitz. [32]

It was hoped that such raids might disrupt the fragile rail co-ordination required to get masses of people to Auschwitz. The possibility that the cooperation between the Eichmann *Sondereinsatz-kommando*, which directed the operation, and the Hungarian administrative apparatus which carried it out, would be disrupted by a physical manifestation of Allied concern, could not be ignored. There was some evidence that the air raids struck terror in the hearts of many officials in the Axis satellites. In June, for example, the Bulgarian Minister in Ankara, Nicholas Balabanoff, was careful to parrot the Goebbels line regarding the barbarism of saturation bombing, but added parenthetically that Bulgaria expected that its Jewish situation would reach a completely normal state when the bombing was halted. [33] The dread of bombing was especially prevalent in Budapest and led to the countermanding of the deportation order by Horthy. The Budapest regime literally frightened itself to death after several raids on the capital during the last weeks of June. Ironically, it was a threat arising from within Hungary, a threat which would be rejected by Allied authorities, which helped turn the tide.

The Hungarian authorities worried needlessly, for even while evidence accumulated that the mere threat of bombing could achieve a great deal, an attempt by Nahum Goldmann, A. Leon Kubowitzki, and John Pehle to convince John J. McCloy, Assistant Secretary of the Army, of the need for such bombing failed.[34] McCloy's reply to the request for bombing is one of the most tragic documents to come out of the Holocaust:

After a study it became apparent that such an operation could be executed only by diversion of considerable air support essential to the success of our forces now engaged in decisive operations elsewhere and would in any case be of such doubtful efficacy that it would not warrant the use of our resources. There has been considerable opinion to the effect that such an effort, even if practicable, might provoke more vindictive action by the Germans.[35]

What "more vindictive action" than Auschwitz was possible remained the secret of the War Department. Had Auschwitz been bombed in time, or retaliatory bombing of German cities undertaken, not only would the Final Solution have been opened to public scrutiny during the war but the destruction of German cities, considered by some today as wanton, might have been given some meaning. As it was, the Final Solution was surrounded by an eerie silence, which helped the relatively small number of Nazi officials involved to carry it through. In 1944 the means of counter terror were at hand and were being used against German cities. What might have occurred had the leveling of Hamburg in the massive incendiary raid of July 1943, which did not succeed in lowering war production in that city, instead been labeled a retaliatory raid for Auschwitz, is an open question. One thing is certain, the Goebbels propaganda ministry would have had to spend some time and energy explaining what had happened to the Jews.

THE WRB AND THE RESCUE ACTIVITIES
OF RAOUL WALLENBERG

One incidental result of Pehle's request to the neutrals "to take immediate steps to increase to the largest possible extent the number of . . . diplomatic and consular personnel in Hungary" deserves special mention because the plea, made "in the interest of the most elementary humanity," led to the saving of at least 20,000 lives.[36] The enlargement of the Swedish diplomatic mission led to the recruitment of Raoul Wallenberg. Wallenberg was first approached for the mercy mission by Herschell Johnson, the American Minister in Stockholm, who was apprised of Wallenberg's sterling qualities by Hillel Storch, agent of the World Jewish Congress, and Chief Rabbi Marcus Ehrenpreis. After some hesitation, Wallenberg became convinced that he could play an important humanitarian role in Hungary. Iver Olsen, WRB agent in Stockholm, gave him a detailed briefing of the situation of the Hungarian Jews and the names of forty Hungarian officials who could, for various and sometimes ignoble reasons, be relied upon for assistance. Wallenberg, who was familiar with Budapest, having been there on business in 1942 and 1943, was ideal for the job Olsen outlined to him, since he had contacts in the Jewish community as well as in the government. Wallenberg was to establish an escape apparatus by enlisting Danube skippers and railroad workers along the Budapest-Mohacs line. He would also organize a special department for the protection and relief of Jews.[37] Wallenberg was given $100,000 to begin the task.

Once in Budapest, Wallenberg proved to be a one-man rescue operation. Thousands of Hungarian Jews were saved by the simple device of extending Swedish diplomatic protection to them even though many had not the remotest connection with Sweden. He leased blocks of apartment houses and placed 13,000 Jews under the "extended protection" of the Swedish mission. Another 7,000 were simply furnished Swedish identification papers.

His determination to save his clients was so great that on one occasion when troops, on orders from the *Sondereinsatzkommando*, arrived at the apartment block ("the quarter," as it was called), to begin rounding up Jews for deportation, Wallenberg physically intruded his own body, stating to the officer in charge that they would have to shoot him before a soul would pass from Swedish protection. Later, when the Germans did succeed in sneaking six of his clients out of the quarter and placed them on a train bound for Auschwitz, Wallenberg raced by auto to the border, intercepted the train, and removed the victims.[38] During the last ordeal of Hungarian Jewry, the marches to the Reich, Wallenberg snatched about 2,000 marchers from an almost certain death under the pretext that they were entitled to Swedish protection. Wallenberg was last seen in mid-January 1945, escorted by Russian soldiers. He was on his way to see General Malinovsky in Debrecen to inquire about the release of AJJDC funds. Before he vanished into the labyrinth of the Soviet penal system, he wrote a letter of appreciation to Iver Olsen, who transmitted the AJJDC funds which financed the elaborate relief system which Wallenberg established in Budapest: "Mr. Ollsen [*sic*] believe me your donation in behalf of the Hungarian Jews has made an enormous amount of good. I think they will have every reason to thank you for having initiated and supported the Swedish Jewish action the way you have in such a splendid manner." [39] This was typical of Wallenberg's modesty.

The enlistment of Wallenberg in the rescue cause represented a rare combination of the right man in the right place at the right time. Such coincidences did not occur with great frequency. The Wallenberg example served to spur the Swiss to similar action. They too began to extend diplomatic protection to Hungarian Jews. The CIRC agent in Budapest began a long-delayed food distribution program for the Jews of Budapest and even Carlton Hayes, who heretofore had refused to cooperate with the WRB, succeeded in getting Madrid to extend Spanish diplomatic protection for several hundred Sephardic Jews who for centuries had lived outside Spain. The number rescued by these devices was small compared to the number destroyed in Auschwitz. The protection of Jews within Hungary, which was the objective of WRB strategy, was proving a failure but removal of Hungarian Jewry from the scene seemed equally impossible in 1944. Neither the United States nor other neutrals appeared ready to accept such a mass immigration.

THE CIRCUMVENTION OF A RESCUE ROAD BLOCK: FREE PORTS

Since 1938 those opposed to American involvement in the refugee problem had hidden behind the restrictive immigration law. We have seen that the inability of the Administration to make a contribution in this area inhibited its ability to request neutrals to be more generous in their admission policy. In 1944 as in 1938 and 1939, it was imperative for rescue advocates to break through this road block in order to rescue at least part of Hungarian Jewry. John Pehle urged repeatedly: "The necessity for unilateral action by this government lies in the fact that we cannot expect others to do what we ourselves will not do and if we are to act in time we must take the lead." [40] Pehle was aware that if some way were not found to neutralize the immigration law, at least symbolically, the reenergized rescue effort of 1944 would remain a mockery and the WRB, like the IGC, would become a monument to the Administration's insincerity.

The opportunity to at least partly circumvent the immigration law lay with the revival of an idea as old as the refugee-rescue problem itself—temporary havens. First suggested by prominent German refugees in 1938, it became popular currency in almost every non-Zionist rescue proposal up to 1944. It received some attention at the Bermuda Conference and was, almost incidentally, incorporated into the executive order which established the WRB.

One of Pehle's earliest tasks as director of the new agency was to dissolve the series of administrative road blocks in the visa procedure which Breckinridge Long had laboriously erected over a period of years. Arrangements were made to give nonquota preference to relatives of citizens and aliens already in the United States. The private rescue agencies were enlisted to provide lists of such persons who might qualify. Efforts were made to relax Long's tight antiinfiltration policy in Latin America,[41] and almost immediately there arose the old problems of corruption in the sale of visas, the fear of commercial competition from refugees, and rumors of spies among the refugees. Spruile Braden, Ambassador to Argentina, was particularly anxious to avoid the contemplated relaxation.[42] On July 1, the Administration, prompted by Pehle, went one step further by offering to revalidate all visas issued up to July 1940 and not claimed. At the same time the neutrals were encouraged to follow suit. Such steps, while they represented a softening of the Administration's policy, were hardly enough to convince neutrals like Sweden and Switzerland, who had in some cases gone far beyond the United States in their rescue efforts, that there had been a real change of heart.

Until Samuel Grafton, popular columnist of the *New York Post* presented the original idea of temporary havens under the rubric "free ports" no one had conceived of a way to circumvent the immigration law. Grafton, by simply giving an old idea a new twist, was able to catch the popular fancy. His logic was compelling: "A free port," he wrote, "is a place where you can put things down for a while without having to make a final decision about them. . . . We do it in commercial free ports for cases of beans so that we can make some storage and processing profit; it should not be impossible to do it for people." [43] There was some reason to believe that such a scheme might be within the purview of the immigration law. Rescue advocates had for some time been aware of Breckinridge Long's scheme to rid Latin America of thousands of unfriendly aliens by interning them in the United States. If such aliens could be admitted outside the quota why not refugees? In his anxiety to keep refugees out and his overreaction to the security problem, Long had inadvertently given an important precedent to rescue advocates. For months Eleanor Roosevelt, Isador Lubin, Sam Rosenman, and other rescue advocates within the Administration, had been struck by the paradox of allowing thousands of POW's to be interned in the United States while friendly refugees could not be. But unaware of the significance of interning unfriendly aliens from Latin America, they never were able to find a legal way to deal with the problem until Samuel Grafton popularized the free-port idea. Roosevelt was informed of the various schemes to intern refugees but 1944 was an election year, a poor time to tangle with the restrictionists. Pehle, aware that without such a breakthrough the continued cooperation of nations like Spain and Turkey, who were acting as conduits for refugees, could not be depended upon, wrote a memorandum to the President in which he explained the importance of making at least a symbolic gesture toward temporary havens in the United States. [44] At the same time he persuaded his former boss, Henry Morgenthau, to intercede personally with the President. Morgenthau subsequently did much to convince Roosevelt of the feasibility of having at least one temporary haven in the United States. Roosevelt did not care much for the "free port" label, but began to prepare the political groundwork for a change in policy. The temporary haven idea already had some support within the Administration and the introduction of identical resolutions in both houses of Congress in November 1943 (H.J. Res. 154 and S.J. Res. 85) assured the President that some congressional support could be mustered should the Administration decide to go that route.

Predictably, there was strong opposition to the proposal from the other members of the Board, Secretary of War Henry L. Stimson and Howard Travers, former head of the State Department's Visa Division. Stimson insisted that the President simply did not have the power to act unilaterally on an issue which "concerns a very deeply held feeling of our people." [45] Congress should be consulted. Stimson was convinced that the term "temporary havens" was misleading. No nation would repatriate these people. Moreover, he shared with the British Foreign Office and Breckinridge Long an apprehension that Hitler would dump huge masses of starving refugees on the Allies in an attempt to damage their war effort.[46]

Meanwhile, Pehle tried to muster public sentiment. At a special news conference he revealed some of the reasoning behind the proposal. He linked the success of the new agency to the implementation of an idea like free ports. Without it, he reasoned, no nation could be expected to follow our lead. Ira Hirschmann, the highly effective WRB agent in Ankara, related some of the drama of the rescue operation in Turkey. At the same time, Pehle sounded a more cautious note, pointing out that geographical factors would militate against large numbers of refugees coming to the United States.[47]

The free port idea began to pick up some public support. During March and April hundreds of letters were sent to the White House favoring the proposal. In April, the first anniversary of the Warsaw Ghetto uprising, there were numerous memorial meetings, few of which missed the opportunity to adopt a resolution in favor of free ports. The group of prominent Americans headed by Al Smith pressed the Administration to make the idea a reality. The *New York Times* assured its readers that "the plan had nothing to do with unrestricted and uncontrolled immigration. It is simply a proposal to save lives of innocent people." [48] The publicity-wise Emergency Committee to Save the Jewish People of Europe, which had already tangled with Zionist organizations over the strategy of separating mass rescue from the notion of a Jewish commonwealth in Palestine, ran a full page ad in the *Washington Post* under the caption: "TWENTY-FIVE SQUARE MILES OR 2,000,000 DEAD—WHICH SHALL IT BE?" [49]

Despite the outpouring of public support, Roosevelt reacted with caution. He accepted Morgenthau's suggestion of by-passing a potentially harmful congressional debate and used an executive order to implement the idea. Roosevelt, however, insisted that a careful groundwork be laid before he made an official announcement. He desired above all to avoid the impression that he was concerned with an exclusively Jewish problem lest the charge of "Jew Deal" frequently heard in 1938, be used again. The preparatory instructions sent to Robert Murphy, Roosevelt's special agent in North Africa, whence it was planned to draw the first contingent of refugees, were specific about the matter of selection. He was to be certain to "include a reasonable proportion of the categories of persecuted minorities who have fled Italy." [50] Meanwhile, Roosevelt hinted at a news conference that he did not expect temporary havens to be confined to the United States. The American lead would be symbolic and the neutrals and Allies would be expected to carry the major burden, since geography and the continued shipping shortage would effectively limit the number of refugees who could find shelter in the United States.[51] A few days later Roosevelt announced that he had ordered the preparation of certain "obsolete" facilities for refugees but hastened again to add that it would be wasteful to bring large groups of refugees across the ocean. He suggested that the Sicilian resort of Taormina was ideally suited for a refugee haven.[52] Finally, on June 9, in the midst of intense public interest in the successful Allied invasion of Europe, Roosevelt almost casually made the official announcement. A temporary haven was being prepared in Oswego, New York, where a maximum of 1,000 refugees would temporarily reside. Similar camps were contemplated for Cyprus and Tripoltania. It was to be an international operation and the refugees would be repatriated after the war.[53] Three days later Congress was faced with the *fait accompli*. Using arguments drawn primarily from a memorandum prepared by Pehle, Roosevelt's explanation was a shrewd amalgam of military necessity and humanitarianism. He stressed the potential interference of refugees in the war zone with the prosecution of the war. Congress was reminded of the urgent need to counteract the ferocious will of the Nazis to complete the annihilation of the Jews before their own demise. "In the face of this attitude of our enemies we must not fail to take full advantage of any opportunity, however limited, for the rescue of Hitler's victims. We are confronted with a most urgent situation." [54] Ultimately these havens would be financed through UNRRA, but until then the War Relocation Authority would handle the camp at Oswego. Within the next week the WRB persuaded Mexico, Curacao, Dutch West Indies, Surinam, Jamaica and the British West Indies to follow the Administration's lead.[55]

The restrictionist uproar, though muted by the war news, came in due course. Senator Robert R. Reynolds (Democrat, North Carolina), who, it will be recalled, had taken a leading role in closing the door to refugees in the early period, fired off a letter to Francis Biddle, the Attorney General: "Will you please be good enough to advise me as to just what ground the President based his authority to set aside the laws permitting refugees . . . to enter this country outside our quotas?" [56] Biddle, doubtless expecting the challenge, cited the precedent which must have shocked Reynolds. His friend Breckinridge Long, in admitting unfriendly aliens from Latin America, had furnished the precedent. If unfriendly aliens could be interned in Texas why not friendly ones in Oswego? Both help the war effort.[57]

ZIONISM, TEMPORARY HAVENS, AND CONTINUED
DISUNITY OF AMERICAN JEWRY

One source of opposition to temporary havens was not so easily understood. The joyful reception of the free ports plan in the Jewish community was not fully shared by some of the Zionist organizations, who sensed that free ports, like mass resettlement outside Palestine, would take the edge off agitation for the revocation of the British White Paper and the eventual establishment of the Jewish commonwealth in Palestine. One Zionist spokesman, sensing that the rescue issue had been separated from the Palestine national homeland goal, labeled the plan an "Audobon Society for Jews." [58] When the Zionists advocated temporary havens they never failed to couple it with demands for unlimited immigration to Palestine. The situation between the Emergency Committee and the Zionist organizations became more embittered after the establishment of the camp at Oswego. The Zionists, who were doing much of the actual rescue work in Hungary and Slovakia, considered the Emergency Committee all thunder and no lightning. "They are not to be trusted," explained Wise to a Zionist colleague, "they are not decently honest or trustworthy." [59] When the Committee attempted to recruit Sol Bloom, whose prestige had declined but whose position as Chairman of the House Foreign Affairs Committee gave him considerable leverage in the Administration, Wise cautioned him that Peter Bergson was "dangerously ruthless." [60] Zionists hardened their attitude when the precipitous intervention of Henry L. Stimson caused the defeat of a move to get Administration support for a Commonwealth resolution. The loss was partly recouped by including pro-Zionist planks in both party platforms. In August new commonwealth resolutions were introduced in Congress. But Zionists were disturbed when a cross current was established by the Emergency Committee's introduction in Congress of a competing resolution which called for a temporary haven in Palestine. Here was additional evidence of the wrecker role of the Emergency Committee. Why urge temporary asylum, reasoned Zionists, when Whitehall still had 14,000 unused visas available? Zionists were more interested in having the White Paper revoked than in circumventing its effects by means of temporary havens. Pehle, however, in keeping with the general policy of encouraging temporary havens wherever they might spring up, supported the idea of a camp in Palestine.[61]

American Zionists must have felt some relief in the last months of 1944 when they were able to observe the dream of temporary havens turn into something of a nightmare. At Oswego, near Fort Ontario in New York State, on August 4, 1944, Harold Ickes welcomed 987 carefully selected refugees to the eighty-acre former army post. Almost immediately the project ran into trouble. The refugees, most of whom had come from camps situated in the mild climates of North Africa and Italy, found it difficult to adjust to the cold isolated northern location. Moreover, the conditions under which they had gained admittance proved to be so confining that the refugees were little more than prisoners. For people who did not feel that they had committed a crime, such treatment seemed irrational. A number of physical and mental breakdowns occurred. The unwholesome conditions, due mainly to a rigid interpretation of the regulations as administered by the Army, were fully revealed by a congressional investigation in 1945.[62] But little could be done to improve conditions in 1944. Several requests by Joseph Chamberlain, director of the National Refugee Service, and Harold Ickes were rejected by Attorney General Francis Biddle, who felt strongly that Roosevelt's original commitment left no room for liberalization of the conditions.[63] The refugees remained internees rather than immigrants.

Temporary havens turned out to be another illusion. The gates of America were not open wide. In practice few refugees owe their lives directly to the existence of such havens. But in the case of the rescue of the Jews of Hungary the symbolic value of circumventing the immigration law can hardly be overestimated. It helped galvanize the neutrals and may have contributed significantly to a startling turn of events in Hungary itself.

HORTHY HALTS THE DEPORTATIONS:
A PROSPECT CREATES A PROBLEM

On July 6, after several days of rumors and just as the deportations were about to begin in Budapest's large Jewish community, Horthy ordered the deportations halted and the Hungarian gendarmes, who were to carry out the operation, to leave Budapest. The order was followed by a startling offer from the Regent, transmitted through the CIRC, which had become one of the agencies which brought pressure to bear on the regime. Hungary would release "certain categories" of Jews who held visas to other countries provided that such persons were accepted for resettlement in Allied or neutral countries. Berlin, then in the midst of engineering its own ransom proposal, had consented to give safe passage to such "special category" Jews.

The WRB was faced suddenly with an unforeseen reward for its effort. Nevertheless, rescue advocates were wary. What would happen to the majority of Jews who were not visa holders? What was behind the offer? Doubtless much of the offer was part of Horthy's continuing opposition to solving the Jewish question according to the Nazi timetable and techniques. Not until March when Hungary lost its leverage as a cobelligerent, was Hitler successful in carrying out his plans. Now several things had occurred that may have served once again to prop up Horthy's courage. Since April the Horthy government had been battered by a constant flow of representations from the neutrals and from the Allies, through intermediaries. Especially telling was the Pope's intercession, finally made on June 25, and an earlier message from King Gustaf of Sweden which presented Horthy with a detailed graphic description of what was actually happening to the deported Hungarian Jews. At the same time Max Huber, President of the CIRC, changed his strictly hands-off policy to join the chorus of protest. A CIRC representative was finally sent to Budapest. The protests were being made amidst constant repetition of the threat of specific retribution for those who participated in the anti-Jewish actions. Such threats suddenly took on a new meaning when *Festung Europa* was reached on June 6, 1944.

It was one thing to order a halt to the deportations and another to explain it to Berlin. Edmund Veesenmayer, the German plenipotentiary in Hungary, seemed willing to acknowledge the fear sweeping Hungarian officialdom that reprisals were being prepared for Hungarian-Americans; but Ribbentrop, whose enthusiasm for the Final Solution had not yet begun to weaken, needed more information for the Fuehrer. Sztójay then produced the three underground messages which listed names of Hungarian officials involved in the Final Solution and urgently requested precision bombing of strategic railroad junctions as well as certain buildings in Budapest.[64]

Washington was informed of Horthy's action through Alfred Zollinger, representative of the CIRC, who attached an urgent request that the Administration accept the offer immediately and publicize the number of persons it planned to admit. The Sztójay regime, argued Zollinger, needed "a visible sign of a favorable reaction to their decision to cease their persecution of Jews." [65] The Administration had already given its consent to the establishment of a temporary haven in Oswego but such a test of its sincerity was not foreseen. Involved in the Hungarian proposal were about 9,700 families and an additional 1,000 children below the age of ten, a total of about 17,000 to 20,000 souls. There was, moreover, some suspicion that the offer represented a *quid-pro-quo* between Budapest and Berlin. Hitler had threatened to revoke the concession if the deportations were not continued. The concession for "special category Jews" may have represented the price Berlin was willing to pay to deport the remainder of Hungarian Jewry.

A contingent of 20,000 Hungarian Jews in addition to the thousands that were available in Rumania and Bulgaria would have forced a reopening of the resettlement and the Palestine questions, which were no nearer solution in 1944 than in 1940. The United States had become more flexible on the admission of refugees and had in the interim assumed responsibility for thousands of German POW's taken by the British. Much therefore depended on whether London would momentarily relax its Palestine policy. Late in July, Morgenthau and Josiah DuBois, Jr., the assistant general counsel of the Treasury, went to London to work out a joint Anglo-American response to the offer. The British proved extremely reluctant to make more Palestine certificates available and preferred to leave the Horthy offer unanswered.

Eden, according to DuBois, raised arguments which were "inhumanly political." What Britain would do with so many refugees, he could not imagine.[66] Morgenthau and DuBois then turned to Parliamentary Undersecretary George Hall for redress, but to no avail. London was adamant in its rejection of the Horthy offer and the German ransom proposal. Moreover, it was clear that Whitehall did not take the creation of the WRB and the establishment of a temporary haven as anything more than gestures to American Jewry. Washington would have to go ahead on its own. Pehle, conscious of the tenuousness of the offer and exasperated by Whitehall's reluctance to go along, cabled London in August that continued delay "might prove tragic." [67] Eventually the threat of a unilateral response spurred the Foreign Office to action. Eden privately informed Washington that the Horthy offer was acceptable provided it remained limited to the categories announced and due recognition be given to Britain's limited ability to absorb more refugees.[68] A full month had passed and the situation in Hungary was again taking a turn for the worse. Not until August 11 was Pehle able to inform the Hungarian government that "this Government now repeats its assurances that it will arrange for the care of all Jews permitted to leave Hungary in the present circumstances who reach the United Nations or neutral territory and will find such people temporary havens of refuge where they may live in safety." [69] But word of a new wave of deportations created some apprehension. Were the Hungarian authorities interpreting the acceptance of the Horthy offer as a sign that the remainder of Budapest Jewry could now be deported without fear of retaliation? Clarification was requested from Budapest.[70]

If the situation in Hungary could be stabilized the rapid development of events in the war might prove a boon for the surviving Jews of Hungary. The successful D-Day landing had been supplemented by a Soviet offensive which forced the Rumanian King Mihail to sue for peace. Devastating air raids on German cities were taking their toll and on July 20 an unsuccessful attempt on Hitler's life gave observers the first solid evidence of a breach between the German Army and the Nazi leadership. But in Hungary the Germans continued to retain absolute physical control and as long as that was so, the situation of the surviving Jews remained precarious. In Berlin there were some signs of a weakening of the will to see the Final

Solution through to the bitter end but die-hards like Eichmann seemed
more determined than ever to win this final victory—the destruction
of Hungarian Jewry. Himmler, a prime architect of the Final Solution,
began to weigh the possibility of obtaining some consideration for
himself in the forthcoming peace negotiations while acquiring much
needed war material for the *Wehrmacht* through a ransom deal for
the surviving Jews of Hungary. Even the German Foreign Office
began to show signs of an uncommon concern for world opinion
by urgently requesting the *Einsatzkommando* to find some pretext
such as Jewish attacks on policemen as a pretext for future deportations.[71] But Eichmann showed distress at Berlin's agreement to
Horthy's offer to release "special category" Jews. He complained to
Berlin that if the Horthy offer were allowed to stand "important
biological material" would escape his net.[72] He flew to Berlin to push
his case in person and when that failed he took matters into his own
hands and smuggled out an extra transport from the detention camp
at Kistarcza, seventeen miles outside of Budapest.

On August 23 it appeared as if the German occupation of Hungary
was about to be broken. The Soviet Army broke through the German
lines and the *Wehrmacht* was given three days to leave Rumania. The
change in the fortunes of war undoubtedly encouraged Horthy to
depose the collaborationist Szkójay regime and replace it with a group
headed by General Geza Lakatos, who was more willing to withstand
Berlin's mania for liquidating Jews even while its own house was
caving in. Indeed one of Lakatos' early actions was to order the
removal of the Eichmann *Sondereinzatskommando*. Berlin, in the
midst of ransom negotiations and informed by Veesenmayer that the
Budapest authorities were under extreme pressure to disassociate themselves from the Final Solution in Hungary, ordered Eichmann to
comply. As one German newspaper put it: "Pressure from enemy and
neutral countries has become so strong that those circles in Hungary
that are friendly to Jews . . . influence the Hungarian government
to prevent any further measures against the Jews." [73] It seems apparent
that by August 1944, even the heretofore ineffective psychological
warfare which was the strategy of the WRB, was beginning to pay
dividends. The "special category Jews" were split up, 1,200 prominent
Orthodox rabbis were "kept on ice" in Bergen Belsen, from where
most of them ultimately reached Switzerland, as a first payment of the

renewed ransom negotiations, 15,000 others were interned in Strass-hof, Austria, and 600 were confined in Budapest.[74]

Nazi speculation that its logistical support might be shored up by ran-soming the Jews of Hungary preceded Horthy's order revoking de-portation. The several ransom proposals which marked the *Götter-dämmerung* period of the Third Reich were a return to the commer-cial mindedness of the 1939 period when Nazi moderates negotiated a "Statement of Agreement" with George Rublee and Robert Pell which was, in fact, an offer to ransom German Jewry. Ransom offers anchored at both ends gives the Holocaust a ghoulish symmetry.

The biological destruction of the Jews, while it was touted in the Reich in highly idealistic terms and evoked in men like Eichmann a zeal which might best be described as religious, was never too far removed from a sure instinct for profit. Eichmann's commitment was matched by "businessmen" like Dieter Wisliceny from whom Gizi Fleischmann was able to buy time for the Jews of Slovakia or Kurt Becher, who was a business agent for Himmler's SS. Even a prime architect of the Final Solution, Heinrich Himmler, was by 1944, no longer averse to ransom. The Manfred Weiss family was ransomed from under the nose of the Hungarian authorities, who naturally had first claim on their property, so that the SS might become virtually independent for certain types of military hardware.[75] In one instance, Pehle became apprehensive of involvement with ransom. He cautioned against the ransoming of the rabbis of Satmar and Nitre and their retinues because the bad precedent the ransoming of specific indi-viduals might establish.[76]

The principal ransom proposal during the Hungarian crisis was the so called "blood for trucks" offer and the protracted Mayer-Becher negotiations, which sustained it in different terms. The WRB was involved in both. The Hungarian origins of the "blood for trucks" offer need not concern us here except to note that by April 1944 Himmler, perhaps through the benevolent influence of Kurt Becher, had taken a personal interest in the prospect of arranging a ransom for Hungarian Jewry. On the part of Hungarian Jewry the idea of ransom as a rescue alternative emanated from the Vaadat Ezra Vehatzala, the Zionist-oriented Assistance and Rescue Committee, which may have had in mind the example of Gizi Fleischmann's successful dealings with Dieter Wisliceny. On May 17, in the midst of the first wave of deportations, Joel Brand, a member of the Vaadat, and Bandi Grosz, formerly a Jewish member of the German counterintelligence, left for Istanbul to bring the offer to the attention of the representatives of the Jewish Agency. Details of the ransom offer reached Washington from Istanbul. As described by Steinhardt, the German price was 2,000,000 cakes of soap, 200 tons of cocoa, 800 tons of coffee, 200 tons of tea and 10,000 trucks.[77] Later the luxury items, soap, tea and coffee, were replaced by military hardware which would be used exclusively on the "eastern front." In turn for this the Germans would release 100,000 Jews upon Brand's return and ultimately, according to Eichmann's testimony in Jerusalem, 1,000,000 Jews would be given their freedom.[78] But Berlin had not changed its mind about Palestine, which would receive only "limited" numbers while neutrals such as Spain would receive "unlimited" numbers.[79]

Not surprisingly, the astonishing offer placed the WRB and the rescue advocates into something of a quandary. What was the meaning of the offer, which an interrogation of Grosz indicated originated in the highest Nazi echelons? Was it a last-minute attempt to implicate the Allies in the Final Solution? [80] Was Himmler perhaps trying to redeem himself at this late date? Was he anxious to establish a direct line to the Anglo-American bloc for future peace negotiations? Such conjecture was dismissed by Allied intelligence which viewed the offer as a shrewd attempt to split the Allied camp. This was the meaning of Eichmann's emphasis on the claim that the equipment received by the *Wehrmacht* would be used exclusively against the Russians. Rescue advocates came to a similar conclusion.[81] In 1964, while testifying at the trial of Otto Hunsche and Hermann Krumey, Eichmann's lieutenants in Hungary, Joel Brand, who transmitted the original offer, confirmed that this was the meaning of the offer. "It is now clear to me," he observed, "that Himmler sought to sow suspicion among the Allies as a preparation for his much desired Nazi-Western coalition against Moscow." [82] Apparently the ransom offer was based at least partly on the fact that the Nazis had swallowed their own propaganda on the imminence of an Anglo-American-Soviet split.

Such questionable motivations did not mean that the offer might not be used for rescue purposes. Rescue advocates were virtually unanimous in their agreement that it could. It was clear from the outset, however, that the British Foreign Office could muster little enthusiasm for the proposal. The moment Brand moved to Aleppo in Syria he was arrested and held incommunicado. The State Department was informed of London's distrust of the offer and without awaiting a reply disclosed news of the offer and an indignant refusal to the *London Times*, which published it under banner headlines on July 20—"A Monstrous Offer—German Blackmail—Bartering Jews for Munitions." The threat of even a limited release of Jews threw the Foreign Office into turmoil. What would London do with so many Jews? [83] Churchill too was adamant about accepting the offer even on a tactical basis. He preferred a simple declaration to the effect that anyone connected with the Final Solution "will be hunted down and put to death." [84] Almost before rescue advocates could determine how to handle the new rescue opportunity, the doors were being closed on it. The WRB, which was coming under some pressure to investigate the Brand mission, decided to send Ira Hirschmann to Cairo for a first-hand examination of the case. Before he left, Morgenthau escorted the prize agent of the WRB to the White House where Hirschmann again related stories of what could be done on the rescue front. Roosevelt gave the mission his personal endorsement. [85]

After overcoming the opposition of Lord Moyne, who preferred Hirschmann to go through proper Foreign Office channels in London, the agent succeeded in interviewing the distraught Brand on June 11. Hirschmann's report of the interview allayed much of the distrust for the mission generated by the British. He was impressed with Brand's stature and sincerity. Though the offer might have been "pulled out of a hat," Hirschmann observed, there could be little doubt that it was *bona-fide* and originated with the highest authorities in Berlin. It was important therefore to permit Brand to return to Budapest and "keep the door open." [86] Hirschmann's recommendation coincidentally paralleled that the Jewish Agency, whose head of the Political Division, Moshe Shertok, had also interviewed Brand in mid-June and advised Nahum Goldmann that "though the exchange proposition may be mere eye wash and the possibility of ulterior motives must be assumed, it is not improbable that even preliminary negotiations might result in salvation of substantial numbers." [87] Goldmann needed no advice from Shertok. He had already been told by Stettinius that the "Germans must be made to think that we take them seriously." [88] The opinion of rescue advocates thus contrasted sharply with the continued insistence of Whitehall that "the offer was not serious" and claimed as evidence the insignificant channel through which it was made.[89]

The WRB and the British Foreign Office had taken contrasting positions on the "blood for trucks" offer. London held the trump card, for in order to convince the authorities in Berlin that the offer was being seriously considered, it was necessary to comply strictly with Eichmann's instructions that Brand must be returned to Budapest. This the British would not do. As the time expired and neither Brand's return nor an Allied gesture materialized, anxiety grew into despair in Budapest. "Now he sits there, instead of returning . . . willy nilly," wailed one member of the rescue committee, "and we here and every day 12,000 Jewish men leave our ranks." [90] While the British were holding Brand the deportations were rapidly moving ahead. Desperate pleas were made to bring the British into line. Chaim Weizmann, well known for his anglophilia, attempted to exert his special influence in London by urging Eden to send either Brand or Menahem Bader, a representative of the Jewish agency in Istanbul, back to Budapest.[91] Morgenthau and Pehle pleaded the same cause to Roosevelt.[92] The Jewish Agency, thwarted in its attempt to get the Foreign Office to take some action, turned desperately to the White House. Goldmann again appealed to Roosevelt "not to allow this unique and possibly last chance of saving the remains of Jewry to be lost. . . ." [93] The same response to the offer was suggested by all the appeals—the use of dilatory tactics such as a promise to negotiate if the Germans would call off the Hungarian deportations. That at least held out the promise of saving some lives.

In the end, however, it was not these desperate pleas which led to halting of the deportations, but Horthy's initiative. Thereafter the rescue advocates remained concerned about the safety of the surviving Jews of Budapest. The Jewish Agency attempted to keep the proposal alive through Joel Schwartz, its agent in Lisbon, who had established contact with Freiherr Von Schroeder, chief of the SS main office. The idea that it might be possible to work around the British by moving the negotiations to Lisbon came from Chaim Barlasz, a Jewish Agency representative in Ankara, who had received word that the SS intended the Brand mission only as a feeler.[94] But Pehle quickly rejected the Jewish Agency's request to work through Lisbon.[95] New developments made it clear that the offer was a divisive one, even if Berlin had not intended it to be.

The Soviet Union's reaction to the offer made any hope of utilizing it futile. The State Department informed Moscow of the ransom proposal on June 9.[96] Soviet suspicions that a separate peace feeler was in the making were immediately aroused. On June 19, the Soviet Deputy Foreign Minister informed Ambassador Averill Harriman that his government "does not consider it permissible or expedient to carry on any conversations whatsoever with the German Government. . . ."[97] The State Department hastened to assure Moscow "that neither this Government nor the British Government have been deceived as to the character of this alleged offer . . . [they] were convinced from the outset that the offer is part and parcel of the German psychological warfare effort."[98] But Soviet suspicions were not so easily allayed. As late as February 1945, the new American Ambassador, George Kennan, fearing a further undermining of confidence, recommended keeping the Kremlin in the dark about such proposals "in view of the extreme suspicion with which the Soviet Government views all financial transactions with Germany conducted through Swiss channels. . . ."[99]

Whether a real opportunity to ransom Hungarian Jewry existed is doubtful. Despite promises to the contrary the mills of Auschwitz kept grinding throughout the Brand mission and even after the Nazi leaders seem to have lost their taste for the Final Solution. On the operational level, where Eichmann reigned supreme, the Final Solution appeared to have achieved an independent momentum. But the offers, when properly exploited by rescue agents, could be instrumental in salvaging at least some lives. The negotiations in the final months of 1944 give some evidence of this possibility.

A RENEWED THREAT TO THE JEWS OF BUDAPEST

The actions of the Lakatos regime in dismissing Eichmann's *Sodereinzatskommando* gave some grounds for optimism. But the situation did

not remain stable. Berlin, suspecting that the Lakatos regime, like the
Kállay regime before it, was seeking a separate peace, began to tighten
its hold on Hungary. One of the earliest signs was a renewal of the
alarms from the Jewish community of Budapest. In late August the
Vaadat Ezra Vehatzala sent word to the WRB that small groups of
Jews were being secretly deported despite Horthy's order.[100] Another report from Sweden told of a particularly cruel deportation
from Budakalasz in which Hungarian gendarmes participated.[101] In
September the Horthy offer to release "special category" Jews was
modified by the Nazi authorities on the grounds that even the limited
number of Jews earmarked for Palestine would disturb German-
Arab relations. The offer would henceforth be limited to Jews bound
for Britain and the United States and even here, McClelland was informed by the Swiss Foreign Minister who acted as intermediary,
the names of the Jews involved would have to be submitted to Berlin
beforehand.[102]

The respite for Budapest's Jews ended officially in October when
the Soviet Army broke into southern Hungary. A German armored
division occupied Budapest on October 14, toppling the Lakatos
regime. In the wings again was Eichmann, prepared this time to complete the job. Otto Skorzeny's movie scenario operation of kidnapping Horthy's son proved sufficient to break the dictator's spirit.
Ferenc Szálazi, leader of the fascist Arrow Cross, became the new
Prime Minister. Reports of new concentrations of Jews outside Budapest, which were customarily preparatory to actual deportation, soon
reached the WRB.[103] An inquiry was made concerning the new
measures. It contained a strong threat; "None who participate in these
acts of savagery shall go unpunished . . . all who share the guilt shall
share the punishment." [104] But the Szálazi regime proved far less sensitive to pressure from abroad. Its response came almost two months
later and included one cover story which stated that Jews were being
integrated into the German economy according to prearranged plans.
Another stated that Jews were being concentrated outside Budapest
to protect them from Allied bombing and Soviet invasion.[105] Intercession by the Budapest agent of the CIRC and Angelo Rota, the
Papal Nuncio, were no more successful.

By October 20, Eichmann had succeeded in rounding up approximately 27,000 Jews who were to be marched to Austria 150 miles

away and thence to Germany. The destruction of the rail lines and the dismantling of Auschwitz would not be allowed to interfere with the liquidation of Hungarian Jewry. Wallenberg and a CIRC delegation followed behind the long columns, trying to give succor to the marchers, and Wallenberg immediately extended diplomatic protection to about 2,000 of them. Hundreds of the aged, sick, women, and children were simply shot when they could no longer keep up.[106] "There were grandmothers and small children among us," reads the testimony of one survivor, "we walked the whole day under the supervision of the Arrow Cross men. They were often shooting or throwing hand grenades; . . . after the first day many fell; those who could not move were shot or left to die on the spot. . . . We got no food, only some dirty water in the evening which they called soup. . . ." [107] Himmler's order countermanding the foot marches was not put into effect until mid-November when Eichmann was summoned to Berlin and in face to face confrontation with Himmler was ordered to stop all murder programs. Himmler had already ordered all extermination in the camps to be halted. Even then the ordeal of Budapest's Jews was not over. They remained at the mercy of the Arrow Cross until the surrender of the German garrison to Marshall Malinovsky in February 1945.

THE MAYER BECHER NEGOTIATIONS

While Hungarian and Slovakian Jewry were undergoing their last agonies there arose an opportunity for continuing the negotiations with the SS through Saly Mayer, the Swiss representative of the AJJDC. As a Swiss citizen, Mayer had more maneuverability than a citizen of a belligerent or a member of the Jewish community to be ransomed, such as Joel Brand. The negotiations lasted throughout the final months of 1944 and were in a sense a substitute for the fruitless "blood for trucks" venture.

The motivation of the rescue advocates remained the same. They wanted to buy time rather than Jews. Each day the liquidation process could be delayed, each Jew that was released as a token of good will was an asset. The Nazi motivation is more difficult to surmise. The German Foreign Office was not apprised of "the deal" by Himmler. When the London radio broke the news of the "blood for trucks" offer, Ribbentrop was forced to inquire of Veesenmayer about what was going on.[108] Veesenmayer apparently believed that the Reuters message and the well-publicized British indignation were only a ruse to dupe the Russians who would naturally oppose an offer which smacked of a separate peace feeler.[109] Directly involved in both offers is the enigmatic figure of Rudolf Kastner, a leading member of the Jewish Council, and his relation to Kurt Becher. It was Kastner who originally began the movement for ransom through his connection with Dieter Wisliceny and it was Kastner who kept the idea alive when Brand failed to return through his connection with Kurt Becher. Becher, who had singlehandedly incorporated the giant Weiss works into the SS state, was lured to further ransom negotiations by the bait of 3,000,000 Swiss francs, collected from local Jewish sources, and a promise that additional money would become available. He apparently had successfully converted Himmler to the idea of using captive Jews as a bargaining wedge with the Allies.

The negotiations began auspiciously with the arrival in Basel in August of a token of "good faith," a transport of 318 "special category" Orthodox Jews from the Bergen Belsen camp. Thereafter between August 1944 and April 1945, the austere Mayer and the business-minded SS Colonel, Kurt Becher, would meet periodically at the Swiss border town of St. Margarethen to discuss, according to Kastner, who frequently witnessed the negotiations, "the price of abandoning the gassing." [110] Becher soon broadened the negotiations by revealing that he had Himmler's authority to bargain for the lives of all Jews in German hands. The Nazi price again was matériel and money.

The price demanded by the Germans placed Mayer in an awkward position. There was not the remotest possibility that the Allies would allow military equipment or money to reach the Axis. Yet the talks had somehow to be kept going since every passing day lessened the leverage of the SS negotiators and brought the day of salvation closer. Mayer's task was to convince Becher that his price could be paid under certain conditions while at the same time steering the talks to an alternate scheme which would permit the Allies to assume the cost of extending the Red Cross program of relief packages to the camps. The strategy was approved by Pehle after the third meeting, providing there was no consummation of the ransom offer.[111] Progress was very slow but the talks were kept going. Perhaps the Germans too had some use for simply maintaining a connection to the West. The news that Slovakian Jewry, relatively secure heretofore, was being readied for its final ordeal lent to the negotiations a special urgency.[112]

One tactic utilized by Mayer to stretch out the talks was to request Becher for a specific list of types and quantities of foodstuffs desired by the Security Ministry. This required that Becher return to Berlin for consultation which meant time for Mayer. But by September such dilatory tactics seemed to have been exhausted. "My personal opinion and that of Saly Mayer also," McClelland informed Pehle, "is that all the time possible has now been gained and that in all probability the Gestapo has lost patience so that these negotiations can be considered as having lapsed, negotiations which were after all ultimately doomed to failure." [113] But Pehle, aware that the deportations of Budapest Jewry might be resumed at any time, encouraged Mayer to keep talking. Such advice was easier given than put into practice. It was impossible to put off talk of money indefinitely and yet the Administration's policy of not allowing deposits to be made in blocked Swiss bank accounts made it virtually impossible to bait the negotiations properly. Pehle's judgment proved wise. In December, after Mayer and McClelland had abandoned hope that the Germans would continue the negotiations, Becher agreed to abandon the quest for military hardware and money and allow the Allies to furnish the medical and food requirements of those inmates still in the camps. The reason for the new-found generosity was not hard to find.

No one could doubt that it was only a question of time before Allied victory. Paris had been liberated in August. In a single day in October more tons of bombs had been dropped on the Ruhr town of Duisburg than on London in the entire war. German steel production had been cut in half, fuel was running low, and the Russians were in the midst of a new offensive which would sweep German troops out of Hungary. On October 20, Tito's partisans liberated Belgrade and by December it was apparent that the Ardennes offensive on which the Nazi high command had banked so much had run out of steam. Little stood in the way of invasion of the German homeland from both east and west.

On December 6 Mayer's persistence was rewarded further by the arrival in Basel of two transports of 1,355 Orthodox Jews. At the same time there was a loosening on the question of depositing money in blocked Swiss accounts. In January Pehle finally gave his approval for the depositing of 20,000,000 Swiss francs, the equivalent of $5 million, in such blocked accounts. The money would come from the AJJDC. The precedent for granting such licenses was established in December 1943, when license number W-2115 was granted to the World Jewish Congress for rescue operations in France and Rumania. McClelland had for weeks requested such a license to enhance Mayer's credibility as a bargaining agent.[114] Unknown to Becher, no withdrawals could be made without express consent of Mayer and McClelland and their approval, in turn, could not be granted without the consent of the WRB. None of these funds ever fell into Nazi hands.

The death agony of the Reich saw an increase in probes regarding bargains for the surviving Jews in Nazi hands. There was the offer of Dr. Bruno P. Kleist, head of the Eastern Affairs Division of the German Foreign Office, and General Walter Schellenberg, chief of Himmler's Office of Information and Dr. Felix Kersten, a Swedish physiotherapist whose most notable patient was Heinrich Himmler, all of whom carried Himmler's offer to release thousands of surviving Jews and authority to permit food and medical supplies to the camps in the early months of 1945. Iver Olsen, the WRB agent in Stockholm, was involved in all these contacts. Jean Marie Musy, a former Swiss federal counselor, leader of the Catholic Conservative Party and editor of a right-wing newspaper *Le Jeune Suisse*, claimed major credit for influencing Himmler's change of mind. The token transport of rabbis which arrived in Basel in August was supposedly Musy's doing. In August he also carried a ransom offer for 700,000 souls for an initial payment of $1 million. The offer was handled through Isaac Sternbach, WJC agent in Switzerland, whose request for funds to be transferred by the AJJDC was referred to Pehle.[115] Pehle was skeptical, but advised that the Mayer precedent for granting a license be followed.[116] In February 1945 the Musy deal came to the attention of the Jewish press which promptly condemned Musy for his fascist leanings, thereby endangering the negotiations.[117] In March Himmler ordered his SS Brigades to deliver all surviving inmates of the camps. When Hitler heard that the liberated inmates of the Buchenwald concentration camp were plundering Weimar, he countermanded Himmler's order and decreed instead that no camp inmate in the southern half of Germany be allowed to fall into Allied hands alive.[118] A meeting of Felix Kersten and Nobert Masur with Himmler at Harzfeld, near Berlin, on the night of April 21, ultimately led to the release of 4,500 Jewish women from the Ravensbruck concentration camp and renewed promises of handing over the camps without further killings.[119]

The ransom offers did not in themselves fulfill their promise of saving the lives of thousands of Jews. The initiative usually came from Berlin, where the most steely nerved proponent of the Final Solution, Heinrich Himmler, was having second thoughts about it. The WRB, unprepared for this particular form of rescue, moved sluggishly in response. Only at the very last moment did Pehle grant authority to deposit money in blocked Swiss accounts. But even with a more rapid response there was no guarantee that more lives might have been won. Few of the road blocks to rescue in 1940 had been removed in 1944. That was especially true of the bitter strife among the Jewish organizations, which reached its peak in the midst of the Hungarian crisis.

JEWISH DISUNITY AND THE RESCUE OPERATION, 1944

The Hungarian crisis appears to have had little effect in healing the divisions within American Jewry. The dispute between the Emergency Committee and the Zionist-oriented organizations seems, in fact, to have grown more intense. The Emergency Committee, at one point, went as far as urging the use of poison gas against the Nazis in retaliation for the gassing of Jews. Zionists, no less bitter, counseled against opening up such a Pandora's box.

For some time the Zionists had observed the activities of Eri Jabotinsky, son of the Zionist revisionist leader, Vladimir Zev Jabotinsky, who was working for the Emergency Committee in Ankara. Jabotinsky had been granted permission to travel to Ankara in an American bomber with the help of Congressman Will Rogers, Jr., who was closely linked to the Committee. On a stop-over in Jerusalem, Jabotinsky had given the impression at a news conference that he was traveling as an agent of the WRB. The Zionists lost no time in bringing the hoax to Pehle's attention.[120] An inquiry brought confirmation from Laurence Steinhardt, who informed Pehle that Jabotinsky "had sought and given this impression." [121]

In October the *Washington Post* published an exposé entitled "Bergson Admits $1,000,000 Fund Raised, Vague On Its Use." [122] The article went on to label Bergson a "self styled nuisance diplomat" and questioned the Committee's financing and its claim to having rescued 40,000 illegals (immigrants being smuggled into Palestine). Bergson was revealed to be a Palestinian Jew who had not served in the Army. The Committee's recent troubles with some of its charter members, Dean Alfange, former cochairman, and Pierre Van Paassen, a writer and publicist for the Committee, were used as indications of its instability. Both had resigned from the Committee and the latter had denounced it as "a cruel hoax perpetrated on the American public." [123] In response the Committee published a special pamphlet which characterized the American Zionist leadership as "defeatist" and "malicious libelers who hold lucrative jobs at exaggerated salaries of $20,000 a year." [124] The pamphlet singled out for attack the publisher of the *Washington Post*, Eugene Mayer. He was characterized as a stooge for the Zionists. He eventually, in fact, retracted much of what had been said concerning the Emergency Committee. [125]

Such feuding in the midst of the Hungarian rescue crisis might simply have passed as something endemic in the Jewish community if it had not spilled over into rescue operation itself. It posed a particular problem, for the WRB which was little more than a coordinator and conduit of a concerned Administration for the private, largely Jewish, rescue agencies. Precious time had to be spent distinguishing between groups who were doing effective rescue work and those who were in the rescue business for dubious purposes. The Emergency Committee, for example, was denied a license to finance its activities in Ankara because it was "dictated by previous experience acquired by the Board." [126]

Additional evidence of bad feeling among Jewish groups involved in rescue soon became available to the Board. In Ankara, for example the dispute concerned the composition of the refugee transports. The Jewish Agency in control of the rescue apparatus which filtered Jews out of Hungary, Bulgaria and Rumania, was accused of showing preference to refugees with Zionist backgrounds. Ira Hirschmann, who was himself formerly a member of the Emergency Committee, informed Pehle of this problem, adding the thought that the Agencies selection of refugees threw a "highly significant light upon the attitude of the Jewish Agency toward the refugee problem." [127] Accusations that Zionists took care of their own first, often at the expense of other Jews, became a *cause célèbre* in Israel when Malkiel Grünwald, a Hungarian refugee, brought suit against Rudolf Kastner, chairman of the Zionist Council of Hungary, for collaborating with Gemans and rescuing a handful of Zionists from his own home town of Kluj at the expense of Hungarian Jewry. Following Kastner's assassination in 1957, the Supreme Court of Israel in 1958 reversed a lower court decision, and cleared Kastner of any wrongdoing.[128] Laurence Steinhardt, the American Ambassador in Turkey, had established a close working relation with Hirschmann. He recommended to Pehle that the solution for the bickering among the rescue groups was to give the WRB agent Hirschmann authority to coordinate the activities of all rescue agencies operating in Turkey.[129] The sticky problem of selection was not so easily solved. Two months later we hear Jabotinsky boasting that he has succeeded in giving preference to his own clients in selecting those who would be placed on transports.[130] After the assassination of Lord Moyne, the British Ambassador requested the Turkish government to deport Jabotinsky. He was interned by the British on his return to Palestine. The British were concerned lest his plan to independently shuttle 2,500 refugees a week from the Balkans to Palestine, for which he had succeeded in chartering a Turkish boat, be carried out.[131]

At the same time the smouldering feud between the Jewish Agency and the WRB in Turkey broke out on the question of credit for those who were being rescued. The Jewish Agency became distressed when Ira Hirschmann, on his return to the United States in March, drew publicity for the Turkish rescue operation and placed himself and Ambassador Steinhardt at its center. At that time he was held up by Morgenthau and Pehle at various press conferences as an example of what could be done in rescue. The news stories spurred Moshe Shertok, political secretary of the Jewish Agency, to cable Nahum Goldmann that he was "compelled to state the truth that not a single refugee yet owes his escape to the Board's initiative or activity.[132] Hirschmann charged that Shertok had shamelessly taken credit for the activities of the Jewish Agency in the occupied areas. The

Agency, claimed Shertok, would not ordinarily involve itself in such disputes if Hirschmann's overriding concern with publicity had not in one instance prematurely exposed certain rescue operations, which led to a refusal by Nazi authorities to grant safe conduct.[133] Interestingly enough, Hirschmann, in his account of the events in Turkey, *Caution to the Winds*, and the WRB, in its unpublished three-volume history of its activities, are careful to acknowledge the primacy of the Zionist rescue effort in occupied Europe.[134]

Friction with Zionists was not the only source of disunity in Turkey. The Vaad Hahatzala, the rescue agency representing Orthodox Jewry, pressed relentlessly for better representation on the refugee transports. So exasperating did their claim for special treatment become that Steinhardt felt compelled to cable the New York Headquarters of the group to request that the rabbis be ordered to be less obtusive. But Eliezer Silver, president of the organization, did not share Steinhardt's apprehension regarding the activities of its agents. Instead, Steinhardt was reminded that in the rescue business it was a "dog eat dog world." [135] Jacob Rosenheim, an official of the Vaad, observed that "the interest of religious Jews [is] always menaced by the preponderance of the wealthy and privileged Jewish organizations, especially the Agency and the Joint." [136] Clearly for the Orthodox wing of Jewry, Nazis were not the only enemy.

A parallel phenomenon occurred in Stockholm where Iver Olsen encountered bickering among the various private rescue agencies. By June things had become serious enough to warrant a special dispatch to Pehle. "A major obstruction has been the jealousies between the various relief organizations and the difficulties of persuading them to work together." [137] Olsen's difficulties were compounded by the necessity to rely on various Balkan underground groups representing all shades of the political spectrum. The Latvian group, for example, was felt by Jewish organizations to be virulently anti-Semitic and opposed to the idea of rescuing Jews. The Baltican Committee of the World Jewish Congress observed that the rescue clients of the Latvian group were all rightists and suspected that some had actually participated in the Final Solution. Olsen was informed of these suspicions.[138]

As in Turkey, the dispute between the private rescue agencies in Portugal was concerned primarily with the touchy question of credit.

As usual the rescue apparatus itself had been established by a Zionist group, the World Jewish Congress, and the Jewish Agency. Employing Maquis groups and paid smugglers, they specialized in bringing primarily the Jewish children, who had been stranded in Vichy as a result of the collapse of the negotiations with the Vichy government in 1940 and 1941, across the Pyrenees to Portugal. After arrival in Portugal the children would be sent as a matter of course to the AJJDC for food and shelter. But Isaac Weissmann, the agent of the WJC in Lisbon, under whose auspices the children's rescue program had been initiated in October 1943, became incensed when it appeared that the JDC was anxious to claim some credit for the program. As in the case of Shertok's claim about the absence of genuine WRB activity, Weissmann cabled Stephen Wise to inform him that "Joint has not brought out a single person, rather once the WJC brings out the children they are sent to the Joint for support." [139] Jacques Chaillan, a former French diplomat, who served as one of the contacts with the French underground and M. Croustillon, the delegate of the Jewish section of the Maquis, were cited as witnesses to the veracity of this claim. The WRB agent in Portugal, Robert C. Dexter, while acknowledging that Weissmann "seems to get results," found him "impractical and visionary." [140] Subsequent events seem to have borne out that judgment. In mid-May tragedy struck when a group of twelve children and their underground guides were arrested by Nazi border guards while trying to cross the Portuguese frontier. Rather than attributing the misfortune to the vagaries of a particularly dangerous rescue operation, Weissmann chose to lay the blame on the JDC, which he claimed had been guilty of a "thwarting maneuver." [141] Despite such setbacks the rescue operation was distinctly successful. Between October 1943 and October 1944, 1,350 children and adolescents reached Switzerland, 770 children reached Spain together with 200 parents, 700 children were hidden in Vichy France itself as well as 4,000 to 5,000 adults. Lisbon also was one of the principal centers for the distribution of baptismal and false birth certificates as well as Latin-American passports.[142] The problem between the two agencies did not appear to affect the rescue operation. Nevertheless, it was not finally resolved until Portugal was outflanked as an escape center by the fast-moving military developments in France.

THE HIRSCHMANN-STEINHARDT LIAISON

The highly successful rescue route through Turkey, from the Balkans and Rumania to Palestine owes some measure of its effectiveness to Ira Hirschmann and Laurence Steinhardt. Steinhardt was one of the most enigmatic figures on the American rescue scene.

Steinhardt was a rarity, a Jew who occupied an important post in the State Department's Foreign Service. Educated at Columbia, where he took a law degree in 1915, Steinhardt, after serving overseas in World War I, established himself as a successful attorney in the firm of Guggenheim, Untermeyer, and Marshall. At the same time he was active in Zionist causes, first becoming director of the American Federation of Zionists and then of the American Zionist Commonwealth. Like Breckinridge Long, with whom he maintained a correspondence throughout his career, Steinhardt's debut as a diplomat came about in 1933 as a reward for his fund-raising activities for the Democratic campaign in 1932. He was rewarded with the position of Minister to Sweden in April 1933. In 1937 he was appointed Ambassador to Peru. In 1939 he became Ambassador to Moscow. From that remote post he became involved in the rescue refugee crisis when he assumed a highly legalistic position on the issuance of visas, the power of the consuls, and the inviolability of the immigration laws. Long, delighted with the strong support he was receiving from a Jewish Ambassador, gleaned from his dispatches much evidence to support his antirefugee position. Steinhardt became a staunch supporter of Long in his 1940 campaign to establish a rigid screening procedure. He seemed anxious to adapt himself to the official anti-refugee position of the State Department in the early phase and there was not a hint of his involvement in the Zionist movement in the 1920s.

In 1941 it was clear that Steinhardt went further than other State Department officials in his hostility to refugee advocates. When it was apparent that some consuls were refusing visas because of their distaste for Jews, Steinhardt nevertheless insisted that consuls rightfully had the final word.[143] During the bitter dispute with the PACPR over the Department's administration of visa regulations, Long used a Steinhardt dispatch of October 1940 from Moscow, detailing with devastating effect the dangers of a more liberal visa list procedure. He left the dispatch with Roosevelt, who was so impressed with it that when James G. McDonald and Francis Biddle appeared before him shortly thereafter to press for liberalization, they had no effective retort. Steinhardt lent strong support to Long's "close relatives" ruling in June 1941, and buttressed Long's already strong anti-Semitic predilections by articulating his own prejudices against "eastern" Jews. Long was so impressed with Steinhardt's slurs against "eastern" Jews, that he recalled them in his diary:

Steinhardt is an able man and has decisiveness and courage. He took a definite stand on immigration in large numbers from Russia and Poland of the Eastern Europeans whom he characterizes as entirely unfit to become citizens of this country. He says they are lawless, scheming, defiant—and in many ways unassimilable. He said the general type of intending immigrant was just the same criminal Jews who crowd our police dockets in New York and with whom he is acquainted and whom he feels are never to become moderately decent American citizens.[144]

Such sentiments may not have been unknown among "uptown" Jews but few would have revealed them to men of Long's temperament and opinions. Long had little use for eastern people in general. "I think he [Steinhardt] is right not as regards the Russian and Polish Jew alone," he confided in his diary, "but the lower level of all that slav population of Eastern Europe and Western Asia—the Caucasus, Georgia, Ukraine, Croat, Slovene, Carpatho-Ukraine, Montenegro, etc. . . ."[145] At least the Jews were in good company.

In January 1942 Steinhardt was transferred from Moscow to Ankara, a post that had attached to it some tradition for being filled by a Jew. The transfer seems also to have spurred a remarkable change in Steinhardt's position on refugees and rescue. Ankara was a strategic rescue outpost and he was able to witness the catastrophe to European Jewry from a ringside seat. Part of that change of heart may have also been caused by the assiduous wooing of the Zionists, who at one time had claimed Steinhardt as one of their own. Stephen Wise was warned by a Zionist colleague Bernard Rosenblatt that "the initiative must not be lost with Ambassador Steinhardt as it has been in some other case [Since he] . . . may prove of the greatest importance to our cause."[146] What Rosenblatt meant was that Turkey was the natural route for Jews from occupied Europe to Palestine. The initiative lost in some other cases was hinted at by Rosenblatt, who felt strongly that in the Zionist failure to advocate a separate Jewish army they had missed an opportunity on which the revisionists, the Emergency Committee, had been able to capitalize. The Jewish Agency did place Emanuel Neuman, one of its representatives, in touch with the Ambassador. He briefed Steinhardt on the Agency's broad rescue program and gave him the names of its representatives in Turkey.[147] His previous record notwithstanding, Steinhardt was not receptive to such wooing. "You have introduced me to Zionism many years ago," he replied to Rosenblatt, "and I have not forgotten it. I have not changed." [148] But since his early contact Steinhardt had in fact changed; he was deeply involved in his professional career and was fully aware that a conspicuous link to the Jewish organizations could be a liability. He cautioned that his usefulness would be compromised should his link and sympathy to the Zionist cause become known.[149] Thus when Ira Hirschmann joined Steinhardt in February 1944, the Ambassador had for two years led a kind of double life. In the State Department he was known as a staunch restrictionist while the Zionists considered him sympathetic to their cause. It was the latter role that would win out in 1944.

Throughout 1942 and 1943 Steinhardt proved himself an effective negotiator with the Turks. In April 1943 he was instrumental in getting Turkey to accept approximately 30,000 Balkan Jews, including many from Rumania, for transit to Palestine. Early in 1944 he was successful in getting the Turkish government to intercede for Jews of Turkish extraction living in France. Only the shipping problem seemed to thwart him.

In February 1944 Steinhardt's burden was lightened by the timely arrival of Ira Hirschmann, an energetic New York Department store executive whose interest in the refugee crisis harked back to the futile Evian Conference which he had witnessed personally. He left the Conference in disgust and proceeded to Vienna, in July 1938, the most critical point of the refugee crisis, where he began to underwrite dozens of affidavits. He became, on his return, chairman of the board of the University in Exile, and in 1943 became involved with the most militant of all the rescue organizations, the Emergency Committee to Save the Jewish People of Europe.

Steinhardt and Hirschmann were impressed with each other's ability and worked well together. Hirschmann's first cables mentioned

Steinhardt in laudatory terms. "It is essential that you give Steinhardt top Washington backing for immediate resultful action as now I know Turkey is a bottleneck. . . ."[150] The Turks permitted about forty persons a week to move through Turkey and the delay in granting exit visas sometimes lasted two months.

After two months of intensive activity in which Hirschmann was instrumental in streamlining the procedure by which refugees moved through Turkey, Hirschmann returned to the United States to resume his position at Bloomingdale's department store. He began an active campaign to publicize the Turkish rescue operation and incidentally his own role in it. Wherever possible he praised the activities of Steinhardt. The story of the Turkish rescue operation thus became popular currency among rescue advocates. Stephen Wise was impressed enough to jestingly offer Hirschmann, who was associated with the rival Emergency Committee, a "real job" when his mission was over.[151] Doubtless Pehle found Hirschmann's flair for publicity an asset to the Board. A dramatic story of Hirschmann's activities was released to the press in April to aid the campaign for temporary havens.[152] Morgenthau, gratified that his contention that more could be done in the rescue operation had proved correct, brought Hirschmann's story to Roosevelt's attention with the observation that "he really accomplished wonders while in Turkey."[153] Isador Lubin with whom Hirschmann maintained close contact, followed suit.[154]

Steinhardt, for whom the establishment of the WRB was undoubtedly a sign that the State Department officials to whom he looked for support had fallen from grace, heard welcome echoes of Hirschmann's publicity. Paul Baerwald, one of the most influential figures in American Jewry, informed him that "everybody was much impressed by the stories of success which Mr. Hirschmann presented to us."[155] Hirschmann, too, exulted about his public relations *coup*. "There is a new connotation to your name," he informed the Ambassador, "which is only as it should be."[156] Steinhardt returned the favor by bringing his influence to bear with the Board and Bloomingdale's to permit Hirschmann to return to Ankara.

The two men seemed to have reached some kind of agreement whereby Hirschmann would employ his considerable public relations talent to refurbish the Ambassador's tarnished reputation in the rescue camp in return for Steinhardt's continued active cooperation with the rescue effort. "You have sacrificed some public acceptance for complete loyalty and appreciation by the State Department," wrote Hirschmann to his mentor, "I can say with modesty that I have succeeded better than I ever dreamed in executing the first step in the job we agreed on." [157] Thus was the fragile rescue operation in Turkey held together.

On balance, Hirschmann's emphasis on getting the rescue story popularized benefited the rescue effort, Shertok's complaint notwithstanding. Dramatic publicity was imperative if the idea of a special government effort to rescue non-Americans was to be accepted by the American public. Most Americans had little idea of what the "Final Solution" was and simply to inform them proved difficult because the story was dismissed as "atrocity mongering." A. Leon Kubowitzki, in trying to bridge the credibility gap, attributes it to the "incredibility and incomprehensibility to the normal human mind of the German determination to exterminate our people." [158] A public opinion poll taken in December 1944 found that a majority of Americans were aware that Hitler had been cruel to the Jews, but few fathomed the extent of the killing. Twelve percent believed the stories of mass murder of Jews to be totally untrue, 27 percent believed that it involved only 100,000 people and only 4 percent believed that over 5,000,000 Jews had been put to death.[159] Hirschmann's special flair for publicity, while it may have had ulterior motives, hardly went far enough to dramatize rescue.

OTHER RESCUE ROAD BLOCKS

Lack of physical control of the scene and disunity among the rescue agencies were only two of the road blocks to effective rescue. The rescue operation from Hungary, Rumania, Slovakia, and Bulgaria was adversely affected by Berlin's reluctance to grant safe passage for vessels sailing the Black Sea route, without which the Turkish authorities would not permit their ships, the *Tari* and the *Constanca*, and the Swedish ship *Bardeland*, all of which had been leased after difficult negotiations, to make the dangerous voyage. If Berlin's determination to liquidate the Jews was waning in 1944, it still was not prepared to cooperate in what it saw as an attempt to create a new Jewish population center from which to subvert the world. Moreover, the State Department's claim of a shipping shortage was not without substance in the Black Sea area. It was for this reason that Myron Black, field director of the War Shipping Board, arrived in Ankara on March 2. Ultimately Hirschmann became convinced that it would be cheaper to buy ships outright than to pay the exorbitant prices to lease unseaworthy vessels, like the *Bellacita*, the *Milka*, the *Maritza*. On his way to the United States, Hirschmann attempted to publicize the shipping shortage by calling for a "bridge of ships." The use of the World War I slogan did not improve the situation.

Compounding the difficulty was London's reluctance to grant Palestine certificates. The British had taken a leaf from the State Department's book and were running cursory security checks on all applicants. It took from six to ten weeks to gain clearance. This in spite of the fact that according to the provisions of the White Paper 32,000 certificates were still available in 1944 for entry into Palestine. Once the British gauntlet was run the refugees still had to face the creaking corrupt Turkish bureaucracy which was painfully slow in granting exit permits and allowed only limited numbers to enter each week and then only if an equal number of refugees left Turkey.

Attempts to wring greater cooperation from the Turkish government officials proved only partly successful. The WRB turned for help to the agents of the American tobacco companies who purchased a commanding share of the Turkish crop. Friedrich Seckel, an agent of the tobacco companies, soon informed Pehle of their reluctance to become involved in politics. He was pessimistic about any attempt to wring cooperation from the outside since there was "plenty of opposition to rescue . . . especially [among] the new Ankara crowd." [160]

In August 1944 Sol Bloom introduced a resolution in Congress urging the State Department to use its influence in Turkey to facilitate the entrance of Jews and to establish a temporary haven in that country. The move was not solicited by the WRB and was withdrawn when Bloom was informed that the resolution might prove detrimental to the rescue operation. [161] The most effective way to keep the operation running was through personal influence. Steinhardt's good reputation and friendship in high government circles, especially with Turkey's Foreign Minister Noman Menenencioglu, went far in unraveling some of the bureaucratic snarls. It was through Steinhardt that Hirschmann was able to establish contact with Kemel

Aziz Payman, the Turkish official who administered the issuance of visas and exit permits. He was able to wring some concessions from him but the primary suggestion, the issuance of a mass transit visa by the Turkish consuls in Bulgaria, Hungary, and Rumania, and the technical arrest of refugees moving into Turkey through the Bulgarian overland route so that they might be interned in Turkey, were not accepted by the Turkish government.

In August, when the Hungarian situation was again deteriorating, London suddenly halted the issuance of entrance certificates altogether, breaking its secret agreement with the State Department. London did not bother to inform Steinhardt of the change in policy. It was primarily the uncertainty of the flow of such certificates that stimulated the Jewish Agency's program of illegal immigration into Palestine. Precise figures of the number rescued through Turkey are difficult to come by. The World Jewish Congress has estimated that a total of 14,164 came through Turkey in 1944 alone.[162] This figure, however, does not take into account the numerous illegals who were smuggled out through the Rumania-Turkey conduit.

EVALUATION

In early 1945 it became apparent that far from overestimating the extent of the catastrophe to European Jewry, rescue advocates had been persistently too low in their estimates. When the full extent of the Holocaust became known one of its effects was to reveal in stark relief the magnitude of the need and the paucity of the rescue effort.

The early evaluations of the role of the WRB therefore naturally sounded a note of despair. The effort, it was clear, never remotely approached in energy and resources the Nazi commitment to liquidate the Jews. The cry of "too little and too late" reflected the anguish of the rescue advocates. Typical was the evaluation of A. Leon Kubowitzki, a principal figure in the rescue program of the World Jewish Congress. He regretted that the Board had not established a consultative body where the private agencies might have expressed their views. The secrecy with which the Board shrouded many of its operations proved counterproductive in the long run, according to Kubowitzki, because it blocked full cooperation with the private agencies on whom success depended. "The consensus of those who watched the work of the Board," he observed, "[was] that, had it been set up two years earlier, it might have spared humanity much agony and many, many lives."[163] That sentiment was echoed by most of the Anglo-Jewish press. The opinion from within the Board was not far different. Shortly before Iver Olsen resigned, he confided to Pehle that he "wished it could have been thousands more and think[s] it could have been had we started much sooner."[164] On the scene, too, there were similar sentiments. When Ira Hirschmann concluded his negotiations with Alexander Cretzianu, the Rumanian minister in Turkey, for the rehabilitation of the 48,000 survivors of the concentration camps of Transnistria, the minister told Hirschmann, "If this means so much to you why didn't you come sooner? You could have saved more lives."[165] It is in this light that Breckinridge Long's effective holding action between 1940 and 1943 gains its full significance.

It is clear from the Hungarian experience that once the problem of generating a will to rescue had been overcome there remained that of making that will effective on the scene. That brings us to one of the irreducible realities. As long as Nazi Germany physically controlled the scene she determined the rescue options. While the WRB was forced to act by remote control and devise a strategy of changing minds, Berlin held the trump card. Eichmann's zeal required a physical deterrent which, with the exception of bombing, was not available. It is in this context that the War Department's decision not to bomb the camps and the railroad lines leading to them stands out as especially tragic. The evidence is irrefutable that Hungary and the satellites were highly sensitive to pressure to disassociate themselves from the Final Solution when it was linked to a threat of bombing. There seems little doubt that bombing, or even the threat of retaliatory bombing, offered some hope of undoing the delicate strands of cooperation which made the Final Solution possible.

Several circumstances combined to prevent full use of existing opportunities. Most of these have already been discussed. A word should be added regarding the posture of the victims and the people in occupied Europe as well as the difficulties involved in an effort which combined many independent components. This last factor was of critical importance in Hungary. In order to undertake a successful mass rescue effort in 1944 it was not only necessary to vitalize the American government's effort but to mobilize and coordinate at least a half-dozen nations and agencies which composed the rescue forces. Included was Britain, the neutrals, the Vatican, the CIRC, the private rescue organizations, the people in the occupied areas, and the victims themselves. The existence of several components tended to lessen the feeling of urgency for rescue within each one. Collective responsibility like collective guilt proved far easier to bear. In the Hungarian operation, for example, the Administration's new-found enthusiasm for rescue was not shared by the British. London continued to resist pressure to issue Palestine certificates. Its recalcitrance contributed to the delay of one precious month in dealing with the Horthy offer to release "special category" Jews. The delay allowed Berlin to reassert its first priority, the destruction and then the ransoming of the surviving Jews.[166] What was true of Britain was to some extent true of the Vatican and the CIRC. We have seen that both bodies followed their own policies. What might have happened had the CIRC pressed for inspection of all camps or for a change of status of the inmates, or even to expand its food package program, remains an unanswered question. Such steps were not taken until it was too late. And there seems little doubt that a condemnation of the liquidation program by the Pope might have helped, especially in Slovakia and Hungary.

The concentration-deportation-liquidation sequence which everywhere came to be the pattern of the Final Solution and it was actually managed by a relatively small nucleus of administrators. The process required not only the collaboration of local police forces but of the victims themselves. The speed with which the Hungarian deportations were executed reflected the *Sondereinzatskommando's* success in winning cooperation of all concerned, including the victims. Hungarian gendarmes and middle echelon officials contributed notably to the success of the operation. The posture of Hungarian Jewry, however, is a more complex phenomenon, especially the activities of the Jewish Council which has caused some consternation among Holocaust researchers. It falls within the scope of this work only in so far as the posture of the victims affected the rescue operation.

It proved impossible, for various reasons, for the Hungarian Jewish community to heed the warnings beamed by the OWI to destroy community lists and discard the tell-tale Jewish stars. Whereas WRB strategy to change minds proved moderately successful on the highest government levels it put too much confidence in the possibility of organizing civil disobedience in the totally dependent Jewish population. Each Hungarian Jew faced the onslaught alone once Jewish organization and communication had been captured by the *Sondereinzatskommando* and converted into an instrument to deport the Jews. Moreover, such tactics required a sympathetic native population. Despite the WRB campaign to change minds, "eighty percent of Hungary's metropolitan population [were] quite unmoved," Wallenberg informs us.[167] Nor was the WRB campaign to dissuade Hungarian officialdom and gendarmes from cooperating with the Germans noticeably effective. Thus many Jews in desperation chose to believe the SS story that they were bound for the Reich to alleviate the labor shortage, and they entered the Auschwitz-bound cattle cars, according to one SS observer, "without resistance and in submission." [168] Wallenberg, a sympathetic observer, was dismayed at the "total lack of courage" among the Jews of Budapest.[169] But he also observed a classic reaction of a defenseless civilian population facing overwhelming odds. "The Jews," he noted, "are so terrified that they are simply hiding in their houses." [170]

For Hungarian Jews the thousands saved by negotiations, by Horthy's order halting the deportations, by baptismal certificates, by the activities of Wallenberg and members of the Swiss delegation, and even by the CIRC, barely gave solace for the enormity of the tragedy. Of the 725,007 Jews in greater Hungary, according to a census taken in 1941, barely 219,000 survived the war.[171] In any terms, therefore, the rescue operation in Hungary was a failure. The question for historians is how much greater that failure would have been had there been no change in the Administration's rescue policy in 1944.

10

Rescue in Retrospect

On those occasions during the Holocaust years when mass rescue appeared possible, it required of the nations a passionate commitment to save lives. Such a commitment did not exist in the Roosevelt Administration, although there were many individuals who wanted to do more.

Between 1938 and 1941 refugee-rescue advocates, most of whom were supporters of the New Deal, undoubtedly believed that the humanitarian concern which characterized Roosevelt's handling of domestic problems could be projected to the refuge crisis. That assumption was buttressed by the statements of concern which accompanied each White House announcement that visa procedures had been liberalized. Those who might have questioned the authenticity of the Administration's concern would have been hard pressed to explain other steps taken by Roosevelt in this early period. The President had, after all, taken the initiative in calling an international refugee conference to meet at Evian. The establishment of the IGC which resulted from that conference was primarily an Administration-supported endeavor as were the Rublee-Schacht negotiations, which were designed to bring order into the refugee chaos. Moreover, a special procedure to rescue the cultural and scientific elite of Europe had been established and the Administration was busily occupied in searching for areas where the refugees might find new homes. What more could be asked?

PROMISE AND REALITY

What refugee-rescue advocates could foresee only with some difficulty at the time was that all these steps would remain largely gestures which the Roosevelt Administration would not and sometimes could not follow up. There developed a gulf between the professed good intentions of the Administration and the implementation of policy. The hope of bringing refugees to the United States was severely circumscribed by the seemingly immutable immigration law. The invitation to the nations to meet at Evian was so qualified that from the outset there seemed little hope of solving the problem of where to put the growing number of refugees. Once at the Conference the American delegation was in the embarrassing position of lacking the bargaining power to convince others to undertake a serious effort to provide for refugees or the will to do so itself. The Intergovernmental Committee for Political Refugees which grew out of the Conference became a monument to the Administration's impotence on the rescue front. The IGC remained throughout those years to clutter and confuse the effort. The attempt by Breckinridge Long to resurrect this ineffective agency after the Bermuda Conference was little more than an effort to thwart more energetic rescue activity.

The Administration's search for resettlement havens shows a similar tendency to degenerate into mere humanitarian gestures. While the President dreamed of a United States of Africa and proposed visionary schemes of nation-building, a visible manifestation of the Administration's concern, a proposal to make Alaska and the Virgin Islands available to a limited number of refugees, was ultimately rejected. When the political risk of circumventing the immigration laws was finally taken in July 1944 by the establishment of a temporary haven in Oswego, New York, it was too late to make a difference.

The struggle over the administration of the visa procedure and the special visa lists throws some light on the conflicting tendencies within the Administration. The visa system became literally an adjunct to Berlin's murderous plan for the Jews. The quotas were underissued until 1939 and after June 1940 a skillful playing on the security fear resulted in ever more drastic reduction of refugee immigrants. In the critical year of 1941 only 47 percent of the German-Austrian quota was filled. A similar pattern is discernible in the procedure by which prominent refugees could receive special visitors' visas. Here again, the good intentions of the Administration were thwarted by the State Department and the consuls.

The calling of the Bermuda Conference in mid-1943 marks the fullest development of what might be called a politics of gestures. Held in inaccessible Bermuda, officials in London, where the initiative to hold such a conference developed, and Washington saw in the idea of holding another refugee conference the possibility of muting the growing agitation for a more active effort. The State Department confined the delegates to dealing with a group it called "political refugees," a euphemism for Jews, who bore the brunt of the Nazi liquidation program. The Conference was thereby confined to discussing ways and means of "rescuing" a handful of refugees who had found a precarious safety in Spain and other neutral havens and who were, in fact, already rescued, while those who faced death in the camps were ignored.

REASONS FOR THE GAP IN IMPLEMENTING RESCUE POLICY

The gulf which often exists between decision makers and administrators was especially wide in the case of rescue because the coterie of middle echelon career officers headed by Breckinridge Long and located primarily in the Special Problems Division of the State Department consistently opposed the professed humanitarian intentions of the Administration. The mobilization of a countervailing influence within the Administration which might have come from the Department of Interior, the Justice Department, and the Treasury Department, as well as numerous Jewish officials, did not materialize until the final months of 1943 when Henry Morgenthau, Jr., took up the cause. Before that time, Breckinridge Long, by his own account, usually had his way. He was able to capitalize on the weakness of White House leadership, so that the making and the administration of what amounted to the rescue program fell naturally in the purview of the State Department. An effective coalition of restrictionists and conservative legislators and Long's control of the flow of information to the White House abetted anti-rescue activities. After 1940, Breckinridge Long, by use of what I have called the security gambit, a playing on the fear that spies had infiltrated the refugee stream, was able to curtail the humanitarian activity of the Roosevelt Administration.

To place the responsibility for the failure of the Administration's rescue activity on Breckinridge Long alone would be to oversimplify. Roosevelt did intrude intermittently into the arena of rescue activity. We have seen that he was especially enthusiastic about the search for resettlement havens and he had some firm ideas about the form such ventures should take. Occasionally he mediated squabbles between rescue advocates and opponents within the Administration. But usually his suggestions, especially in the resettlement area, had an "above the battle" quality, being nowhere bound to the reality of the circumstances. Much of the inconsistency between the rhetoric of the Administration and the actual implementation of policy can be traced to the chief executive's uncertain mandate. Bound by a restrictive immigration law and perhaps an oversensitivity to the "Jew Deal" label which had been applied to his Administration on the one hand, and yet anxious to help the Nazi victims on the other, Roosevelt sought a balance between the opponents and advocates of a more active rescue policy. Such a middle road was never found, and to this day it is difficult for researchers to determine Roosevelt's personal role. They must turn to the State Department for answers, and repeat the journey made by American Jewish leaders during the Holocaust.

THE ROLE OF AMERICAN JEWRY

There have been times when "hyphenate" groups have exercised considerable influence over American foreign policy. The role of the Irish and the Germans in "twisting the Lion's tail" or the role of American Jews in Truman's *de facto* recognition of Israel are good examples of successful projection of influence in the foreign policy area. On the surface, few groups appeared better equipped to exert pressure on the Roosevelt Administration than American Jewry. Yet between 1938 and 1943 Jews were not notably successful in influencing the establishment on rescue ground rules and that failure proved catastrophic. In one sense the rescue battle was lost in the first round. Why they did not have more influence on the making and administration of rescue policy is only partly answered by what was happening within the American Jewish community during those terrible years.

The role that fell to American Jewry was difficult, perhaps impossible, to fill. It was called upon not only to attempt to change restrictive immigration policies which a majority of American Jews had supported in 1938, but also to challenge the State Department's administrative fiat further limiting the number which might come to these shores. They had to counteract a hysterical fear of Nazi espionage which was abetted by Congress, the State Department, the White House, and the communications media. No "hyphenate" group had ever been faced with the prospect of total annihilation of its European brethren and, while there was great urgency to use its influence, it proved to be extremely difficult to impress the urgency for action on the Administration. The rescue case concerned the disposition and treatment of a foreign minority, took place largely during the war years and, most important, required Roosevelt to tangle with powerful restrictionists in Congress and his own Administration. The kind of influence required was not available to Jewish leaders.

When catastrophe threatened, the deep fissures between its "uptown" and "downtown" elements had barely been bridged. Jews were anxious to continue their rapid movement into the mainstream of American life and did not readily accept the mantle of leadership which for centuries had been worn by European Jewry. Much of their formidable organizational resources were dissipated in internal bickering until it seemed as if Jews were more anxious to tear each other apart than to rescue their coreligionists. One has only to read Long's description of the numerous Jewish delegations, each representing a different group, to realize how tragic the situation of American Jewry was. That a community which desperately needed to speak to Roosevelt with one voice remained in an organizational deadlock is no small tragedy, and when one realizes how appallingly irrelevant the issues and personalities dividing them were, one can only shake one's head in disbelief. The Jews had achieved higher positions in the New Deal than in any prior Administration, but even with such resources they could not fully mobilize.

It is, of course, easy to know by hindsight what might have been done by American Jews. Disunity and powerlessness were characteristic of Jewish communities everywhere and the United States was no exception. The political behavior of American Jewry, moreover, exacerbated the situation. American Jews, who would paradoxically require concrete evidence of the authenticity of New Deal humanitarianism, supported Roosevelt because they thought his program evidenced concern for the "forgotten man." Such concern was a traditional part of the Jewish belief. When the New Deal moved further to the left after the election of 1936, the Jewish "love affair" with Roosevelt, in sharp contrast with other hyphenate groups, grew more ardent. The delivery of a voting bloc, the most potent weapon in any political arsenal, was not available to Jewish leaders. They could not gain leverage by threatening a withdrawal of votes and were therefore dependent on less certain rewards for political loyalty. If American Jews detected any failing in the rescue program it was not reflected in their voting. Such devotion seems puzzling. London and Berlin, who also enjoyed close familiarity with the Administration's rescue program, soon learned to dismiss a good deal of it as politically motivated and without serious intent. But American Jewry, perhaps because not even for them did rescue have the highest priority, remained faithful to the New Deal and still cherishes the memory of Roosevelt.

The growth of Zionist sentiment among American Jews as the crisis deepened was an additional factor interfering with the focusing of Jewish pressure on the White House. The new power relationship naturally gave those organizations with Zionist inclinations reason to hope that Jewry might be unified under their auspices. But other organizations stubbornly protected their organizational integrity. The crisis posed a special dilemma for the Zionists, for while it convinced many Jews of the need for a Jewish national homeland it also gave the old territorialists a new lease on life. Roosevelt was only one of many world leaders who were taken with visionary resettlement schemes. For Zionists a national homeland in Palestine was so clearly the answer that to divert money and energy to resettlement elsewhere was akin to heresy. When one considers today what was being offered, British Guiana, Mindanao, and other remote areas, it remains difficult to challenge the Zionist position. Resettlement outside Palestine was, even under the most favorable circumstances, only remotely possible, while in contrast the *Yishuv* was firmly established. Yet a gnawing doubt remains. Is it possible that there was an element of truth in the contention of the Bergson group that the goal of rescue and the national commonwealth goal worked at cross purposes during the war? Might the diversion of some resources to resettlement schemes such as the Sosua experiment in the Dominican Republic have made a difference for the doomed Jews of Europe? The Zionist movement had, after all, fashioned the only successful mass resettlement venture in the twentieth century. It possessed the zeal, the pioneering skill, and the support of the masses of Jews that might have gone far in overcoming the serious demographic difficulties found elsewhere. The Zionists faced an agonizing choice. There were not enough resources to support both expensive resettlement ventures and the pioneering effort in Palestine. The bitter truth seems to be that in order for mass rescue to have succeeded, the effort in Palestine would not only have had to be supplemented by other resettlement ventures but also by mass infiltration into established states. Had the last two alternatives been realized before 1942 there is some reason to believe that the Wannsee decision to liquidate the Jews of Europe might not have been taken. In any case, more Jews might have been rescued.

Unfortunately, the strife between Zionists and other groups did not remain merely academic. It not only interfered with the mobilization of American Jewry but spilled over into the largely Zionist-administered operation which maintained listening posts around the periphery of occupied Europe. The bickering between agents over credit for the handful that were brought out, which could be heard in Lisbon, Ankara and Stockholm, possesses an irony all its own. While the Nazi overlords endlessly projected a picture of a well-coordinated international Jewish conspiracy, the rescuers were in continuous conflict over questions of which Jews should be saved and who should get the credit.

PERSPECTIVE ON THE ROOSEVELT ADMINISTRATION
AS HOLOCAUST WITNESS

To view the Administration's failure to do everything that might have been done to save Jewish lives in perspective, an appreciation of the domestic and international problems involved in mass rescue is necessary. The rescue of European Jewry, especially after the failure to act during the refugee phase (1939 to October 1941), was so severely circumscribed by Nazi determination that it would have required an inordinate passion to save lives and a huge reservoir of good will toward Jews to achieve it. Such passion to save Jewish lives did not exist in the potential receiving nations. In the case of the United States, one can readily see today that a projection of human concern inwards to its own domestic problems such as alleviating the misery of its own Negro minority had barely been begun by the New Deal. What hope of better treatment could be held for a foreign minority? But this was not the only reason that the energy and organization of the Administration's rescue effort, even at its apogee in January 1944, never remotely approached the effort Berlin was willing to make to see the Final Solution through to its bitter end.

There were factors on the domestic political scene that further circumscribed action on the Administration's part. We have noted the continued strength of the restrictionists who remained alert during the refugee phase to the slightest infringement of the quota system. The anti-Jewish thrust of the anti-refugee sentiment did not escape the notice of Jewish leadership, who had become sensitized to the mood in the nation in the thirties. Supported by the Depression-created tensions and the example and financial support of the Reich, Jews found it difficult to dismiss the rantings of Father Charles E. Coughlin and other spokesmen of anti-Semitism. In Congress, for example, the negative response to the Wagner-Rogers Bill to save German-Jewish refugee children as contrasted to the favorable response to the evacuation of non-Jewish British children was too apparent to escape notice. The growth of domestic anti-Semitism projected against what was happening in Europe brought out the latent insecurities of American Jewry and sharpened internal divisions. The bitter disputes over the boycott of German goods and other "emotional" forms of agitation as well as the continued apprehension about dual loyalties in some sections of American Jewry become more understandable in the light of this insecurity.

A hidden casualty to the renewed vigor of domestic anti-Semitism may have been Roosevelt's willingness to strengthen his Administration's strong link to American Jewry. Roosevelt's appointments of Jews to high positions were a far cry from extending a helping hand to a foreign minority whose coreligionists in America were not winning medals for popularity. Such a commitment entailed a political risk which Roosevelt was not willing to take, and the Administration's response was to go through the motions of rescue without taking the political risk of implementing them. Undoubtedly this partly explains the paradox of the State Department's use of the innocuous label "political refugees," and maintaining it long after it had become apparent that the Reich meant to liquidate Jews and was converting all "enemies," including Roosevelt, to the Jewish faith. By concealing the anti-Jewish character of the Nazi depredations behind a neutral or interdenominational cover, Roosevelt may have sought to lessen the predictable outcry about favoritism towards Jews at home. For example, he expressed disappointment at the specific mention of Jews when Rublee revealed the provisions of the statement of agreement to him in February 1939. Again in October 1939 Roosevelt told Ickes about his hope to admit ten thousand refugees to Alaska on the same nationality ratio by which the quota system admitted immigrants to the mainland. That would limit entrance to one thousand Jews, a figure which Roosevelt hoped "would avoid the undoubted criticism" which would surely result "if there were an undue proportion of Jews." In May 1944 Roosevelt was still worrying about such "undue proportions" when he instructed Robert Murphy, who was to make the selection for the camp in Oswego, to make certain that he gets "reasonable proportions" of all categories of persecuted minorities. Beyond traumatizing American Jewry, the startling growth of anti-Semitism in the thirties may have alerted Roosevelt, whose sensitivity to the ethnic strain in American politics was well known, to the perils of further strengthening his ties to American Jewry.

Aside from such domestic political considerations, there were other roadblocks in the way of rescue. In the refugee and later the rescue phase, certain legal technicalities plagued the rescue effort. Admittedly there is a certain unreality in talking of legal technicalities while mass murder is being committed, but the witnesses and the perpetrators of the Holocaust were affected by such considerations. Before being deprived of their national citizenship the Jews were an "internal problem," and after they had been stripped of their national rights and citizenship they were not legally the responsibility of the nations who might have acted as rescue agents. As much as France, Britain, and the United States were directly involved in Germany's extrusion policy by having to become receiving nations, they had no power to force her to cease and desist. When there was a clear legal responsibility or an opportunity to utilize international law, the nations often did act. Thus when the Nazis threatened American Jewish property in Germany with confiscation before December 1941, the State Department did make strong representations. When Hungarian Jews in France were forced to wear the yellow star and later concentrated to be deported, Hungary did intercede in Berlin. Italian Jews were not forced to wear the yellow star. As cobelligerents Hungary and Italy maintained their sovereignty and therefore control of the fate of their Jews. A neutral like Turkey was able to protect its Jewish nationals in France and Spain's willingness to extend citizenship to Sephardic Jews saved some lives. Often Latin-American legal papers could make the difference between life and death, for paradoxically, even in the midst of their bloody operation, Nazis observed certain legal niceties. When there was no clear-cut legal responsibility, it proved difficult to elicit from the nations a voluntary response on humanitarian or moral grounds. Nation states like the United States are man-made institutions, not man himself. They have no souls and no natural sense of morality, especially when it concerns a foreign minority which is clearly not their legal responsibility. It is difficult to separate the charge that the Roosevelt Administration did not do enough to rescue Jews during the Holocaust years from the assumption that modern nation-states can make human responses in situations like the Holocaust. One wonders if the history of the twentieth, or any other century, warrants such an assumption, especially when the nation-state feels its security threatened.

In those rare cases where governments are able to make human responses to catastrophes they do so at the behest of an aroused public opinion. The shipping of relief supplies to Biafra is a case in point. In the case of the Jews the Roosevelt Administration had no popular mandate for a more active rescue role. Public opinion was, in fact, opposed to the admission of refugees, because most Americans were not aware of what was happening. A Roper poll taken in December 1944 showed that the great majority of Americans, while willing to believe that Hitler had killed some Jews, could not believe that the Nazis, utilizing modern production techniques, had put millions to death. The very idea beggared the imagination. Perhaps there is such a thing as a saturation point as far as atrocity stories are concerned. In the American mind the Final Solution took its place beside the Bataan Death March and the Malmedy massacre as just another atrocity in a particularly cruel war. Not only were the victims unable to believe the unbelievable, but those who would save them found it extremely difficult to break through the "curtain of silence." The State Department's suppression of the details compounded the problem of credibility.

The Administration's reluctance to publicly acknowledge that a mass murder operation was taking place went far in keeping American public opinion ignorant and therefore unaroused while it helped convince men like Goebbels that the Allies approved or were at least indifferent to the fate of the Jews. Psychological warfare techniques such as threats of retribution and bombing did have some effect in Hungary. A statement by Washington that the massive raid on Hamburg in July 1943 was made in retribution for a Treblinka or better yet a bombing of the rail lines and crematoria would have gone far to pierce the "curtain of silence," not only in the United States but among the people of occupied Europe. Specific mention of the crime against Jews was omitted from war-crimes statements and not until March 1944 could Roosevelt be prevailed upon to make some correction in the Moscow War Crimes Declaration. That statement promised vengeance for crimes against Cretan peasants but neglected to mention the Final Solution. From that point of view the failure of John J. McCloy, then Assistant Secretary of War, to favorably consider a joint request by the World Jewish Congress and the WRB to bomb the crematoria because it would be of "doubtful efficacy" was especially tragic. It might have gone far to alert world opinion to the mass murder operation as well as disrupting the delicate strands which made it possible. Washington maintained its silence for fear, in McCloy's words, that it might "provoke even more vindictive action by the Germans." Berlin, it was felt, was fully capable of escalating the terror. But for European Jewry, at least, it is difficult to imagine a terror greater than that of Auschwitz.

An effective rescue effort required not only inordinate energy and will but also coordination with other nations and agencies. It required the collective effort of the Vatican, the Committee of the International Red Cross (CIRC), other neutrals, the Allied governments, the governments in exile and the people of the occupied areas. While a determined effort by the Roosevelt Administration would have set a good precedent it did not mean that other nations and agencies would have automatically fallen in line. Latin America, for example, showed little propensity to follow Washington's advice regarding resettlement havens. The Taylor mission to the Vatican did not result in a change of Vatican policy and the CIRC was not fully activated until mid-1944. All maintained their own measure of commitment which they could claim fully matched that of the United States. The mere existence of separate national rescue efforts presented a problem of coordination. The IGC, which was established after the Evian Conference, might have furnished such coordination but, as we have seen, it became instead the first casualty of the lack of will. The early rescue effort was literally strangled by red tape, a reflection of the general lack of will to save lives. The State Department and Whitehall played a game which might be called "you've got the moral onus now" throughout the crisis.

The Holocaust was part of the larger insanity of World War II, and few world leaders possessed the foresight to comprehend that Auschwitz was a separate tragedy, a lethal combination of the most primitive atavism with the most advanced technology, a combination which summed up the agony of the twentieth century. Instead, there was a certain annoyance at the priority demanded by the Jews when the entire civilized world hovered on the brink of totalitarian domination. It was difficult for France to muster enthusiasm for a mass resettlement for refugees, which was suggested by Roosevelt at the meeting of the officers of the IGC in Washington in October 1939, when the existence of the French nation itself hung in the balance. Nor was Britain, while fighting for its life, anxious to accept more refugees. The priorities were for national survival and victory, and the rescue of Jews would be considered only if it could be accommodated to these priorities.

In the three years before America's entry into the war it faced no threat to its continued national existence as did France and Britain. But it acted as though it did and ordered its priorities accordingly. By June 1941 a nonbelligerent United States had more rigid screening procedures for refugees than Britain, which had been at war for almost two years. The security psychosis which was generously abetted by the State Department was the Administration's version of the national survival argument and had much the same effect on rescue activity. Once the war began the mania about spies having been infiltrated among the largely Jewish refugees could be muted in favor of the argument that the fastest road to rescue was to defeat Hitler. Nothing must be done to divert energy and resources from that goal. As it turned out, almost anything that could be done for rescue would cause such a diversion. Ships to transport refugees, which came back empty, could not be diverted because they were in short supply. Relief supplies could not be sent to camps because, according to Breckinridge Long, it would relieve the Reich from responsibility of feeding people under its control. Camps could not be bombed because aircraft could not be diverted to tasks of "doubtful efficacy." If one argued, as many rescue advocates did, that by the time victory came all Jews in Europe would be dead, one revealed a greater concern for Jewish survival than for the survival of the United States. Breckinridge Long's diary is full of charges that the rescue advocates, in pressing for a more humanitarian visa procedure or relief shipments to the camps, were really acting as Berlin's agents and subverting the nation's war effort. Counteracting such arguments proved to be a nigh impossible task.

These, then, were some of the reasons why the Roosevelt Administration responded only half-heartedly to the challenge of saving Jewish lives. But even if the problems that prevented rescue had been solved—if Breckinridge Long had been converted to the rescue cause; if the divisions within American Jewry had been magically healed; if the immigration laws had been circumvented earlier; if Alaska had been made available for resettlement; if Whitehall had abandoned its inhumanely political attitude towards Jewish immigration into Palestine; if the Pope had spoken out; if the CIRC had been more courageous; in short if there had been a will to save lives, we still have no assurance that mass rescue could have been realized, although many thousands more might have been saved. Something like such a miracle occurred in Hungary in 1944. Yet within full view of the world and when the Nazi authorities could no longer doubt that they had lost the war, the cattle cars rolled to Auschwitz as if they had a momentum of their own. Over half of Hungary's Jewry went up in smoke.

Appalling as it may sound, the saving of lives was a far more formidable task than the practice of genocide. Even a passionate will to save lives could prove insufficient, given Nazi determination to liquidate the Jews of Europe. Something more was required, something to soften the hearts of those in Berlin who were in physical control of the slaughter. Such a miracle was never in the power of the Washington policy makers. It belongs to a higher kingdom whose strange indifference has become an overriding concern of the theologians.

Notes

Abbreviations used for all published and archival sources are listed below. Publication data and locations of archival collections are listed in the Bibliography.

Annals	*Annals of the American Academy of Political and Social Science*
AJYB	*American Jewish Year Book*
Bloom MSS	Papers of Solomon Bloom
British Documents	*Documents on British Foreign Policy,* 3d series, III
Chamberlain MSS	Papers of Joseph Chamberlain
CJR	*Contemporary Jewish Record*
CR	*Congressional Record*
FDRL	Papers at Franklin D. Roosevelt Library
FDRL/OF	Official File
FDRL/PPF	President's Personal File
FDRL/PSF	President's Secretary File
FDRL/WRB	Papers of the War Refugee Board
FRUS	*Foreign Relations of the United States*
German Documents	*Documents on German Foreign Policy, 1918–1945,* series D, IV, V
Hull MSS	Papers of Cordell Hull
Long MSS	Breckinridge Long Papers
Long Diary	Breckinridge Long Diary

Moffat MSS   J. Pierrepont Moffat Papers
Moffat Diary   J. Pierrepont Moffat Diary
NA/SDDF   National Archives, State Department
                     Decimal File
Wise MSS   Stephen S. Wise Papers

Abbreviated titles used to cite documents, committee reports, proceedings with especially long titles.

Bermuda Conference Final Report—*Report to the Government of the United States and the United Kingdom from the Delegates to the Conference on Refugee Problems held at Bermuda*, April 19–28, 1943.

Evian Proceedings—Proceedings of the Intergovernment Committee, Evian, July 6–15, 1938, Verbatim Record of the Plenary Meetings of the Committee, Resolution and Reports.

Final Summary Report, WRB—Final Summary Report of the Executive Director of the War Refugee Board.

House Rescue Commission Hearings—Hearings on Resolutions Providing for the Establishment . . . of a Commission to . . . Rescue the Jewish People of Europe.

Footnoting procedure: An abbreviated procedure of documentation which affords the reader the fullest publication data is followed. A list of abbreviations of frequently used published and original archival sources is provided. Full information on these sources is provided in the bibliography. The same procedure is followed in the case of books. The initial citation omits publication data which may be found in the bibliography. Where two citations follow each other directly the normal practice of using *Ibid.* is followed. However, where other citations intervene I have preferred to use the last name of the author and an abbreviated version of the title followed by dates and page references.

Chapter 1

1. Throughout the 1930's numerous warnings by Hitler and other Nazi leaders regarding the annihilation of the Jews were issued. When Ambassador Dodd presented his credentials on March 7, 1933, Hitler coldly informed him that the Jews would be liquidated in case of war. William

E. Dodd, *Ambassador Dodd's Diary*, ed. William E. Dodd, Jr., and Martha Dodd, 89. A similar warning was given to James G. McDonald on April 3, 1933. *New York Times*, July 17, 1944, 14. For the persistency of the annihilation thread in Nazi thinking see Alan Bulock, *Hitler; A Study in Tyranny*, 407.

2. Department of Commerce, Bureau of the Census, *Historical Statistics of the United States, 1789–1943*, 36–37.

3. A description of the reaction of German Jewry is found in Mark Wischnitzer, *To Dwell in Safety: The Story of Jewish Migration Since 1800*, 175.

4. Edward N. Peterson, *Hjalmar Schacht: For and Against Hitler—A Political-Economic Study of Germany, 1923–1945*, 246.

5. Gerald Reitlinger, *The Final Solution: The Attempt to Exterminate the Jews of Europe, 1934–1945*, 18.

6. There is little agreement on the number of Jews in Germany after the Anschluss. One-half million is the approximate figure sometimes cited. Bruno Blau, "The Jewish Population of Germany, 1939–1945," *JSS*, XII (April 1950), 161–172, calculates that in September 1938 there were only 343,552 Jews of all categories in the Reich. If his calculations are correct, the figure used for resettlement purposes was overestimated by at least 150,000. Blau also presents an important statistical description of occupation categories: In 1931, 1.7 percent were in agriculture, as compared to 52.5 percent in trade and commerce and 23.1 percent in industry.

7. Stephen S. Wise, *As I See It*, 98.

8. Raul Hilberg, *The Destruction of the European Jews*, 30, quoting from the press release of Reichsbund Judischer Frontsoldaten, March 27, 1933, and *Central-Verein Zeitung*, March 23, 1933. A full description of the antiagitation posture of German Jewish leadership is also presented in British Diplomatic dispatches. See especially *British Documents*, 2nd Ser., Vol. V, 14 (March 31, 1933).

9. Rudolph Stahl, "Vocational Retraining of Jews in Nazi Germany," *JSS*, I (April 1939), 171. See also Blau, "Jewish Population."

10. The evaluation belongs to Thomas A. Bailey, *The Man in the Street: The Impact of American Public Opinion on Foreign Policy*, 24.

11. For a complete statistical description of American Jewry in 1939 see H. S. Linfield, "Jewish Communities of the United States," *AJYB*, XLII (1940–1941), 215–266.

12. Alfred O. Hero, *Voluntary Organization in World Affairs Communication*, vol. V: *Studies in Citizen Participation in International Relations*, 72.

13. Nathan Glazer, "The American Jew and the Attainment of Middle

Class Rank," *The Jews: Social Patterns of an American Group,* ed. Marshall Sklare, 141.

14. The Editors of *Fortune, Jews in America,* 5.

15. Werner Cohn, "The Politics of American Jews," in Sklare, *The Jews,* 614–626. Lawrence H. Fuchs, *The Political Behavior of American Jews,* 171 ff.

16. *Reconstructionist,* January 11, 1935, editorial.

17. Fuchs, *Political Behavior,* 201.

18. *Ibid.* 129.

19. A parallel observation is made about the position of world Jewry by Samuel Halperin, *The Political World of American Zionism,* 29. A provocative analysis of American Jewish political behavior is found in Daniel J. Elazar, "Jews and American Political Ideas," *Congress Bi-Weekly,* 36, No. 1, January 13, 1969, pp. 3–7.

20. *Fortune, Jews in America,* 2.

21. Donald Strong, *Organized Anti-Semitism in America: The Rise of Group Prejudice During the Decade 1930–1940,* 21 ff.

22. *Public Opinion Quarterly,* IV, 1, p. 94 (November 1939). Italians received 22.5 percent of the vote for worst citizen, Jews 6 percent, and Germans 4.1 percent.

23. Samuel Lubell, *The Future of American Politics,* 82–83.

24. *New York Times,* November 17, 1938, 7. A full discussion of the effects of the boycott is presented in A. Leon Kubowitzki, *Unity in Dispersion: A History of the World Jewish Congress,* 108 ff.

25. The anti-boycott argument is well developed in Nathan Schachner, *The Price of Liberty: A History of the American Jewish Committee,* 11 ff.

26. For a description of these activities see Cyrus Adler and Aaron M. Margalith, *With Firmness in the Right: American Diplomatic Action Affecting Jews, 1840–1945.*

27. See for example Max J. Kohler, *The United States and German Jewish Persecution: Precedents for Popular and Government Action* and *The Jews in Nazi Germany: The Factual Record of Their Persecution by the National Socialists.*

28. Stephen S. Wise, *Challenging Years,* 314, quoted from a speech by Nahum Goldmann, president of the World Jewish Congress.

29. Halperin, *Political World,* 20, and Rufus Learsi, *The Jews in America: A History,* 286.

30. A. Ginsburg, "Our Protest," *Forwards,* April 1, 1933, p. 8.

31. Sumner Welles, *Time for Decision,* 314.

32. Roosevelt listened attentively to Brandeis' plea against the British White Paper in October 1939. Alpheus T. Mason, *Brandeis,* 635.

33. David Brody, "American Jewry: The Refugees and Immigration Restriction, 1932–1942," *Publications of the American Jewish Historical Society, XLV* (June 1956), 219–247.

34. "Twenty-eighth Annual Report of the American Jewish Committee, 1935," 59–60. (Published in pamphlet form by American Jewish Committee.)

35. *B'nai B'rith Magazine*, July 1935, 354.

36. FDRL/OF 133, James G. McDonald to Felix Warburg, October 10, 1935.

37. Long Diary, January 11, 1944.

38. Dodd, *Diary*, 5. FDR's personal instructions to Dodd, June 16, 1933.

39. Out of the yearly quota allowance for Germany of 25,957, 2,273 immigrants entered in 1932; 1,445 in 1933; 3,744 in 1934; 5,532 in 1935; 6,642 in 1936; 11,536 in 1937. Not until 1939 was the now combined German-Austrian quota of 27,360 fulfilled. See Louis Adamic, *America and the Refugees*, 10–11. Also Read Lewis and Marian Shibsby, "Status of the Refugee Under American Immigration Laws," *Annals*, CCIII (May 1939), 78 ff.

40. FDRL/PSF Lehman Folder, Herbert Lehman to FDR, June 5, 1935 and FDR to Lehman, November 13, 1935.

41. *The Public Papers and Addresses of Franklin D. Roosevelt*, ed. Samuel Rosenman, VII, 603.

42. FDRL/PSF Hull Folder, Hull memo to FDR, April 21, 1936.

43. Particularly successful at chiding the Nazis was Fiorello H. La Guardia, the irrepressible mayor of New York City. Others who succeeded on touching the raw nerves of Nazi officialdom so that official request that they be silenced followed were Harold Ickes and William E. Dodd, Jr.

44. For a review of Dodd's troubles in Berlin see Franklin L. Ford, "Three Observers in Berlin, Rumbold, Dodd, and Francois Poncet," *The Diplomats, 1919–1939*, ed. Gordon Craig and Felix Gilbert, II, 447–460. A more favorable evaluation of Dodd's effectiveness is presented by Robert Dallek, *Democrat and Diplomat: The Life of William E. Dodd*.

45. Cordell Hull, *The Memoirs of Cordell Hull*, I, 237.

46. Adler and Margalith, *Firmness*, 27.

47. *FRUS*, II, 374, June 2, 1938, Hugh Wilson to Hull.

48. *New York Times*, February 4, 1938, 12.

49. Henry Morgenthau, Jr., "The Morgenthau Diaries VI—The Refugee Run Around," *Collier's*, November 1, 1947, 22.

50. Hull, *Memoirs*, II, 471.

51. *FRUS*, I, 752, July 2, 1938, Wallace Murray to George Wadsworth in confidential memo.

52. FDRL/OF 3186 Marvin McIntire to Sumner Welles, June 3, 1938.

53. Hull, *Memoirs*, II, 1936. *See also* Frank E. Manuel, *The Realities of American-Palestine Relations*, 315.

54. Bartley Crum, *Behind the Silken Curtain*, 36–39.

55. A complete description of the defense and oil factors in the Administration's Palestine policy may be found in Herbert Feis, *Petroleum and American Foreign Policy*. See also Manuel, *The Realities*, 234.

Chapter 2

1. *New York Times*, March 26, 1938, 1.

2. FDRL/OF 3186, FDR to Herbert Lehman, March 28, 1938.

3. *FRUS*, I, 740–741, March 23, 1938.

4. Gideon Hausner, *Justice in Jerusalem*, 34–40, 44–47. See also Dorothy Thompson, *Refugees, Anarchy or Organization*, 92, and Hannah Arendt, *Eichmann in Jerusalem*, 43–45.

5. Frances Perkins, *The Roosevelt I Knew*, 92.

6. Thompson, *Refugees*, xi (Introduction), Hamilton Fish Armstrong, chairman of the Foreign Policy Association, credits Miss Thompson with having been the principal influence on Roosevelt. Miss Thompson reiterated this belief in her testimony. She claimed that her powerful article on the refugee crisis in *Foreign Affairs*, XVI (April 1938), 375–378, entitled "Refugees, A World Problem," convinced Roosevelt that something had to be done. *Joint Hearings before a Subcommittee of the Committee on Immigration, United States Senate, and a Subcommittee of the Committee on Immigration and Naturalization*, House of Representatives, 16th Cong., 1st Sess. (April 20, 21, 22, and 24, 1939) (Wagner-Rogers Resolution), 160 ff.

7. Letter from Lubin to author, September 26, 1963.

8. Perkins, *Roosevelt*, 92.

9. This was especially true after *Krystallnacht*, November 9, 1938. For speculation on this point see David S. Wyman, *Paper Walls: America and the Refugee Crisis, 1938–1941*, 44–45.

10. FDRL/OF 3186, January 3, 1940, Observation made by Adolf Berle in memorandum.

11. FDRL/OF 3186, Lehman to FDR, March 28, 1938; FDR to Lehman, March 30, 1938.

12. FDRL/OF 3186, March 26, 1938. The organizations involved were the American Jewish Congress, the American Jewish Committee, B'nai B'rith, the Zionist Organization of America and the Jewish Labor Council.

13. *New York Times*, April 11, 1938, 4.

14. *CR*, 75th Cong., 3rd Sess., XXLIII, part 4, p. 4227. March 28, 1938.

15. FDRL/OF 3186, April 8, 1938, Invitation to White House meeting.

16. Chamberlain MSS, Minutes of the Executive Board of the National Coordinating Committee, October 1, 1935.

17. FDRL/OF 3186, Armstrong to FDR, April 26, 1938.

18. *FRUS*, I, 750–751, June 27, 1938, William C. Bullit to Hull.

19. Replies to the invitation are printed in Department of State, *Press Releases*, XVIII, Nr. 44, April 1938 and *FRUS*, I, 741 ff. March–April, 1938.

20. *New York Times*, March 27, 1938, 25.

21. FDRL/OF, April 11, 1938, Sumner Welles memo to FDR.

22. *Evian Proceedings*, preface, 8.

23. FDRL/OF, April 11, 1938, Welles memo to FDR.

24. *New York Times*, July 6, 1938, 1 (Clarence E. Streit column).

25. *Evian Proceedings*, July 6, 1938, 11.

26. *British Documents*, 3rd Series, III, 294–296, November 24, 1938, Neville Chamberlain–Edouard Daladier conversations.

27. *Evian Proceedings*, July 6, 1938, 13.

28. *Ibid.*, Annex IV, Final Resolutions. The term "involuntary emigrant" was substituted for "political refugee" and a pledge was made to carry on the work of the soon to be disbanded Nansen Office which provided stateless refugees with documents.

29. *Ibid.* A good account of the conflicts at the Evian conference is available in Erick Estorick, "The Intergovernmental Committee and the Evian Conference," *Annals*, CCIII (May 1939), 136–141. The entire League of Nations effort is examined in Louise W. Holborn, "The League of Nations and the Refugee Problem," *Annals*, CCIII (May 1939), 124–136.

30. Chamberlain MSS, June 16, 1938, Avra Warren to George Brandt.

31. *Evian Proceedings*, July 6, 1938, 13.

32. *FRUS*, I, 787, September 13, 1938; I, 772, August 25, 1938, Rublee to Hull.

33. *Evian Proceedings*, July 9, 1938, 31.

34. *Ibid.*, 25.

35. *Ibid.*, 32.

36. *Ibid.*, July 11, 1938, 30.

37. *Ibid.*, July 9, 1938, 25.

38. The press survey is contained in *CJR*, I (September 1938), 55 ff.; Ira Hirschmann, *Lifeline to a Promised Land*, 102.

39. *FRUS*, I, 778–780, August 30, 1938, Anthony Biddle to Hull.

40. *Evian Proceedings,* July 15, 1938, 42, Earl Winterton's closing address.

41. A highly dramatized fictionalized account of the Neumann mission serves as the basis of Hans Habe's, *The Mission.* The ransom motif for individuals and masses is not uncommon during the Holocaust and can be found as early as 1936 and as late as 1944.

42. Mark Wischnitzer, *Visas to Freedom, The History of HIAS,* 153.

43. *New York Times,* July 9, 1938, 4. Repeated warnings of the worsening situation in Poland and Rumania were given by Stephen Wise, Nahum Goldmann, and Norman Bentwich.

44. *FRUS,* I, 778–780, August 30, 1938; 835–836, November 19, 1938.

45. *Ibid.,* 810, October 19, 1938, Rublee to Hull.

46. James A. Farley, *Jim Farley's Story: The Roosevelt Years,* 159.

47. Estimate made by Taylor at the London conference of the IGC. Arthur D. Morse, *While Six Million Died: A Chronicle of American Apathy,* 218. Taylor's estimate seems rather high and is at variance with one given by Adamic, *America and Refugees,* 11, 19. Adamic estimates that during the 1938–1939 quota period the number of German Jews receiving visas was between one half and two thirds of the total issued.

48. *Evian Proceedings,* July 11, 1938, 34. He was the Swedish delegate M. G. Engzell, who was also head of the Legal Department of the Swedish Ministry of Foreign Affairs.

49. *German Documents,* D, IV, July 8, 1938, 894–895.

50. Quoted in *New York Times,* July 13, 1938, 13.

51. *FRUS,* I, July 9, 1938, Hugh Wilson to Hull.

52. *FRUS,* I, 772, August 25, 1938, Rublee to Hull.

53. *Public Papers of FDR,* VII, 169.

54. *Fortune Quarterly Survey,* XX, 4, p. 104 (April 1939).

55. *FRUS,* I, 796–798, October 12, 1938.

56. *Ibid.*

57. *Public Papers of FDR,* VII, 173, Hugh Wilson to FDR, reporting on conversation with Weizsäcker on October 18, 1938.

58. *Evian Proceedings,* July 6, 1938, 13 and also Annex IV. See also, Minutes of the Meeting of the National Coordinating Committee, October 20, 1938 for an expression of the same association with the appeasement policy in the thinking of leading refugee advocates.

59. Department of State, *Press Releases,* XX, Nr. 47 (October 1938), 245–255.

60. *Public Papers of FDR,* VII, 172–173, October 5, 1938.

61. *Ibid.,* 173.

62. *New York Times,* January 22, 1939, 32.

63. *Nazi Conspiracy and Aggression*, III, 277–278, November 9, 1938.

64. *New York Times*, November 11, 1938, 1.

65. *German Documents*, D, V, November 14, 1938, 639–640, Dieckhoff to Weizsäcker.

66. *Ibid.*, IV, November 17, 1938, 643, Dirksen to Weizsäcker.

67. Philip E. Jacob, "The Influence of World Events on the United States Neutrality Opinion," *Public Opinion Quarterly*, IV, Nr. 1, 51 ff.

68. The precedent was established by Theodore Roosevelt when he was Police Commissioner of New York City in 1895.

69. *The Moffat Papers*, ed. Nancy Harrison Hooker, 221–222.

70. *FRUS*, II, 396–397, November 14, 1938, Messersmith to Hull.

71. *New York Times*, November 15, 1938, 1.

72. FDRL/OF 3186, Rosenman to Taylor, November 23, 1938.

73. *Fortune Quarterly Survey*, XX, 4, p. 104 (April 1939).

74. Wyman, *Paper Walls*, 37.

75. *British Documents*, 3rd Series, III, 270, November 13, 1938, Forbes to Halifax.

Chapter 3

1. *German Documents*, D, V, October 20, 1938, 902.

2. Gordon A. Craig, "The German Foreign Office from Neurath to Ribbentrop," Craig & Gilbert eds., *The Diplomats*, II, 434.

3. *German Documents*, D, V, November 12, 1938, 904.

4. *Ibid.*, November 16–21, 1938, 908–910.

5. *British Documents*, 3rd Ser., III, 278, November 17, 1938, Forbes to Halifax.

6. *German Documents*, D, V, December 12, 1938, 910.

7. *Ibid.*, December 9, 1938, 347–348. *FRUS*, I, 862–863, December 8, 1938, Rublee's despatch to Hull based on Berenger's report to the executive committee of the IGC.

8. FDRL/PPF, December 12, 1938, Welles Folder.

9. For details of the original scheme see, *American Hebrew*, January 10, 1936, 253.

10. FDRL/PSF, November 14, 1938, Guenther Folder, Franklin Mott Guenther to FDR.

11. *FRUS*, I, 760, August 5, 1938, Taylor to Hull.

12. *British Documents*, 3rd Ser., III, 270, November 11, 1938, Forbes to Halifax.

13. *FRUS*, I, 776–777, August 12, 1938, Wilson to Hull, Wilson, his successor Gilbert, and Pell were continuously reminded usually by Weizsäcker, that the absence of resettlement opportunities made negotia-

tions futile. In contrast to Schacht the German Foreign Office insisted that such havens be available beforehand.

14. *Ibid.*, 821, November 11, 1938, Rublee to Hull.

15. Chamberlain MSS, Minutes of the Board of Directors of the NCC (National Coordinating Committee), October 20, 1938 (typed copy).

16. *AJYB*, vol. 49 (1947–1948), 751. See also Wyman, *Paper Walls*, 33.

17. The description of the Schacht proposal is taken from NA/SDDF, 840.48 Refugees/1119, December 15, 1938, Rublee memorandum, 840.48 Refugees/1125, December 16, 1938, Rublee to Hull; *German Documents*, D, V, 900–903; *British Documents*, 3rd Ser., III, 675–677; Lewis L. Strauss, *Men and Decisions*, 113–129.

18. *FRUS*, I, 755, August 25, 1938, Hull to Rublee. On September 19, 1938 George Messersmith again communicated with Rublee about this concern. *Ibid.*, 788–790.

19. *Public Papers of FDR*, VII, 174, December 15, 1938, FDR to Taylor FDR's adverse reaction did not, however, mean that he favored rejecting the proposal. If anything, Roosevelt agreed with Taylor that the road should be kept open and the initiative passed to London.

20. *New York Times*, January 17, 1939, 1.

21. Dorothy Thompson, *Let the Record Speak*, 273

22. Strauss, *Men and Decisions*, 121.

23. Wise MSS, August 17, 1938, Tenenbaum to Wise.

24. *Ibid.*, August 21, 1938, Wise to McDonald.

25. *FRUS*, II, 66–67, January 14, 1939, Roosevelt Memorandum.

26. *German Documents*, D, V, 912, December 20, 1938.

27. *Ibid.*, 913–914.

28. Strauss, *Men and Decisions*, 121, Letter from Norman to Strauss.

29. *German Documents*, D, V, July 7, 1938, 912 ff. Schacht to Wilhelm Frick in memorandum, "The Final Elimination of Jews from German Economic Life."

30. *FRUS*, II, 71, January 20, 1938, Rublee to Hull.

31. *German Documents*, D, V, 925, January 20, 1939.

32. Quoted in Reitlinger, *Final Solution*, 21.

33. *Ibid.*, 935, February 11, 1939, Circular of Foreign Office to all embassies. See also, *Nazi Conspiracy and Aggression*, VI, 87–89, January 31, 1939, "The Jewish Question as a Factor in German Foreign Policy in the Year 1938."

34. *Ibid.*

35. Quoted by Hilberg, *The Destruction*, 259.

36. Strauss, *Men and Decisions*, 121; *FRUS*, II, 73, January 21, 1939, Rublee to Hull; Moffat MSS, February 6, 1939, Gilbert to Pierrepont Moffat.

37. *Nazi Conspiracy and Aggression*, IV, 451.

38. *New York Times*, March 10, 1939, 5; *FRUS*, II, 82–84, February 6, 1939, Rublee to Hull.

39. *Ibid.*, 83; Department of State, *Press Releases*, XX, Nr. 493, 184, March 11, 1939.

40. Kubowitzki, *Unity in Dispersion*, 116.

41. New York *Herald Tribune*, February 17, 1939, 21.

42. Moffat Diary, February 13, 1939.

43. *FRUS*, I, 883, December 28, 1938. FDR and Welles opposed the idea but a few weeks later approved it.

44. *Ibid.*, II, 84–87, February 8, 1938.

45. *Ibid.*, 85; *Public Papers of FDR*, VII, 174–175.

46. *Ibid.*

47. *German Documents*, D, V, 937, February 18, 1939, Dirksen to Weizsäcker.

48. Moffat Diary, February 12, 1939.

49. *FRUS*, II, 97–98, March 14, 1939, Welles to Pell.

50. Department of State, *Press Releases*, XX, Nr. 493, 184, March 11, 1939.

51. *FRUS*, II, 98–99, March 22, 1939, Welles to Rublee.

52. *Ibid.*, 110–112, May 18, 1939, Pell to Hull.

53. *Ibid.*

54. Jewish Black Book Committee, *The Black Book; The Nazi Crime Against the Jewish People*, 121.

55. See Nathan Eck, "The Rescue of Jews With the Aid of Passports and Citizenship Papers of Latin American States," *Yad Washem Studies*, I, 1957, 125–152.

56. *New York Times*, August 5, 1939, 6.

57. The most complete account of the *St. Louis* incident is contained in Morse, *While Six Million Died*, 270–288.

58. International Military Tribunal, *The Trial of Major War Criminals Before the International Military Tribunal*, XXII, 389, Schacht testimony. See also *Nazi Conspiracy and Aggression*, Supplement B, 517, Schacht's final plea and statement of Dr. Dix.

59. *German Documents*, D, V, 906, November 12, 1938.

60. Moffat MSS, February 6, 1939, Gilbert to Moffat.

Chapter 4

1. FDRL/OF 3186, May 4, 1939, Welles memo to FDR; also *FRUS*, II, 105–107, May 14, 1939.

2. NA/SDDF, 840.48 Refugees/1514, Memorandum, Division of European Affairs, March 15, 1939.

3. Strauss, *Men and Decisions*, 120. See also *FRUS*, II, 133, July 13, 1939.

4. *Ibid.*

5. Committee on Immigration and Naturalization, House of Representatives, *Hearings on the Joint Resolution to Authorize the Admission of a Limited Number of Refugee Children*, 76th Cong., 1st Sess., May 25, 1939, 246.

6. Wise MSS, April 1, 1939, Paul Baerwald to Wise.

7. Moffat Diary, May 11, 1939.

8. *FRUS*, II, 115–118, June 6, 7, 1939.

9. *Ibid.*, 108, May 12, 1939.

10. See David H. Popper, "A Homeland for Refugees," *Annals*, CCIII (May 1939), 175.

11. Wise MSS, January 5, 1939, Judge Proskauer to Wise.

12. *Ibid.*, May 26, 1939, Silver to Wise.

13. NA/SDDF, 840.48 Refugees/1514, Memorandum, Division of European Affairs, March 15, 1939.

14. A summary of the agreement is included in Wise, MSS "Minutes of the 26th Meeting of the Presidential Advisory Committee on Political Refugees," June 29, 1939.

15. Wise MSS, June 17, 1939, Baerwald, Jaretzki, Hyman to Linder.

16. *Ibid.*, June 13, 1939, Baerwald to Wise.

17. *FRUS*, II, 123–124, June 9, 1939, Pell to Hull.

18. *Ibid.* See also Moffat Diary, June 12, 1939.

19. Moffat MSS, April 17, 1939, Pell to Moffat.

20. *FRUS*, II, 130, July 1, 1939, Pell to Hull.

21. *Ibid.*, 131.

22. Moffat Diary, May 12, 1939.

23. *Ibid.*

24. Moffat MSS, July 25, 1939, Moffat to Theodore Achilles.

25. Wise MSS, May 19, 1939, Wise to McDonald.

26. *FRUS*, II, 131, July 31, 1939, Pell to Hull.

27. *Ibid.*, 134.

28. *Ibid.*, 127, June 25, 1939, Taylor to FDR.

29. *Ibid.*, 134, July 1, 1939, Pell to Hull.

30. *Ibid.*, 135, June 25, 1939, Hull to Pell.

31. Hull MSS, Container 44, Folder 18, July 17, 1939, verbatim transcript of trans-Atlantic telephone conversation between Dunn and Taylor.

32. The management council included American and British names of unusual prominence. John W. Davis, Democratic candidate for President (1924); Dr. Rufus Jones, president of Swarthmore College and an outstanding Quaker leader; Nathan I. Miller, former Governor of New York;

David H. Morris, former Ambassador; Judge Joseph Proskauer, former justice of the Supreme Court of New York State and soon to be head of the American Jewish Committee; Lessing J. Rosenwald, prominent American industrialist; Rabbi Stephen S. Wise, president of the American Jewish Congress; Owen D. Young, chairman of the board of the General Electric Company. On the British side there was the Earl of Bessborough, former Governor General of Canada; Viscount Bearsted, head of Shell Oil Company; Jarold Butler, warden of Nuffield College; Lionel L. Cohen, leader of the British Bar; Simon Marks, successful merchant; Lionel de Rothschild, of the Rothschild banking firm; Sir Horace Rumbold, former British Ambassador to Berlin; Sir John Hope Simpson, of the Royal Institute of International Affairs and expert on Refugees. Lewis Strauss and Paul Baerwald of the AJJDC were also included. The French did not participate.

33. *FRUS*, II, 138, August 18, 1938, Pell to Hull.

34. FDRL/OF 3186, June 8, 1939, FDR to Taylor.

35. The Jewish community of Poland was the largest and fastest growing Jewish community in the world. At the time of the invasion in September 1939 it consisted of 3,325,000 souls which was about 10 percent of the population of Poland. About 1,250,000 were able to find safety on the Soviet side of occupied Poland. The Reich thus received anywhere from 2,000,000 to 2,400,000 additional Jews.

36. *Public Papers of FDR*, VII, 1004, March 7, 1940, FDR to Hull.

37. *FRUS*, II, 150, October 2, 1939.

38. FDRL/OF 3186, September 26, 1939, McDonald Memorandum.

39. *Ibid.*

40. *FRUS*, II, 145–146, September 25, 1939.

41. FDRL/OF 3186, Official Minutes of the Meeting of the Officers of the IGC held in Washington, October 16, 17, 18 and 26, 1939, 36.

42. *FRUS*, II, 149, September 28, 1939.

43. Wischnitzer, *Visas to Freedom*, 160.

44. *German Documents*, D, VIII, September 12, 1939.

45. *FRUS*, II, 150, September 29, 1939.

46. FDRL/OF 3186, June 8, 1939, FDR to Taylor.

47. FDRL/PSF, Hull File, October 2, 1939, Confidential Memo, FDR to Hull. Also found in *Public Papers of FDR*, VIII, 930–932.

48. See Guenter Lewy, "Pius XII, the Jews, and the German Catholic Church," *Commentary*, XXXVII (February 1964), 29–30 and his *The Catholic Church and Nazi Germany*, 292. For the strange career of Kurt Gerstein see Saul Friedländer, *Kurt Gerstein: The Ambiguity of Good*.

49. Moffat Diary, July 27, 1939.

50. FDRL/OF 3186, Official Minutes of the Meeting of the Officers of the IGC, October 17, 1939, 19. See also Wise MSS, Minutes of the Twenty-ninth Meeting of the President's Advisory Committee on Political Refugees, October 23, 1939.

51. *Ibid.* See also *State Department Press Releases*, I, No. 17, 397–398.

52. Moffat Diary, October 18, 1939.

53. *New York Times*, October 22, 1939, 26.

54. Wise MSS, Minutes of the Twenty-seventh Meeting of the President's Advisory Committee on Political Refugees, September 14, 1939.

55. *New York Times*, October 18, 1939, 17.

56. Wise MSS, October 4, 1939, Wise to Benjamin Cohen.

57. *Ibid.* October 17, 1939, Wise to Frankfurter.

58. Moffat Diary, October 23, 1939.

59. *New York Times*, November 2, 1939, 10. See also *The Black Book*, 127.

60. Chamberlain MSS, Minutes of the National Coordinating Committee, October 30, 1939.

Chapter 5

1. Strauss, *Men and Decisions*, 124–125.

2. FDRL/PSF, State Department File, June 3, 1938, FDR letter to Gonzales.

3. NA/SDDF, 840.48 Refugees/1115, December 5, 1939, Leo Sack to FDR.

4. Wise MSS, Minutes of the Third Meeting of the PACPR, June 2, 1938.

5. NA/SDDF, 840.48 Refugees/1531, March 3, 1939, Memorandum, Division of American Republics.

6. *Ibid.*

7. FDRL/OF 3186, January 5, 1939, Sumner Welles to FDR.

8. NA/SDDF, 840.48 Refugees/2159A, Hull to Jefferson Caffrey; 840.48 Refugees/2543, April 19, 1941, Jefferson Caffrey to Hull.

9. NA/SDDF, 855.55 J/1 February 8, 1939, Leopoldville to State Department.

10. Wise MSS, December 8, 1938, Report on special meeting of the PACPR (typed).

11. *AJYB*, XLII, 1940/41, 600.

12. Wise MSS, Minutes of the Third Meeting of the PACPR, June 2, 1938.

13. For the American Jewish resettlement precedent see, Abraham Ducker, "Jewish Territorialism: An Historical Sketch," *CJR*, II (March–April, 1939, No. 20, 14–20; Oscar Handlin, *Adventures in Freedom, Two*

Hundred Years of Jewish Life in America, 34–35; Gabriel Davidson, *Our Jewish Farmers and the Story of the Jewish Agricultural Society*, 12.

14. Refugee Economic Organization, *Annual Reports*, 1939–1943.

15. Wise MSS, Minutes of the Fifth Meeting of the PACPR, June 10, 1938.

16. FDRL/OF 3186, November 18, 1938, Buckley to FDR; December 7, 1938, FDR to Buckley (via State Department).

17. *The Problem of Alaskan Development*, 38–41.

18. FDRL/OF 3186, October 18, 1939, Ickes to FDR, with enclosures.

19. *Ibid.*, October 19, 1939, FDR to Welles.

20. *Ibid.*, November 23, 1938, FDR to Ickes (composed by Welles).

21. Harold L. Ickes, *The Secret Diary of Harold L. Ickes:* vol. III, *The Lowering Clouds, 1939–1941*, 56–57.

22. FDRL/OF 3186, Report of the Jewish Telegraph Agency, August 21, 1938.

23. NA/SDDF, 840.48 Refugees/116½, December 16, 1938, Memorandum of conversation, Paul V. McNutt and Welles; see also *Interpreter Releases*, XV, 308, September 2, 1938.

24. *FRUS*, II, 77, January 25, 1939.

25. *New York Times*, April 23, 1939, 33.

26. Wise MSS, Minutes of the 28th Meeting of the PACPR, October 13, 1939; FDRL/OF 3186, mimeographed copy of survey commission's report, October 17, 1939.

27. *New York Times*, February 4, 1939, 19. While the growth of restrictionist sentiment varied, virtually every Latin American Republic passed some sort of restrictive legislation. Argentina in October 1938; Bolivia in August 1939; Cuba in January and May 1939; Costa Rica in December 1939; Chile in May and October 1939; Colombia in May 1939; Paraguay in January 1939; and Uruguay in May 1939.

28. NA/SDDF, 710.H Continental Solidarity/10, December 8, 1938, Hull to Pell. See also Hull MSS, Bx. 42, File 109, December 10, 1938, Welles to Hull.

29. FDRL/OF 3186, July 3, 1940, FDR to Hull.

30. Arthur Prinz, "The Role of the Gestapo in Obstructing and Promoting Emigration," *Yad Washem Studies*, II, 1958, 209.

31. Nathan Eck, "The Rescue of Jews with the Aid of Passports and Citizenship Papers of Latin American States," *Yad Washem Studies*, I, 1957, 125–152.

32. *AJYB*, XLII, 1940/41, 600.

33. NA/SDDF, 840.48 Refugees/2350, December 10, 1940, memorandum of conversation between Berle, Wise and Goldmann.

34. Nathan Goldberg, "Immigration Attitudes of Mexicans: An In-sight," *Rescue*, II (July/August 1945), 3.

35. *Ibid.*, quoting from the Inter-American Monthly, December 1942.

36. NA/SDDF, 840.48 Refugees/2543, November 9, 1941, Jefferson Caffrey to Hull.

37. *Ibid.*, 822.00/1314, May 13, 1940, Quito to State Department.

38. Morse, *Six Million*, 278–280.

39. Long Diary, January 28, 1942.

40. Strauss, *Men and Decisions*, 125–126.

41. *Ibid.*

42. FDRL/PPF 64, Rosenman memorandum to FDR, December 5, 1938. Rosenman confided to Roosevelt that he believed that Baruch could be persuaded to take the lead in implementing the scheme.

43. Isaiah Bowman, *Limits of Land Settlement: A Report of Present-day Possibilities*, 1.

44. FDRL/PPF 5575, November 4, 25, 1938, Bowman to FDR.

45. *Public Papers of FDR*, VII, 1938, 597–598, Press conference, No-vember 15, 1938. *New York Times*, November 16, 1938, 22.

46. FDRL/OF 76-C, November 26, 1938; NA/SDDF, 840.48 Ref-ugees/985½, November 26, 1938.

47. Elliot Roosevelt, ed., *FDR: His Personal Letters, 1928–1945*, II, 951, November 1, 1938.

48. *FRUS*, I, 796, October 10, 1938, Rublee to Welles.

49. *German Documents*, D, IV, 333–341, November 18, 1938, Inter-view of Oswald Pirow, South African Minister of Defense with Hitler. *British Documents*, 3rd Ser., III, 295–296, November 24, 1938.

50. FDRL/OF 3186, January 12, 1939, Welles memorandum to FDR.

51. NA/SDDF, 840.48 Refugees/1232, January 5, 1539, Taylor to Rublee.

52. *FRUS*, II, 67–69, January 14, 1939, FDR to Taylor for delivery to Chamberlain.

53. *Ibid.*

54. *Ibid.*

55. *Ibid.*, II, 134, July 13, 1939.

56. *Ibid.*, II, 87–88, February 9, 1939, Taylor to Hull.

57. *Ibid.*, II, 90, February 15, 1939, Hull to Taylor.

58. *Ibid.*, II, 91, February 16, 1939, Taylor to Hull, and 102, April 15, 1939, Moffat Memorandum.

59. NA/SDDF, 840.48 Refugees/1640 May 26, 1939, Theodore Achilles to Bowman.

60. *FRUS*, II, 154, November 8, 1939, Pell memorandum of conversation with Van Zeeland; Wise MSS, Minutes of the 27th Meeting of the PACPR, September 14, 1939. Van Zeeland's troubles in Lisbon were discussed.

61. NA/SDDF, 840.48 Refugees/4022, June 10, 1943, Charles Liebman to Taylor.

62. *FRUS*, II, 64, June 12, 1939.

63. NA/SDDF, 840.48 Refugees/1319½, December 10, 1938, William Phillips to FDR (confidential); see also *Ciano Diaries, 1939–1943*, p. 5, and *German Documents*, D, IV, 548.

64. *New York Times*, October 17, 1939, 25.

65. NA/SDDF, 840.48 Refugees/4967, December 12, 1943, Letter to Roosevelt announcing organization of new group.

66. "Large Scale Settlement in the Eastern Mediterranean," *Bulletin of the Economic Research Institute of the Jewish Agency*, II, No. 9–10 (September/October, 1938), 159. See also David H. Popper, "A Homeland for Refugees," *Annals*, CCIII (May 1939), 175.

67. Wise MSS, Minutes of the 12th Meeting of the PACPR, November 21, 1938. *FRUS*, II, 139–140, July 17, 1939.

68. FDRL/PSF, Hull Folder, November 21, 1939, Bowman to FDR.

69. Wise MSS, May 26, 1939, Rothschild to Warren.

70. NA/SDDF, 840.48 Refugees/1607, May 9, 1939, London to State Department.

71. Wise MSS, February 6, 1939, Bowman to Wise.

72. *Report of the British Guiana Refugee Commission to the President's Advisory Committee of Political Refugees of the United States of America*, May 1939.

73. Moffat Diary, June 1, 1939.

74. *New York Times*, May 13, 1939, 3.

75. *FRUS*, II, 70, January 18, 1939, Hull to Rublee.

76. Official Minutes of the Meeting of the Officers of the Intergovernmental Committee for Political Refugees, October 17, 1939.

77. Joseph B. Schechtmann, "Failure of the Dominican Scheme," *Congress Weekly*, January 15, 1943, 8–9. For a more realistic appraisal of DORSA made in 1941 see *Refugee Settlement in the Dominican Republic: A Survey Conducted Under the Auspices of the Brookings Institute*, 1942.

78. FDRL/OF 3186, June 8, 1939, FDR to Taylor.

79. *FRUS*, II, 154–155, December 1, 1939, Van Zeeland to Hull.

80. FDRL/PSF-Box 24, December 4, 1939, FDR memorandum to Welles.

81. NA/SDDF, 840.48 Refugees/2184½, July 8, 1940, Strauss to Welles. See also Strauss, *Men and Decisions*, 129.

82. *Ibid.*, July 12, 1940, Welles to Strauss.

83. *FRUS*, II, 217, February 29, 1940, Memorandum from the Assistant Chief, Division of European Affairs (Pell).

84. *Ibid.*, 219, March 7, 1940, FDR to Hull.

85. Roosevelt, ed., *Personal Letters*, II, 1022, May 4, 1940, FDR to Eleanor Roosevelt.

86. Wise MSS, Minutes of the 27th Meeting of the PACPR, June 17, 1940. Wise asked the PACPR to draw up an *aide-mémoire* to the State Department stressing the temporary nature of the settlement and the hope of government financial assistance in establishing them.

87. Wyman, *Paper Walls*, 59.

88. Long MSS, May 27, 1942, Hrdlička to FDR.

89. *Ibid.*, May 30, 1942, Long to Hull for FDR.

90. *Ibid.*

91. See David H. Popper, "A Homeland for Refugees," *Annals*, CIII (May 1939), 165–176. Included in this group were Hendrik Van Loon, the historian, and Dorothy Canfield Fisher, a prominent refugee advocate.

92. Long MSS, July 5, 1942, Bowman to FDR.

93. Hannah Arendt, *Eichmann in Jerusalem, A Report on the Banality of Evil*, 4.

94. *German Documents*, D, V, 932–933, January 25, 1939.

95. *Nazi Conspiracy and Aggression*, VI, 87–89, January 31, 1939, "The Jewish Question in German Foreign Policy."

96. Philip Friedmann, "The Lublin Reservation and the Madagascar Plan," *YIVO Annual of Jewish Social Science*, VIII, 167 ff.

97. *Ibid.*, also E. Hevesi, "Hitler's Plans for Madagascar," *CJR*, IV (1941), 381–395.

98. *Ibid.* The Winghen pamphlet, "Aryan Race, Christian Culture and the Jewish Problem," was generally ignored but the report of the Lepecki Commission caused considerable furor because the Polish members and the Jewish members of the Commission did not agree on the resettlement potential of Madagascar.

99. See Chapter III.

100. *The Black Book*, 91, *New York Times*, February 9, 1938, 17.

101. Friedmann, "Lublin Reservation."

102. *Ibid.*, see also Hausner, *Justice*, 57–62, 89–90.

103. A. G. Price, "Refugee Settlement in the Tropics," *Foreign Affairs*, XVIII (July 1940), 659–670.

104. John Gunther, "Hispaniola," *Foreign Affairs* (July 1941), 772–773; Long Diary, September 12, 1942.

105. NA/SDDF, 840.48 Refugees/6351, June 1944, hand carried letter, J. E. Hoover to A. E. Berle.

106. *Ibid.*, 840.48 Refugees/2387, January 31, 1940, Hull to Jefferson Caffrey.

107. *Ibid.*, 840.48 Refugees/5247, February 11, 1944, Lima to State Department, /2117, April 1, 1940, Caffrey to State Department. There were in addition dozens of despatches from the consuls in Europe which warned of spies among the refugees.

108. *Ibid.*, 840.48 Refugees/5846, May 25, 1944. The government of South Africa, for example, was especially concerned that such refugees would not be able to maintain a proper attitude of white supremacy.

109. Bruno Blau, "The Jewish Population of Germany, 1939–1945," *JSS*, XII (April 1950), 161–172.

110. *FRUS*, II, 127, June 25, 939, Taylor to Welles.

111. Moffat Diary, February 15, 1939, Dr. Muñoz in conversation with Moffat.

112. NA/SDDF, 840.48 Refugees/4839, December 1, 1942, Unsigned memorandum.

113. A full account of problems involved in Jewish settlement in Latin America is presented by S. G. Inman, "Refugee Settlement in Latin America," *Annals*, CCIII (May 1939), 183–189 and Gerhardt Neumann, "German Jews in Colombia: A Study in Immigration Adjustment," *JSS*, III (1941), 189–206.

114. Bowman, *Limits*, 1.

115. Wise MSS, July 19, 1937, Wise to Pesach Rosenblatt.

116. *Ibid.*, May 9, 1938, Wise to Pesach Rosenblatt.

117. Committee on Foreign Affairs, House of Representatives, *Hearings on Resolutions Relative to the Jewish National Home in Palestine*, 78th Cong., 2nd Sess., February, March, 1944, 25. Evidence taken from the article "Palestine's Role in the Solution of the Jewish Problem," *Foreign Affairs*, January, 1942.

118. Wise, *As I See It*, 110. The same sentiments are expressed in a letter to Myron Taylor, Wise MSS, November 23, 1938.

119. *Ibid.*, 130.

120. Long MSS, memorandum submitted to the Bermuda Refugee Conference by the World Jewish Congress, April 14, 1943.

121. *Jewish Forum*, May 1942.

122. Wise MSS, May 26, 1939, A. H. Silver to Wise.

Chapter 6

1. That is the approximate figure which results from totaling the following relevant national quotas:

Poland	6,524
Netherlands	3,153
France	3,086
Czechoslovakia	2,874
Soviet Union	2,712
Norway	2,337
Belgium	1,304
Denmark	1,181
Hungary	869
Yugoslavia	845
Lithuania	386
Rumania	377
Germany (incl. Austria)	27,370
Total	53,018

2. Maurice R. Davie, *Refugees in America*, 14. This figure departs slightly from that given by Wyman, *Paper Walls*, 209. There is also little agreement on how many Jews were among the refugees admitted. The Rescue Commission of the American Jewish Conference estimated the total to June 1943 as 166,843 and 44,889 on emergency visas. *Interim Report of the Rescue Commission of the American Jewish Conference*, Appendix I, 1944, 43–45, the Estimate of the Immigration and Naturalization Service for the same period was lower: 476,930 Refugees were admitted of whom 165,756 were Jews. Solomon Dingol estimates 157,927 Jews admitted for the same period. "How Many Refugees from Nazi Persecution were admitted to the United States," *Rescue*, I, February 1944, p. 1.

3. FDRL/OF 133, October 29, 1935, James G. McDonald to Felix Warburg.

4. See Read Lewis and Marian Shibsby, "Status of Refugees Under American Immigration Regulations," *Annals*, CCIII (May 1939), 74–82; Henry Smith Leiper, "Those German Refugees," *Current History*, L (May 1939), 19–22.

5. *New York Times*, May 26, 1940, 1.

6. Robert E. Sherwood, *Roosevelt and Hopkins*, II, 712–713; Also *FRUS*, II, 38–39, March 27, 1943, Hopkins Memorandum.

7. NA/SDDF, 832.00N/124, May 31, 1940, Jefferson Caffrey to Hull. Similar reports came from Brazil, Cuba, Chile and Bolivia.

8. Long MSS, May 31, 1940, George Messersmith to Long.

9. NA/SDDF, 840.48 Refugees/3489, December 16, 1942, Censorship Daily Report No. 700.

10. *Nation*, August 31, 1940, pp. 167–168, quoted by Heinz Pol, "An Open Letter to Ambassador Bullitt."

11. *Ibid.*

12. Charles Weighton and Guenther Peis, *Hitler's Spies and Saboteurs*, 37.

13. Samuel Lubell, "War by Refugee," *Saturday Evening Post*, CCXIII (March 29, 1941).

14. *Ibid.* See also Karl H. Abshagen, *Canaris*, 74.

15. NA/SDDF, 840.48 Refugees/3179, October 5, 1942, Lowenstein Memorandum.

16. Quoted in *CJR*, May–June, 1940, 24.

17. Alfred Wagg, III, "Washington's Stepchild," *The New Republic*, April 28, 1941, 592–594.

18. Long MSS, March 26, 1941, Long to Wise.

19. Gilbert H. Stuart, "The Special War Problems Division," *Department of State Bulletin*, XI (July 2, 1944), 6–12.

20. Long Diary, April 22, 1942.

21. Long MSS, June, 1933, Long to Joseph Davies.

22. *Ibid.*, June 27, 1933, Long to FDR.

23. *Ibid.*, August 11, 1933, Long to Homer Cummings.

24. *Ibid.*, February 3, 1935, Long to FDR.

25. *Ibid.*, November 29, 1935.

26. Fred Israel, ed., *The War Diary of Breckinridge Long, Selections From the Years 1939–1944*, xi–xxv.

27. Long Diary, March 13, 1938.

28. *Ibid.*, February 1, 1939. Long had a tendency to make bad predictions. His master's thesis written in 1908 was titled, "The Impossibility of India's Revolt from England."

29. *Ibid.*, June 13, 1939.

30. *Ibid.*

31. *Ibid.*, February 6, 1938.

32. *Ibid.*

33. *Ibid.*, February 15, 1941. (The characterization was specifically made of Ben Cohen, an economic adviser and assistant to John Winant.)

34. *Ibid.*, June 13, 1944.

35. *Ibid.*, December 9, 1940.

36. *Ibid.*, September 4, 1941.

37. *Ibid.*

38. *Ibid.*, December 29, 1940.

39. *Ibid.*, September 13, 1943.

40. *Ibid.*, April 11, 1939.

41. For a contemporary account of the rescue of scholars see Norman Bentwich, *The Rescue and Achievement of Refugee Scholars*, and Stephen Duggan, *The Rescue of Science and Learning*. Recent interest in the contribution of this category of refugees to developments in physics, mathematics, psychology, art, and architecture has produced a spate of new studies. Especially noteworthy is Donald Fleming and Bernard Bailyn, eds., *Perspectives in American History*, Vol. II, *The Intellectual Migration: Europe and America, 1930–1960*.

42. Long Diary, November 27, 1939.

43. Moffat Diary, February 8, 1939.

44. FDRL/PSF, Welles Folder, July 1, 1941, Memorandum to Rabbis Schneersohn and Teitelbaum. This group was placated when Raymond Geist, Chief of the State Department's Division of Commercial Affairs, interceded with Admiral Canaris, chief of the German Intelligence Service, to extricate a leading Rabbi from Warsaw.

45. *FRUS*, II, 232–233, July 24, 1940.

46. NA/SDDF, 840.48 Refugees/2183, June 18, 1940, Freda Kirchway to FDR.

47. FDRL/OF 3186, June 14, 1940, Edwin Watson to Robert Pell.

48. Perkins, *Roosevelt*, 361.

49. *Public Opinion Quarterly*, IV (September 1940), 544.

50. Long MSS, July 30, 1940, Messersmith to Long.

51. *The New Republic*, August 18, 1941, 208.

52. Freda Kirchway, "Nightmare in France," *Nation*, August 27, 1940, 124.

53. Wise MSS, Minutes of the 40th Meeting of the PACPR, September 12, 1940.

54. Long MSS, June 26, 1940, Long memo to Berle and Dunn. Also *FRUS*, II, 178–179, 194–195, June 26, 1940.

55. FDRL/OF 3186, December 21, 1940, Carlton Hayes to Hull.

56. Long Diary, September 18, 1940.

57. *Ibid.*

58. *Ibid.*, October 3, 1940.

59. FDRL/OF 3186, September 6, 1940, Herbert Pell to FDR.

60. Long Diary, October 3, 1940.

61. *Ibid.*

62. *Ibid.*

63. FDRL/OF 3186, October 8, 1940, McDonald to FDR.

64. *Ibid.*

65. Wise MSS, Minutes of the 41st Meeting of the PACPR, October 30, 1940.

66. Long Diary, October 10, 1940.

67. FDRL/OF 3186, November 23, 1940, Long to Jackson.

68. Long Diary, November 27, 1940.

69. Wise MSS, Minutes of the 42nd Meeting of the PACPR, December 19, 1940.

70. Freda Kirchway, "The State Department Versus Political Refugees," *Nation*, December 28, 1940, 648–649.

71. Long Diary, July 12, 1940.

72. *New York Times*, February 19, 1939, 32.

73. Committee on Immigration and Naturalization, House of Representatives, *Hearings on the Joint Resolution to Authorize the Admission of a Limited Number of Refugee Children*, 76th Cong., 1st Sess. (May 24, 25, 31 and June 1, 1939) (Wagner-Rogers Resolution), 197.

74. Moffat Diary, May 25, 1939.

75. Committee on Immigration and Naturalization, *Hearings on the Joint Resolution to Authorize the Admission of a Limited Number of Refugee Children*, 76th Cong., 1st Sess. (May 24, 25, 31 and June 1, 1939) (Wagner-Rogers Resolution), 2.

76. NA/SDDF, 150.01 Bills/99, Messersmith memorandum to Moffat and Achilles.

77. FDRL/OF 3186, June 2, 1939, Watson to FDR.

78. Weyman, *Paper Walls*, 117–118.

79. Long Diary, June 19, 1940.

80. Wise MSS, June 18, 1940, McDonald to FDR. (Duplicate copy to each member of the PACPR.)

81. Long Diary, July 12, 1940.

82. *New York Times*, July 27, 1940, 16.

83. Long Diary, August 22, 1940.

84. *New York Times*, July 27, 1940, 4. The *Times* reported the sinking of a French liner while repatriating French nationals.

85. FDRL/OF 3186, Copy of column, "Let's Save the Children," *Washington Daily News*, July 6, 1940.

86. FDRL/OF 3186, July 8, 1940, FDR memo to Early.

87. *Ibid.*, August 12, 1940, FDR to O'Day and *New York Times*, July 27, 4.

88. *Ibid.*, August 14, 1940, O'Day to FDR.

89. An interesting discussion of the effects of anti-Semitism on the disposition of the two measures is presented in Wyman, *Paper Walls*, 127.

90. Long Diary, September 12, 1940.

91. *Ibid.*, September 26, 1942; Wise MSS, September 26, 1942, Avra Warren memorandum to PACPR.

92. *Ibid.*, (Wise MSS)

93. Long Diary, November 13, 1940.

94. *Ibid.*

95. FDRL/OF 3186, December 18, 1940, FDR to Ickes.

96. *Ibid.*, November 25, 1940.

97. *Ibid.*, December 16, 1940.

98. *Ibid.*, November 25, 1940.

99. FDRL/OF 3186, December 18, 1940, FDR to Ickes.

100. *American Hebrew*, December 20, 1940.

101. Long MSS, February 25, 1941, Hull to FDR.

102. Long Diary, April 22, 1941.

103. *The New Republic*, July 28, 1941, 105–106.

104. *Ibid.*, June 23, 1941, 843.

105. *Ibid.*, June 30, 1941, 873.

106. *Department of State Bulletin*, III, 564, December 21, 1940. See also Long Diary, December 18, 1940.

107. *Nation*, December 28, 1940, 648–649.

108. Long Diary, February 18, 1941.

109. Quoted in *Interpreter Releases*, XVIII, 199, July 1940.

110. Wise MSS, Minutes of the 42nd Meeting of the PACPR, December 19, 1940.

111. See William E. Leuchtenberg, *Franklin D. Roosevelt and the New Deal, 1932–1940*, 37.

112. Long MSS, May 5, 1941, Long to McDonald.

113. Robert H. Jackson, "Alien Registration and Democracy," *Interpreter Releases*, XVII, 423, June 1940.

114. Long Diary, June 17, 1941.

115. *Ibid.*, June 25, 1941.

116. Graham H. Stuart, "Wartime Visa Control Procedure," *Department of State Bulletin*, XI, 271–272 (September 10, 1942).

117. Wischnitzer, *HIAS*, 32.

118. Long Diary, June 17, 1941.

119. Long MSS, July 3, 1941, Long to Biddle.

120. Long MSS, August 8, 1941, McDonald to FDR. The cable was forwarded by Watson to Long with an inquiry about whether Long wished McDonald to see the President.

121. *The New Republic*, July 28, 1941, 105–106.

122. Long Diary, August 19, 1941.

123. FDRL/OF 3186, August 20, 1941, State Department memorandum to FDR.

124. Long Diary, August 27, 1941.

125. Wise MSS, Minutes of the 50th Meeting of the PACPR, September 4, 1941.

126. Long Diary, September 4, 1941.

127. Arieh Tartakower and Kurt Grossman, *The Jewish Refugees*, 94.

128. Long Diary, November 27, 1941.

129. Varian Fry, *Surrender on Demand*, 148 ff.

130. Long Diary, January 29, 1942.

131. *New York Times*, September 10, 1942, 4. The offer was supposedly made to S. Pinkney Tuck, counselor for the American embassy.

132. *Ibid.*

133. FDRL/OF 3186, October 13, 1942, Welles to Celler.

Chapter 7

1. Rolf Hochhuth, *The Deputy*, 312.

2. Jan Ciechanowski, *Defeat in Victory*, 117.

3. *Ibid.*, 118–119.

4. Kubowitzki, *Unity*, 261–262.

5. *The Goebbels Diaries*, 1942–1943, ed. and trans., Louis P. Lochner, 241, December 12, 1942.

6. NA/SDDF, 840.48 Refugees/3080, September 2, 1942, Wise to Welles, with enclosures. Riegner cabled Wise simultaneously but the cable was withheld by the State Department.

7. *Ibid.*

8. Wise MSS, September 4, 1942, Rosenheim to Wise.

9. *Ibid.*, September 16, 1942, Frankfurter to Wise.

10. *Jewish Telegraph News Bulletin*, October 9, 1942.

11. Wise, *Challenging Years*, 275–276.

12. Wise MSS, April 1, 1942, Wise to Eleanor Roosevelt.

13. Long Diary, September 13, 1942. Long showed Bendiner's work to Homer Cummings, former Attorney General, with a view to bringing a libel suit but Cummings discouraged the action.

14. Wise MSS, September 18, 1942, Wise to Frankfurter.

15. *Goebbels Diaries*, 254, December 20, 1942. Emil Ludwig Cohn refers to Emil Ludwig, the renowned biographer.

16. *FRUS*, I, 48, August 5, 1942, Winant to FDR.

17. *Ibid.*, 59, October 5, 1942.

18. NA/SDDF, 740.00116 EW 1939/994, April 19, 1943, FDR to Hull.

19. *FRUS*, I, 61–67, December 17, 1942. The reservation is found in *Department of State Bulletin*, VII, 797, October 10, 1942.

20. *Ibid.*, VIII, 351, April 17, 1943.

21. *CJR*, IV, 45, *Report of the Executive Committee*, "25th Annual Report of the American Jewish Committee, 1942," Speech of Maurice Wertheim.

22. Wise MSS, March 1, 1943, copy of Wise's speech at "Stop Hitler Now" rally.

23. FDRL/PPF 5029, March 1, 1943, Wise to FDR, contains copy of resolutions and Wise's covering letter to the President.

24. NA/SDDF, 840.48 Refugees/3860, March 29, 1943, Taylor to Long.

25. *Ibid.*, /3819, March 23, 1943, Ronald Campbell to Long.

26. Long MSS, May 14, 1943, Long Intradepartmental Memorandum.

27. Wischnitzer, *HIAS*, 107.

28. FDRL/PPF 2748 Celler File, March 28, 1943.

29. Wise MSS, Copy of column reprinted in *Jewish Advocate* (Boston), January 26, 1940.

30. *FRUS*, II, 870, November 2, 1941, Franklin Gunther to Hull.

31. *Ibid.*, 875–876, November 12, 1941, Memorandum by Cavendish Canon.

32. *Ibid.*

33. *Ibid.*, 864–865, October 17, 1941, Gunther to State Department.

34. See for example Long Diary, February 17, 1940 and April 3, 1943. Also several of the spy stories appearing in the popular magazines were indirectly sponsored by the State Department. On May 7, 1943, he suggested planting an article in *Collier's* to counteract renewed rescue agitation. Long MSS, May 7, 1943, Confidential intradepartmental memorandum.

35. "The Morgenthau Diaries," 23 (February 10, 1943).

36. Morse, *Six Million*, 9.

37. NA/SDDF, 862.4016/2268, April 20, 1943, Harrison to Hull.

38. The best account of this episode is "The Morgenthau Diaries." Arthur Morse, *Six Million*, and Stephen Wise, *Challenging Years*, also contain complete accounts of the episode.

39. NA/SDDF, 840.48 Refugees/3055, October 1, 1942, Buenos Aires to State Department.

40. Hilberg, *Destruction*, 370.

41. Reitlinger, *Final Solution*, 407 ff.

42. *New York Times*, February 13, 1943, 5.

43. NA/SDDF, 840.48 Refugees/3603, February 5, 1943, Hull to Stein-hardt. "Morgenthau Diaries," 23.

44. "Morgenthau Diaries," 23.

45. Long Diary, March 23, 1943.

46. "Morgenthau Diaries," 23. A full account of the Rumanian rescue opportunity is also found in Joseph Tenenbaum, "They Might Have Been Rescued," *Congress Weekly*, February 2, 1953, 5–7.

47. *Ibid.*

48. *FRUS*, II, 38–39, March 27, 1943, Hopkins Memorandum. Also Sherwood, *Roosevelt and Hopkins*, II, 712–713.

49. *Ibid.*

50. *Ibid.*

51. Kubowitzki, *Unity*, 181.

52. *New York Times*, April 18, 1943, 13. There were of course other problems involved including shipping and Turkish recalcitrance.

53. Kubowitzki, *Unity*, 182.

54. *FRUS*, I, 292–293, April 19, 1943, *Aide-Mémoire* from British Embassy.

55. Kubowitzki, *Unity*, 182.

56. *FRUS*, I, 70–71, December 17, 1942, Harold Tittman to State Department via Harrison.

57. *Ibid.*, II, 911–913, January 5, 1943.

58. NA/SDDF, 840.48 Refugees/3723, February 26, 1943, Harold Tittman to State Department.

59. Hilberg, *Destruction*, 429–430; Hausner, *Justice*, 252.

60. FDRL/PPF 5029, March 1, 1943, Copy of Madison Square Garden Rescue Resolutions.

61. Kubowitzki, *Unity*, 174.

62. *Ibid.*

63. *Ibid.*

64. *Ibid.*

65. Long Diary, December 11, 1940.

66. *Ibid.*

67. Long MSS, September 29, 1942, Memorandum of conversation, Long, Acheson, Goldmann, Wise (Jonah). See also Long Diary, September 29, 1942.

68. Long Diary, September 29, 1942.

69. *Ibid.*, October 1, 1942.

70. *House Rescue Commission Hearings*, 78th Cong., 1st Sess., November 26, 1943, 37 ff. NA/SDDF, 140–48 Refugees/4542, September 29, 1943, Memorandum of conversation, Long and Goldmann.

71. Kubowitzki, *Unity*, 176.

72. *FRUS*, I, 134, January 20, 1943, *Aide-mémoire* from British Embassy to State Department.

73. *Ibid.*

74. *Ibid.*

75. *Ibid.*

76. *Ibid.*

77. *Ibid.*, I, 144–146, February 6, 1943, Welles to H. Freeman Mathews (chargé in London).

78. *Ibid.* For Long's hostility toward the British see particularly Long Diary, January 29, 1942.

79. *Ibid.*, 138–140, February 20, 1943, Mathews to Hull.

80. *Ibid.*, 140–141, February 25, 1943, Hull to Halifax.

81. *Ibid.*

82. Long Diary, March 19, 1943.

83. *Ibid.*, February 16, 1943.

84. Hull MSS, March 22, 1943, Memorandum of conversation Eden, Halifax and Hull.

85. *Ibid.*

86. Long Diary, March 22, 1943.

87. *Ibid.*

88. *Ibid.*

89. *Ibid.*

90. *Ibid.*, March 28, 1943.

91. Long MSS, March 22, 1943, Memorandum of Agreement, Atherton, Long and Strang.

92. *FRUS*, I, 146–147, March 23, 1943, Hull to FDR.

93. FDRL/OF 3186, April 2, 1943, Dickstein to FDR.

94. Long Diary, June 20, 1940.

95. Long MSS, April 13, 1943, Long to Wise.

96. Long Diary, April 13, 1943.

97. *Ibid.*, March 28, 1943.

98. Long MSS, April 7, 1943, Long to Law.

99. Wise MSS, April 14, 1943, Wise to Welles.

100. Long MSS, April 19, 1943, Murray to Welles.

101. *State Department Bulletin*, VIII, 386, April 26, 1943.

102. Long MSS, April 17, 1943, Memorandum to American Delegation.

103. Long Diary, April 20, 1943.

104. *Ibid.*

105. *New York Times,* April 20, 1943, 1.

106. *Department of State Bulletin,* VIII, 351, April 17, 1943.

107. Long MSS, Minutes of the Meeting of the American Delegation, April 25, 1943.

108. *Ibid.*

109. Bloom MSS, April 9, 1943, Kalmanowitz to Bloom.

110. Long MSS, Confidential memorandum from the chairman, April 20, 1943.

111. Long MSS, Minutes of the Bermuda Conference, April 21, 1943.

112. *Ibid.,* April 20, 1943.

113. Long MSS, Minutes of the American Delegation, April 28, 1943.

114. Long MSS, *Bermuda Conference Final Report,* April 19–29, 1943.

115. Long MSS, Minutes of the Bermuda Conference, April 21, 1943. *FRUS,* I, 153, April 19, 1943, Harold Dodd to Long.

116. *Ibid.,* 156, April 21, 1943, Long to Dodd.

117. *New York Times,* April 22, 1943, 10.

118. Long MSS, Minutes of the Bermuda Conference, Morning Session, April 23, 1943.

119. Long MSS, *Bermuda Conference Final Report,* Recommendations.

120. *Ibid.*

121. *FRUS,* I, 253–254, January 20, 1943, Taylor to Welles.

122. Long MSS, Minutes of the Meeting of the American Delegation, April 25, 1943.

123. Long MSS, Minutes of the Bermuda Conference, Morning Session, April 23, 1943.

124. Long Diary, April 22, 1943.

125. *FRUS,* I, 167–168, May 14, 1943, Roosevelt to Hull. In April the British had themselves reported difficulty in getting General Giraud to agree to such a camp, 292–293, April 19, 1943, *Aide-mémoire* from British Embassy.

126. *FRUS,* I, 254–255, April 21, 1943, Dodd to Long.

127. *Ibid.,* 176–178, May 7, 1943, Hull to FDR.

128. *Ibid.,* 250, January 4, 1943, Hayes to Hull; Taylor informed the Department of Hayes' overestimate, Hayes estimated that there were 7,000 refugees in Spain but Taylor now informed the Department that there were not many over 1,600 and of these 500 had valid visas to other countries. FDRL/PSF State Department folder, Taylor to State Department. August 31, 1943.

129. Hull MSS, January 5, 1943, Memorandum of conversation, Hull and Halifax.

130. *FRUS*, I, 252, January 16, 1943, Welles to Taylor; 252, January 20, 1943, Taylor to Welles.

131. Long Diary, June 23, 1943.

132. *Ibid.*

133. Long MSS, Minutes of the Bermuda Conference, April 25, 1943.

134. Long MSS, Minutes of the Meeting of the American Delegation, April 25, 1943.

135. Long MSS, Minutes of the Bermuda Conference, April 25, 1943.

136. *Ibid.*

137. *Ibid.*

138. *Ibid.*

139. Long MSS, Minutes of the Meeting of the American Delegation, April 28, 1943.

140. *Ibid.*

141. Emanuel Celler, *You Never Leave Brooklyn*, 89.

142. Quoted in Morse, *Six Million*, 63.

143. *FRUS*, I, 174, April 29, 1943.

144. *Ibid.*, 183–184, May 19, 1943, Final Communique.

145. *Ibid.*

146. Long MSS, May 7, 1943, Confidential intradepartmental memorandum.

Chapter 8

1. Long MSS, May 3, 1943, Long to Carlton Hayes. See also Carlton J. H. Hayes, *Wartime Mission in Spain, 1942–1945*, p. 137.

2. Celler, *Brooklyn*, 88, quoting from his article in *Free World*, July 1943.

3. *American Hebrew*, May 7, 1943.

4. FDRL/PPF 3292, April 28, 1943, Wise to FDR.

5. *New York Times*, April 30, 1943, 9.

6. *FRUS*, I, 176–177, May 7, 1943, Hull to FDR.

7. Long MSS, January 7, 1944, Long to Avra Warren. While explaining his miscalculation to his former underling, Long mentioned that it was the same figure he had been using all along in his briefings of the President.

8. *New York Times*, May 20, 1943, 12. *FRUS*, I, 183–184, May 19, 1943, Winant to State Department.

9. Hausner, *Jerusalem*, 238.

10. The Committee for a Jewish Army of Stateless and Palestinian Jews, *From Evian to Bermuda*, 15.

11. Bloom MSS, May 3, 1943, Dodd to Bloom.

12. Long MSS, June 16, 1943, Dodd to Long.

13. Bloom MSS, December 20, 1943, Leo Steinreich to Bloom, a touching letter from a Quanza refugee whom Bloom helped.

14. *New York Times*, May 24, 1943, 15.

15. Bloom MSS, July 20, 1943, Malkenson, Margoshes, and Manischewitz thank-you letter to Bloom.

16. *Ibid.*, January 26, 1944, Joseph Baldwin to Bloom.

17. *New York Times*, May 4, 1943, 17.

18. Emergency Committee to Save the Jewish People of Europe, *Deliver Us from Evil.*

19. *House Rescue Commission Hearings*, 37.

20. Long MSS, May 7, 1943, confidential memorandum.

21. *Ibid.* Coincidentally Goebbels too claimed that Jewish organizations had stolen his slogan, *"Deutschland Erwache"* (Germany awake), when they supposedly used the slogan "England awake," *Goebbels Diaries*, 243, December 14, 1942.

22. Long MSS, June 16, 1943, Dodd to Long.

23. Long Diary, June 23, 1944.

24. Quoted by Morse, *Six Million*, 60.

25. *FRUS*, I, 211, August 25, 1943.

26. NA/SDDF, 840.48 Refugees/4124, August 10, 1943, Long to Winant.

27. *Records of the Proceedings of the Meeting of the Executive Committee of the Intergovernmental Committee for Political Refugees*, August 4, 1943.

28. Long MSS, May 23, 1943, Memorandum of conversation with Sir Ronald Campbell.

29. *FRUS*, IV, 767, March 3, 1943, Memorandum of conversation, Welles-Hassan Bey.

30. *Ibid.*, 773–775, May 25, 1943, Saud to FDR.

31. Long Diary, January 29, 1942.

32. *FRUS*, 782–785, April 20, 1943, Summary of Hoskins Near East report.

33. *Ibid.*, 784.

34. *Ibid.*, I, 763, March 16, 1943, Memorandum, William L. Parker, Division of Near Eastern Affairs.

35. *Ibid.*, IV, 794–795, June 12, 1943, Memorandum of conversation, Roosevelt and Weizmann.

36. *Ibid.*

37. *Ibid.*, 807–810, August 31, 1943, Hoskins memorandum of Conversation with Ibn Saud.

38. *Ibid.*, 785–786, May 8, 1943, Shullaw (chargé in Jidda) to State Department.

39. *Ibid.*, 812, September 27, 1943, Hoskins memorandum of talk with FDR.

40. *Ibid.*, I, 354, September 9, 1943, Sir Ronald Campbell to State Department.

41. *Ibid.*, 355–356, September 27, 1943, Adolf Berle to Ronald Campbell.

42. NA/SDDF, 840.48 Refugees/4683⅕, October 8, 1943, Memorandum to State Department.

43. *Report of the Interim Committee of the American Jewish Conference*, 1946, 5, Alexander Kohanski (ed.). The American Jewish Conference, *Proceeding of the First Session*, August 29 to September 2, 1943. See also Schachner, *History*, *American Jewish Committee*, 143.

44. Cecil Roth, "The Jewish Problem Today and Tomorrow," *American Hebrew*, September 17, 1943.

45. *American Hebrew*, June 11, 1943.

46. Joseph M. Proskauer, *A Segment of My Time*, 201.

47. Alexander Bittleman, *Jewish Unity for Victory*, 6.

48. Long MSS, October 25, 1943, Long to Hirschmann. See also Ira Hirschmann, *Life Line to a Promised Land*, 131.

49. NA/SDDF, 840.48 Refugees/4435, September 1, 1943, Steve Early to Max Learner.

50. *New York Times*, September 7, 1943, 16.

51. *American Hebrew*, November 26, 1943.

52. NA/SDDF, 840.48 Refugees/4726, October 16, 1943, Memorandum of conversation, Long and Swedish Minister.

53. *New York Times*, October 21, 1943, 18, and November 1, 1943, 5.

54. NA/SDDF, 840.48 Refugees/4683⅕, October 8, 1943, State Department memorandum.

55. *Ibid.*, /4710, October 15, 1943, Memorandum of conversation, Peter Bergson, Henry Pringle and Long.

56. *Ibid.*, 4683⅗, November 17, 1943, Bergson to Stettinius and enclosures of Long's reply.

57. *Ibid.*

58. *House Rescue Commission Hearings*, 2.

59. Long Diary, September 13, 1943.

60. *Ibid.*, September 26, 1943.

61. *FRUS*, I, 370–371, October 25, 1943, British memorandum.

62. Kubowitzki, *Unity*, 182–183. For an interesting account of the rescue of Danish Jewry see Harold Flender, *Rescue in Denmark*.

63. *FRUS*, I, 364–366, October 7 and 11, 1943, Winant to State Department.

64. *Ibid.*, 346, September 8, 1943, Tittman to State Department.

65. Subcommittee of the Senate Committee on Foreign Relations, *A Resolution Favoring Action Looking to Relief for Starving People of Europe*, 78th Cong., 1st Sess., November 1943.

66. *Ibid.*, 112.

67. *FRUS*, I, 374–375, November 11, 1943, Winant to State Department.

68. *House Rescue Commission Hearings*, 37 ff.

69. *FRUS*, I, 594, December 24, 1943, Winant to State Department. Contains enclosures of letters questioning motives behind Long's revelations and Long's denial.

70. *Ibid.*, 392, December 17, 1943, Memorandum of conversation, Howard K. Travers, and Carlton Hayes.

71. *Ibid.*, 393–394, December 20, 1943, State Department to Herschell Johnson.

72. Eck, "Rescue . . . with the Aid of Passports . . . ," *Yad Washem Studies*, 125–152.

73. NA/SDDF, 840.48 Refugees/4969, December 23, 1943, Jacob Rosenheim to State Department.

74. *Ibid.*, December 29, 1943, State Department to Asunción and other Latin American Capitals. Also FDRL/WRB, *History of the WRB* (Latin American Passports), March 31, 1944.

75. FDRL/WRB, April 14, 1944, Morgenthau to Hull.

76. *Ibid.*

77. *Ibid.*, April 19, 1944, Pehle to Morgenthau detailing Vittel case.

78. NA/SDDF, 840.48 Refugees/5136, January 29, 1944, Berle memorandum to Rabbi Riegelmann.

79. Kubowitzki, *Unity*, 164.

80. *Ibid.* Quote is a statement by Reich Deputy Press Chief, Helmut Suendermann, made in July 1944. See *Goebbels Diaries*, 241, December 13, 1942 for Goebbels policy on Allied atrocity stories.

81. *Jewish Comment*, May 28, 1943.

82. *Ibid.*

83. Hull, *Memoirs*, II, 278.

84. NA/SDDF, 840.48 Refugees/4854, November 4, 1943, Bergson to FDR.

85. *Jewish Comment*, November 10, 1943 (editorial).

86. *Department of State Bulletin*, X, 277, March 24, 1944.

87. FDRL/WRB, *History of the WRB* (UN War Crimes Commission). The War Department's reluctance stemmed from its desire to limit crimes to "major" war criminals and to discount all crimes of persecution committed against its own citizenry.

88. *Morgenthau Diaries*, 66.

89. *House Rescue Commission Hearings*, 10–11. See also NA/SDDF, 840.48 Refugees/5029, November 19, 1943, Alfange Testimony.

90. Quoted in *Jewish Comment*, December 17, 1943 from the *Voelkischer Beobachter*, June 20, 1943.

91. *House Rescue Commission Hearings*, 32.

92. *Ibid.*

93. *Ibid.*, 27 ff.

94. *Ibid.*, 29, 40.

95. Long MSS, January 7, 1944, Long to Avra Warren.

96. *Interim Report of the Rescue Commission of the American Jewish Conference*, Appendix I, 1944, 43–45. See also Solomom Dingol, "How Many Refugees from Nazi Persecution Were Admitted to the United States," *Rescue*, I, February 1944, 1. Dingol estimated that only 157,927 refugees falling in this category were actually admitted to the United States.

97. *House Rescue Commission Hearings*, 35.

98. *Ibid.*, 36.

99. Morse, *Six Million*, 96.

100. *House Rescue Commission Hearings*, 34.

101. *Ibid.*, 35.

102. *FRUS*, I, 237–238, December 10, 1943, Cable to all Latin American Republics.

103. *Ibid.*, 594, December 24, 1943, Winant to State Department.

104. *Ibid.*, I, 246, December 29, 1943, Winant to State Department.

105. *Ibid.*, 240, December 22, 1943, Long to Winant.

106. *Ibid.*, 243, December 24, 1943, Long to Winant.

107. *Ibid.*, 246, December 29, 1943, Winant to State Department.

108. *Ibid.*, 247, December 31, 1943, Winant to State Department.

109. NA/SDDF, 840.48 Refugees/5006, December 28, 1943, Joseph Proskauer to Long.

110. *FRUS*, I, 226, November 28, 1943.

111. *Ibid.*, 227, November 30, 1943, Long to Winant.

112. *New York Times*, December, 1943, 8.

113. *Interim Report of the Rescue Commission of the American Jewish Conference*, Appendix I, 1946, 43–45.

114. *PM*, December 20, 1943, 4; *Nation*, December 29, 1943.

115. Long MSS, December 15, 1943, Avra Warren to Long.

116. Long Diary, January 1, 1944; also Long MSS, January 7, 1944, Long to Warren.

117. *New York Times*, December 3, 1943, 4.

118. *Ibid.*, December 31, 1943, 10; NA/SDDF, 840.48 Refugees/5025, December 31, 1943, American Jewish Conference to State Department.

119. *New York Times*, December 31, 1943, 10.

120. *Morgenthau Diaries*, 65.

121. *Ibid.;* and Morse, *Six Million*, 88.

122. *Morgenthau Diaries*, 65.

123. NA/SDDF, 840.48 Refugees/5215, January 1, 1944, Petition of the Inmates of Northeastern Penitentiary, Lewisburg, Pennsylvania.

124. *New York Times*, January 31, 1944, 5.

125. Hull, *Memoirs*, II, 107.

126. Roosevelt (ed.), *FDR, Personal Letters*, II, 913–914.

127. *Morgenthau Diaries*, 65.

128. NA/SDDF, 840.48 Refugees/5007, January 14, 1944, Long to Proskauer.

129. Long Diary, January 20, 1944.

130. *Morgenthau Diaries*, 65.

131. Long Diary, January 24, 1944.

132. *Ibid.*

133. *Ibid.*, also September 7 and 26, 1943.

134. FDRL/OF 5477, Executive Order 9417; *New York Times*, January 23, 1944, 11.

135. *Ibid.*

136. NA/SDDF, 840.48 Refugees/5041, January 25, 1944, State Department to London, Lisbon, Madrid, Stockholm, Bern, Ankara and the Latin American Republics.

137. FDRL/WRB, Projects and Documents File, Box 51, February 1944.

138. FDRL/PPF 5477, January 25, 1944, Celler to FDR.

139. *Ibid.*, 470, January 24, 1943, Lubin to FDR.

140. Hull MSS, January 25, 1944, FDR memorandum to Hull.

141. *Department of State Bulletin*, X, 95 ff, Executive Order 9417.

142. *Ibid.*

143. *Ibid.*

144. Hirschmann, *Lifeline*, 131 ff. Hirschmann describes how Isador Lubin presented him with a secret phone number which he was to use in case of emergency.

Chapter 9

1. *Goebbels Diaries*, May 8, 1943, 357.

2. Béla Vágó, "Germany and the Jewish Policy of the Kállay Government," Randolph L. Braham (ed.), *Hungarian Jewish Studies*, 190.

3. *Ibid.*

4. *Ibid.*, 202.

5. Quoted in Hausner, *Jerusalem*, 134.

6. NA/SDDF, 840.48 Refugees/5157A, February 14, 1944, Stettinius to Leland Harrison requests confirmation of the JTA story.

7. *Ibid.*, /5524, April 11, 1944, Harrison to State Department. See also Kubowitzki, *Unity*, 183.

8. FDRL/WRB, February 11, 1944, Pehle to Stettinius.

9. *Ibid.*, March 7, 1944, Pehle to Harrison for transmission to Budapest.

10. *New York Times*, March 25, 1944, 1.

11. NA/SDDF, 840.48 Refugees/5498C, March 24, 1944, WRB to Stockholm, Lisbon, Madrid, Ankara, etc. . . .

12. FDRL/WRB, March 22, 1944, Morgenthau memorandum to FDR.

13. *New York Times*, March 25, 1944, 4.

14. FDRL/WRB, February 25, 1944, Pehle to Halifax. See also *History of the WRB*, I, 336.

15. *New York Times*, March 31, 1944, 9.

16. FDRL/WRB, April 13, 1944, Roswell McClelland to Pehle.

17. *Ibid.*, May 25, 1944, Pehle to McClelland. A full description of WRB's relations with the CIRC is contained in the mimeographed *Summary Report of the Activities of the WRB with Respect to Jews in Hungary*, October 9, 1944.

18. Some controversy exists on the Church's role during the Holocaust. Rolf Hochhuth's *The Deputy* views the Church as having been morally derelict. To some extent the Hochhuth view is documented by Guenter Lewy, *The Catholic Church and Nazi Germany*. A more recent work by Pinchas Lapide, *Three Popes and the Jews*, takes a far less critical view of the role of the Church.

19. FDRL/WRB, March 24, 1944, Pehle to Cicognani.

20. Quoted by Hilberg, *Destruction*, 539.

21. Hirschmann, *Caution*, 179–188.

22. FDRL/WRB, *History of the WRB*, I, 297.

23. *Ibid.*, June 18, 1944, Hirschmann to Pehle. (The latest of the reports available to the WRB.)

24. Hausner, *Jerusalem*, 141.

25. The first estimate is by the same Rudolf Hoess, the second by Ed-

mund Veesenmayer, the German Minister Plenipotentiary in Hungary. The latest estimate for all deaths including the August forced marches is 516,000. See Ernö Lázló, "Hungary's Jewry: A Demographic Overview, 1918–1945," Randolph L. Braham (ed.), *Hungarian Jewish Studies*, 181.

26. *Interpreter Releases*, XXI, June 1944, 213.

27. FDRL/WRB, June 6, 1944, McClelland and Harrison to Pehle.

28. *Ibid.*, June 6, 1944, Pehle to Harrison for transmission to Budapest.

29. *Ibid.*, Box 69, Records Classified Secret, Receipt #27; Record of Expenditures from Board Discretionary Fund, May 1–October 31, 1944, McClelland to Pehle; *History of the WRB*, I, 54–55.

30. *Ibid.* (Record of Expenditures from Board Discretionary Fund.)

31. *Jewish Forum*, May 1944.

32. FDRL/WRB, June 24, 1944, McClelland to Pehle. A second request containing names of Hungarian officials implicated in the Final Solution emanating from Bratislava on August 28, 1944, is also located in the WRB files. According to Hausner, prosecuting attorney in the Eichmann trial, the message intercepted by Hungarian counterintelligence containing the names of seventy Hungarian officials was one sent by the controversial Rudolf Kastner via Bern. Hausner, *Jerusalem*, 142.

33. *Ibid.*, June 28, 1944, Herschell Johnson to Pehle, "Informal Statement of Bulgarian Minister Balabanoff."

34. *Ibid.*, June 29, 1944, Pehle to McCloy.

35. *Ibid.*, July 4, 1944, McCloy to Pehle; also August 10, 1944, Memorandum of conversation Friedman, Kubowitzki, Goldmann, Mereminski and Pehle; also Kubowitzki, *Unity*, 167.

36. *Ibid.*, May 25, 1944, Pehle to McClelland and Harrison. Similar cables were sent to Madrid, Ankara, Lisbon, and Stockholm.

37. *Ibid.*, July 7, 1944, Olsen to Pehle. Contains account of instructions given to Wallenberg.

38. *Ibid.*, March 7, 1945, Johnson to Pehle with enclosure of translation of Swedish newspaper article on Wallenberg's activities in Budapest, based on interviews with surviors.

39. *Ibid.*, October 12, 1944, Wallenberg to Olsen.

40. FDRL/OF 3186, Memorandum of the Executive Committee of the War Refugee Board to the President, May 8, 1944.

41. FDRL/WRB, State Department to Rio De Janeiro, Havana, Bogota, *et al.*, n.d.

42. *Ibid.*, April 22, 1944, Spruille Braden to Stettinius.

43. *Rescue*, I, May 1944, 9, Reprint of Grafton's article, "What Is Free Ports?" from the *New York Post*, April 5, 1944.

44. FDRL/OF 3186, Memorandum of the Executive Committee of the War Refugee Board to the President, May 8, 1944. Also Chamberlain MSS, February 24, 1944, Memorandum of conversation, Joseph Chamberlain and Pehle.

45. NA/SDDF, 840.48 Refugees/5499, March 31, 1944, Stimson to Pehle.

46. *Ibid.*

47. *New York Times*, April 19, 1944, 1.

48. *Ibid.*, May 4, 1944, 18.

49. *Washington Post*, May 29, 1944.

50. FDRL/OF 3186, May 29, 1944, FDR to Robert Murphy.

51. *New York Times*, May 31, 1944, 4.

52. *Ibid.*, June 3, 1944, 15.

53. *Ibid.*, June 10, 1944, 1.

54. *Ibid.*, June 13, 1944, 1. Pehle's brief which suggested the line the President should follow is found in FDRL/OF 3186, June 8, 1944, Pehle to Steve Early.

55. FDRL/WRB, *History of the WRB*, I, 234.

56. *Ibid.*, June 14, 1944, Robert Reynolds to Francis Biddle.

57. *Ibid.*, June 23, 1944, Biddle to Reynolds.

58. Barnett Hirsch, "Free Ports and the White Paper," *The Jewish Forum* (June 1944), 115–117.

59. Wise MSS, February 17, 1944, Wise to Harry Fuller.

60. *Ibid.*, September 13, 1944, Wise to Bloom.

61. FDRL/WRB, *History of the WRB*, I, 242.

62. Subcommittee of the Committee on Immigration and Naturalization, House of Representatives, *Hearings, Investigation of Problems Presented by Refugees at Fort Ontario Refugee Shelter*, 79th Cong., 1st Sess., June 25 and 26, 1945. See also *Final Summary Report, WRB*, 66 ff.

63. Chamberlain MSS, December 29, 1944, Joseph Chamberlain to Biddle; January 20, 1945, Biddle to Chamberlain.

64. FDRL/WRB, June 24, 1944, McClelland to Pehle. (See note 32.)

65. *Ibid.*, July 25, 1944, Alfred Zollinger to State Department. Simultaneously a similar request was made to the British Foreign Office.

66. Josiah E. DuBois, Jr., *The Devils Chemists*, 198.

67. FDRL/WRB, August 4, 1944, Stettinius (Pehle) to Winant.

68. DuBois, *Chemists*, 199.

69. FDRL/WRB, August 11, 1944, Pehle to Harrison for transmission to Budapest.

70. *Ibid.*, August 23, 1944, Pehle to Harrison for transmission to Budapest.

71. Hausner, *Jerusalem*, 142.

72. *Ibid.*, 143.

73. *Die Lage*, August 23, 1944, reproduced in *Nazi Conspiracy and Aggression*, Supplement A, Doc't. 908, 1062–1063.

74. FDRL/WRB, August 11, 1944, McClelland to Pehle.

75. *Ibid.*, August 6, 1944, Johnson to Pehle. The dispatch describes the stir caused by the arrival of some members of the Weiss family in Lisbon.

76. NA/SDDF, 840.48 Refugees/5077, January 28, 1944, Memorandum of conversation, Pehle and Rabbi Schoen.

77. FDRL/WRB, May 25, 1944, Steinhardt to State Department; May 26, 1944, Jewish Agency (Shertok) to Pehle.

78. Hausner, *Jerusalem*, 357–358.

79. FDRL/WRB, May 25, 1944, Steinhardt to State Department.

80. Hausner, *Jerusalem*, 149; both Eichmann in his trial and Schacht at the Nuremberg trials based part of their defense on the involvement in ransom offers. Both argued that Allied failure to take advantage of the offers was responsible for later happenings. International Military Tribunal (IMT), *The Trial of Major War Criminals Before the Military Tribunal*, XXII, 389, Schacht's Testimony and Final Plea. See Hausner, *Jerusalem*, 408, for defense counsel's Robert Servatius summation, and p. 149 for Eichmann's claim that the Allies were responsible for the failure of a proposal which he had originated.

81. FDRL/WRB, June 1944, Memorandum of Reuben Resnick (AJJDC) to Pehle.

82. New York *Herald Tribune*, May 21, 1964, 18.

83. Those were the sentiments first expressed by Lord Moyne, a Deputy Minister of State, when he interviewed Joel Brand in Cairo: "Save a million Jews? What shall we do with them? Where shall we put them?" Hilberg, *Destruction*, 728.

84. Winston Churchill, *The Second World War; Triumph and Tragedy*, VI, 693.

85. Hirschmann, *Caution to Winds*, 114–116.

86. FDRL/WRB, June 24, 1944, Hirschmann to Pehle.

87. NA/SDDF, 840.48 Refugees/6344, June 19, 1944, Shertok to Goldmann.

88. Hausner, *Jerusalem*, 249. Quoting from a memorandum of conversation between Stettinius and Goldmann, June 7, 1944.

89. FDRL/WRB, July 1, 1944, Eden to State Department.

90. *Ibid.*, June 18, 1944, Hirschmann to Pehle with enclosure of letter from Bratislava.

91. Hausner, *Jerusalem*, 249.

92. FDRL/WRB, July 8, 1944, Pehle memorandum to Leahy for FDR.

93. *Ibid.*, July 11, 1944, Jerusalem to State Department with enclosures.

94. *Ibid.*, June 22, 1944, Stettinius to Pehle.

95. *Ibid.*, July 27, 1944, Pehle to Stettinius.

96. *Ibid.*, June 9, 1944, Hull to Averell Harriman.

97. *Ibid.*, June 20, 1944, Harriman to Hull.

98. *Ibid.*, July 7, 1944, Hull to Harriman.

99. *Ibid.*, February 17, 1945, George Kennan to State Department.

100. *Ibid.*, August 23, 1944, McClelland to Pehle with enclosure from Vaad to Morgenthau. The dispatch also referred to fears by the Orthodox community regarding 320 Rabbis, including the renowned Satmar Rov, who had supposedly been interned in Austria but about whom no news had been received.

101. *Ibid.*, August 22, 1944, Johnson to Pehle.

102. *Ibid.*, September 22, 1944, McClelland to Pehle.

103. *Ibid.*, October 8, 1944, Kubowitzki to Pehle.

104. *Ibid.*, October 6, 1944, Pehle to McClelland for transmission to Budapest.

105. *Ibid.*, December 7, 1944, McClelland to Pehle with enclosure of Budapest's response.

106. *Ibid.*, December 22, 1944, Olsen to WRB based on Wallenberg's detailed description.

107. Hausner, *Jerusalem*, 153, quoting directly from testimony of Aviva Fleischman, a march survivor, at the Eichmann trial.

108. *Ibid.*, 150.

109. *Ibid.* See also FDRL/WRB, June 22, 1944, Stettinius to Pehle. The Jewish agency representative in Ankara, Chaim Barlasz, had word that the SS meant the Brand mission only as a feeler.

110. *Nazi Conspiracy and Aggression*, Supplement B V, 315–325. Kastner testimony at Nuremberg.

111. FDRL/WRB, November 18, 1944, Pehle to McClelland.

112. *Ibid.*, September 15, 1944, McClelland to Pehle.

113. *Ibid.*, September 16, 1944, McClelland to Pehle.

114. *Ibid.*, January 6, 1945, McClelland to Pehle.

115. *Ibid.*, February 27, 1945, Kubowitzki to Pehle.

116. *Ibid.*, *History of the WRB*, I, 218 ff.

117. H. A. Goodman, "Mission to Himmler," *Jewish Life* (November–December, 1952), 335–339.

118. Reitlinger, *Final Solution*, 462.

119. FDRL/OF 3186, July 24, 1944, Smertenko to FDR.

120. FDRL/WRB, July 10, 1944, Montor to Pehle.

121. *Ibid.*, June 30, 1944, Steinhardt to Pehle.

122. *Washington Post*, October 3, 1944, 1.

123. *Ibid.*

124. Hebrew Committee of National Liberation, *Washington Post a Victim of British and Zionist Intrigues?*, October 1944.

125. *Washington Post*, October 13, 1944, 8.

126. FDRL/WRB, *Final Summary Report, WRB*, 5; *History of the WRB*, I, 16.

127. NA/SDDF, 840.48 Refugees/5415, March 23, 1944, Hirschmann to Pehle and Wallace Murray.

128. A highly controversial account of the case is presented in Ben Hecht's *Perfidy*. According to Hecht, Kastner virtually guaranteed order in the delicate deportation precedure by keeping the truth, which he and other Zionist leaders knew to be gassing at Auschwitz, hidden from Jews in the provinces. In turn for this service the *Sondereinzatskommando* permitted the Zionists to select a small group for rescue.

129. NA/SDDF, 840.48 Refugees/6062, May 18, 1944, Steinhardt to Pehle.

130. FDRL/WRB, July 14, 1944, Eri Jabotinsky to Bergson.

131. *New York Times*, June 9, 1969, 47.

132. NA/SDDF, 840.48 Refugees/6299, May 25, 1944, Shertok to Goldmann.

133. *Ibid.*

134. FDRL/WRB, *History of the WRB*, I, 14; *Final Summary Report, WRB*, 9.

135. Steinhardt MSS, August 16, 1944, Jacob Rosenheim to Steinhardt.

136. *Ibid.*

137. FDRL/WRB, June 21, 1944, Olsen to Pehle.

138. *Ibid.*, November 20, 1944, Olsen to Pehle; also Final Report on Operations from Sweden, February 1945.

139. NA/SDDF, 840.48 Refugees/5892, May 4, 1944, Isaac Weissmann to Wise.

140. *Ibid.*, /5961, May 10, 1944, Robert C. Dexter to Pehle.

141. *Ibid.*, /6094, May 23, 1944, Dexter to Pehle (via Norweb); /6116, May 24, 1944, Weissmann to Wise.

142. Kubowitzki, *Unity*, 193.

143. Long MSS, May 8, 1941, Steinhardt to Long.

144. Long Diary, November 28, 1941.

145. *Ibid.*

146. Wise MSS, January 19, 1942, Bernard Rosenblatt to Wise.

147. *Ibid.*, February 6, 1942, Emanuel Neuman to Steinhardt.

148. *Ibid.*, January 19, 1942, Rosenblatt to Wise (quoted in Rosenblatt letter).

149. *Ibid.*

150. NA/SDDF, 840.48 Refugees/5178, February 12, 1944, Hirschmann to Pehle.

151. Steinhardt MSS, April 27, 1944, Hirschmann to Steinhardt.

152. *New York Times*, April 19, 1944, 1.

153. FDRL/PPF 5477, April 19, 1944, Morgenthau to FDR.

154. *Ibid.*, April 29, 1944, Lubin memorandum to FDR.

155. Steinhardt MSS, May 4, 1944, Paul Baerwald to Steinhardt.

156. *Ibid.*, April 4, 1944, Hirschmann to Steinhardt.

157. *Ibid.*, June 10, 1944. Hirschmann to Steinhardt.

158. Kubowitzki, *Unity*, 194.

159. *Public Opinion Quarterly*, VIII, Winter, 1944–1945, 588.

160. FDRL/WRB, June 21, 1944, Friedrich Seckel to Pehle.

161. Bloom MSS, August 21, 1944, Pehle to Bloom.

162. Wischnitzer, *Dwell in Safety*, 246.

163. Kubowitzki, *Unity*, 166–167.

164. FDRL/WRB, October 12, 1944, Olsen to Pehle.

165. Hirschmann, *Life Line*, 159.

166. See Kubowitzki, *Unity*, 186, for an instructive discussion of this point.

167. FDRL/WRB, August 10, 1944, Olsen to Pehle.

168. Hilberg, *Destruction*, 541, quoting SS Sturmbanführer Höttl.

169. FDRL/WRB, August 14, 1944, Olsen to Pehle with enclosure of Wallenberg's observations.

170. *Ibid.*, August 10, 1944, Olsen to Pehle.

171. Laszlo, "Hungary's Jewry," 157, 181. An earlier estimate made by the Anglo-American Committee calculates the number of Hungarian Jews surviving the war as 220,000. The figure includes approximately 60,000 Jews who returned from camps or were in hiding outside Hungary, *AJYB*, 1947–8, XLIX, 740.

Bibliography

I. *Primary Sources*

A. *Manuscript Collections:* The most important manuscript collections on the refugee-rescue story are held in various government depositories. The Franklin D. Roosevelt Papers, located in the Franklin D. Roosevelt Library at Hyde Park, New York, offer a comprehensive collection of material on the Administration's rescue activity. Especially important is *Official File* 3186 which contains the memoranda pertaining to the refugee phase. Various personal files also contain important data. The Roosevelt Library is also the home of the indispensable papers of the War Refugee Board which runs into thousands of pieces. These papers present a full account of government rescue activity during the years 1944 and 1945 when the Administration's attempt to rescue Jews was at its zenith, and also much material on the rescue program in 1943. A two-volume official history (unpublished) which sums up the activities of the WRB is useful.

The best source of information on the Department of State in relation to rescue advocates and the rescue effort is contained in the Breckinridge Long Papers in the Manuscript Division of the Library of Congress. The papers run into many hundreds of pieces which, together with the diary, present the most candid exposure of the State Department's rescue posture. The diary has been edited by Fred L. Israel (*The War Diary of Breckinridge Long; Selections from the Years 1939–1944*, Lincoln: University of Nebraska Press, 1966) but some of the entries concerning refugees were considered of peripheral importance and were omitted. Also at the Manuscript Division are the Cordell Hull Papers. Much of the material in this collection is duplicated in the *Memoirs* and in the State Department's *Foreign Relations* series. The Laurence Steinhardt Papers, which are also in the Manuscript Division, are especially interesting for the insight they give into his activities as Ambassador to Turkey and his connection with Ira Hirschmann, the agent of the WRB.

The fullest running account of the relation between rescue advocates and the State Department and the various activities of the Department during the years in consideration can be culled from the various memoranda and correspondence in the Records of the Department of State in the National Archives in Washington, D.C. Research is facilitated by use of the decimal file system but the State Department reserves the right to review and blue-pencil research notes and it makes use of this authority.

The YIVO Institute for Jewish Research contains two collections relevant for the rescue story aside from the general collection of original Holocaust literature. The Joseph Chamberlain Papers are important because they contain the files of the President's Advisory Committee on Political Refugees. In addition, it has the files of the National Refugee Service, successor to the National Coordinating Committee, which served as the coordinator of the private refugee agencies in the United States. Unfortunately, the papers are closed to researchers but one can examine the early minutes of the NCC and the reports of the Evian conference. The minutes of the PACPR are available in duplicate in the Stephen Wise Papers housed at the Goldfarb library at Brandeis University. Still not completely catalogued, these important papers also contain correspondence to Stephen S. Wise which gives a good inside view of the principal pro-Zionist national organization on the American Jewish scene, the American Jewish Congress. The second collection at YIVO is in files of HIAS–ICA, The Hebrew Sheltering and Immigrant Aid Society, which is the oldest of the nonpolitical refugee-rescue agencies. These papers are especially useful for the picture they give of the activities, domestic and foreign, of an agency deeply involved in the rescue of Jewish refugees.

The papers of Sol Bloom, who occupied a strategic position as Chairman of the House Foreign Affairs Committee and became a controversial member of the American delegation to the Bermuda Conference, are in the Manuscript Division of the New York Public Library. The collection sheds some light on Bloom's activity on behalf of many refugees. The Pierrepont Moffat Papers at the Houghton Library of Harvard University throw some light on the State Department's reaction to public agitation after *Krystallnacht*. Selections from the papers are also available in print. (Nancy H. Hooker, ed., *The Moffat Papers*, Cambridge: Harvard University Press, 1956.)

Three important collections are unavailable to researchers: the papers of James G. McDonald, an important figure in the refugee effort, are in the possession of his daughter, Mrs. Barbara Stewart, who intends to use them as the source of a book on the refugee issue. The papers of Myron C. Taylor are housed at the Franklin D. Roosevelt Library and may not be opened until after the death of Harry S Truman. The papers of Henry Morgenthau, Jr., are in the same depository where they have thus far been the source of two books by Professor Morton Blum. Excerpts from the Morgenthau diaries were published in *Collier's* in November 1947.

B. *Public Documents:* There are four kinds of documents considered under this heading: (1) Documents published by the United States Government, especially the State Department, (2) congressional hearings which bear on the refugee-rescue issue, (3) documents of foreign governments and international conferences and agencies, (4) miscellaneous documents such as the minutes of the American delegation to the Bermuda Conference.

1. U.S. Department of Commerce, Bureau of the Census, *Historical Statistics of the United States, 1789–1943*, gives a complete statistical survey of immigration. The *Department of State Bulletin* (Title changed from *Press Releases* in 1939.) is a running account of the Department's activities. The most important single collection published by the State Department is *Foreign Relations of the United States, Diplomatic Correspondence.* The collection of diplomatic papers and dispatches is issued twenty to twenty-five years after the events have taken place. Also in this category is the *Final Summary Report of the Executive Director, War Refugee Board*, which was issued by William O'Dwyer, the last director of the Board on September 10, 1945.

2. The *Congressional Record* gives an occasional glimpse of how the refugee-rescue issue was viewed from the floor of Congress. The hearings of the committees offer a better insight into the activities of Congress. They are: "Hearings on Joint Resolution to Authorize the Admission . . . of a Limited Number of Refugee Children," *Hearings before the Committee on Immigration and Naturalization, House of Representatives,* 76 Cong., 1 sess. (May 24–25, 31 and June 1, 1939), and under the same title, *Joint Hearings before a Subcommittee on Immigration, United States Senate and a Subcommittee of the Committee on Immigration and Naturalization, House of Representatives,* 76 Cong., 1 sess. (April 20–22, 24, 1939). Also "Hearings . . . to Provide a Temporary Haven . . . for European Children Under the Age of Sixteen," *Hearings of the Committee on Immigration and Naturalization, House of Representatives,* 76 Cong., 3 sess. (August 8 and 9, 1940).

Other congressional hearings used are: "Providing for the Establishment . . . of a Commission to . . . Rescue the Jewish People of Europe," *Hearings of the Committee on Foreign Affairs, House of Representatives,* 78 Cong., 1 sess. (November 26, 1943). "Favoring Action Looking to Relief for Starving Peoples of Europe," *Hearings before a Subcommittee of the Committee on Foreign Relations, United States Senate,* 78 Cong., 1 sess. (November 1943). "Problems Presented by Refugees at Fort Ontario Refugee Shelter," *Hearings before a Subcommittee of the Committee on Immigration and Naturalization,* 79 Cong., 1 sess. (June 1945). "Jewish National Home in Palestine," *Hearings of the Committee on Foreign Affairs, House of Representatives,* 78 Cong., 2 sess., February–March, 1944.

3. In the category of documents of foreign governments and international agencies are included: *Proceedings of the Intergovernmental Committee, Evian, July 6–15, 1938* (verbatim records of the plenary meetings of the committee, resolutions and reports). *Official Minutes of the Meeting of the Officers of the Intergovernmental Committee on Political Refugees,* Washington, October 1939 (mimeographed). *Records of the Proceedings of the Meeting of the Executive Committee of the Intergovernmental Committee on Political Refugees,* London, August 4, 1943 (mimeographed). *Report of the Fourth Plenary Session of the Intergovernmental Committee on Political Refugees,* London, August 15–17, 1944.

Important for data on other governments involved in the refugee crisis are: *Documents on British Foreign Policy, 1919–1939,* 3rd series, III, London, 1950 and *Documents on German Foreign Policy, 1918–1945,* series D, IV, V, Washington, 1951, 1953. The records of the International Military Tribunal, *The Trial of the Major War Criminals Before the International Military Tribunal,* 24 vols., 1950, and the published evidence of the Office of the United States Counsel for Prosecution of Axis Criminality, *Nazi Conspiracy and Aggression,* 11 vols. and two supplements, 1946–1948, offer interesting insights into Nazi motivations.

4. The most revealing set of minutes bearing on the subject are those of the President's Advisory Committee on Political Refugees, usually submitted under the title *Minutes of the Meeting of the President's Advisory Committee on Political Refugees,* by George Warren. The PACPR met at irregular intervals between 1938 and 1943, when it faded out of the picture. Copies are available in the Joseph Chamberlain Papers at YIVO and in the Stephen Wise Papers at the Goldfarb Library at Brandeis University. The *Minutes of the Meeting of the American Delegation at the Bermuda Conference,* held in April 1943 and the *Minutes of*

the Meetings of the Bermuda Conference as well as a series of memoranda entitled "Confidential Memorandum for the Chairman" and also the final report of the Bermuda Conference, *Report to the Government of the United States and the United Kingdom from the Delegates to the Conference on Refugee Problems Held at Bermuda,* April 19–28, 1943, can be found in the Breckinridge Long Papers in the Manuscript Division of the Library of Congress. They are indispensable for the State Department's thinking on the refugee-rescue issue in 1943.

Two government or quazi-government reports are especially relevant: The Refugee Economic Corporation's *Report of the British Guiana Commission to the President's Advisory Committee on Political Refugees,* London, May 1939, and the report on the possibility of linking Alaskan development to the refugee crisis, *The Problem of Alaskan Development.* Sometimes called the Slattery Report, it was released by the Department of Interior in 1939.

C. *Private Documents:* Included in this category are the plethora of reports, minutes, and proceedings of the private agencies which have some bearing on the refugee-rescue question:

American Jewish Committee, *Annual Report of the Executive Committee,* published in the *Contemporary Jewish Record* and the *American Jewish Yearbook.*

American Jewish Conference, *Proceedings of the First Session, August 29– September 2, 1943.*

——, *Proceedings of the Second Session, December 3–5, 1944* (ed. Alexander S. Kohansky).

——, *Proceedings of the Third Session, February 17–19, 1946* (ed. Ruth Hirschmann). Also contains the report of the Interim Committee and the Final Report of the Commission on Rescue.

American Jewish Joint Distribution Committee, *Aiding Jews Overseas: Reports of the American Jewish Joint Distribution Committee,* 1939– 1942.

——, *The Rescue of Stricken Jews in a World at War,* December 1943.

Brookings Institution, *Refugee Settlement in the Dominican Republic: A Survey Conducted Under the Auspices of the Brookings Institution,* 1942.

Committee for a Jewish Army of Stateless and Palestinian Jews, *From Evian to Bermuda,* 1943.

Dominican Republic Settlement Association, Inc., *Sosua, Haven for Settlement in the Dominican Republic,* 1941.

Hebrew Immigrant Aid Society, *Report on Activities in the United States and Overseas,* 1940.

————, *Rescue Through Immigration, Annual Report and Messages*, 1941.
Joint Emergency Committee for European Affairs, *Program for the Rescue of Jews from Occupied Europe*, April 1943.
National Coordinating Committee, *Minutes of the Board of Directors of the National Coordinating Committee, passim*, 1934–1939 (typed).
National Refugee Service, *Quarterly Report*, 1940–1941.
————, *Report of the Executive Director*, 1939. (Joseph Chamberlain, mimeographed.)
————, *Reports of Meetings of the Board of Directors of the National Refugee Service*, 1941–1944, mimeographed.
Refugee Economic Corporation, *Annual Report*, 1939–1943.
————, *Quest for Settlement, Summaries of Selected Economic and Geographic Reports on Settlement Possibilities for European Immigrants*, 1946.
World Jewish Congress, *Report of the Executive, Submitted to the Twenty-second Zionist Congress at Basle*, 1946.

D. *Contemporary Newspapers and Periodicals:* News concerning Jews and the refugee-rescue issue can most easily be culled from the Anglo-Jewish press and two periodicals, *Rescue* published by HIAS after 1942 and *Interpreter Releases*, which concerned themselves largely with refugee and immigration matters. The latter publication, a monthly, offers a complete statistical description of the refugee crisis. The *New York Times* and to some extent the *New York Herald Tribune* and the *Washington Post* cover the major happenings on the issue but in general the liberal press took more interest in refugee matters. The newspaper *PM* and the *New Republic* and the *Nation* were consistently in favor of a more energetic rescue policy and frequently published articles condemning the Department of State. The Yiddish-language daily *The Day* shared that view. Detailed information on refugee-rescue happenings can be culled from the *Daily News Bulletin* of the Jewish Telegraph Agency, a news service which served the Yiddish as well as the Anglo-Jewish press. The German-Jewish weekly *Aufbau*, which began publication in 1934, took a special interest in the refugee issue and the accommodation of refugees to the United States. The opinions of the various sections of the American Jewish community can best be gleaned from the Anglo-Jewish press. Each periodical served as the house organ for a different organization. The oldest of these, the *American Hebrew*, a weekly which began publication in 1879, represents a middle-of-the-road position. The *National Jewish Monthly* is the organ of B'nai B'rith, the *Congress Weekly* (formerly the *Congress Bulletin*) speaks for the pro-Zionist American Jewish Congress, the *Menorah Journal* for the Menorah Association which is primarily interested in the furtherance of Jewish culture, *Jewish Frontier* for the labor Zionists, and *Workmen's Circle Call* for left-wing labor union elements. The most valuable of all periodicals for research purposes is the *Contemporary Jewish Record*. This bimonthly which made its debut in 1938, published by the American Jewish Committee, featured a detailed calendar of all events relating to the welfare of the Jewish community as well as a useful review of the national press on Jewish matters. It was the progenitor of *Commentary* magazine. The *Public Opinion Quarterly* published many surveys and several articles on matters relevant to the refugee-rescue issue. Most of these have now been gathered together under one cover in Charles H. Stember and others, *Jews in the Mind of America* (New York: Basic Books Inc., 1966). Also sponsored by the American Jewish Committee is the *American Jewish Yearbook*, which provides coverage of events as well as indispensable listings and statistical descriptions of the American Jewish community.

E. *Published Memoirs, Correspondence, Diaries:*   Personal memoirs that bear directly on refugee-rescue activity are relatively scarce. The most important of these is the aforementioned *The War Diary of Breckinridge Long* (See under manuscripts collections). Another is Henry Morgenthau, Jr., "The Morgenthau Diaries VI—The Refugee Run-Around," *Collier's*, November 1, 1947. Ira Hirschmann, the WRB agent in Turkey who played a role in opening the Rumanian-Turkey-Palestine conduit has written three books on his experience; *Lifeline to a Promised Land*, New York: Vanguard Press, 1948; *The Embers Still Burn*, New York: Simon & Schuster, 1949 and *Caution to the Winds*, New York: David McKay Co., 1962. Lewis L. Strauss, who was involved in the attempt to establish the Coordinating Foundation, devotes a chapter to his experience in his book *Men and Decisions*, New York: Doubleday & Co., 1962. Page references in the narrative refer to the Popular Library Edition. Other pertinent works are:

Bloom, Sol. *The Autobiography of Sol Bloom.* New York: G. P. Putnam's Sons, 1948.

Celler, Emanuel. *You Never Leave Brooklyn.* New York: John Day Co., 1952.

Ciechanowski, Jan. *Defeat in Victory.* Garden City: Doubleday & Co., 1947.

Dodd, William, Jr., and Dodd, Martha (eds.). *Ambassador Dodd's Diary, 1933–1938.* New York: Harcourt, Brace & Co., 1941.

Fischer, Louis. *Men and Politics.* New York: Duell, Sloan & Pearce, 1941.

Fry, Varian. *Surrender on Demand.* New York: Random House, 1945.

Hayes, Carlton J. H. *Wartime Mission in Spain, 1942–1945*. New York: The Macmillan Co., 1948.

Hull, Cordell. *The Memoirs of Cordell Hull*. 2 vols. New York: The Macmillan Co., 1948.

Ickes, Harold. *The Secret Diary of Harold L. Ickes: Volume III: The Lowering Clouds, 1939–1941*. New York: Simon & Schuster, 1954.

Lochner, Louis P. (ed. and trans.). *The Goebbels Diaries, 1942–1943*. Garden City: Doubleday & Co., 1948.

McDonald, Dwight. *Memoirs of a Revolutionist: Essays in Political Criticism*. New York: Farrar, Straus & Cudahy Co., 1957.

Perkins, Frances. *The Roosevelt I Knew*. New York: Viking Press, 1947.

Proskauer, Joseph M. *A Segment of My Time*. New York: Farrar, Straus & Cudahy, 1950.

Roosevelt, Elliot (ed.), *F.D.R.: His Personal Letters, 1928–1945*. 2 vols. New York: Duell, Sloan & Pearce, 1950.

Roosevelt, Eleanor. *This I Remember*. New York: Harper and Bros., 1949.

Rosenman, Samuel (ed.), *The Public Papers and Addresses of Franklin D. Roosevelt*. 13 vols. New York: the Macmillan Co., 1938–1950.

Weissberg, Alex and Brand, Joel. *Desperate Mission*. New York: Grove Press, 1958.

Wise, Stephen S. *Challenging Years: The Autobiography of Stephen Wise*. New York: G. P. Putnam's Sons, 1949.

F. *Correspondence and Interviews:*   Some of the most important figures involved in refugee-rescue activity are no longer alive. This includes Breckinridge Long, James G. McDonald and Myron C. Taylor. Ira Hirschmann, special agent of the War Refugee Board in Turkey in 1944, shared some of his experiences with the author and was especially instructive regarding his relationship with Laurence Steinhardt, the American ambassador in Turkey. Isador Lubin, a presidential advisor and later Commissioner of Labor Statistics, Samuel Rosenman, a member of the executive of the American Jewish Committee and Roosevelt's speech writer, Frances Perkins, Secretary of Labor, and Admiral Lewis Strauss, involved in trying to organize the Coordinating Foundation and later the director of the Atomic Energy Commission, shared their knowledge of specific events with the author.

II. *Secondary Sources*

No bibliographic guide for the American aspect of the Holocaust is available but there exists a somewhat dated general guide, Jacob Robinson and Philip Friedman, *Guide to Jewish History under Nazi Impact*, New York: YIVO Institute for Jewish Research and Yad Washem, 1960. It replaces Philip Friedman, "Research and Literature in the Recent Tragedy," *Jewish Social Studies*, XII (January 1950), 14–19. In addition there are guides available for Hebrew, Polish and Yiddish publications. A special guide for the Hungarian aspect of the Holocaust has been compiled by Randolph L. Braham, *The Hungarian Jewish Catastrophe: A Selected and Annotated Bibliography*, New York: YIVO Institute for Jewish Research and Yad Washem, 1962.

A. *Books:* The growing number of works on the Holocaust in the last decade undoubtedly gives that subject the distinction of being among the most intensively explored subjects in twentieth century history. Some of the best known general works which deserve special mention are: Raul Hilberg, *The Destruction of the European Jews*, Chicago: Quadrangle Books, 1961. That work supplements and to some extent replaces Gerald Reitlinger's *The Final Solution: The Attempt to Exterminate the Jews of Europe, 1939–1945*, New York: Beechhurst Press, 1953 (page references in text refer to 1961 Perpetua edition) and Leon Poliakov, *Harvest of Hate: The Nazi Program for the Destruction of the Jews of Europe*, Syracuse: Syracuse University Press, 1954. The trial of Adolf Eichmann stimulated a spate of new works of which the most notable is Gideon Hausner's *Justice in Jerusalem*, New York: Harper & Row, 1966. Hannah Arendt in her *Eichmann in Jerusalem: A Report on the Banality of Evil*, New York: Viking Press, 1963, presents an interesting but controversial thesis about the perpetrators and the victims. A point-by-point refutation of Arendt's work is presented by Jacob Robinson in *And the Crooked Shall be Made Straight*, New York: The Macmillan Co., 1965. The two works are best read together.

The refugee-rescue crisis and the reaction of the Roosevelt Administration to it have recently been the subject of two books. Arthur D. Morse, *While Six Million Died: A Chronicle of American Apathy*, New York: Random House, 1967, is a popularized emotional account of what transpired between 1938 and 1945. David S. Wyman, *Paper Walls: America and the Refugee Crisis 1938–1941*, a scholarly account takes the story only to 1941. It concentrates on the public opinion and congressional aspect of the refugee crisis. An early work which contains invaluable information, edited by A. Leon Kubowitzki and others, is entitled *Unity in Dispersion: A History of the World Jewish Congress*, New York: World Jewish Congress, 1948. Very helpful on Jewish population movements and the refugee problem are Mark Wischnitzer's *To Dwell in Safety: The Story of Jewish Migration Since 1800*, Philadelphia: Jewish Publication Society, 1948, and Arieh Tartakower and Kurt Grossman, *The Jewish Refugee*, New York: Institute of Jewish Affairs of the World Jewish Congress,

1944. Other general works on the refugee problem are Sir John Hope Simpson's *The Refugee Problem: Report of a Survey*, London: Oxford University Press, 1939, Malcolm J. Proudfoot, *European Refugees, 1939–1952*, London: Faber & Faber, 1957 and John G. Stoessinger, *The Refugee and the World Community*, Minneapolis: University of Minnesota Press, 1956. The following is a selected list of books relevant to some aspect of the refugee-rescue crisis or to the total-war environment of which it was part:

Abshagen, Karl H. *Canaris*. trans. A. H. Brodnick. London: Hutchinson and Co., 1956.

Acheson, Dean. *Morning and Noon*. Boston: Houghton Mifflin, 1965.

Adler, Cyrus, and Margalith, Aaron M. *With Firmness in the Right: American Diplomatic Action Affecting Jews, 1840–1945*. New York: The American Jewish Committee, 1946.

Bailey, Thomas A. *The Man in the Street: The Impact of American Public Opinion on Foreign Policy*. New York: Macmillan Co., 1948.

Bendiner, Robert. *The Riddle of the State Department*. New York: The Nation Assoc., 1943.

Bentwich, Norman. *The Rescue and Achievement of Refugee Scholars*. The Hague: Martinus Nijhoff, 1953.

——. *Wanderer in War, 1939–1945*. London: Victor Gollancz, 1946.

Bowman, Isaiah. *Limits of Land Settlement: A Report on Present-Day Possibilities*. New York: Council on Foreign Relations, 1937.

Bulock, Alan. *Hitler, A Study in Tyranny*. New York: Harper & Row, rev. ed., 1964.

Celler, Emanuel. *You Never Leave Brooklyn*. New York: John Day Co., 1952.

Churchill, Sir Winston S. *Triumph and Tragedy*. Boston: Houghton Mifflin Co., 1953.

Ciechanowski, Jan. *Defeat in Victory*. Garden City: Doubleday & Co., 1947.

Craig, Gordon A. and Gilbert, Felix (eds.). *The Diplomats, 1919–1930*. 2 vols. New York: Atheneum, 1963.

Crum, Bartley C. *Behind the Silken Curtain*. New York: Simon & Schuster, 1947.

Dallek, Robert. *Democrat and Diplomat, The Life of William E. Dodd*. New York: Oxford University Press, 1968.

Davidson, Gabriel. *Our Jewish Farmers and the Story of the Jewish Agricultural Society*. New York: L. B. Fischer, 1943.

Davie, Maurice R. *Refugees in America*. New York: Harper & Brothers, 1947.

Divine, Robert A. *American Immigration Policy, 1924–1952*. New Haven: Yale University Press, 1957.

DuBois, Josiah E., Jr. *The Devil's Chemists*. Boston: Beacon Press, 1952.

Duggan, Stephen and Drury, Betty. *The Rescue of Science and Learning*. New York: Macmillan Co., 1948.

Farley, James A. *Jim Farley's Story*. New York: McGraw-Hill Book Co., 1948.

Feis, Herbert. *Petroleum and American Foreign Policy*. Stanford: Stanford University Press, 1944.

Fleming, Donald and Bailyn, Bernard (eds.). Perspectives in American History, Vol. II, *"The Intellectual Migration" Europe and America, 1930–1960*. Cambridge: Charles Warren Center for Studies in American History, 1968.

Friedländer, Saul. *Kurt Gerstein, The Ambiguity of Good*. New York: Knopf, 1969.

Friedman, Philip. *Their Brothers' Keepers*. New York: Crown Publishers, 1957.

Habe, Hans. *The Mission*. New York: New American Library, 1967.

Halperin, Samuel. *The Political World of American Zionism*. Detroit: Wayne University Press, 1961.

Handlin, Oscar. *Adventures in Freedom: Three Hundred Years of Jewish Life in America*. New York: McGraw-Hill Co., 1954.

Hecht, Ben. *Perfidy*. New York: Juliun Messner, 1961.

Hero, Alfred O. *Studies in Citizenship Participation in International Relations*. Vol. V. *Opinion Leaders in American Communities*. Vol. VI. *Studies in Citizenship Participation in International Relations*. New York: World Peace Foundation, 1959.

Hochhuth, Rolf. *The Deputy*. New York: Grove Press, 1964.

Jacob, Charles E. *Leadership in the New Deal, The Administrative Challenge*. Englewood Cliffs: Prentice Hall, 1967.

Jewish Black Book Committee. *The Black Book: The Nazi Crime Against the Jewish People*. New York: Duell, Sloan & Pearce, 1946.

Karpf, Maurice. *Jewish Community Organization in the United States*. New York: Bloch Publishing Co., 1938.

Kohler, Max J. *The United States and German-Jewish Persecution: Precedents for Popular and Governmental Action*. Cincinnati: B'nai B'rith, 1934.

Langer, William E., and Gleason, Everett. *The Challenge to Isolation, 1937–1940*. New York: Harper & Bros., 1952.

Learsi, Rufus. *The Jews in America: A History.* Cleveland: World Publishing Co., 1954.

Leuchtenburg, William E. *Franklin D. Roosevelt and the New Deal, 1932–1940.* New York: Harper & Row (Torchbook Edition), 1963.

Lewy, Guenter. *The Catholic Church and Nazi Germany.* New York: McGraw-Hill, 1964.

Lubell, Samuel. *The Future of American Politics.* New York: Doubleday (Anchor Book), 1956.

Manuel, Frank E. *The Realities of American-Palestine Relations.* Washington, D.C.: Public Affairs Press, 1949.

Peterson, Edward N. *Hjalmar Schacht: For and Against Hitler, A Political Economic Study of Germany, 1923–1945.* Boston: Christopher Publishing House, 1954.

Shachner, Nathan. *The Price of Liberty: A History of the American Jewish Committee.* New York: American Jewish Committee, 1948.

Sherwood, Robert E. *Roosevelt and Hopkins.* 2 vols. New York: Bantam Books, 1950.

Shirer, William L. *The Rise and Fall of the Third Reich.* New York: Simon & Schuster, 1960.

Skalare, Marshall (ed.). *The Jews: Social Patterns of an American Group.* New York: Free Press, 1958.

Strong, Donald. *Organized Anti-Semitism in America: The Rise of Group Prejudice During the Decade 1930–1940.* Washington, D.C.: American Council on Public Affairs, 1941.

Stuart, Graham H. *The Department of State: A History of Its Organization, Procedure and Personnel.* New York: Macmillan Co., 1949.

Syrkin, Marie. *Blessed Is the Match.* Philadelphia: Jewish Publication Society, 1947.

Tenenbaum, Joseph. *Underground: The Story of a People.* New York: Philosophical Library, 1952.

———. *In Search of a Lost People.* New York: Beechhurst Press, 1948.

Thompson, Dorothy. *Refugees, Anarchy or Organization.* New York: Random House, 1938.

———. *Let the Record Speak.* Boston: Houghton Mifflin Co., 1939.

Welles, Sumner. *Time for Decision.* New York: Harper & Son, 1941.

Wighton, Charles, and Peis, Guenter. *Hitler's Spies and Saboteurs.* New York: Holt & Co., 1958.

Wischnitzer, Mark. *Visas to Freedom: The History of HIAS.* New York: World Publishing Co., 1956.

Wise, Stephen S. *As I See It.* New York: Jewish Opinion Publishing Corp., 1944.

B. *Articles:* A large number of articles and pamphlets, most written during the crisis, throw some light on what people were thinking at the time as well as clarifying some of the less well-known aspects of the refugee-rescue crisis. Louis Adamic's *America and the Refugees,* New York: Public Affairs Committee, 1939, for example, was designed to assuage public apprehension regarding the influx of refugees, and it contains much important statistical data. The *Annals of the American Academy of Political and Social Science,* CCIII (May 1939), was entirely devoted to the refugee-rescue crisis. The several articles are perhaps the most comprehensive to be found on the subject. They are: Eric Estorick, "The Evian Conference and the Intergovernmental Committee"; Louise W. Holborn, "The League of Nations and the Refugee Problem"; Bernard W. Levmore, "A Stimulus for American Industry: Nonprofessional Refugees"; Read Lewis and Marian Shibsby, "Status of the Refugee Under the American Immigration Laws"; Erika Mann, Eric Estorick, "Private and Governmental Aid to Refugees"; and Bernhard Ostrolenk, "The Economics of an Imprisoned World—A Brief for the Removal of Immigration Restriction"; Samuel Guy Inman, "Refugee Settlement in Latin America"; and David H. Popper, "A Homeland for Refugees." Joseph Tenenbaum was among the first scholars to examine the role of witnesses to the Holocaust. His "They Might Have Been Rescued," *Congress Weekly,* February 2, 1953 and "The Crucial Year, 1938," *Yad Washem Studies,* II (1958), find this writer in general agreement. Edward N. Saveth's "Franklin D. Roosevelt and the Jewish Crisis," *American Jewish Yearbook,* XLVII (1945/1946), is an early descriptive rather than analytic examination of the actions of the Roosevelt Administration on the refugee crisis. The intricacies of the State Department visa administration are examined in Graham H. Stuart, "Wartime Visa Control Procedure," *Department of State Bulletin,* XI (September 10, 1944). It is supplemented by the aforementioned article in *Annals* by Read Lewis and Marian Shibsby. Dorothy Thompson did much to alert American public opinion to the refugee crisis. One of her best efforts was "Refugees, A World Problem," *Foreign Affairs,* XVI (April 1938). Henry Cohen, "Crisis and Reaction," *American Jewish Archives,* V (June 1953) is an early attempt to examine the reaction of American Jewry through the organization press. The following is a list of other articles used in this study:

Bentwich, Norman. "Wartime Britain's Alien Policy," *Contemporary Jewish Record,* V (February 1942), 41–50.

———. "The Evian Conference and After," *Fortnightly,* CL (September 1938), 287–295.

Bittleman, Alexander. *Jewish Unity for Victory* (New York: Workers Library Publishers, 1943). Bound pamphlet.

Blau, Bruno. "The Jewish Population of Germany, 1939–1945," *Jewish Social Studies*, XII (April 1950), 161–172.

Brody, David. "American Jewry, The Refugees and Immigration Restriction (1932–1942)," *Publications of the American Jewish Historical Society*, XLV (June 1956), 219–247.

Craig, Gordon A. "The German Foreign Office from Neurath to Ribbentrop," in *The Diplomats, 1919–1939* (see under section A, II, 406–436.

Cranston, Alan. "Congress and the Alien," *Contemporary Jewish Record*, III (May–June 1940), 245–252.

Dean, Vera Micheles. "European Power Politics and the Refugee Problem," *Annals of the American Academy of Political and Social Science*, CCIII (May 1939), 18–25.

Dijour, Ilja M. "The Preparation of the Bermuda Conference: An Analysis of Two Documents," *Yivo Bleter*, XXI (December 1943). *np.*

Dingol, Solomon. "How Many Refugees from Nazi Persecution Were Admitted to the United States?" *Rescue*, I (February 1944), 1–7.

Duker, Abraham. "Jewish Territorialism: An Historical Sketch," *Contemporary Jewish Record*, II (March/April 1939), 14–30.

Eck, Nathan. "The Rescue of Jews with the Aid of Passports and Citizenship Papers of Latin American States," *Yad Washem Studies*, I (1957), 125–152.

Esh, Shaul. "Between Discrimination and Extermination," *Yad Washem Studies*, II, 79–93.

Feingold, Henry L. "The Roosevelt Administration and the Effort to Save the Jews of Hungary," in *Hungarian Jewish Studies*, Randolph L. Braham (ed.), New York: World Federation of Hungarian Jews, 1969, 211–244.

———. "Roosevelt and the Holocaust: Reflections on New Deal Humanitarianism," *Judaism*, 18, No. 3, Summer, 1969, 259–276.

Ford, Franklin L. "Three Observers in Berlin: Rumbold, Dodd, and Francois-Poncet," in *The Diplomats*, II, 437–476.

Fortune, "Jews in America," bound reprint published New York: Random House, 1936.

Fry, Varian, "Our Consuls at Work," *Nation*, CLIV (May 2, 1942), 507–509.

Glazer, Nathan. "The American Jew and the Attainment of Middle Class Rank: Some Trends and Explanations," in *The Jews: Social Patterns of an American Group*, Marshall Sklare (ed.), New York: Free Press, 1961, 138–146.

Goldberg, Nathan. "Immigration Attitudes of Mexicans: An Insight," *Rescue*, II (July/August 1945), 23–28.

Goodman, H. A. "Mission to Himmler," *Jewish Life* (November/December 1952), 35–39.

Gunther, John. "Hispaniola," *Foreign Affairs*, XVIII (July 1941), 772–773.

Hevesi, Eugene. "Hitler's Plan for Madagascar," *Contemporary Jewish Record*, IV (August 1941), 381–394.

Hirschberg, Alfred. "The Economic Adjustment of Jewish Refugees in São Paulo," *Jewish Social Science*, VI (April 1944), 143–168.

Jackson, Robert H. "Alien Registration and Democracy," *Interpreter Releases*, XVII (June 1944), 423–424.

Jacob, Philip E. "Influence of World Events on United States 'Neutrality' Opinion," *Public Opinion Quarterly*, VI (March 1940), 48–65.

Kirchway, Freda. "Nightmare in France," *Nation* (August 27, 1940), 124.

———. "The State Department Versus Political Refugees," *Nation* (December 28, 1940), 648–649.

"Large-Scale Settlement in the Eastern Mediterranean," *Bulletin of the Economic Research Institute of the Jewish Agency*, II (September/October 1938), 159–167.

Lasker, Bruno. "An Atlas of Hope," *Survey Graphic*, XXIX (November 1940), 583–590.

Lewy, Guenter. "Pius XII, the Jews and the German Catholic Church," *Commentary*, XXXVII (February 1964), 23–26.

Linfield, H. S. "Jewish Communities of the United States," *American Jewish Yearbook*, XLII (1940/1941), 215–266.

Lubell, Samuel. "War by Refugees," *Saturday Evening Post*, CCXIII (March 29, 1941), 12–13, 88–90, 92.

Malin, Patrick M. "The Work of the Intergovernmental Committee on Political Refugees—Its Relation to Government and Private Agencies," *Interpreter Releases*, XXI (June 1944), 209–213.

Neumann, Gerhardt. "German Jews in Colombia: A study in Immigrant Adjustment," *Jewish Social Studies*, III (1941), 189–206.

Ottenheimer, Hilde. "The Disappearance of Jewish Communities in Germany, 1900–1938," *Jewish Social Studies*, III (1941), 189–206.

Patch, Buel W. "Resettlement of Refugees," *Editorial Research Reports*, I (1938), 21–35.

Pozner, V. "Pogroms for Profit: Jewish Money for Nazi Trusts," *Nation* (January 7, 1939), 33–35.

Price, Grenfell A. "Refugee Settlement in the Tropics," *Foreign Affairs*, XVIII (July 1940), 659–670.

Prinz, Arthur. "The Role of the Gestapo in Obstructing and Promoting Jewish Immigration," *Yad Washem Studies*, II (1958), 205–218.

Roth, Cecil. "The Jewish Problem Today and Tomorrow," *American Hebrew* (September 17, 1943), 27–31.

Schechtmann, Joseph B. "Failure of the Dominican Scheme," *Congress Weekly* (January 15, 1943), 8–9.

Stahl, Rudolph. "Vocational Retraining of Jews in Nazi Germany, 1935–1938," *Jewish Social Studies*, I (April 1939), 169–194.

Tartakower, Arieh. "The Jewish Refugees: A Sociological Survey," *Jewish Social Studies*, IV (October 1942), 317–348.

Vágó, Béla. "Germany and the Jewish Policy of the Kállay Government," *Hungarian Jewish Studies*, Randolph L. Braham (ed.), New York: World Federation of Hungarian Jews, 1969, 183–210.

Wagg, Alfred, III. "Washington's Stepchild: The Refugees," *New Republic* (April 13, 1942), 592–594.

Wischnitzer, Mark. "The Historical Background of the Settlement of Jewish Refugees in Santo Domingo," *Jewish Social Studies*, IV (January 1942), 45–58.

Index

Abshageen, Hans, 46
Addams, Jane, 23
Adler, Cyrus, 12, 14
Africa, 176; Belgian Congo purchase proposal, 93; British possessions in, 34, 44, 106, 108, 124; Rumanian Jewish resettlement plan, 179, 180; supplemental homeland scheme and, 91, 97, 102–109, 112, 114, 118, 122, 124
agriculture, 7, 113, 120, 122, 125; Latin American, 32, 9, 121; Philippine, 98; Russian Jewish settlements, 94
Agro-Joint, 111, 121, 123
Aguda Chasidei Chabad, 139
Agudath Israel, 107
Aguinaldo, Emilio, 98
AJJDC, *see* American Jewish Joint Distribution Committee (AJJDC)
Alaska: resettlement issue and, 75, 94–97, 98, 99, 108, 114, 124, 171, 296, 303, 307
Alaskan Development Bill (1940), 95
Alaskan Development Committee, 96
Albania, 133–34
Aleppo, Syria, 272
Alexander, Robert, 194
Alfange, Dean, 281; quoted, 230–31
Alien Registration Act (1940), 141, 160
Aliyah Beth, 124, 204
Alliance, New Jersey, 93–94

Allied Supreme Command, Declaration on War Crimes, 228–29
All Souls College, Oxford, 138
American Committee for the Protection of Minorities, 24
American Federation of Labor (AFL), 175
American Federation of Zionists, 285
American Friends of Jewish Palestine, 174–75
American Friends' Service Committee, 149
American Hebrew, The (periodical), 156–57, 221
American Jewish Committee, 9, 10, 11, 174, 219; Bulgarian Jews and, 184; election proposal of, 12–13; immigration law liberalization and, 42; Intergovernmental Committee Coordinating Foundation and, 73
American Jewish Conference, 238–39; New York meeting (Aug. 1943), 218–20; Rescue Commission of, 189, 220, 233, 236–37
American Jewish Congress, 12–13, 25, 174, 196; Joint Boycott Council, 52; war crimes trials and, 228, 229; Zionism of, 6, 10, 219, 220
American Jewish Joint Distribution Committee (AJJDC), 15, 66, 123, 187; children and, 154, 155, 284;

367